Applications of Econometrics

Applications of Econometrics

Empirics of Limited Dependent Variable, Time Series, and Panel Data Methods

T. Lakshmanasamy

KALPAZ

First Published, 2020

Published by

Kalpaz Publications
C-30, Satyawati Nagar,
Delhi – 110052
Ph.: 011-47034999, 9811692060
www.kalpazpublications.com
E-mail: kalpaz@hotmail.com

Printed at: G. Print Process, Delhi

Cataloging in Publication Data--DK
Courtesy: D.K. Agencies (P) Ltd. <docinfo@dkagencies.com>

Lakshmanasamy, T., author.
Applications of econometrics : empirics of limited dependent variable, time series, and panel data methods / T. Lakshmanasamy.
pages cm
Includes bibliographical references.
ISBN 9789353242442

1. Econometrics. 2. Econometrics--India. 3. India--Economic conditions--Econometric models. I. Title.

LCC HB139.L35 2020 | DDC 330.015195 23

Contents

Section III – Panel Data Econometrics

Preface

Econometrics is interesting in its own right in unraveling the mysteries of data, applied econometrics is challenging in identifying the appropriate estimation method, and the applications of econometric techniques is even more challenging and complex in understanding the issue, applying relevant method and drawing meaning inference. However sophisticated an economic theory may be, empirical support is an integral part of modern-day policies and programmes. Understanding the intricacies and nuances of econometric methods and their applications is an art that comes with sustained practice and deep insights on the issues involved both in theory and in data. Even more challenging is the grasping of empirical knowledge in the identification of appropriate technique, nature and quality of data and drawing meaningful inferences. Any amount of theoretical knowledge in economic theory and econometric methods is inadequate as long as one is superfluous in empirical analysis. An inclination to empirical work is therefore a very essential quality of quantitative research. It is often been the case in empirical works that many methodological challenges are posed by the data itself and the hitherto existing techniques are identified as inappropriate or inefficient. In many instances, the challenges of data analysis lead to many interesting and improved methods and novel econometric techniques to solve many problems. Applications of econometric methods require specialised skills to identify the issues and appropriate methods to solve them.

In this broad sense, the papers in this volume are unique and interesting. This volume comprises papers on applications of econometrics originally carried out by the students as a project work for the masters degree programme in econometrics. As the project work is taken seriously by the students, the hardwork put by them should not go unnoticed. It is only appropriate to make their work known to the outside world. Hence, this is a modest attempt to bring together the works of students on applications of econometrics as a book. Every research work in this book follows strong empirical insights with equally important serious methodological foundations. The research issues are discussed in detail and appropriate econometric methodologies are carefully identified on various issues and methods. All the works on applications of econometrics in this volume use relevant data and empirical methods to substantiate the research issues and derive meaningful insights and inferences.

The aim of bringing together these works on applications of econometrics is to motivate young researchers to better appreciate the quantitative analysis and empirical approach, estimation methodology and apply appropriate econometric techniques on relevant data in order to derive meaningful inferences from empirical estimates. It is heartening to see that many of the so called empirical studies in India do not follow sound methodological base even for the issues that warrant quite a strong systematic analysis of data. Even the available and much tested simple methodological approaches have largely been ignored and it is quite common to find research works that simply add or duplicate the existing works. In this regard, the present volume may serve as a basis for identifying methodological approaches for undertaking rigorous empirical analysis. With the increasing availability of global, cross country and nationwide large scale data sets and user friendly softwares along with the readily accessible upto date literature and computer programming, there is no handicap for the modern day researchers to venture into new vistas in research and empirics. It is hoped that this book will be a stimulant to the young researchers to explore new and ever growing frontiers of knowledge.

It is always a pleasant moment to acknowledge the support and contributions of well-wishers in the academic career of a teacher and a researcher. First and foremost, I thank all my students whose research works comprise this volume for their research insights and analytical skills. Without their involvement and incised discussions, it would not have been possible for me to learn the different econometric methods and their applications in diverse fields of economics and econometrics. Also, many strong academicians have contributed to my academic pursuits over the years in many ways. I am ever thankful to my teachers, colleagues and students who are the sources of inspiration, involvement, understanding and improvement in my academic learnings. They constantly motivate and infuse my research interests in various fields of economics and econometrics and sharpen my understanding of the subjects that form the basis of this present volume. It is a pleasure to recall the academic interactions I had with my research guide Prof. A.M. Nalla Gounden without whose thoughtful academic insights and critical inputs, I would not have become a researcher in applied econometrics. I also acknowledge the academic interactions with my colleagues Prof. U. Sankar, Prof. S.S. Sivakumar, Dr. K. Shanthi, Dr. G. Mythili, Dr. D. Sathiyavan, Dr. P. Mahendra Varman and Dr. R. Mariappan and their encouragement and cooperation throughout my association with the Department of Econometrics in the University of Madras.

Life satisfaction lies in wholehearted involvement in one's work for which some close people sacrifice their own career. Specifically, family members shape one's life, most importantly one's academic career pursuits. In this respect, I place on record the constant encouragement, extraordinary support and untiring cooperation always extended pleasantly by my family for my endeavour. I acknowledge the evergreen wishes of my father Thiru.Thangamuthu Gounder, innocent faith of my mother Thirumathi. Muthayammal, honoured wishes of my brother Thiru.T.Ramasamy, sacrifices of my sisters Thirumathi.Kannammal, Thirumathi. Parvathy, Thirumathi.Rajathi, and the luxury of care and support of my wife Dr. K. Parimala and my son Mr.L.Ashwanth.

T. Lakshmanasamy

List of Tables

List of Figures

Limited Dependent Variable Econometrics

1

The Determinants of Happiness: Ordered Probit Estimation of Life Satisfaction

1.1 Introduction

Happiness is a subjective measure of the quality of life in all domains of life. It is nearly impossible to have an objective textbook definition of any subjective issue and definition of happiness is one such aspect. This is why less emphasis is given on what happiness is and more emphasis on people's own perceptions about happiness and the determinants that determines of such a dimension of happiness. Though happiness research has long been the domains of psychologists and philosophers, the systematic study of happiness has gained some respectability among economists in recent years, out of the growing dissatisfaction of economists with their conventional measures like utility and welfare as a measure of quality of life or well-being. Psychologists and social scientists generally attempt to measure happiness simply by asking people how happy they are. However, economists need to objectively measure happiness on order to have any meaningful interventions and improvements in standards of life of the people. Happiness is usually considered to be the proper measure of social progress and the goal of public policy. Happiness or well-being or life satisfaction analysis is widely undertaken to implement better welfare policies by governments for the people as making people's lives better would be the major objective to achieve through policies. Improving the quality of life might not be the only thing that matters, but such improvement is desirable. Indeed, improving people's lives is the explicit focus of much of the policymaking and regulatory works of the governments.

The World Happiness Report 2018 ranks India at 133rd position. India has witnessed a drop of 11 places from 2017 ranking of 122nd rank. In fact, the happiness index of India has been consistently falling since 2014. The happiness index is based on six key factors-income, health, social support, freedom, trust and generosity. Despite being one of the fastest growing economies in the world, India is well behind its neighbhours China, Pakistan and Bangladesh. In fact, India stands higher in healthy life expectancy and freedom to make life choices compared to these countries. This raises a question: despite economic growth, why happiness does not rise with income growth? Why people are not happy with rising income? Does an individual's happiness increase with an increase in money income? Is raising income inadequate to raise happiness of people? In other words, does money buy happiness? If money can buy material goods for human satisfaction, why money does not buy happiness? If not money, what is that that leads to an individual's happiness? A search for an answer to these perplexing questions has led to a huge literature on the so called economics of happiness with elusive answer. Rather, the studies have produced contradicting results and importantly raised more questions than the answers. Yet the simple question of what makes people could not be resolved so far.

Hence, this paper tries to identify the determinants of happiness among individuals in India. Specifically, this paper examines the relationship between income and life satisfaction in India in an attempt to understand whether money matters for happiness. The data for the empirical analysis is derived from the 6th wave (2010-2014) of the World Value Survey (WVS) pertaining to India. Since the response variable, life satisfaction or happiness, is measured in the WVS as ordered categorical in Likert scale, this empirical analysis is based on the ordered probit method.

1.2 A Brief Review of Recent Studies

In the first research work on the income-happiness relationship in the US in the economics tradition, Easterlin (1974) arrives at a startling finding that money does not buy happiness. It has been observed that the average happiness in the United States in the 1970s was not significantly different from what it was in 1940s despite significant advances and a high rate of growth in income in this period. This has led Easterlin to conclude that, on average, a rise in income raises happiness at a point in time, but over time happiness does not increase with increases in income. Easterlin explains this paradoxical result in terms of relative comparison, which has been subsequently termed as Easterlin Paradox or Easterlin Puzzle. As individuals compare their income with the incomes to others in the society, especially with that of neighbours, a rise in the income levels of all people does not raise the happiness level of individuals. Specifically, a proportionate shift in the relative position does not change happiness level of individuals. Further, happiness level does not vary much between countries though there are wide income gaps between countries. It has been inferred that while the goods aspirations of higher status people probably exceed those of lower status people, the dispersion in reference norms is less than in the actual incomes of rich and poor.

Borooah (2006) conducts an econometric investigation into what makes people happy analysing the relationship between standards of living and levels of happiness in Ireland. The paper adds to the mounting evidence that not only does money not buy happiness, it may not even fully be convertible in terms of satisfaction of having money. A possible reasoning for this is that satisfaction of one's standard of living depends on comparison with standard of living of others. The study also points to the importance of social capital for life satisfaction emphasising the social environment; the area we live in, the people we have as our neighbours are important in lifting happiness levels.

Litchfield et al. (2012) attempt to investigate the objectives of life satisfaction using the ordered probit model using a cross-section data from Albania. The study finds that absolute household welfare measure plays an important role but there is no role for a relative measure in determining life satisfaction.

Yushkina (2010) explore the determinants of life satisfaction and its changes in modern Russia, analysing the effect of living space, perceive economic rank, other subjective attitudes and perceptions on well-being. The empirical estimates use a panel data and the ordered logit model. The bias due to unobserved personality factors are corrected by instrumenting permanent happiness. The results show that subjective attitudes that describe an individual's perceived power rank, respect rank and economic value in society have consistent and positive significant effects on happiness.

Como (2011) uses three proxies for happiness in examining the relationship between happiness and income: positivity, self-esteem and self-satisfaction. To avoid the endogeneity problem and the direction of causality between happiness and income, the happiness levels of individuals before they earned regular career income and their happiness levels based on the income they earn are compared. While positivity and self-esteem turned out to be highly significant, self-satisfaction is not significant for earning income. But self-esteem is the most accurate predictor of income. Therefore, individuals should pursue courses of actions that make them more positive and have higher self-esteem.

Hajdu and Hajdu (2014) examine the association between subjective well-being and income using various estimation methods. The results of OLS regression are compared with quantile regression, ordered probit and generalised ordered probit estimates. It has observed that income has a strong positive effect on life satisfaction under OLS regression and the quantile regression results reveal that this association is less strong at the upper end and stronger at the lower end of the conditional distribution of life satisfaction. The standard ordered probit model predicts a moderate positive income effect: higher income decreases the probability of dissatisfaction and increases the probability of satisfaction. Contrary to this result, the generalised ordered probit model shows a more negative effect on lower satisfaction levels and income does not affect the probability of the highest satisfaction level. The findings draw attention to the importance of modeling and estimation in life satisfaction research.

In India, Lakshmanasamy (2010) analyse the relationship between income and happiness in India empirically using a primary sample data. An important question raised for the analysis is 'If money does not buy happiness, why most people are after money and material pursuits?' Ordered Probit model has been used to estimate the income-happiness relationship. The estimated ordered probit results show a significant positive effect of both absolute and relative income on happiness, suggesting that money does influence happiness and well-being and the individual's life satisfaction is also influenced by his relative status. It has also been observed and an increase in absolute income may raise happiness but beyond a certain threshold level people develop aspirations for status positions and hence more money may not bring more happiness.

Majumdar and Gupta (2015) elicit the literature on the economics of happiness and survey the relationship between happiness and several correlates of happiness such as unemployment, poverty, literacy rate, life expectancy, inflation rate, crime rate and political stability. The survey shows that employed are more satisfied than unemployed, married are more happy than divorced, separated and widowed, etc. It has also been inferred that the Easterlin Paradox – the nil relationship between income and happiness on average, does not hold in the case of India. This implies that in India happiness may be more sensitive to absolute than to relative income. A justification is also provided for the results in the Indian scenario.

In a global comparison that includes India as well, Inglehart et al. (2008) challenge the view that happiness levels of entire society remain fixed with growing income due to relative comparison. Based on cross-section analysis of 52 nations for which substantial time series are available, they show a positive relationship between income and happiness at the aggregate level in most developing countries. The shift towards rising happiness spans the spectrum from low income to high income countries and cuts across cultural zones. It has been noted that the difference between rich and poor countries must be due to some fixed cultural differences in the meaning of happiness. Among the countries, India, a low income country, shows a steep rise in happiness.

Deaton (2008) using the 2006 Gallup World Poll data analyse the effects of income and age on self-reported well-being in 132 countries, including India. Because the survey used the same questionnaire in all countries, it provides an opportunity to make cross-country comparisons, while at the same time providing enough data to permit within-country disaggregation, for example, by age, sex, ethnicity or education. It is observed that India is less happy than rich countries. Clark et al. (2008), Stevenson and Wolfers (2008) and Clark and Senik (2011) have also mention about happiness in India in their studies that are conducted on a world basis in analysing the income-happiness relationship.

1.3 Data and Methodology

The World Value Survey (WVS) is the largest source of cross-national public opinion surveys in this world in terms of countries covered and years for studying the subjective well-being related issues. The WVS has been administered 6 times worldwide so far. The first wave was conducted during 1980-84 in 21 countries and sixth wave conducted in between 2010 and 2014 includes 60 countries. The WVS consists of nationally representative surveys and covers almost 90 percent of the world's population, using a common questionnaire. The WVS methodology is face-to-face interviews with a detailed questionnaire consisting of about 250 questions with some 400 to 800 measurable variables. The WVS provides information on various aspects of the respondents' life, ranging from income to employment status, religion, education, health status and religion, besides information on personal values and attitudes towards a wide range of social issues such as life satisfaction, family, work and democracy. The years of survey for India are 1990, 1995, 2001, 2006 and 2014.

The WVS is being conducted in all major states and union territories of India. The 1990 (second) wave included 12 states and 2 union territories (Delhi and Chandigarh) in India. The sixth wave (2010-2014) includes 22 states and 2 union territories (Delhi and Puducherry). Same states are sampled in all waves with additional states added overtime. The WVS respondents are asked to give a qualitative assessment on their happiness on a Likert scale. The question in WVS that measures the feeling of happiness is: "Taking all things together, would you say you are: 1 - very happy, 2-rather happy, 3 - not very happy and 4 - not at all happy". The data for this study consists of 1581 observations from the sixth wave (2010-1014) of WVS for India. Since the dependent variable in the study is a qualitative variable or an ordinal variable measured on a Likert scale, the ordered probit model is used to analyse the determinants of happiness in India.

Ordered Probit Method

The ordered probit model is usually used to estimate the relationship between an ordinal dependent variable and a set of independent variables. The ordered probit model assumes an underlying a latent ordinal dependent variable (y*) which is related linearly to the set of independent variables as:

$$y_i^* = \beta x_i + u_i \tag{1.1}$$

The latent dependent variable (y*) is the feeling of happiness which is not directly observed, instead the feeling of happiness is measured in ordinal form y (1=not happy, 2=happy, 3=very happy). The respondents choose appropriate category that describes best their feeling of happiness(y*). The y ranges between the ordinal categories 1 and 3. Assuming j answer categories, (j=3), the observed happiness function is:

$$y_i = j \quad if \ \lambda_{j-1} \le y_i^* < \lambda_j \tag{1.2}$$

where λ_1, λ_2, λ_3 are the cutpoints, certain threshold values of the latent variable at which the outcome variable changes.

The probability of observing y=j for given values of the independent variables is:

$$\Pr(y_i = j|x_i) = \Pr(\lambda_{j-1} \le y_i^* < \lambda_j|x_i) = \Pr(y_i^* < \lambda_j|x_i) - \Pr(y_i^* < \lambda_{j-1}|x_i) \tag{1.3}$$

If the true satisfaction y* falls below the thresholdλ_1, then the individual chooses the lowest category; if the true satisfaction falls between λ_1 andλ_2, the individual will pick the second category; if the true satisfaction falls above the cut point λ_2 the individual chooses the highest category of happiness. Hence, the observed feeling of happiness would be as follows:

$$y_i = 1 \ if \ y_i^* \le \lambda_1; \ \ y_i = 2 \ if \ \lambda_1 \le y_i^* \le \lambda_2; \ \ y_i = 3 \ if \ y_i^* > \lambda_2 \tag{1.4}$$

The probability of feeling of happiness for each category is given by:

$Pr(y_i = 1|x_i) = Pr(y_i^* < \lambda_1|x_i)$ = Not happy
$Pr(y_i = 2|x_i) = Pr(\lambda_1 \leq y_i^* < \lambda_2|x_i) = Pr(y_i^* < \lambda_2|x_i) - Pr(y_i^* < \lambda_1|x_i)$ = Happy
$Pr(y_i = 3|x_i) = Pr(\lambda_2 \leq y_i^* < \lambda_3|x_i) = Pr(y_i^* < \lambda_3|x_i) - Pr(y_i^* < \lambda_2|x_i)$ = Very happy

The β coefficients are the probabilities of the effect of independent variables on the individual's happiness levels. If there are J categories of the ordered outcome variable, there will be j−1cutpointsor threshold values dividing the range of possible values for the latent variable y*. Using the CDF and the linear relationship between the latent dependent variable and the independent variables, the predicted probabilities can be expressed as:

$$Pr(y_i = 1|x_i) = \Phi(\lambda_j - \beta x_i) - \Phi(\lambda_{j-1} - \beta x_i) \quad (1.5)$$

The coefficients β and cutpoints λ are obtained by maximising the following log likelihood function:

$$LogL = \sum_{i=1}^{n} \sum_{j=1}^{j} I(y_i = j) log[\Phi(u_j - \beta x_i) - \Phi(u_{j-1} - \beta x_i)] \quad (1.6)$$

where i is a binary indicator function that equals 1 if y_i = j and 0 otherwise. The marginal probability effects (MPE) are the partial effects of the independent variables on the outcome probability. Since marginal probability effects measure the change in the outcome probabilities, the sum of these effects will be zero. The MPE for outcome *j* can be calculated as:

$$MPE_j(x_i) = \frac{\partial Pr(y_i = 1|x_i)}{\partial x_i} = [\phi(u_{j-1} - \beta x_i) - \phi(u_j - \beta x_i)]\beta \quad (1.7)$$

The empirical specification for estimating the feeling of happiness is given as:

$$Feeling\ Happiness_i = \beta_0 + \beta_1 Income + \beta_2 Gender + \beta_3 Emplyment + \beta_4 Marital\ Status + \beta_5 Social\ Class + \beta_6 Health\ Status + \beta_7 Religion + \beta_8 Education + \beta_9 Age + \beta_{10} Children + u_i \quad (1.8)$$

The Table 1.1 presents descriptive statistics of the variables used in the empirical analysis. Nearly 80 percent of the respondents self-reported happiness, compared to only 19 percent reporting unhappiness. Only one-fifth of the samples are higher educated. Most respondents belong to lower and middle income households. Nearly two-thirds of respondents belong to middle social class, the backward community, and reported good health. About half of the respondents are unemployed and have more than two children. Majority of the respondents are married and Hindus.

Table 1.1: Descriptive Statistics of Variables in the Happiness Analysis.

Variable	*Mean*	*Variable*	*Mean*
Very happy	0.35 (0.47)	Upper social class	0.14 (0.35)
Happy	0.46 (0.50)	Middle social class	0.62 (0.48)
Not happy	0.19 (0.39)	Lower social class	0.24 (0.43)
Hindu	0.70 (0.46)	Male	0.62 (0.49)
Non-Hindu	0.30 (0.46)	Female	0.38 (0.48)
Primary education	0.47 (0.50)	Low income	0.39 (0.49)
Secondary education	0.42 (0.49)	Middle income	0.37 (0.48)
Higher education	0.11 (0.31)	High income	0.24 (0.43)
Married	0.81 (0.39)	Employed	0.49 (0.50)
Single	0.19 (0.39)	Unemployed	0.51 (0.50)
Poor health	0.31 (0.46)	No child	0.27 (0.44)
Good health	0.62 (0.49)	One child	0.18 (0.38)
Very good health	0.07 (0.25)	More than two children	0.55 (0.50)
Age	39.88 (14.19)		

Note: Standard deviations in parentheses.

1.4 Empirical Analysis

The Table 1.2 shows the association between the feeling of happiness and the socioeconomic and demographic variables. The chi-square values show that education, income and health of respondents are significantly associated with feeling happiness, whereas there is no statistically significant associated between feeling happiness and gender, marital status and social class.

Table 1.2: Association between Personal Characteristics and Feeling of Happiness.

Variable	*Category*	*Not happy*	*Happy*	*Very happy*	*Chi-square*
Gender	Male	182 (60.1)	471 (64.6)	329 (60.5)	Chi-sq. = 3.068
	Female	121 (39.9)	258 (35.4)	215 (39.5)	Prob. = 0.216
Marital status	Married	246 (81.2)	600(82.3)	531(79.2)	Chi-sq. =1.924
	Single	57(18.8)	129(17.7)	113(20.8)	Prob. = 0.382
Employment status	Employed	109(38.7)	375(56.6)	238(45.7)	Chi-sq. = 29.81
	Unemployed	173(61.3)	287(43.4)	283(54.3)	Prob. = 0.000
Education	Primary	146(49.8)	291(41.1)	288(53.7)	Chi-sq. =20.55*
	Secondary	111(37.9)	329(46.5)	203(37.9)	Prob. = 0.000
	University	36(12.3)	88(12.4)	45(8.4)	

(Contd...)

Social class	Upper	48(16.1)	101(14.0)	67 (12.4)	Chi-sq. = 4.527
	Middle	171(57.2)	454(63.1)	337(62.5)	Prob. = 0.193
	Lower	80(26.8)	165(22.9)	135(25.0)	
Income class	Low	130(43.5)	246(34.1)	225(41.7)	Chi-sq. =11.26*
	Middle	110(36.8)	283(39.3)	192(35.6)	Prob. = 0.004
	High	59(19.7)	192(26.6)	123(22.8)	
Health status	Poor	47(15.6)	219(30.2)	226(41.7)	Chi-sq. =18.14*
	Good	193(63.9)	480(66.1)	296(54.6)	Prob. = 0.000
	Very good	62(20.5)	27(3.7)	20(3.7)	

Note: Column percentages in parentheses.

The Table 1.3 presents the results of the ordered probit estimation of the social, economic and demographic determinants of the feeling of happiness in India. The probability of reporting happiness increases with education, health and social class. The probability of middle class and lower class to be happy is higher by 0.172 and 0.102 respectively compared to the upper class respondents. Primary education is more important to happiness than higher education. The probability of happiness is higher by 0.151 for unmarried/single individuals than for married respondents. The probability of happiness is higher by 0.284 for primary education than for higher education. While income has negative effect on the probability feeling happiness, but its effect is statistically insignificant. Similarly, neither employment nor age has any significant effect on happiness. Also, religion has no effect on the feeling of happiness in India. The probability of being happy is less by 0.023 for males. The number of children has no statistical effect on the probability of happiness. The estimated cutpoints show that at 0.34, the self-reported feeling of happiness changes from not happy to happy and 1.64, the feeling of happiness changes from happy to very happy in India. The Pseudo R^2log-likelihood values imply better fit of the ordered probit estimation of the socioeconomic and demographic determinants in explaining the feeling of happiness in India.

Table 1.3: Ordered Profit Estimates of Happiness in India.
Dependent variable: Feeling happiness

Variable	*ORPROBIT with social variables*	*ORPROBT with economic and demographic variables*	*ORPROBT with social, economic and demographic variables*
Non-Hindu	0.020(0.063)	-	-0.005(0.065)
Primary education	0.253*** (0.097)	-	0.284*(0.103)
Secondary education	0.148(0.097)	-	0.194(0.100)
Single/unmarried	0.140*(0.075)	-	0.151*(0.082)

(Contd...)

Poor health	1.236*(0.126)	-	1.23*(0.128)
Good health	0.790*(0.120)	-	0.786*(0.122)
Middle social class	0.156*(0.087)	-	0.178**(0.089)
Lower social class	0.072(0.098)	-	0.102(0.101)
Age	-	0.0003(0.002)	0.0007(0.002)
Male	-	-0.036(0.064)	-0.023(0.067)
Low income	-	-0.049(0.077)	-0.051(0.080)
Middle income	-	-0.078(0.077)	-0.083(0.079)
Employed	-	0.050(0.062)	0.83(0.064)
No child	-	0.019(0.035)	0.004(0.038)
Cutpoint 1	0.288(0.156)	-0.873(0.117)	0.334(0.197)
Cutpoint2	1.617(0.159)	0.364(0.116)	1.638(0.199)
Log-likelihood	-1527.1246	-1523.5879	-1431.4233
Pseudo R^2	0.0391	0.0007	0.0419
No. of observations	1527	1460	1431

Note: Absolute t-values in parentheses.*** significant at 1 percent level ** significant at 5 percent level * significant at 10 percent level.

The ordered probit estimation only shows the probability of reporting happiness and it does not reveal the effects of the covariates on the changes in the probability. The marginal probability effects show the change in probability when the predictor or independent variable increases by one unit. The marginal effect of an increase in a regressor on the probability of selecting an alternative j, as given by equation (1.7), is presented in Table 1.4. The change in probability of being happy when income changes from high income to low income increases 2percentage points and increases by 2 points to middle class. The change in probability of being happy when health status changes from very good health to good health and poor health decreases by 22 percentage points and 26points respectively. The change in probability of reporting happy decreases by 4 percent and 2 percentage points when social class changes from upper class to middle class and lower class respectively. The probability of being happy when marital status changes from married to single decreases by 3 percentage points. The change in probability of being happy when health status changes from very good health to good health and poor health decreases 22 percentage points and 26 points respectively. The change in probability of being happy when employment status changes from unemployed to employed decreases by 1 percent.

Table 1.4 Marginal Effects of Social, Economic and Demographic Variables on Happiness

Variable	*ORPROBIT with social variables*	*ORPROBT with economic and demographic variables*	*ORPROBT with social, economic and demographic variables*
Non-Hindu	-0.005(0.016)	-	0.001(0.017)
Primary education	-0.066*(0.025)	-	-0.074**(0.026)
Secondary education	-0.038(0.025)	-	-0.050(0.025)
Single/unmarried	-0.035**(0.182)	-	-0.037**(0.055)
Poor health	-0.260***(0.022)	-	0.259***(0.023)
Good health	-0.223***(0.036)	-	-0.221***(0.036)
Middle social class	-0.041**(0.023)	-	-0.047**(0.024)
Lower social class	-0.018(0.024)	-	-0.026(0.025)
Age	-	-0.0001(0.0005)	-0.0001(0.0006)
Male	-	0.009(0.175)	0.006(0.017)
Low income	-	0.013(0.021)	-0.026(0.021)
Middle income	-	0.021(0.021)	0.022(0.021)
Employed	-	-0.013(0.017)	-0.021***(0.036)
No child	-	-0.005(0.009)	-0.0009(0.010)

Note: Standard errors in parentheses.*** significant at 1 percent level ** significant at 5 percent level * significant at 10 percent level.

1.5 Conclusion

Identifying the determinants of happiness, both theoretically and empirically, had always been a puzzling question for social science. The concept is happiness is not easily amenable for defining as well as for quantification as there is not a single set of approach to understand what constitutes happiness and what the dimensions of happiness are. However, most people agree that happiness is a feeling and it can be clearly understood by the subject himself and therefore self-reported measures of happiness are valid and reliable for empirical analysis. The main aim of this paper is to estimate the effects of the socioeconomic and demographic determinants on feeling happiness in India individuals. The econometric technique of ordered probit model is applied to the sixth wave (2010-1014) World Value Survey data of India as happiness is a qualitative variable measured by a four point Likert scale and the responses are in an ascending order. The covariates considered in this study as determinants of happiness in India gender, social class, marital status, income, health status, employment status, education, number of children, age, and religion. The estimated ordered probit results show that the probability of reporting happiness increases with education, health and social class whereas age, income, employment, children and gender have no statistical effect on happiness in India. Changes in the marginal effects are reported in the case of primary education, health, employment and middle social class. As income changes from high income to low income, people tend to become unhappier.

2

The Determinants of Child Health: Logit Estimation of the Effect of Mother's Education on Child Immunisation

2.1 Introduction

General education is important because it often enhances not only productivity and output, but also confers many non-market social benefits, especially for women and the marginalised. An added benefit of raising school enrollment and literacy, particularly for girls and females, is the spillover effects on own health and health of the family, especially child health. Many outcomes demonstrate that education improves both health-seeking behaviour and health outcomes (Caldwell, 1979). Education is the only tool with which a girl or a woman can empower herself, her family and her child, the next generation. Therefore, by declaring education as a fundamental right, India ensures constitutional provisions for providing free and compulsory education to all children between 6 to 14 years of age and special considerations for educating girl children. There are numerous schemes in India to bring girl child to school as well as providing incentives to mothers to send children to school. The central and state governments also provide free health services both for mothers in neonatal periods and for girl child in school, apart from general health services and health insurance.

Among the various schemes aimed at increasing health and reducing mortality, child immunisation has been regarded as the most cost effective intervention for child health, which is vigorously promoted by World Health Organisation (WHO). Immunisation at the early childhood significantly reduces costs of treating diseases, thus providing a healthy childhood and reducing poverty and suffering. Immunisation or vaccination is the injection of a small amount of viruses/bacteria into the human body to stimulate the immune system to make antibodies against them. Childhood vaccination has saved millions of lives and prevents many more millions from suffering debilitating illness and lifelong disability. Despite the huge success in vaccination across countries, WHO estimates that 1.5 million children under 5 years die from vaccine-preventable diseases annually.

As a signatory of the Sustainable Development Goals (SDGs) agenda, India is committed to ensure healthy lives and promote well-being for all, at all ages. To foster the global efforts, India tries to make rapid headway in achieving universal health coverage, particularly in the provisioning of essential health care services (Rudra, 2017). The Universal Immunisation programme (UIP), started as early as 1978, is one of the key interventions for protection of children from life threatening conditions, which are preventable. It is considered to be one of the largest immunisation programmes around the world and a major public health intervention in the country. Since 2005, the immunisation has been one of the key areas under National Rural Health Mission (NRHM). Under the Universal Immunisation programme, the Government of India is providing vaccination to prevent seven vaccine preventable diseases i.e. Pertussis, Tetanus, Polio, Measles, Childhood Tuberculosis, Hepatitis B, Heamophilus influenza type b (Hib) and Diarrhea (National Health Mission, 2014).

In December 2014, India's Ministry of Health and Family Welfare launched the Mission Indradhanush with an ambitious target to vaccinate at least 90 percent of pregnant women against tetanus and ensure that all children are fully vaccinated against seven vaccine-preventable diseases before they reach an age of two years with a rigorous focus on remote and inaccessible rural areas, urban slums and migrant and mobile communities. Subsequently, general improvements in the delivery of routine immunisation services are also critical in the successful efforts to interrupt polio transmission in India and remain a key component in attempts to eliminate measles from the country by 2020. Different campaigns and awareness programs through anganawadis and panchayats at grass root levels of the society are also vigorously undertaken to spread knowledge of immunisation and health benefits.

The Figure 2.1 presents trend of child immunisation in India between 1999 and 2013 showing shows a gradual increase in child immunisation over the period. The estimated changes are from 74 percent to 91 percent for BCC (Bacilli Calmette-Guerin) vaccine; from 74 percent to 90 percent and from 59 percent to 83 percent for DTP1 and DTP3, respectively; from 57 percent to 82 percent for the third dose of oral polio vaccine; and from 56 percent to 83 percent for the first dose of vaccine against measles.

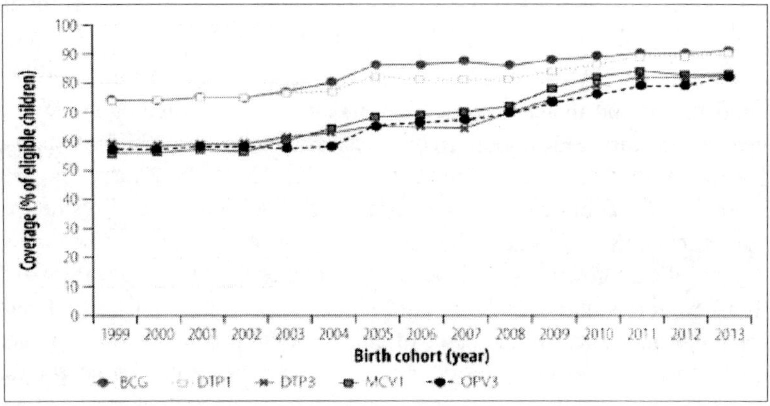

Source: WHO (2016).

Figure 2.1: Trend of Child Immunisation in India

Despite the all-round efforts by the governments in India and significant progress, still India could not achieve the target and is away from the goal of full immunisation. One of the important factors in child immunisation is the role of mother's education. Illiteracy among mothers is the primary cause for poor health of the family. Improving maternal education is important for increasing childhood vaccination uptake and coverage. Therefore, this paper examines the determinants of child immunisation, focusing the home of the child itself, especially the maternal education. The study also incorporates other maternal characteristics, socioeconomic and demographic characteristics that are closely related to child immunisation in a family. The 6th round survey data of DHS (2015-16) is used in this study. The empirical analysis is based on a sample of 12817 observations out of a total sample of 259628 of DHS. The paper analyses the relationship between maternal education and child immunisation status for children in the ages between 12 to 23 months. The econometric method followed are univariate and multivariate logistic regression (LOGIT) analysis as the dependent variable, child immunisation status, is a categorical variable with two possibilities - whether the child is fully vaccinated or not.

2.2 A Brief Review of Recent Studies

The studies on the relationship between child health and maternal education goes back to early 1970's when Caldwell (1979) demonstrates that "ceteris paribus, children of educated mothers experience lower mortality than do children of uneducated mother". Many studies have established the link between maternal education and different aspects of child health in every country both developing and developed.

Desai and Alva (1998) analyse the casual relationship between child health and maternal education, using a panel of demographic and health data for 22 developing countries. The study uses child mortality, immunisation status and height for age as dependent variables and mother's education, children's age, father's education, area of residence, marriage status and some environmental factors as independent variables. Among the 22 countries, in 11 countries mother's primary education and in 15 countries mother's secondary education are statistically significant for infant mortality, an indicator of child health. The education variables are jointly significant in 14 countries. When accounting for height for age, maternal education coefficients are significant as well as positive. Out of 20 countries, in 9 countries maternal primary education and in 11 countries mother's secondary education has a significant positive effect on children's immunisation status regardless of the community effects and other socioeconomic factors.

Basaleem et al. (2010) evaluate the Expanded Programme on Immunisation (EPI) in Yemen which vaccinates children in 12-23 months in Aden region of Yemen. In contrast to many studies, the outcome of this study finds that mother's education has no significant impact in determining the immunisation status of child in Yeman. On the other hand, father's occupation, birth order of child and place of residence account more for the immunisation status.

Forshaw et al. (2017) attempt a meta-analysis on 37 studies to examine the correlation between increasing maternal education and vaccine uptake in an attempt to know whether this relationship varies between continents, setting and time. The analysis shows increasing child vaccination uptake with increasing maternal education, the odds of full childhood vaccination are 2.3 times greater in children whose mother received secondary or higher education when compared to children whose mother with no education. Vaccination of children is most likely in highly educated women in rural areas, with an odds ratio of 2.17. There is no statistically significant difference in the odds ratios between the rural and urban settings.

Though many studies assert the positive relationship between maternal education and child immunisation, only few studies explore the pathway through which maternal education increases child immunisation uptake. Merely having heard the term immunisation does not necessarily imply having accurate knowledge of the functions of specific types of immunisation. While the pattern of knowledge of immunisation in general increases slightly with higher education, the level of correct knowledge about which diseases the immunisation prevents rises with increasing education. Illiteracy, socioeconomic status and empowerment of women are significant factors linked to poor uptake of routine polio vaccination.

Streatfield et al. (1990) finds in two villages in Indonesia, the levels of knowledge of the function of anti-polio vaccine are much higher than for the BCG and DPT vaccines, probably because the name of the vaccine incorporates the name of the disease. About 51.7 percent of mothers with primary school or more are much more likely to obtain their immunisation knowledge from a medical source (doctor, nurse, vaccinator) than led educated women (34.3 percent). Further, the levels of complete coverage do not follow a clear linear pattern according to educational level. The study finds that mother's with primary education are around 7 times less likely to have their children immunised than those having either no formal education or secondary education. While more than half (55 percent) of children of mothers with secondary school have complete immunisation, illiterate group and the highly educated group have higher coverage levels (45 percent) than the primary (31 percent) or completed primary (34 percent) groups. All education groups have an equally small proportion (1.1-3.5 percent) whom never obtained any immunisation for their children. Thus, mother's education has nonlinear relationship described earlier.

Abuya et al. (2011) and On somu et al. (2015) analyse the effect of maternal education on immunisation and nutritional status in Kenya, where the child mortality rate is 115/1000 children compared to 88/1000 average for Sub Saharan African countries. The data from Kenya Demographic Health Survey (KDHS)-2003 shows that 80 percent of children in Kenya are (nutritionally) stunted and only 49 percent are immunised. Children born to mothers with only a primary education are 2.17 times more likely to be fully immunised compared to those whose mothers lacked any formal education.

Kim et al. (2007) assess the effects of maternal and provider characteristics on children's up-to-date status on age-appropriate immunisation. The study observes that vaccination completion rates vary according to mother's socio-demographic characteristics, especially educational attainment. Lower vaccination completion rates are associated with single motherhood. The rate among children of mothers who are never married is 14 percent, whereas the rate among children of mothers in all other marital status categories combined is 17 percent.

Babalola (2008) introduces household characteristics in the relationship between child immunisation and maternal education and finds that motherly elements are underrated as compared to household characteristics such as income, residence area, etc. Further, children whose mothers have primary education are less likely to be immunised than those whose mothers are illiterate. Another finding of the study shows that mother's knowledge, decision taking power and ideation play crucial role in giving immunisation to their child than the number of years she sat in the classrooms.

Khan et al. (2017) study polio vaccination coverage in Pakistan using DHS data and show that only 56.4 percent of children received complete polio vaccination and it is attributed to maternal education. Women with no education had significantly higher odds of their children receiving no polio vaccination and incomplete vaccination. Further, un-empowered women also have significantly higher odds of not taking their child for any polio vaccination and incomplete vaccination. The multivariate analysis on the relationship between mothers' level of education and polio vaccination uptake for their children shows that 74.4 percent of children of mothers with higher education are completely vaccinated compared to 66.9 percent of those with secondary education and 62.3 percent and 47.1 percent of those with primary and with no education respectively.

Balogun et al. (2017) try to capture the mediating role of maternal literacy and socioeconomic status on the link between maternal education and complete immunisation of children under the age of one in Nigeria. The ability to read and write is considered to be maternal literacy while household expenditure is treated as the measure of socioeconomic status. Using prevalent ratios and regression analysis, the study concludes that the relationship between maternal education and immunisation uptake is substantially explained by maternal literacy. Household economic status is another pathway through which maternal education improves immunisation uptake. The indirect effect of the socioeconomic status is lower compared to maternal literacy skills.

In India, Yadav and Singh (2004) study immunisation status of children and maternal education in Madhya Pradesh in the context of Universisal Immunisation Programme (UIP). The multivariate analysis shows an increasing full vaccination with increasing level of maternal education i.e. significant differences has been observed among the fully immunised children of literate parents especially for literate mother as compared to illiterate parents. Lack of information is main obstacle of non-immunisation.

Phukan et al. (2008) study takes into account the fact that in North Eastern regions of India immunisation coverage is poor. In analysing the factors associated with immunisation coverage of child over the first year of life in Assam, the study observes that only about 62.2 percent of children only are fully immunised. Mother's education level and urban region show significant role in immunisation coverage. Lack of information among the parents is one of the major causes of poor vaccination in North Eastern India.

Patra (2012) analyse the determinants of immunisation coverage in India concluding a strong positive relationship between mother's education and children's immunisation coverage. The study observes that the chance of that the child is immunised is almost three times higher for the children of mothers with high school or above education than the children of illiterate mothers. Mother's awareness about immunisation also has significantly strong positive effect on vaccination. The chance of child immunisation is 58 percent for children of mothers with some awareness of immunisation, whereas it is only 33 percent for children of mothers unaware of vaccination. This study also finds that empowerment of women, exposure of mother towards mass media, mother's employment and her communication skills and fathers education show positive and significant relationship with child vaccination.

Sharma et al. (2013) examine the status and performance of child immunisation programmes in Uttar Pradesh and Uttarakhand during the period 1980-2004 and try to identify the factors stimulating immunisation coverage. The study observes a positive relationship between mother's education and children's vaccination coverage. While 74 percent of children are fully vaccinated whose mothers have completed at least high school, 56 for mothers educated below high school level, only 28 percent of children of non-literate mothers are fully vaccinated. Further, the relationship between vaccination coverage and birth order is consistently negative for almost all vaccinations. About 69 percent of children have received polio vaccine at the time of birth in urban areas whereas this proportion is only 33 percent in rural areas. Full vaccination is likely for male children (47 percent) than for female children (45 percent). A large majority of first-order births occur to younger women who are more likely than order women to utilise child healthcare services. The children from Hindu households are much more likely (47 percent) than children from Muslim families (36 percent) to have received each of the recommended vaccinations.

In a comparative study of India and Pakistan, Subhani et al. (2015) figure out impact of maternal education on child immunisation. Using multinomial logistic model on the categorised variable, fully vaccinated, partially vaccinated and non-vaccinated, the study concludes that the uneducated females living in villages immunised their children less than the educated mothers living in cities. Child immunisation is higher in female headed family than in male headed family. Though both India and Pakistan show the same pattern in odds ratios, there is significant difference in each estimate between the two countries.

Thus, the relationship maternal education and child immunisation, both coverage and full vaccination, has been consistently positive in all studies and immunisation coverage increases with rising female education. Further, the studies also show that lack of information is the main cause for poor vaccination in most studies. Therefore, improvement in female literacy coupled with fostering awareness of immunisation especially among females is suggested as the basic issue in full coverage of child immunisation.

2.3 Data and Methodology

The main focus of this study is to understand the impact of maternal education on child immunisation status. This paper uses the 6th round of the nationally representative Demographic and Health Survey of India for the year 2015-16 (DHS-VI). The global DHS Program, of which India is a part, collects and disseminates nationally representative data on population, family planning, maternal and child health, HIV/AIDS, malaria, nutrition, etc. along with household demographic data for most of the countries. The DHS survey covers information on 3540 variables including data on child characteristics, household characteristics, health history, etc. To study child immunisation coverage, children between the ages of 12 to 23 months are considered. The criterion for selecting samples is whether the sample household holds immunisation card or not. A child is considered to be completely vaccinated if he or she has received a dose of BCG, three doses of DPT and three doses of Oral polio vaccine (OPV) within the age of 12-48 months. The data set for this paper consists of 12817 samples out of a total of 259628 in the DHS-IV survey of India.

In the empirical analysis on the effect of maternal education on child immunisation, this paper takes complete immunisation i.e. if he or she has received a dose of BCG, three doses of DPT and three doses of oral polio vaccine (OPV) within the age of 12-48 months. Therefore, the outcome measure of children immunisation is dichotomous in nature which takes value of 1 for complete immunisation and 0 otherwise. Hence, the logistic regression is identified as the estimating model.

Logit Regression Method

Given the basic regression equation:

$$y_i = \beta_0 + \beta_1 x_i + u_i \tag{2.1}$$

The logistic regression model can be derived as:

$$E(y_i|x_i) = \beta_0 + \beta_1 x_i = p_i \tag{2.2}$$

$$p_i = E(y_i = 1|x_i) = \beta_0 + \beta_1 x_i \tag{2.3}$$

$$p_i = E(y_i = 1|x_i) = \frac{1}{1 + e^{-\beta_0 + \beta_1 x_i}} = \frac{1}{1 + e^{-z_i}} = \frac{e^{z_i}}{1 + e^{z_i}} \tag{2.4}$$

which represents the cumulative logistic distribution. The value of z ranges from -∞ to +∞, p, 0< p <1 is non-linearly related to z. The logistic model cannot be estimated by the OLS method as p is non-linear not only in x but also in β. Therefore,

$$1 - p_i = \frac{1}{1 + e^{z_i}} \tag{2.5}$$

and hence,

$$\frac{p_i}{1-p_i} = \frac{1+e^{z_i}}{1+e^{-z_i}} = e^{z_i} \tag{2.6}$$

Taking log,

$$L_i = ln\left(\frac{p_i}{1-p_i}\right) = lne^{z_i} = z_i = \beta_0 + \beta_1 x_i \tag{2.7}$$

That is L, the log of odds ratio, is not only linear in *x*, but also linear in the parameters. The L_i is the logit and a positive logit means that when the value of regressors increases, the odds that the regressand equals 1 (complete immunisation) increases and if L_i is negative, the odds that the regressand equals 1 decrease as the value of *x* increases. Taking the antilog of L, the odds ratio is obtained and the odds ratio ranges from 0 to ∞.

From the Odds Ratio (OR), estimated through the logistic regression, the probability that a child is fully vaccinated is calculated as:

$$OR = \frac{p}{1-P} \Rightarrow p = OR - (OR)p \Rightarrow OR = p + OR(p) \Rightarrow OR = p(1 + OR)$$
$$\Rightarrow p = \frac{OR}{1+OR} \tag{2.8}$$

As the logit model is non-linear in parameters and variables, the logistic regression is estimated by the maximum likelihood estimation approach.

For a random sample of n observations, let $f_i(y_i)$ denote the probability that $y_i = 1$ or 0, the joint probability of observing the *ny* values $f(y_1, y_2, \dots, y_n)$ is given as:

$$L_i = f(y_1, y_2, \dots, y_n) = \prod_{i=1}^{n} f_i(y_i) = \prod_{i=1}^{n} p_i^{y_i} (1-p_i)^{(1-y_i)} \quad (2.9)$$

The joint probability density function is a product of individual density functions because each y_i is drawn independently and each y_i has the same (logistic) density function, which is the likelihood function. Taking natural logarithm, the log-likelihood function is obtained:

$$\ln(y_1, y_2, \dots, y_n) = \sum_{i=1}^{n} [y_i ln p_i + (1-y_i) ln(1-p_i)] \quad (2.10)$$

$$= \sum_{i=1}^{n} [(y_i ln p_i - y_i ln(1-p_i) + ln(1-p_i)] \quad (2.11)$$

$$= \sum_{i=1}^{n} \left[y_i ln \left(\frac{p_i}{1-p_i} \right) \right] + \sum_{i=1}^{n} \ln(1-p_i) \quad (2.12)$$

Therefore,

$$(1-p_i) = \frac{1}{1+e^{z_i}} \quad (2.13)$$

$$ln\left(\frac{p_i}{1-p_i}\right) = ln e^{z_i} = \beta_0 + \beta_1 x_i \quad (2.14)$$

The log-likelihood function is a function of parameters β_0 and β_1, since the x_i are known. Once the numerical values of β_0 and β_1 are obtained by maximising the log-likelihood function, then the probability and odds ratios are obtained.

Empirically, as the measure of a child immunisation is a binary variable that indicates whether a child had all six vaccinations or not, binary logit regression is estimated. The estimated β coefficients shows how the probability that the discrete dependent variable $y_i = 1$ is predicted to a change from 0 to 1 in a covariate and the marginal effects are calculated using the cumulative logistic distribution function. The estimating logit model is specification as:

Complete Immunisation$_i$ = β_0 + β_1*Mother education* + β_2*Father education* + β_3*Residence* + β_4*Gender of child* + β_5*Age of child* + β_6*Socioeconomic status* + β_7*Community* + β_8*Religion* + β_9*Birth order* + β_{10}*Age of mother* + β_{11}*Birth interval* + β_{12}*Access to information* + u_i (2.15)

2.4 Empirical Analysis

The Table 2.1 presents the descriptive statistics of the variables used in the estimation of the effect of maternal education on child health in India. The descriptive statistics includes mean and standard deviations and proportions for the variables with 12817observations. The mean of education of mothers is 6.69 years with a standard deviation of 5.19 years. The mean of father education is slightly higher, 7.84 years with a dispersed of 4.86 years. The mean age of children is 20.42 months and standard deviation is 5.17 months.

The proportion of children received all course of immunisation in time is 67 percent, while 32 percent of children failed to receive complete vaccination. Surprisingly, more female children (88 percent) has been immunised compared to male children (68 percent). New born babies have higher chances (74 percent) of receiving complete vaccination than older children (60 percent). About 77 percent of children from higher income class received immunisation, while only 59 percent of children in poor families have received full immunisation. While child immunisation is almost complete in urban households, only 88 percent of children are vaccinated in rural areas. There is not much difference by community or religion in child immunisation. But significant difference exists by sources of knowledge as a sizable number of mothers do not read newspapers and watch television which are the main channels of information.

Table 2.1: Descriptive Statistics of Variables in the Analysis of Child Immunisation and Maternal Education in India.

Variable	*Description*	*Mean*	
Complete immunisation	If a child is completely vaccinated i.e. if the child has received a dose of BCG, three doses of DPT and three doses of oral polio vaccine (OPV) within the age of 12-48 months = 1, 0 otherwise i.e. if the child missed any of these five vaccines	0.67 (0.32)	
Child's age	Age of the child between 12 and 23 months	20.42 (5.17)	
Birth order of child	Birth parity/order from the first birth to the last birth of children	2.24 (1.45)	
Mother's education	Completed education of mother (years)	6.69 (5.19)	
age	Age of mother (years)	26.6 (4.94)	
Father's education	Completed years of education of father (years)	7.84 (4.86)	
Proportions		Complete vaccination	No full immunisation
Child's gender	Male child =1 Female child - 2	67.89 88.27	32.05 21.73
Birth interval	≥ 48 months = 1 25–47 months =2 ≤ 24 months = 3	60.24 67.09 73.87	27.72 32.91 38.71
Socioeconomic status	Poor income= 0 Middle income = 1 High income = 2	58.92 70.49 76.78	41.08 29.51 23.22

(Contd...)

Community	SC = 1 ST = 2 Other backward class = 3 Others = 4	68.42 60.15 68.86 70.27	31.56 39.85 31.39 29.72
Religion	Hindu = 1 Muslim = 2 Christian = 3 Others = 4	68.56 68.03 59.60 76.39	31.44 40.86 40.40 23.51
Residence	Urban = 1 Rural = 0	99.00 88.12	1.00 11.46
Information source	Mother reads newspaper = 1 Not reading newspaper = 0	63.17 37.55	32.43 68.78
Information source	Mother watches television = 1 Not watching television = 0	78.56 21.78	21.45 77.96
Observations		12817	

Note: Standard deviations in parentheses.

The Table 2.2 presents the logistic regression estimates of complete immunisation with alternative specifications. The primary interest is to identify the effect of maternal education on child immunisation. In the first specification where the maternal education alone is regressed on child immunisation, the estimated coefficient is positive and statistically significant. An increase of a year of mother's education, the probability of child getting immunised increased by 0.0214. Controlling for confounding effects of socioeconomic and demographic characteristics also, the effect of mother's education is attenuated, in such a way that the probability of child immunisation is almost the same, ranging from 1.3 percent to 1.8 percent. In all specifications the coefficients are still positive and statistically significant. Thus, maternal education is important for complete vaccination of children.

The estimated results show that father's education also play a positive and statistically significant role in child immunisation, though its effect is somewhat lower than maternal education. Age of the children has no statistically significant effect on child immunisation, whereas age of mother influences child immunisation positively and significantly. The birth order effect on the probability of child receiving complete immunisation is significantly negative the birth interval has no significant effect. Older children have about 3 percent less chances of completely immunised. The probability of receiving complete immunisation is significantly higher for male child and urban residence. The probability of male child getting immunised is higher by 1.6 percent than the female child. Another significant variable in child vaccination is the income status. While the probability of child immunisation is significantly negative for poor families, other income groups have statistical impact on child vaccination.

The community background has little effect on complete immunisation of children, whereas the effect of all religion on child immunisation is significantly negative. The effect of knowledge of immunisation helps higher chances of child getting complete vaccination in time as the positive and significant coefficients of reading newspaper and watching television reveals.

Thus, the overall estimated logistic regression results show that maternal education dominates over all other factors in generating a significant impact on child immunisation coverage. The estimates also show a consistent attenuation of positive measure of probability of getting child immunised as the maternal education increases in all specifications considered.

Table 2.2: Logistic Regression Estimates of Child Immunisation in India.

Variable	*Speci.1*	*Speci.2*	*Speci.3*	*Speci.4*	*Speci.5*
Mother's education	0.0214*** (0.0008)	0.0183*** (0.001)	0.0165*** (0.001)	0.0165*** (0.001)	0.0138*** (0.001)
Father's education	-	0.0045*** (0.001)	0.0026** (0.001)	0.002** (0.001)	0.0019** (0.001)
Age of child	-	-0.0003 (0.0008)	0.0003 (0.0008)	-0.0006 (0.0008)	-0.0007 (0.0008)
Male child	-	0.013** (0.084)	0.0163** (0.0084)	0.0162** (0.0084)	0.016** (0.0084)
Urban	-	0.0217** (0.010)	0.0089 (0.011)	0.0078 (0.011)	0.0067 (0.011)
Poor income	-	-	-0.059*** (0.013)	-0.0450*** (0.013)	-0.036* (0.013)
Middle income	-	-	-0.010 (0.013)	-.0048 (0.013)	-0.003 (0.013)
SC	-	-	-0.064 (0.074)	-0.0508 (0.075)	-0.0508 (0.076)
ST	-	-	-0.1006 (0.088)	-0.087 (0.087)	-0.087 (0.087)
OBC	-	-	-0.022 (0.085)	-0.020 (0.085)	-0.019 (0.085)
Hindu	-		-0.07* (0.023)	-0.066* (0.023)	-0.066* (0.023)
Muslim	-	-	-0.131*** (0.028)	-0.116*** (0.028)	-0.113*** (0.028)
Christian	-	-	-0.162*** (0.032)	-0.145*** (0.032)	-0.152*** (0.032)
Birth order	-	-	-	-0.029*** (0.004)	-0.029*** (0.004)
Mother's age	-	-	-	0.004*** (0.001)	0.004*** (.001)
Birth interval ≥ 48 months	-	-	-	-0.003 (0.011)	-0.001 (0.011)

(Contd...)

Birth interval ≤ 24 months	-	-	-	0.0028 (0.011)	0.0039 (.011)
Mother reads newspaper	-	-	-	-	0.023* (.023)
Mother watches television	-	-	-	-	0.036* (0.11)
Log- likelihood	-7772.74	-7759.67	-7709.92	-7679.22	-7670.91
LR chi2(1)	689.48	715.64	815.13	876.53	893.14
Prob.> chi²	0.000	0.000	0.000	0.000	0.000
Pseudo R- square	0.045	0.044	0.050	0.054	0.055

Note: Standard errors in parentheses. *** significant at 1 percent level ** significant at 5 percent level * significant at 10 percent level.

2.5 Conclusion

Education makes a woman empowered and this empowered woman is central for fruitful decisions, especially on health and education of children. Female education builds strong mindsets and is effective in improving communication and maintaining relations with the society. The crucial role of women education especially in intrahousehold allocation of resources specifically towards girl child is well documented in the literature. The effect of female education of the utilisation of government services especially on healthcare is also well recognised. Maternal education is the crucial factor in seeking both neonatal and post-natal care of both the mother and the child. This focus of this paper is to understand the effect of maternal education on child health in India. The paper measures child health in terms of complete immunisation, the child receiving all vaccinations - a dose of BCG, three doses of DPT and three doses of Oral Polio Vaccine (OPV) within the age of 12-48 months. To study the impact of maternal education on child immunisation status, this paper uses the 6th round of the Demographic and Health Survey of India for the year 2015-16 (DHS-VI), the nationwide survey consisting of 12817 samples out of a total of 259628 in the DHS-IV survey of India. Empirically, as the dependent variable is binary - whether the child received complete immunisation or not, logistic regression is used.

The logit estimates show that the effect of maternal education on complete child vaccination is significantly positive. Woman with at least formal education is better placed in seeking child healthcare. This positive effect is further facilitated by knowledge and awareness of immunisation programmes. The information on child vaccination is enhanced with maternal education. Socioeconomic status, father's education, birth order, urban residence and religion also show significant influence on child immunisation status. Significantly, more boys receive complete immunisation than girls, showing some form of neglect of female children. The estimated results also show that community and births are not important for child immunisation in India. Therefore, an integrated approach that improves female schooling, increasing the level of health knowledge, and developing positive attitudes toward modern healthcare among mothers are beneficial for complete vaccination of children in India. This is also a key to improving child health and reducing child mortality in India bringing India a step closer to achieving the SDG goals.

3

The Determinants of Demand for Education: Ordered Logit Estimation of Educational Attainment

3.1 Introduction

The human capital embodied in human beings, specifically education, is valued as one of the significant catalysts to economic growth and social development of a country (Bhaumik and Chakrabarty, 2010). It is widely accepted education and economic growth are positively related and that education helps to improve the living standards of people improving the occupation and earnings of individuals. Educating more people in the country means positive change of the society as well. The new theory of economic growth postulates that government should invest more on human capital to encourage economic growth in the country through increased productivity and improved technology and innovations. Therefore, both public and private expenditures on education are viewed as investments just like as investments in manufacturing and land. Human capital investments have not only private returns to the investor, but also generate social returns in the form of healthy society and responsible citizens. The ever increasing household expenditure on education implies that households value education as an investment as they regard investing in education yields high returns in the future. This view tempts to suggest that individuals who commit higher budgets towards their education expenses are likely to progress to higher levels of education as well as completing at the expected age as opposed to those who receives less to nothing towards their schooling expenses.

However, some groups such as religious and social groups and culturally conservative groups prefer educating or sending boys to school over girls and invest less in the education of girl child. Education bias can be one of the major challenges that individuals might face. Such challenges might be inflicted by individuals, social phenomena such as culture, religion and society. This means that there will be more educated men than women, creating an education gender gap between men and women. Such practice has come a long way, and it still practiced in some societies and the end result is that women find it hard to complete even the first level of education. Tilak (2002) refers to various social and cultural reasons and households might spend or may have a preference to spend on education of their sons than their daughters or vice versa. Household characteristics, such as religion, caste, household size, educational levels of the parents, occupational of parents, etc. embedded in the so called social, cultural, religious and regional biases are viewed as the main influences on the nature and quantum of household investments on the education of their children. Therefore, it is very important to understand the role of household expenditure, gender, religion and economic and social groups in determining the education attainment of individuals in the household.

Further, due to difference in social organisation, different states in India have different levels of commitments towards education system as well as its performance in their states and regions. Hence, this paper aims to investigate the determinants of education attainment in the major 17 states of India. In the empirical investigation, this paper uses the 2012 NSSO data at the individual level comprising 2,48,098 individuals in these 17 states. To capture education level completed, all levels of education from the lowest to the highest level of education are ordered, primary education being the lowest level of education and post-graduation being the highest level of education. Since the educational attainment is an ordered category that is, attaining each level of education is conditional on not exiting the education process after completing the previous level of education, the ordered logit model of estimation is used in the empirical analysis.

3.2 A Brief Review of Recent Studies

Bhaumik and Chakrabarty (2008; 2009) analyse the differential role of human capital or educational attainment in explaining earnings differentials by gender and socioeconomic groups. They note that while the earnings differentials by religion or social constructs such as caste or between Indian wage earners and their counterparts in other emerging markets are well documented (Bargain et al. 2009), the inter-group differences in educational attainment, specifically the issue of transition from one educational level to the next remains relatively unexplored (Bhalotra and Zamora, 2010). The estimated results suggest that in both rural and urban areas, the transition probabilities for men are higher than for females for all educational levels. The difference in transition probabilities of men and women is particularly higher in rural areas. There also exists is a significant rural-urban divide. Transition probabilities of urban females, while significantly lower than those of their urban male counterparts is comparable to, and marginally better than, those of their rural male counterparts. They attribute these differentials to poor economic conditions that decrease the funding from state tax revenues, availability of student loans, chances of working a part time job as well as increases in tuition fees and other private costs of education.

Bhaumik and Chakrabarty (2010) investigate the relative impact of personal household and state level characteristics including government policy on the likelihood of transition educational levels using the 61st round of the NSSO survey. The data used contains 14332 individuals in the 25-30 age group cross classifying as Hindus and Muslims and the levels of education considered are primary education, middle education, higher education and tertiary education. The order logit model has been applied for analysing the odds of transitions from primary education level to tertiary education. The estimated results show that the transition to a higher level of education of Hindu individuals is influenced by the household characteristics or family background, government policy and the economic environment prevailing in the state at the time of the relevant decision. The educational attainment of the household head and the socioeconomic status of the household have a significant and positive impact on the likelihood of the transition at each level of an individual's educational attainment and such influences are more effective at the first level of education. Both government policy and the stage of economic development of the state have a positive impact on the likelihood of transition to middle school and higher secondary level of education. However, the level of development does not have any influence for moving to the tertiary education but government expenditure has a negative influence. In the case of Muslim individuals, household head and economic status have significant positive impact on individual transition likelihood at each level of educational attainment while household head educational attainment has a less influence especially at lower level of transitions. Compared to a Hindu, Muslim individual transition likelihood is inversely related to literacy rate of the resident state. For woman, the likelihood to move to the next higher level of education declines from primary to middle school or higher level of education and government policy and state level economic environment influence the transition likelihood as well.

Bhaumik and Chakrabarty (2012) examine high school dropout rates in India, which has a negative effect for human capital formation and as a result poor long-term economic growth potential. Using the 2004-05 NSSO employment-unemployment survey data, the transition probabilities of moving from a number of different educational levels to higher educational levels are estimated by a sequential logit model. The transition probabilities and educational attainment of males and females in rural and urban areas are estimated as a function of family background, gender, ethnicity and religion. The sequential logit model to estimate the transition probabilities are also used by Sander (1992) and Tansel (1997; 2002). The estimated results suggest that the overall probability of reaching tertiary education is very low. Further, the results reveal that women are significantly worse-off even by the overall standards particularly in rural areas.

Chaudhri and Jha (2011; 2012) studying child poverty, demographic transition and gender bias in education identify some of the major characteristics of demographic transition and child education and their relation to household poverty status in India. The evidence from their analysis of the census data (1951-2001) and the NSSO surveys of 1993-94 (50th round) and 2004-05 (61st round). They stress that even though total fertility rates have declined for the country as a whole including all the states, there is a considerable variation by space, poverty status and education of women in the household in the two cross-sections. The probit and logit estimates also reveal evidence for gender bias in education. The sequential logit model indicates that children (under 15 years of age) growing up in poor and/or nutritionally deprived households also live with a number of challenges of deprivations that stifle their freedom to actively participate in and benefit from early or elementary school education. Lack of health care, limited access to quality schooling and opportunity cost of participation in education are some of the layers that prohibit girl child education in India.

3.3 Data and Methodology

In the empirical analysis of the determinants of completion of education level by an individual, this paper uses individual level data from the 2012 NSSO 68^{th}round data for 17 major states in India. States included in the study are Andhra Pradesh, Bihar, Jharkhand, Gujarat, Haryana, Karnataka,

Kerala, Madhya Pradesh, Chhattisgarh, Maharashtra, Orissa, Punjab, Rajasthan, Tamil Nadu, Uttar Pradesh, Uttarakhand and West Bengal. The 17 major states in India account for 87 percent of India's population and over 85 percent of India's GDP. The left out states are the North Eastern states and Jammu and Kashmir, as major political uncertainties and insurgencies in these states impacts educational outcomes differently compared to the 17 states where the educational outcomes are generally from theses exigencies. Some other states are later carved out of an existing state or clubbed with other states in the educational system. Therefore, it is empirically difficult to include them with the chosen states. The sample for these 17 states consists of 2,48,098 observations. The data contains individual information such as gender, religion, urban/rural location, monthly household expenditure on education, community, education and age. All education levels completed from the lowest primary education to the highest level of education are considered. As the educational attainment is an ordered category, the empirical analysis uses ordered logit regression estimation method.

The focus is on individuals in the 6-34 age groups. At the age of 6 an individual should have completed the first level of education which is the primary level. One year is added to this age to make provision for any other event that may have occurred to delay finishing primary level on time. That makes the individual to complete lower level of education at (6+1)=7 years of age. If an individual did not complete it at that age, then it is treated as failure or exit. For instance, someone who is 34 years of age in year 2012 should have completed his primary education in the year 1985, at the age 7, and it is assigning a dummy=1 otherwise 0. After completing primary level, individual can choose to continue to the next level and is expected to complete the 12th standard at age of 18 (17+1), that is by the year 1996, if not will exit, and go for three years of under graduate completing at the age 21 by year 2002. Then, the individual may choose to continue to post graduate education for 2 years completing at age 24 (2+1). Hence, at the age of 34 an individual should have completed all 6 levels of education, possibly still higher levels like Ph.D. degree. Therefore, the upper age limit is influenced by the availability of data and the upper age limit is chosen as 34 years. All educational decisions by the individual is taken to move from the lower level (j^{th}) education level to the next upper level of education ($j+1^{th}$) is influenced by the individual, household and economic conditions prevailing at the time at which the decision is taken. To account for economic and other environmental influences, this paper uses the states of India as indicators for appropriate data on economic conditions prevailing in different states of India at different times going back from 1985 to 2012.

As the education level completed by an individual is ordered from the lowest level of education to the highest education level conditional on age, the ordered logistic regression model is used in this paper. The progression through educational levels is conditional on not exiting the process after completing the previous level of education. The individual can drop out of the education system after completing one level of education or some years of education within the level. Further, not all those who completed the primary level continue into secondary level and only few of the secondary level enter and complete the tertiary or higher education in India. Thus, there is a well-defined sequence and order in education - tertiary education is higher than high school education and the sequence and the risk of not making the transition from one level of education to the next cannot be ignored. Following Bhaumik and Chakrabarty (2010), the completed education level of individuals is modeled as an ordered logit model, specifying four levels of education - primary, middle school, higher secondary, and tertiary (diploma/certificate, undergraduate, post graduate) levels of education that exists in the Indian education system.

The ordinal structure of the education levels in India is depicted in Figure 3.1which presents the probability table in an order from the first/ lowest level of education (primary) to the highest level of education (post graduate) and the probability of completing the highest grade at the right age (p) and probability of not completing the next high level of education at the expected age (1-p). After completing any level of education j, an individual i has a choice to progress to the next higher level of education with a probability pj or drop out of school with the probability of (1-p)j.

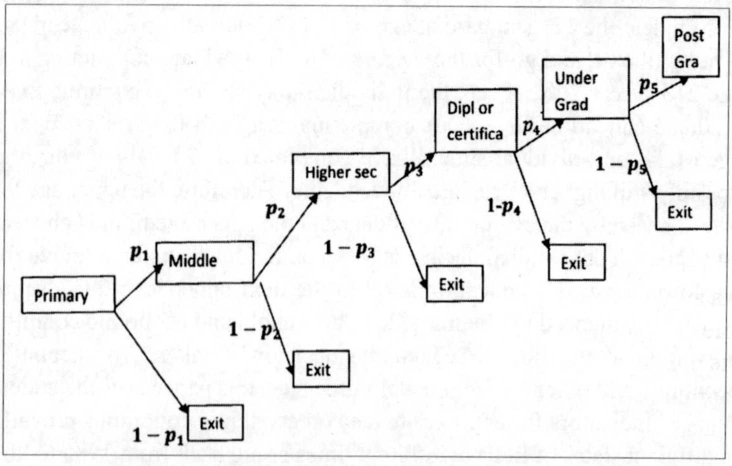

Figure 3.1: Ordered Structure of Education Levels in India

According to Long and Freese (2001), while categories of an ordinal variable can be ranked, the distances between the categories are unknown. Ordinal variables are often coded as consecutive integers from 1 to the number of categories, from 1 indicating primary level of education completed to 6indicating post graduates which is the highest level of education to be completed. As a consequence of this coding, ordinal outcomes may be analysed with the linear regression model. However, as the distance between ordinal categories is not uniform, an ordinal dependent variable violates the assumption of the linearity of OLS estimation which can lead to incorrect conclusions Therefore, with ordinal outcomes, it is much better to use models that avoid the assumption that the distances between categories are equal. While many different models have been designed for ordinal outcomes, the logit and probit versions of the ordinal regression model introduced by McKelvey and Zavoina (1975) in terms of an underlying latent variable and by McCullagh (1980) who referred to the logit version as the proportional odds model. The ordered regression model is nonlinear and the magnitude of the change in the outcome probability for a given change in one of the independent variables depends on the levels of all of the independent variables. The estimated coefficient summarises the effects of the independent variables in a way that fully reflects key substantive processes without overwhelming and distracting detail.

Ordered Logit Regression Method

The ordinal regression model starts from a latent variable (structural) model. Defining y as a latent i.e. an unobserved variable, the underlying structural model is specified as:

$$y_i^* = \beta x_i + u_i \tag{3.1}$$

The observed model for a discrete outcome is specified as:

$$y_i = \begin{Bmatrix} 1 & if \ \ \beta x_i > 0 \\ 0 & if \ \ \beta x_i \leq 0 \end{Bmatrix} \tag{3.2}$$

The measurement model for j outcomes is expanded to divide y_i^* into J ordinal categories:

$$y_i = j \ \ if \ \ \kappa_{j-1} \leq y_i^* < \kappa_j \qquad j = 1, \dots, J \tag{3.3}$$

where the cutpoints or thresholds κ_1 through κ_{J-1} are to be estimated. The threshold value represents the level of x at which y changes its value. In the present study, the outcome variable completed educational level takes four possible outcome categories: 1=primary education (PED), 2=middle education (MED), 3=high secondary education (SED), and 4=higher/

tertiary education (HED). These observed response categories are tied to the latent variable by the measurement model as:

$$y_i = \begin{cases} 1 = PED \;\; if\; \kappa_0 = -\infty \le y_i^* < \kappa_1 \\ 2 = MED \;\; if\; \kappa_1 \le y_i^* < \kappa_2 \\ 3 = SED \;\; if\; \kappa_2 \le y_i^* < \kappa_3 \\ 4 = HED \;\; if\; \kappa_3 \le y_i^* < \kappa_4 \end{cases} \tag{3.4}$$

For one independent variable, the structural model is specified as:

$$y_i^* = \beta x + u_i \tag{3.5}$$

The Figure 3.2 plots such a model along with the cutpoints for the measurement model. The plot is similar to that for the binary regression model except that there are now three horizontal lines representing the cutpoints κ_1, κ_2, and κ_3 and the three cutpoints lead to four observed outcomes of the observed variable y. In terms of graph, the probability of an observed outcome for a given value of x is the area under the curve between a pair of cutpoints.

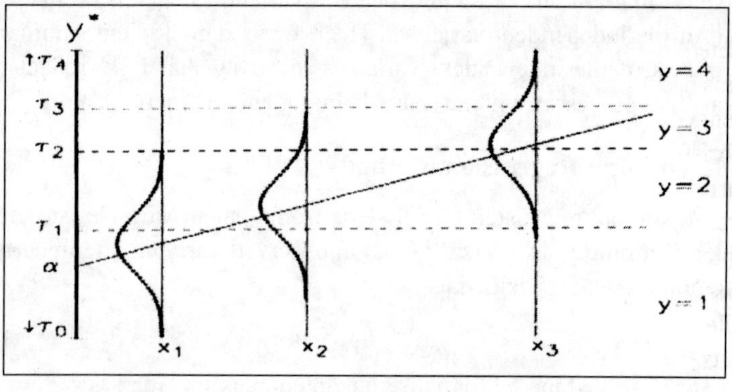

Figure 3.2: Plot of Latent Variable Model with Cutpoints.

For example, the probability of observing y=j for given values of x corresponds to the region of the distribution where y falls between κ_{j-1} and κ_j:

$$P(y = 1|x) = P(\kappa_{j-1} \le y_i^* < \kappa_j|x) \tag{3.6}$$

Substituting $\beta x + u$ for y^* and some algebra yields the standard formula for the predicted probability of the ordered response model:

$$P(y = 1|x) = \Phi(\kappa_j - \beta x) - \Phi(\kappa_{j-1} - \beta x) \tag{3.7}$$

where Φ is the cumulative density function. For y=1, the second term on the right drops out since Φ(-∞-βx)=0 and for y=J, the first term equals Φ(-∞-βx)=1.

The ordinal regression model can also be developed as a nonlinear probability model without appealing to the idea of a latent variable. The odds (π) that an outcome is less than or equal to j versus greater than j for given x can be defined as:

$$\pi \leq j|x = P(y \leq j|x)m = 1, \ldots, J-1 \tag{3.8}$$

The log of the odds equals:

$$\ln(\pi \leq j|x) = \kappa_j - \beta x \tag{3.9}$$

For one independent variable and multiple outcome categories, the odds ratio is specified as:

$$ln\left[\frac{P(y \leq j|x)}{P(y > j|x)}\right] = \kappa_j - \beta x \qquad j = 1, \ldots, J \tag{3.10}$$

3.4 Empirical Analysis

The Figure 3.3 and Table 3.1 show that not just there are more Hindus than any other religion in the 17 states, but more Hindus also complete the expected level of education at the right/expected age. About 80 percent of Hindus have completed primary level of education, compared to around 20 percent of Muslims, almost three times less than Hindus. Only 5 percent of Christians have completed their first highest level of education and in other religions only 4 percent have completed primary education level at the relevant age. In middle education level, 71 percent of Hindus have completed middle level of education at the expected age (18), while only 15 percent of Muslims and 9.5 percent of Christians have completed middle level of education. At the under graduate level, 77 percent of Hindus, 10 percent of Muslims and 8 percent of Christians have completed under graduate at the expected age. In regard to post graduate level, 80 percent of Hindus, 9.5 percent of Muslim and 5.5 percent of Christians have completed post-graduation at the expected age.

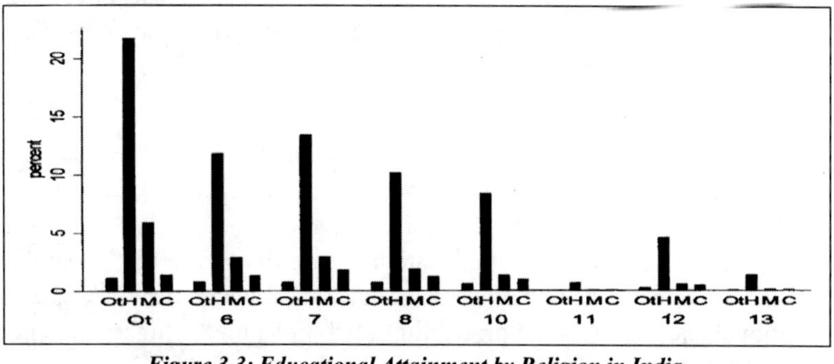

Figure 3.3: Educational Attainment by Religion in India.

Table 3.1: Educational Attainment in India by Religion.

Education level	*Hindus*	*Muslims*	*Christians*	*Others*	*Total*
No formal education	53969 (71.99) [30.08]	14709 (19.62) [37.51]	3493 (4.66) [18.90]	2795 (3.73) [25.41]	74996 (100) [30.22]
Primary	29377 (70.1) [16.38]	7215 (17.22) [18.40]	3342 (7.98) [18.08]	1971 (4.70) [17.92]	41905 (100) [16.89]
Middle	33433 (71.12) [14.04]	7234 (15.39) [18.45]	4459 (9.49) [24.13]	1885 (4.01) [17.92]	47011 (100) [18.95]
Secondary	25188 (72.38) [14.04]	4720 (13.56) [12.04]	3075 (8.84) [16.64]	1816 (5.22) [16.51]	34799 (100) [14.03]
Higher secondary	20806 (73.89) [11.60]	3304 (11.73) [8.43]	2459 (8.73) [13.30]	1590 (5.65) [14.46]	28159 (100) [11.35]
Diploma / Certificate	1788 (79.71) [1.00]	181 (8.07) [0.46]	211 (9.41) [1.14]	63 (2.81) [0.57]	2243 (100) [0.90]
Under graduate	11381 (77.42) [6.34]	1442 (9.81) [3.68]	1198 (8.15) [6.48]	680 (4.63) [6.18]	14701 (100) [5.93]
Post graduate	3453 (80.23) [1.92]	408 (9.48) [1.04]	245 (5.69) [1.33]	198 (4.6) [1.8]	4304 (100) [1.73]
Total	179395 (72.31) [100]	39213 (15.81) [100]	18482 (7.45) [100]	10998 (4.43) [100]	248098 (100) [100]

The estimating ordered logit regression equation is specified as:

$$P(y_i = j|x) = \beta_1 Age + \beta_2 HHIncome + \beta_3 HHSize + \beta_4 Gender + \beta_5 Religion + \beta_6 Community + \beta_7 Residence + \beta_8 Occupation + \beta_9 State + u_i \quad (3.11)$$

The y_i is conditional that the probability for y to occur given x is only if j has been completed. The j-1 in J is the previous or lower level of education that should be completed before moving to the next higher level of education. The determining variables include age, gender, occupation and employment, household size, religion, community, and state dummies to capture the economic and physical environment that affects an individual's educational progress. The Table 3.1 describes the variables in the empirical analysis of the determinants of educational level completion by an individual.

The estimated ordered logit regression coefficients are presented in Table 3.2 along with odds ratio. The coefficients of ordered logit regression are the estimates of the probability of moving from the primary education to any of the further levels of education. The estimated results show that almost all the estimated coefficients are statistically significant. A year of additional age increases the probability of completing the highest level of education by 0.123 units and the odds ratio is 0.132. Similarly, an increase in monthly per capita expenditure, proxy for household income, increases the probability of the highest education completion by 2.75 percent and the corresponding log of odds is 0.317. An addition of a family member is expected to increase the log odds of highest education level completed by 0.018. If an individual is Hindu or Muslim, the probability of completing the highest education decreases by 0.153 and 0.676 while the log odds of completing higher level of education at the expected age increases by 0.131 for a Christian compared to other religious groups. Males have 0.282 higher probability of completing the highest level of education at the right/ expected age relative to females. Similarly, the rural background depresses the probability of completing education at the expected age by 1.82 percent.

Table 3.2: Ordered Logit Estimates of Educational Attainment in India.

Variable	*Coefficient*	*Std. error*	*z-value*	*Odds ratio*
Age	0.124***	0.0005	25.76	1.132
Monthly household per capita expenditure	0.275***	0.003	82.32	1.317
Household size	0.018***	0.001	7.60	1.018
Male	0.282***	0.007	38.05	1.325
Hindu	-0.153***	0.020	7.60	0.857
Muslim	-0.676***	0.022	30.41	0.508
Christian	0.123***	0.023	5.15	1.131
SC	-0.051***	0.012	41.15	0.600
ST	-0.539***	0.015	37.28	0.583
Rural	-0.181***	0.009	20.79	0.834
Agriculture	-0.421***	0.020	20.93	0.654
Non-agriculture	-0.458***	0.019	24.37	0.632
Salary	-0.093***	0.019	4.89	0.911
Agricultural casual labour	-0.566***	0.026	37.03	0.381
Non-agricultural casual labour	0.018***	0.021	52.22	0.340
State dummies	Yes			
Cutpoint 1	0.769			
Cutpoint 2	1.707			
Cutpoint 3	2.752			
Log-likelihood	-383997.99			
LR chi^2	99242.4			
Prob.>chi^2	0.000			
Pseudo R^2	0.115			
Obs.	248098			

Note: Standard errors in parentheses. *** significant at 1 percent level.

The transition probability of completing education levels by religion, gender and residence are reported in Table 3.3. It can be observed that the probability of educational transition is higher at lower levels of education completed than at higher levels. Irrespective of religion or gender or residence, the mean probability of completion of primary education level is consistently higher than the completion of the college level education. Similarly, the Hindus have higher mean probability of completion of each level of education compared to Muslims and urban residents have higher mean probability of completion of education level relative to the rural residents.

Table 3.3: Mean Transition Probabilities of Completion of Education Level in India.

Education level	*Hindu*				*Muslim*			
	Male		*Female*		*Male*		*Female*	
	Rural	*Urban*	*Rural*	*Urban*	*Rural*	*Urban*	*Rural*	*Urban*
Primary	0.179	0.129	0.173	0.127	0.172	0.221	0.173	0.217
Middle	0.227	0.269	0.223	0.263	0.234	0.298	0.267	0.291
Secondary	0.208	0.213	0.208	0.214	0.209	0.216	0.208	0.291
Under graduate	0.104	0.148	0.108	0.150	0.077	0.105	0.082	0.107
Post graduate	0.032	0.054	0.032	0.053	0.020	0.031	0.022	0.031

The Hindu males from urban areas have a less probability of completing primary level than their rural counterparts (0.129 vs 0.179). The mean probability of a Hindu from rural area completing primary education is also higher (0.173) compared to their urban counterparts (0.127). However, the urban Muslim females have higher mean probability of completion of primary education (0.217) relative to the rural Muslim females (0.173). The Hindu males from rural areas have a higher mean probability of completing post graduate education (0.032) compared to male Muslims in rural areas (0.020). The same can be said for Hindu females in urban areas who have higher mean probability to that of Muslim females from urban areas.

3.5 Conclusion

Education is an engine that stimulates and accelerates economic growth and development of any type of country as well as for the individual development and progress. Therefore, individual' spending on education is regarded as an investment. Apart from government and private spending on education, the general environment including demographic characteristics and government policies are important determinants of individual. Individuals' educational choice and performance are to be viewed from a broader perspective not only limited to what the government supply in the form of grants to schools or other forms of benefits to schools. Individual's educational choice as well as performance is influenced by regional differentials in economic policies as well as different environmental factors. The effects of household expenditure, household size and composition, gender, religion, community, social groups, regional aspects and state policies on both educational investments as well as education attainment are well documented. It is also well researched that both governments and households spend increasingly on education. However, can it be concluded that individuals who receive higher budgets towards their education expenses are likely to progress to higher levels of education completing at the expected age as opposed to those who receive less to nothing towards their schooling expenses? An answer to this is complex and the evidences are less convincing.

Therefore, this paper investigates the determinants of education attainment in the major 17 states of India using the 2012 NSSO data applying the ordered logit model. The estimated logit estimates show that age, household income, and household size increase the probability of completing the educational levels. The males have higher probability of completing the highest level of education relative to females. The Hindu and Muslim individuals have lower probability of completing the highest education while the log odds of completing higher level of education is higher for Christians. The rural background depresses the probability of educational attainment. The community backgrounds have a negative effect on the level of education completed. The probability of completing education level is relatively higher for scheduled castes compared to scheduled tribes. All employments have negative effects on completion of education levels, except the non-agricultural casual labour. The salary workers have slightly higher probability of completing the highest education level than dependents of agriculture. Individuals belonging to states of Tamil Nadu, Kerala, Maharashtra or Karnataka have better chances of completing the highest grade compared to individuals in other states of India. The probability of educational transition is higher at lower levels of education than at higher levels. Irrespective of religion or gender or residence, the mean probability of completion of primary education level is consistently higher than the completion of the college level education. The Hindus have higher mean probability of completion of each level of education compared to Muslims and urban residents have higher mean probability of completion of education level relative to the rural residents.

4

The Determinants of Financial Inclusion: Multinomial Logit Estimation of Bank Account Holding and Sources of Credit

4.1 Introduction

In the more and more monetising economy, without access to financial services in various forms offered by various institutions, the economically poor individuals and small business enterprises rely on their own limited savings and earnings and to a significant extent the local moneylenders and informal monetary transactions. Including the entities that are hitherto excluded from financial services i.e. financial inclusion serves as an effective tool for reducing poverty and income inequality as well as improving welfare. However, the nature, scope and ways and means of financial inclusion vary according to the place and sources. There is no universally accepted definition of financial inclusion. Financial inclusion is generally understood as the access and uptake of affordable financial services, which allows an individual to store money in a safe place, access credit, insurance products and managing risks. The Consultative Group to Assist the Poor (CGAP) (2009) defines financial inclusion as "a state in which all working age adults have effective access to credit, savings, payments and insurance from formal service providers" and effective access is defined as "convenient and responsible service delivery, at a cost affordable to the customer and sustainable for the provider". The World Bank (2017) defines financial inclusion as the "means that individuals and businesses have access to useful and affordable financial products and services that meet their needs - transactions, payments, savings, credit and insurance – delivered in a responsible and sustainable way".

The concept of financial inclusion has become the buzz word and gained momentum in the context of developing economies with the development of the concept and institutions of microfinance and with the ambitious launching of the Millennium Development Goals (MDGs) and the Sustainable Development Goals (SDGs) by the World Bank. Though the access of finance has not been directly spelt, it is an important contributor (direct or indirect) for achievement of most of these goals. Access to financial services also improves income opportunities and thus the possibility of obtaining health and education services. It also contributes to gender equality by letting women to have direct access which also makes them financially independent. According to Demirguc Kunt et al. (2015), out of 143 economies, 63 percent have a mandate to promote financial inclusion and more than 50 countries have set formal targets and goals for financial inclusion. Given the importance of financial inclusion for development, international institutions including the G20 and the World Bank have also initiated to formulate strategies to promote financial institution. Improved financial services would lead to increased economic activities and employment opportunities for rural households, as more economic activities raise the disposable income, leading to more savings and a robust deposit base for the bank, resulting in inclusive economic growth (Khan, 2011). The role of financial institutions in addressing issues such as global poverty, income inequality, underdevelopment and welfare are well documented. With more and more people coming under the purview of financial system, their combined impact contributes to faster development process. Further, formal financial services reduce the dominance of informal financial institutions, which are exploitative in nature and access to formal financial services increases efficiency of the resource allocation and reduces cost of capital (Sarma and Pais, 2011).

The iconic story of microcredit in Bangladesh continues to thrive as a force across the regions. The microcredit helps to narrow down the gender disparity in account ownership and advance financial literacy and capability among women. In India, the launch of the Pradhan Mantri Jan Dhan Yojana (PMJDY) program in 2014 has been one of the world's largest financial inclusion initiatives to date and is a prominent example of India's commitment of advancing financial inclusion. The PMJDY has dramatically expanded access to formal financial services. Beyond this traditional microfinance, the availability of technology has started to promote a new wave of branchless banking. The African countries have made significant strides toward advancing financial inclusion through digital technology. Developing countries adopt the internet technology very fast with several microfinance banks, mobile operators and more recently the commercial banks pursuing the business very diligently. The rapid proliferation of digital financial platforms and services, particularly mobile money, has been a key driver of financial inclusion progress across the region. But, the main barriers to using mobile money services include the limited mobile phone ownership as well as a lack of understanding surrounding mobile money.

Despite the rapid expansion of financial services, in absolute terms financial inclusion remains limited and significant gap prevails including a quite prominent gender disparity with women being excluded from formal financial services. In India, though the PMJDY program has enormously expanded access to financial services and ensure access to financial services such as accounts, credit, remittances, etc. to the people who are often excluded from the formal financial sector, further efforts still remain to ensure that individuals can efficiently leverage these services. As of 2016, around a quarter of accounts opened under PMJDY are dormant indicating the benefits of the initiative were unrealised. An earlier initiative, the Swabhiman Campaign (self-respect) introduced in 2004, also aimed at inculcating self-respect and confidence to people by making them aware of financial sectors and banking services. It especially focused on including rural people in banking services and linking them to the financial sector of India in an organised way. On its part, the RBI has advised all banks to open Basic Saving Bank Deposit (BSBD) accounts with minimum common facilities such as no minimum balance, deposit and withdrawal of cash at bank branches and ATMs, receipt/credit of money through electronic payment channels, facility of providing ATM card. It has also relaxed and simplified KYC norms to facilitate easy opening of bank accounts, especially for small amount. The RBI has also made it compulsory for banks to set up rural branches in un-banked villages and banks are directed to allocate at least 25 percent of the total number of branches in the rural centres.

The extent of financial inclusion in India can be gauged from the trend in the sources of borrowing by the people over the years. The Figure 4.1 which depicts the trend of sources of borrowing shows that in the initial phase from 1950s to 1970s, people were more susceptible to informal borrowings, from sources like moneylenders, unauthorised lending services and friends. After the nationalisation of banks and opening of the economy, the trend of borrowing has been changing. The tendency of borrowing from formal sources increases whereas borrowing from informal sources has gone down. This change in pattern of borrowing indeed is an indication of financial inclusion and such growth in financial services contributes to a financial progress in the economy.

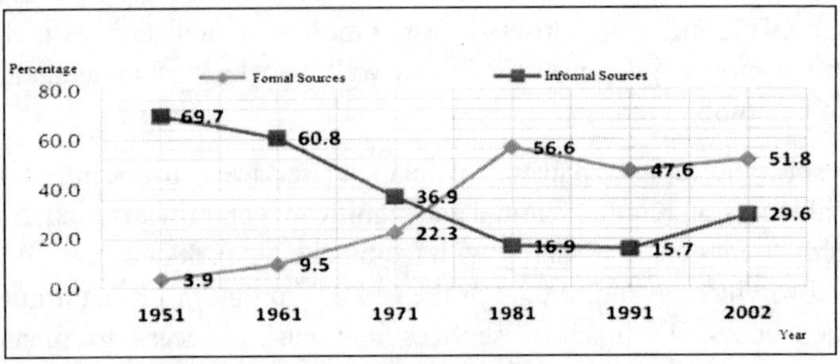

Figure 4.1: Trend in Sources of Borrowing in India.

With nearly 70 percent of Indian population living in villages and a significant proportion of villages without a single bank branch, India's development hinges on this segment's growth- banking the unbanked population under the purview of financial services. In a place where poverty still affects 22 percent of the population, credit access in India is difficult for many of its people. Though financial inclusion has become a recent focus for policymakers, 40 percent of people still lack access to basic financial services. While there are programs formulated to improve access to credit in India, there remains a gender bias. Though loan approval or rejection is at an equal rate to both men and women, women tend to seek financial services less often. Therefore, this paper attempts to analyse the degree of financial inclusion in India. Specifically, this paper examines the factors influencing financial inclusion in India in terms of account penetration and credit access in formal financial institutions. An added objective is to identify the determinants of source of borrowing by individuals. The World Bank Financial Inclusion Index (Global Findex) micro level data of 2014 pertaining to financial inclusion is used to address the objective. The data covers 3000 individuals across India with different wealth classes, occupations, geographical locations, and gender. Among the various dimensions of financial services, account holding in formal financial institution and access to institutional credit are taken as two primary aspects of financial inclusion. Empirically, the logit and multinomial models are applied to analyse the account holding status and source of borrowing respectively.

4.2 A Brief Review of Recent Studies

United Nations (2006), in its study on "Building Inclusive Financial

Sectors for Development" highlight the importance of inclusive financial sectors for developing countries. It is noted here that many developing countries majority are deprived of the basic financial services. The providers of financial services consider certain factors while selecting the potential customers that include cultural norms, gender age, legal identity, limited financial literacy, proximity to formal financial institution, type of occupation and level of income. The United Nations reports that the retail financial institutions can serve the poor in a better way.

Similarly, the CGAP/World Bank (2009), in its report "Financial Access Measuring Access to Financial Services Around the World", observes the poor incidence of financial inclusion in developing countries. It notes that the number of bank deposits per adult and the value of bank deposits (percent to GDP) are high in developed than in developing countries. But, the average bank deposit (percentage of GDP per capita) is higher in developing countries. Further, the amount of loan per capita in developing countries is a quarter of the loans per person of developed countries. The rich people have easy access to financial services even in poor countries. The poor are mainly served by non-bank suppliers of deposit and credit services which mainly include cooperatives, specialised state financial institution and MFIs. The most common and convenient alternative source of credit for the poor is relatives, friends, vendors, money lenders and savings clubs. The report reveals that some of the countries with large proportion of population suffer from lower financial access in terms of deposit or in loans (per 1000 adults) and lower outreach of bank branches and also low density of branches per 1,00,000 adults with varying degrees.

Beck et al. (2007) finds that financial inclusion not only reduces income inequality but also benefits the poor disproportionately and is strongly related with poverty alleviation. Financial inclusion enhances growth and reduces inequality through trickle down effects.

Chen and Jin (2017) study the usage of credit by individuals in China using the 2011 China Household Financial Survey applying the multinomial logit model. While over half of the sample (53.21 percent) reported using credit, about 20 percent only used formal credit. The use of formal credit is associated with socioeconomic characteristics of households. The findings suggest that promoting financial inclusion in China involves expanding access to formal credit among socially and economically disadvantaged households.

Ulwodi and Muriu (2017) explore the factors that determine an individual's account holding in sub-Saharan Africa using the 2014 Global Findex data and multilevel regression analysis. The key variables used include debit card ownership, domestic remittances, having borrowed and saved in the last year. This study makes in the SSA region. The multilevel regression analysis results show that owning a formal account is related to the level of income of an individual. From lowest to highest income quintiles, the impact turns from negative to positive.

Gitaharie et al. (2014) analyse the access of household credit in Indonesia using the 2008 and 2012 Susenas data. The multinomial logit estimates on household access business credit from several sources, namely bank, non-bank and individual sources show that the probabilities for household to obtain business credit is affected by the demographic and social-economic factors and the effectiveness of the implementation of banking public education program.

Fanta and Mutsonziwa (2016) examine the extent of financial inclusion of women in the South African Development Region which includes the countries Botswana, Swaziland, Mauritius, South Africa, taking account holding, access to credit and savings penetration as measures of financial inclusion. The logit estimates of gender gap in financial inclusion show that gender gap in account usage is wider than account ownership, females who even own account mostly go dormant. Both the descriptive statistics and economic analysis point out that financial inclusion is strongly related with income generating capability. The suggestions are to promote financial literacy through financial education especially in rural areas, enabling females to develop skills and mitigating risk related to informal services in order to provide safety.

Rajput (2017) attempts to measure the inter-state variations in access to finance using credit and deposit penetration ratios and analyse the determinants of financial inclusion using panel data of 29 states spanning over a period from 2006 to 2014 in India. The study corroborates the theory of importance of regional economic conditions on the level of financial inclusion and suggests that access to finance by the poor which is a prerequisite for poverty reduction and sustainable economic development of a country.

Asare et al. (2016) study the determinants of household savings option for African households. The multinomial probit estimation show that the highest probabilities that individuals would hold savings products is observed within informal savings mechanisms and secret place or home than through formal and semi-formal savings mechanisms. The financial services providers need to adopt market-led savings mobilisation strategies to attract micro-savers from informal savings mechanisms to formal and semi-formal financial institutions.

In India, Dutta (2015) uses the logit regression and correlation analysis to understand the impact of financial inclusion on financially deprived rural and semi-urban poor of West Bengal on two major factors, the dependency on bank loans and preferences for keeping savings in banks. In consonance with the greater amount of evidences that exist all over the world, the study finds that the poor in West Bengal lack access to basic financial services. On supply side, the study points out understanding towards financial literacy as one of the requisites for dependency on bank loans, and on demand side, safety is the major issue in keeping savings in bank.

Sahoo and Gomkale (2015) aim to reason out for the unaccounted un-organised sector in Gujarat dealing with primary data on different parameters of financial Inclusion pertaining to unorganised sector of Gujarat and logit regression model. The study reveals that in Gandhinagar district a significant proportion of respondents were out of the coverage of financial services and biasness against females in terms of access to financial services. About 60 percent have taken credit from formal sources of finance and 25 percent have taken credit from informal sources like local money lenders, relatives and family friends, while 15 percent have not taken any loan from any sources.

4.3 Data and Methodology

This paper analyses the socioeconomic factors affecting financial inclusion in India. The proxies for financial inclusion have been taken as whether an individual holds an account in a formal financial institution and an individual's source of borrowing. The micro level data on 3000 individuals across India from the World Bank Financial Inclusion Index (Global Findex) for the year 2014 has been used in the empirical analysis. Since the dependent variables are categorical in nature the logit model of the probabilities of account holding and sources of credit are estimated and the marginal effects calculated.

Binary Logistic Regression Method

In order to analyse the determinants of account holding, binary logistic regression has been used. A logit model is based on cumulative logistic distribution function. For the basic regression function:

$$y_i = \beta x_i + u_i \tag{4.1}$$

y_i=1 if the individual is an account holder in a formal financial institution and y_i=0 if he doesn't. The probability of such a binary choice for all individuals is given by:

$$p_i = Pr(y_i = 1|x,\beta) = \Phi(\beta x_i) \tag{4.2}$$

where p_i is the probability of an individual holding formal institutional account. Therefore,

$$(1\text{-}p_i) = Pr(y_i = 0|x,\beta) = 1 - \Phi(\beta x_i) \tag{4.3}$$

is the probability of an individual not holding account in formal financial institutions. The logit model uses logistic cumulative distribution function Φ. The logistic curve resembles a sigmoid curve, as depicted in Figure 4.2.

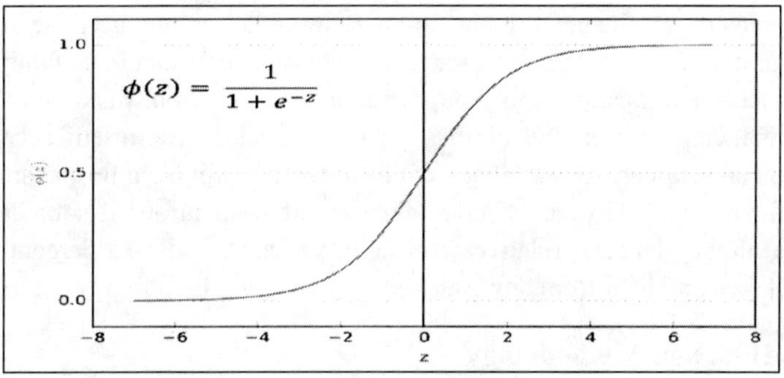

Figure 4.2: The Logistic Distribution Curve.

Given the logistic distribution, the probability can be specified as:

$$Pr(y_i = 1) = e^{\beta x_i}/(1 + e^{\beta x_i}) \tag{4.4}$$

The logistic function specifies the odds ratio as:

$$\frac{Pr(y_{i=1})}{Pr(y_{i=0})} = e^{\beta x_i} \tag{4.5}$$

Taking natural logarithm on both sides of the equation (4.5) yields the log of odds ratio:

$$L_i = \ln\left(\frac{p_i}{1-p_i}\right) = lne^{\beta x_i} = \beta x_i \tag{4.6}$$

Since the logit model is in terms of probabilities, the logit model is estimated by maximum likelihood estimation method.

Multinomial Logit Regression Method

The multinomial logit model follows when there are various categories of dependent variable in a model. The multinomial logit analyses a single decision among multiple alternatives, ordered or unordered (two or more).

The way every category is being influenced by the factors is reflected by multinomial logit model. For a random utility model:

$$U_{ij} = \beta z_{ij} + \varepsilon_{ij} \tag{4.7}$$

where j is the choice alternative, the probability that choice j is made if the prob(U_{ij}>U_{ik}) for all j≠k. Given that the J disturbances are independently and identically distributed (Mc Fadden, 1973):

$$F(\varepsilon_{ij}) = \exp\,(e^{\varepsilon_{ij}}) \tag{4.8}$$

As in other forms of linear regression, the multinomial logistic regression uses a linear predictor function to predict the probability that observation *f(j, i)* has outcome j:

$$f(j,i) = \beta_{0j} + \beta_{1j}x_{1i} + \beta_{2j}x_{2i} + \cdots\cdots + \beta_{mk}x_{mi} \tag{4.9}$$

One fairly simple way to arrive at the multinomial logit model is to imagine, for J possible outcomes, running J-1 independent binary logistic regression models, in which one outcome is chosen as a pivot and then the other J-1 outcomes are separately regressed against the pivot outcome. If outcome *K* (the last outcome) is chosen as the pivot, the modeling is:

$$\begin{aligned} \ln\left[\frac{Pr(Y_{i=1})}{Pr(Y_{i=J})}\right] &= \beta_1 x_i \\ \ln\left[\frac{Pr(Y_{i=1})}{Pr(Y_{i=J})}\right] &= \beta_1 x_i \\ &\ldots\ldots\ldots\ldots\ldots \\ &\ldots\ldots\ldots\ldots\ldots \\ \ln\left[\frac{Pr\ (Y_{i=J-1})}{Pr(Y_{i=J})}\right] &= \beta_{J-1} x_i \end{aligned} \tag{4.10}$$

Taking exponential on both sides, and solving for probabilities:

$$\begin{aligned} &\Pr(y_i = 1) = \Pr(y_i = j)\, e^{\beta_1 x_i} \\ &\Pr(y_i = 2) = \Pr(y_i = j)\, e^{\beta_2 x_i} \\ &\ldots\ldots\ldots\ldots\ldots \\ &\ldots\ldots\ldots\ldots\ldots \\ &\Pr(y_i = J-1) = \Pr(y_i = j)\, e^{\beta_{K-1} x_i} \end{aligned} \tag{4.11}$$

Given that all J of the probabilities must sum to one:

$$\Pr(y_i = J) = 1 - \sum_{j=1}^{J-1} e^{\beta_j x_i} \tag{4.12}$$

$$\Pr(y_i = J) = 1/\left(1 + \sum_{j=1}^{J-1} e^{\beta_j x_i}\right) \tag{4.13}$$

The individual probabilities are then calculated as:

$$\begin{aligned}
\Pr(y_i = 1) &= \frac{e^{\beta_1 . x_i}}{1 + \sum_{j=1}^{J-1} e^{\beta_j . x_i}} \\
\Pr(y_i = 2) &= \frac{e^{\beta_2 . x_i}}{1 + \sum_{j=1}^{J-1} e^{\beta_j . x_i}} \\
&\dots\dots\dots \\
&\dots\dots\dots \\
\Pr(y_i = J-1) &= \frac{e^{\beta_{J-1} . x_i}}{1 + \sum_{j=1}^{J-1} e^{\beta_j . x_i}}
\end{aligned} \tag{4.14}$$

The model implies the log-odds ratios:

$$\ln\left[\frac{P_{ij}}{P_{iJ}}\right] = (\beta_j - \beta_k)x_i \tag{4.15}$$

4.4 Empirical Analysis

The Table 4.1 presents the definition and distribution of the variables used in the empirical analysis. About 55.6 percent of individuals reported having a formal account in financial institutions whereas the rest do not hold an account. The reasons that respondents cite for not borrowing from formal institutions are lack of necessary documents, lack of money, distance, etc. Among the borrowers, 13.1 percent borrow from formal sources like authorised banks, insurance companies, and financial institutions and 32.8 percent resort to informal borrowing which includes store credit, family, friends, private lender, pawn shop, etc. Borrowing from informal or non-institutional sources involve high interest rate and highly risky. A sizable 40.2 percent have not borrowed from any source at all. Majority people are with just primary level of education are (58.4 percent) and about 25.1 percent are poor, but a sizable 11.4 percent are rich. Only 41.4 percent reported savings in the past 12 months. The mean age is 37.50 years.

Table 4.1: Descriptive Statistics of Variables in Financial Inclusion Analysis.

Variable	*Description*	*Frequency*	*Percent*
Account holders	If owning an account in any bank or any financial institutions =1, 0 otherwise	1332	44.4
Non-account holders		1668	55.6
Borrowed from formal sources only	Proxy for access to credit and borrowing	393	13.1
Borrowed from informal sources only		984	32.8
Borrowing from both formal and informal sources		417	13.9
No borrowing		1206	40.2

(Contd...)

Female	If gender is female = 1, 0 otherwise	1655	55.2
Male		1345	44.8
No education	Highest level of education attained - no education, primary education, secondary education and tertiary education	1	0.00
Primary education		1754	58.4
Secondary education		986	32.9
Tertiary education		259	8.6
Poor class	Economic status in five categories in quintiles - poorest 20%, lower middle class (20%), middle class (20%), wealthy or upper middle class (20%), richest (top 20%)	343	11.4
Lower middle class		578	19.3
Middle class		692	23.1
Wealthier class		635	21.2
Richest class		752	25.1
Non-saver	If saved in the past 12 months in a bank, financial institution, formal and informal, household savings =1, 0 otherwise	1759	58.6
Saver		1241	41.4

The association of account holding status and source of credit with explanatory variables are tested with chi-square test for the null hypothesis that the variables do not have any association. The chi-square test results presented in Table 4.2 rejects the null significantly.

Table 4.2: Association of Socioeconomic Status with Account Holding Status and Source of Credit.

Variable	*Account holding status*	*Source of credit*
Gender	91.64*** (0.00)	170.77*** (0.00)
Education	167.45*** (0.00)	93.82** (0.02)
Income	99.04*** (0.00)	250.09*** (0.00)
Savings	196.77*** (0.00)	-
Wage earnings	34.03** (0.04)	-
Obs.	3000	

Note: χ^2 (chi square) values in parentheses. *** significant at 1 percent level ** significant at 5 percent level.

In the empirical analysis of the determinants of account holding status is specified as a logit function:

$$\ln\left[\frac{\Pr(y_i=Having\ an\ account)}{\Pr(y_i=Not\ having\ an\ account)}\right] = \beta_0 + \beta_1(age) + \beta_2(female) + \beta_3(primaryeducation) + \beta_4(secondaryeducation) + \beta_5(tertiaryeducation) + \beta_6(lowermiddleclass) + \beta_7(middleclass) + \beta_8(uppermiddleclass) + \beta_9(rich) + \beta_{10}(wage\ earner) + \beta_{11}(saver) + u_i \quad (4.16)$$

The maximum likelihood estimates of the binary logit regression on account holding status in formal financial institutions along with the calculated marginal effect, the change in probability of predictive margin, is presented in Table 4.3.

Table 4.3: Binary Logit Regression Estimates of Account Holding Status in India.

Variable	*Coefficient*	*Std. error*	*p>z*	*Marginal effect*
Age	0.020*	0.07	0.003	0.005
Female	-0.540***	0.000	0.0475	-0.131
Primary education	-17.371***	0.000	0.007	-0.998
Secondary education	16.576***	0.000	0.012	0.995
Tertiary education	15.598***	0.000	0.002	0.802
Lower middle class	-0.083	0.547	0.127	-0.020
Middle class	-0.179	0.185	0.113	-0.044
Upper middle class	0.038	0.787	0.145	0.009
Rich	0.333**	0.018	0.019	0.080
Wage earners	0.332***	0.002	0.015	0.079
Savers	0.961***	0.000	0.022	0.228
Pseudo R^2	0.592			

Note: Reference category variables are male, illiterate, poor, non-wage earners and non-savers. *** significant at 1 percent level ** significant at 5 percent level* significant at 10 percent level.

The results show that the probability of females having account ownership in formal financial institutions is significantly lower than that of males. As age increases, it is more likely for the individual to own an account. In terms of marginal effects, an extra year of age of individuals increases the probability of financial inclusion in formal financial market by about half a percent. All educational coefficients are statistically highly significant. People only having just primary education would be less likely have an account. The relative probability of a low educated person to own an account compared to not having an account is about 99 percent lower than the high educated people. Individuals with secondary and higher levels would have a higher relative probability of being financially included and the effect rises by 99 and 80 percent respectively. The income or economic status coefficients are not significant except the rich class. A negative influence has been observed of the middle classes whereas the upper middle class have a positive effect on account holding. The probability of holding financial account increases by 8.02 percent for the rich class. The probability of financial inclusion significantly increases with wage earnings and savings, the relative probability of account holding rises by 7.9 percent and 22.8 percent respectively.

This study also analyses the factors which impact individual's access and sources of borrowing using the multinomial logit method. The dependent variable is classified into four categories: (i) formal institutional source only (ii) informal sources only, (iii) both formal and informal sources, and (iv) no borrowing at all.

The estimation empirical specification of the multinomial logit model is given as:

$$\ln\left[\frac{\Pr(y_i = Formal\ institution)}{\Pr(y_i = No\ borrowing)}\right] = \sum_{j=1}^{4} \beta_j x_{j-1}$$
$$\ln\left[\frac{\Pr(y_i = Informal\ institution)}{\Pr(y_i = No\ borrowing)}\right] = \sum_{j=1}^{4} \beta_j x_{j-1} \qquad (4.17)$$
$$\ln\left[\frac{\Pr(y_i = Both\ sources)}{\Pr(y_i = No\ borrowing)}\right] = \sum_{j=1}^{4} \beta_j x_{j-1}$$

Taking antilog on both sides and solving for probabilities:

$$\Pr(y_i = 1) = \Pr(y_i = 4)\, e^{\sum_{j=1}^{4}\beta_j x_{j-1}}$$
$$\Pr(y_i = 2) = \Pr(y_i = 4)\, e^{\sum_{j=1}^{4}\beta_j x_{j-1}}$$
$$\Pr(y_i = 3) = \Pr(y_i = 4)\, e^{\sum_{j=1}^{4}\beta_j x_{j-1}} \qquad (4.18)$$
$$\Pr(y_i = 4) = 1/(1 + e^{\sum_{j=1}^{4}\beta_j x_{j-1}}$$
$$\Pr(y_i = 4) = \frac{1}{1+\sum_{j=1}^{4} e^{\beta_j x_{j-1}}}$$

The empirical specification of the multinomial logit model is specified as:

$$\ln\left[\frac{\Pr(Credit\ source = j)}{\Pr(No\ borrowing)}\right] = \beta_0 + \beta_1(age) + \beta_2(female) + \beta_3(primaryeducation) + \beta_4(secondaryeducation) + \beta_5(tertiaryeducation) + \beta_6(lowermiddleclass) + \beta_7(middleclass) + \beta_8(uppermiddleclass) + \beta_9(rich) + \varepsilon_i \qquad (4.19)$$

The estimation method is maximum likelihood estimation which maximises the likelihood function. The value of the estimated coefficient β reveals the direction of the relationship between x and logits of y. When β>0, larger (or smaller) x values are associated with larger (or smaller) logits of y and the distribution curve will resemble an increasing sigmoid (or S-shape). Conversely, if β<0, larger (or smaller) x values are associated with smaller (or larger) logits of y and is show by a reverse sigmoid curve. In other words, an increase in x is associated with a decrease in logits of y and vice versa.

The Table 4.4 presents the estimated multinomial logit model along with the marginal effects. Age significantly and positively influences availing credit from formal sector and not from informal sources. Individual's gender influences sources of borrowing considerably. Females have lesser access to borrowing irrespective of sources. The male dominance can be attributed to the very less penetration of bank branches in India especially in rural areas and to the male dominating Indian patriarchal society. Also, females lack knowledge of benefits of being financially included since literacy rate is lower among them. The relative probability of females borrowing from formal sources goes down by 9.21 percent compared to no borrowing if the individual is female. In the informal borrowing sources also women have lower access and the relative probability decreases by 2.22 percentage. Compared to formal sector sources, females have slightly higher tendency to borrow informally as these sources are close to them and easily accessible to women.

Table 4.4: Multinomial Logistic Regression Estimates of Source of Credit in India.

Variable	*Formal credit*		*Informal credit*		*Both formal and informal credits*	
	Coefficient	*Marginal effect*	*Coefficient*	*Marginal effect*	*Coefficient*	*Marginal effect*
Age	0.006** (0.004)	0.0003	0.002 (0.003)	-0.0002	0.013*** (0.004)	0.004
Female	-1.264*** (0.134)	-0.092	-0.320*** (0.087)	-0.022	-1.162*** (0.129)	0.129
Primary education	-16.592*** (0.365)	-0.9994	0.303* (0.176)	0.406	0.708** (0.311)	0.311
Secondary education	-11.354*** (0.353)	-0.966	0.169*** (0.167)	0.356	1.078*** (0.296)	0.296
Tertiary education	4.110*** (0.385)	0.332	-0.044 (0.229)	-0.044	1.091*** (0.339)	0.339
Lower middle class	-0.669* (0.362)	-0.068	0.073* (0.146)	0.023	-0.226 (0.307)	0.307
Middle class	-1.551*** (0.337)	-0.170	.052** (0.145)	-0.115	1.115*** (0.278)	0.278
Upper middle class	2.026*** (0.337)	0.196	0.385** (0.152)	-0.118	1.851*** (0.275)	0.275
Rich	2.376*** (0.332)	0.268	0.239 (0.153)	-0.154	1.717*** (0.275)	0.275
Pseudo R^2	0.473					

Note: Standard errors in parentheses. *** significant at 1 percent level ** significant at 5 percent level* significant at 10 percent level. Reference category variables are male, illiterate and poor.

With regard to education, there is an interesting implication. As far as formal borrowing is concerned, only higher education has a positive impact, while the lower levels of education drifts people towards non-institutional sources due to lack of financial education. The relative probability that an individual would borrow from formal sector financial institutions than not to borrow increases by about 33 percent with higher the education. But the probability of the same goes down drastically if the person has less education. Instead, people with low education tend to go for informal borrowing which they find it apparently convenient. If an individual is primary educated then the relative probability informal borrowing increases by almost 40 percent. Similarly educated people have a lower probability of resorting to informal sources of borrowing and this probability falls by around 4 percentages compared to not having borrowed. Probability of people borrowing from both the sources also decreases for low level of education and increases with rise in education.

Similarly, the MNL estimates show that rich people borrow from formal financial institutions. As the people move from low income class to high income class they tend to have credit from institutional finance. The relative probability that high income individual would have formal borrowing is almost double than low income people. Rich people have an increased probability of almost 26 percent for formal borrowing from no borrowing which drastically falls as income falls and it is negative for poor. But lower middle class and poor tend to borrow from informal institutions more than the rich. The probability for a rich individual to borrow informally falls by almost 15 percent from no borrowing. Limited income therefore is a major factor for such an adverse scenario. For poor households, limited assets restrict them from formal sector borrowing as they have insufficient assets to put as collateral.

4.5 Conclusion

This paper analyses the determinants of financial inclusion in India, taking account holding and source of borrowing as proxies for financial penetration in India. The study uses the 3000 observations from the World Bank financial inclusion survey (Global Findex) for the year 2014. The binary logit model is applied to estimate the impact of various factors on account holding status, while the multinomial logit model is applied to understand the choice of borrowing from formal and informal financial institutions. It is noted that through the initiatives of financial inclusion in India by the government through PMJDY and RBI, the usage of formal financial sources by people has been increasing. However, the extent of financial inclusion is quite severe and disproportionate in India, especially there exists gender divide. Financial inclusion is disproportionately low among relatively poor and low education households and among females.

Even a significant percentage of rich households in India are also financially excluded. The estimated results show that individual's savings frequency and wage earnings also influence their account holding status in formal financial institutions. Females have lesser access in owning bank accounts as well as borrowing from formal sources. Low educated people and poor mostly resort to informal borrowing as they are not exposed to financial market, and even if exposed, they do not have collateral security for formal institutional credit.

The initiatives taken by government seem to have paid off and the flow of institutional credit has increased significantly in real terms. However, the presence of informal sources of borrowing is still intact, despite legal curbs and it is well known that their interest rates are high and there exists usury. Therefore, the formal financial institutions should develop more flexible products and services that are less restrictive for poor, women and illiterate to avail them. Further, the financial institutions should be more proactive in spreading financial literacy to overcome the hurdles posed by the low level of education of the prospective borrowers. And simplification of the procedures of lending and making the credit accessible are required. The new initiative Jan Dhan Yojana is expected to further improve financial inclusion in rural areas and such efforts need to be consolidated.

5

The Determinants of Demand for Nutrition: Tobit Estimation of Meat Consumption

5.1 Introduction

The human body needs protein and other nutrients such as vitamins and minerals like phosphorus, sodium, iron, and potassium for both growth and repair of human body cells. Much of the protein requirements for humans come from the animal protein consumed by humans as meat products. A healthy person in developing countries requires an average of 35 grams of animal protein intake per day (Sichilima et al. 2015). Generally, the household food consumption pattern is influenced by a number of factors like economic (income and price changes), social (urbanisation leading to dietary changes), culture (exotic lifestyle influences) and market development that makes new foods available (Zhou et al. 2005). Among these factors income and price are seen to be the most influential in determining the choice of food, especially meat, consumption pattern. The increase of consumer income in the developing countries tends to induce greater changes in the composition of food consumption (Gould, 2002). At the same time, the much higher prices of mutton, fish and chicken relative to others meats and vegetables are constraints on the required meat consumption. As a substitute, the beef consumption among consumers of non-Hindus is on the rise (Gandhi and Zhang, 2010).

Nearly 73 percent of the Indian consumers are living in rural areas and their lifestyle is changing at greater pace and large levels due to increased connectivity and availability of junk foods and delivery mechanisms. The buying behaviour of the rural consumers is influenced by several factors such as socioeconomic conditions, culture, environment, literacy level, occupation, geographical location, efforts on the part of sellers, exposure to media, etc. The consumer movement in India started with the middle-class citizens in urban areas has spread among the masses in rural area also. Such changing consumption scenario has been largely overlooked in India in the studies of consumption in India. Especially, very few Indian studies have focused on the pattern of animal product consumption by households. For instance, studies on animal product consumption in India like Sinha and Giri (1989) examine the consumption of livestock products in three states of Gujarat, Punjab and Tripura, Raghavendra et al. (2009) analyse the preference for and consumption pattern of meat types by individual households in Dharward, Karnataka, Jagadeesh Babu et al. (2010) study the meat consumption patterns of the rural households in the Chittoor district of Andhra Pradesh, and Kavithaa et al. (2014) investigate the seasonal variation in the consumption of meat in the Erode District of Tamil Nadu using the primary survey data.

The limited number of available Indian studies have confined to specific regions of India are largely primary survey based. Moreover, they do not use quantitative methods in analysing the determinants of household meat consumption or the expenditure on meat. Hence, this paper tries to fill this gap using the 68th round NSSO (2011-2012) data and applying the quantitative method of Tobit model.

5.2 A Brief Review of Recent Studies

Jung and Koo (2000) analyse the demand system for meat and fish products consumption in Korea, using three sets of time series data the three-stage least squares method. The estimated results show the changing consumption pattern between 1980 to 1998 from cereals to more livestock products, vegetables and fruits. The demand for meat products has increased from 0.4 million metric tons in 1980 to1.3 million metric tons in 1996 along with the growth of national income. In Korea, meat production accounted for 19 percent of total agriculture production in 1980 which has grown to 25 percent in 1996. As fish products are important sources of protein in Korea, the 1998 per capita fish product consumption has been 28 kg, higher than per capita consumption of all other meat combined (25 kg). In the empirical estimation, meat price has a significant effect on Han woos beef, pork, chicken and fish, and insignificant effect on imported beef, crustacean and mollusk. The expenditure variable is significant in the share equation for Han woo beef, imported beef, pork, and fish, and insignificant in the share equations of chicken and crustacean.

Aepli and Finger (2013) study the influence of different meat prices, socio-demographic and geographic variables on sheep and goat demand in Switzerland, using the Switzerland Household Expenditure Survey from 2000 to 2005 and applying the Tobit model. The estimated results show that the consumption of sheep and goat meat is determined by meat prices, total expenditure, expenditure for food, and household characteristics like presence of children and education. Further, the results indicate that rising prices of sheep and goat meat lead to a decline in the demand for sheep and goat meat. For an increase in the price of pork, the household demand for sheep and goat meat increases by 0.38 units, suggesting that for Switzerland households, pork is substitute but beef is complementary for sheep and goat meat. Also, the effect of total, food and meat expenditures and the socio-demographic variables are statistically highly significant. The Switzerland households with higher total expenditure or higher income have elastic demand for sheep and goat meat. Importantly, education has a positive influence on sheep and goat meat consumption indicating that education plays a crucial role in the choice of healthy dietary intake as the sheep and goat meat have several health benefits in comparison to other red meat.

Karli and Bilgic (2007) try to identify the determinants of demand for red and white meat using a primary data for 2003 and applying the censored regression analysis. The Tobit estimates of the demand for red and white meat demand shows that the total food expenditure has a significant effect on the purchase of red meat. As the price of red meat increases, its quantity decreases significantly. On the other hand, the price of white meat has a significant positive effect on the quantity demanded of the red meat, but negative effect on white quantity meat consumption. This indicates that consumers substitute white for red meat as the price of the white meat increases. The food expenditure has a significantly positive effect on the quantity consumed of the red meat and an increase in the proportion of food expenditures in income increases the quantity of the red meat product consumed. While the red meat quantity demand is elastic with respect to the age and size of household, the white meat quantity demand is inelastic with social, individual and product characteristics.

Hupkova and Bielik (2009) estimate price and income elasticity of meat demand in Slovakia using the household budget survey of the Slovak statistical data for the period 1993-2007 and applying the regression method. The data consists of yearly observation of beef, pork and poultry consumption, average annual consumer price of beef, pork and poultry meat, and net income. In Slovakia, during this period, the aggregate average consumption of beef meat is 52549 tons and the beef market prices have increased ranging between 10 to 30 percent. The pork meat consumption is stable as it continues to be favored by Slovak people and the poultry production remains relatively positive with respect to other meats. The empirical results show that the beef meat demand is inelastic with respect to own price and income and the price of poultry meat has no effect on beef consumption. Further, a decline in the purchasing power of population and a reduction in the consumer subsidies have significant effect on the meat consumption in Slovakia.

Maina and Baba (2012) examine the socio-economic determinants of ruminant meat demand in Maiduguri in Nigeria using a 2011 primary survey data. According to the survey, about 92 percent of the households demand ruminant meat. Adetunji and Rauf (2012) also study the household demand for meat in selected states in the Southwest Nigeria. In the study area, for 43.7 percent households, beef is the most preferred meat. Applying the Almost Ideal Demand System (AIDS) demand function for a primary dataset, the estimates show income levels and tastes of respondents influenced the type of meat preferred. The budget share of beef decreases with an increase in the price of chicken. The budget share of pork increases with an increase in the price of mutton but it decreased with an increase in its own price. The budget share of chevon, chicken and mutton also increase with an increase in their prices. The results suggest that one percent increase in the prices of beef, cheven and chicken would result in 8, 5, and 7 percent reduction in the quantity demanded respectively. For households in southwest Nigeria, mutton and pork are luxury goods while chicken, beef and chevon are normal goods.

Emokaro and Dibiah (2014) analyse demand for chicken, beef and fish among urban households in Edo and Delta states of Nigeria. In these areas, the chicken meat has a sizable budget share of 20 percent and beef has a 57 percent. The Linear Approximate Almost Ideal Demand System applied to a primary dataset shows that the total expenditure elasticity of chicken meat is significantly positive, own price elasticity is significantly negative and cross price elasticity with respect to beef is a significant positive. Salawu et al. (2014) examine the consumption and consumer preference for poultry meat types - broiler, cockerel, layer and turkey - in Ibadan metropolis, using a primary dataset and applying descriptive statistics and multinomial logit regression method. The respondents show different level of preference for the types of poultry meat - broiler is the most preferred with 40 percent, followed by turkey (33.3 percent), layers (14.7 percent and cockerel (12 percent). The multinomial logit regression estimates show that age, educational level, gender, availability of substitutes, appearance of meat and taste are the significant factors that influence consumer preference for poultry meat types.

In India, Raghavendra et al. (2009) examine the household preference and consumption pattern of meat types while analysing the economics of meat retailing using a 2006-2007 primary survey of urban and rural households in the Dharward district of Karnataka. The average chicken meat consumption varied from 40 gm sperday to 384g per day in urban areas and 25g per day to 129g per day in rural areas. While most urban households ranked mutton first and chicken second, it is other way round in rural areas. Both urban and rural households assigned third and fourth ranks respectively to beef and pork. The important factors considered by urban households while purchasing meat is the nutritive value, followed by taste, freshness, tenderness, source, price, fat content and ease of availability. In rural area, the factors in the descending order of importance are taste, nutritional value, price, freshness, source, fat content, tenderness and ease of availability.

Jagadeesh Babuet al. (2010) study the meat consumption patterns of rural households in Chittoor district of Andhra Pradesh, using a primary survey collected in 2009. The study shows that the most preferred meat is poultry meat (70 percent), followed by mutton (21 percent), chevon (7 percent) and few preferring pork (1 percent) and beef (1 percent). The major reasons for consumption of meat types are taste (88 percent) and habituation (8.5 percent), and consume chicken once in a week (60.5 percent) followed by fortnightly (34.5 percent). Majority of the rural people prefer to consume mutton once in a month (60.0 percent) followed by fortnightly (36.0 percent) because of its high cost. The frequency of consumption of chicken and mutton are attributed to individual taste, specific occasions like festival and cost. Even though the cost of pork and beef is less compared to the cost of mutton, the poor percentage consumption of pork and beef is attributed to religion (91.5 percent) followed by individual taste (6.0 percent) and less availability (2.5 percent).

Kavithaa et al. (2014) analyse the seasonal variation in the consumption of meat, in the Erode District of Tamil Nadu, using a rural primary survey data. According to the survey, majority of people are consuming more meat during winter (53.33 percent) followed by rainy season (35 percent) and only 11.66 percent of people prefer meat in summer. With respect to the type of meat consumed by the rural people, most prefer chicken

(56.25 percent), followed by mutton (34.38 percent), fish (6.25 percent) and pork (3.13 percent).

5.3 Data and Methodology

The data used in the empirical analysis of meat consumption in India is the secondary data set related to the consumption expenditure from the 68th round (2011-2012) of the National Sample Survey Office (NSSO). The NSSO conducts the nationwide household consumer expenditure surveys at regular intervals as part of its 'rounds', each round normally of a year's duration conducted through interviews of a random sample of households covering the entire geographical area of the country. The NSSO data contains information on consumption expenditure for nine groups of consumption items: (i) cereals and cereal substitutes, (ii) milk and milk products, (iii) edible oils, (iv) meat, fish and egg, (v) sugar etc., (vi) other food items (spices, salt, beverages, prepared food, etc.), (vii) clothing,(viii) fuel and light, and finally (ix) other non-food items (medicine, personal care, education, transport, recreation, rents, taxes, etc.). This paper uses the meat consumption expenditure of 6646 households in Tamil Nadu from the 68th round data of NSSO collected during the period July 2011 to June 2012 by the NSSO.

Tobit Regression Method

One of the major issues in modeling household consumption is that some households in the sample might not consume some kinds of foods during the survey periods. In the 68th round NSSO data also, there is considerable number of households that do not consume all meats. With sizable number of zeros in the dataset on meat consumption, the OLS estimates of household meat consumption is biased and inconsistent as there is a censoring of data at the zero values. A censored regression model by maximum likelihood estimation method that deals with both zero and non-zero values of the dependent variable is the appropriated estimation procedure. Such a technique, the Tobit model, proposed by Tobin (1958), is employed widely to estimate the expenditure and consumption patterns with censored data. The Tobit model is specified by a latent regression as:

$$y^* = \beta x + u \tag{5.1}$$

where $u \sim N(0,\sigma^2)$, y^* is a latent variable that is censored and observed for values greater than some threshold, say λ. The observed y is defined by a measurement equation:

$$y = \begin{Bmatrix} y & if\ y^* > \theta \\ \lambda y & if\ y^* \leq \theta \end{Bmatrix} \quad (5.2)$$

In typical Tobit model, θ is assumed to be zero i.e. the data are censored at 0. Thus, the estimating Tobit model is specified as:

$$y = \begin{Bmatrix} y & if\ y^* > 0 \\ 0 & if\ y^* \leq 0 \end{Bmatrix} \quad (5.3)$$

Assuming normal distribution of the error term u, the likelihood function for the maximum likelihood estimation of the censored regression model is specified as:

$$L = \prod_{i}^{N} \left[\frac{1}{\sigma}\phi\left(\frac{y-\mu}{\sigma}\right)\right]^{\theta} \left[(1-\phi)\left(\frac{y-\mu}{\sigma}\right)\right]^{(1-\theta)} \quad (5.4)$$

where θ is the censoring point. In the Tobit model, with θ=0 and parameter rising μ as βx, the likelihood function for the Tobit model is specified as:

$$L = \prod_{i}^{N} \left[\frac{1}{\sigma}\phi\left(\frac{y-\beta x}{\sigma}\right)\right]^{\theta} \left[(1-\phi)\left(\frac{y-\beta x}{\sigma}\right)\right]^{(1-\theta)} \quad (5.5)$$

The log-likelihood function for the Tobit Model is specified as:

$$lnL = \sum_{i=1}^{N} \left\{\theta\left[-ln\sigma + ln\phi\left(\frac{y-\beta x}{\sigma}\right)\right] + (1-\theta)ln\left[(1-\phi)\left(\frac{\beta x}{\sigma}\right)\right]\right\} \quad (5.6)$$

In the log-likelihood function, the first part corresponds to the classical regression for the uncensored observations and the second part is relevant for the censored observation.

As Sigehnan and Zeng (1999) point out, there are three expected values from the Tobit model which is of interest:

The expected value of the latent variable y*: $E(y^*) = \beta x$ (5.7)

With censoring at 0, the expected value of y:

$$E(y|y^* > 0) = \beta x + \sigma\lambda\lambda = \frac{\phi(\beta x/\sigma)}{\Phi(\beta x/\sigma)} \quad (5.8)$$

where λ is the inverse mills ratio, ϕ and Φ are the marginal density and cumulative distribution functions.

The expected value of y: $E(y)=\Phi(\beta x/\sigma)(\beta x+\sigma\lambda)$ (5.9)

This is the probability of being uncensored multiplied by the expected value of y conditional on y being uncensored. Given that there are three expected values, there is no consensus on appropriate expected value. If the data is always censored, then focusing on the latent variable is not particularly useful, especially if a corner solution model is employed. If interested in the effects of explanatory variables that may or not be censored, probably E(y) may be interesting. If interested in just the uncensored observations, probably the conditional expectation $E(y|y^* > 0)$ is to be looked at.

5.4 Empirical Analysis

In the 2011-2012 68th round NSSO sample of Tamil Nadu, out of 6646 households, 50 percent households have consumed chicken meat, followed by 31 percent fish, 16 percent of mutton and 3 percent beef meat. Only 10 sample households in Tamil Nadu consumed pork. The Table 5.1 presents the descriptive statistics of the variables used in the empirical analysis of meat consumption. The descriptive statistics indicate that majority of households both in rural and urban areas of Tamil Nadu prefer chicken and mutton consumption irrespective of religious background. The average monthly per capita meat expenditure of households in Tamil Nadu is Rs.2442.84. On average, the household consumption of fish, chicken, mutton and beef are 0.99, 0.79, 0.66 and 0.74 kgs respectively and the average price of fish, mutton, chicken and beef are Rs.101.51, 320.61, 121.19, 124.02 and 120 respectively.

Table 5.1: Descriptive Statistics of Variables in Household Meat Consumption Analysis.

Variable	*Description*	*Mean*	*Std. dev.*
MPCE	Household monthly per capita consumption expenditure (Rs.)	2442.84	1981.16
Household size	No. of household members	3.67	1.65
Fish meat	Fish consumption (kg)	0.99	0.71
Mutton meat	Mutton consumption (kg)	0.66	0.37
Chicken meat	Chicken consumption (kg)	0.79	0.42
Beef meat	Beef consumption (kg)	0.74	0.32
Pork meat	Pork consumption (kg)	0.75	0.50
Fish price	Fish price (Rs.)	101.51	39.38
Mutton price	Mutton price (Rs.)	320.61	48.71
Chicken price	Chicken price (Rs.)	121.19	20.34
Beef price	Beef price (Rs.)	124.03	30.92
Pork price	Pork price (Rs.)	120.00	15.63
Hindu	If religion is Hindu=1, 0 otherwise	0.87	0.33
Muslim	If religion is Muslim=1, 0 otherwise	0.06	0.23
Rural	If household resides in rural area=1, 0 otherwise	0.50	0.50
Urban	If household resides in urban area=1, 0 otherwise	0.50	0.50
N	No of observations	6646	

The maximum likelihood Tobit estimates of household meat consumption in Tamil Nadu are presented in Table 5.2, and rural and urban Tamil Nadu separately in Table 5.3. The Tobit results show that the price effect is negative and income effect is positive on meat consumption and both are statistically significant. The coefficients of monthly per capita consumption expenditure, used as a proxy for household income, have statistically significant positive effect on the consumption of all types of meat. However, both income elasticity and own price elasticity of meat products are only marginal quantity changes. The Tobit coefficients of household size on consumption of all types of meat are significantly positive implying addition of members in a household will increase meat consumption and hence household consumption expenditure. The estimated coefficients on religion are negative but are statistically insignificant showing no impact of religion on meat consumption in Tamil Nadu.

Table 5.2: Tobit Estimates of Household Meat Consumption in Tamil Nadu.

Variable	*Fish*	*Chicken*	*Mutton*	*Beef*
MPCE	0.007***	0.005***	0.004***	0.005**
	(7.48)	(10.37)	(6.93)	(2.37)
Household size	0.111***	0.129***	0.087***	0.076***
	(8.09)	(7.85)	(9.55)	(4.06)
Price	-0.004***	-0.001**	-0.008***	-0.003***
	(7.05)	(2.44)	(2.75)	(2.78)
Hindu	-0.310***	-0.006	-0.007	0.069
	(5.11)	(0.19)	(0.89)	(0.89)
Muslim	-0.067	0.037	-0.017	-0.010
	(0.84)	(0.87)	(0.79)	(1.12)
Constant	0.935***	0.264***	0.414***	0.624***
	(9.87)	(3.99)	(3.55)	(3.89)
Log-likelihood	-1182.84	-828.04	-207.43	-20.63
LR chi2	160.27	457.30	106.92	22.88
Pro>chi2	0.00	0.00	0.00	0.00
Pseudo R-square	0.06	0.22	0.21	0.36
Obs.	1172	1910	623	106

Note: Absolute t-values in parentheses. *** significant at 1 percent level ** significant at 5 percent level * significant at 10 percent level.

Table 5.3: Tobit Estimates of Meat Consumption in Rural and Urban Tamil Nadu.

Variable	*Rural*			*Urban*		
	Fish	*Chicken*	*Mutton*	*Fish*	*Chicken*	*Mutton*
MPCE	0.002*** (7.55)	0.001*** (10.63)	0.006*** (5.47)	0.005*** (5.11)	0.003*** (5.78)	0.003*** (4.65)
Household size	0.117*** (5.36)	0.136*** (15.86)	0.089*** (5.24)	0.106*** (6.41)	0.122*** (15.45)	0.082*** (3.66)
Price	-0.002** (2.39)	-0.009 (1.56)	-0.009 (1.63)	-0.004*** (7.02)	-0.001** (2.18)	-0.004 (1.11)
Hindu	-0.148 (1.47)	-0.068 (1.15)	-0.127 (1.14)	-0.418*** (7.04)	0.018 (0.47)	0.028 (0.48)
Muslim	0.310** (2.05)	-0.137 (1.52)	-0.157 (1.03)	-0.262*** (3.05)	0.096** (2.01)	0.052 (0.82)
Constant	0.556*** (3.19)	0.198** (1.98)	0.514** (2.34)	1.049*** (9.88)	0.326*** (3.71)	0.229* (1.68)
Log-likelihood	-557.801	-421.95	-163.19	-582.51	-378.85	-69.15
LR chi2	83.02	264.58	42.93	128.02	235.26	70.41
Pro>chi2	0.00	0.00	0.00	0.00	0.00	0.00
Pseudo R-square	0.07	0.24	0.12	0.10	0.24	0.34
Obs.	511	897	273	661	1013	350

Note: Absolute t-values in parentheses. *** significant at 1 percent level ** significant at 5 percent level * significant at 10 percent level.

For both rural and urban samples, the Tobit coefficients of household size and monthly per capita consumption expenditure have positive effect on all types of meat consumption are positive and statistically significant at 1 percent level. The coefficients of prices are negative, but statistically significant at 5 percent level only for fish consumption in both rural and urban areas and insignificant in the case of mutton consumption. The coefficients of Hindu dummy are negative for rural households and positive for urban households, but insignificant except for fish in the urban case. However, the Muslim dummy has a significant effect on meat consumption and it is significantly positive for fish demand and insignificantly negative in other types of meat demand in rural households. In urban households, The Muslim religion is associated with significant negative fish consumption and a significant positive chicken consumption and an insignificant effect on mutton consumption in the urban area of Tamil Nadu.

5.5 Conclusion

The human body needs energy, especially proteins, for growth as well as to do work. Much of the protein requirements for humans come from the animal protein consumed by humans as meat products. The household demand for meat products such as fish, mutton, chicken, beef and pork are determined chiefly by the market prices of the meats, availability of meats, household income, family size and consumer tastes, and by factors such as demographic characteristics, socioeconomic status and importantly religion as well. This paper has analysed the consumption of different types of meat, fish, chicken, mutton, beef and pork in Tamil Nadu using the 68th round NSSO survey data for the year 2011-12 and employing the censored Tobit regression model. The estimated Tobit regression results indicate that the meat consumption in Tamil Nadu is generally inelastic, though the income and price elasticities are positive and negative respectively and are statistically significant. The household size matters for meat consumption, whereas the religion has no effect on meat consumption in general.

6

The Determinants of Private Investment on Education: Quantile Regression Estimation of Household Education Expenditure

6.1 Introduction

The essence of human development is education which is significant in balancing the socio-economic fabric of a country. Quality education is the foundation for furthering knowledge, discoveries, innovation and entrepreneurship that triggers growth and prosperity of an individual as well as of a nation. Therefore, both individuals and governments invest heavily in education. Individual investment refers to the investment made by the students and/or their parents on their education and is referred to as household investment in education or private expenditure on education. The government investment in education is mostly institutional investment and is referred to as government or public investment in education. Both public and household investments in education are highly significant not only because of their magnitudes, but also because of their nature and characteristics. While public investment provides educational facilities, only household investment enables its utilisation. Though at lower levels of education, considering its publicness, the public expenditure needs to be higher than the household expenditure, the pattern gets reversed at the higher levels of education. However, either in the absence of adequate government expenditure in school education and/or ability of the household to pay to school education necessitates the substitutability between the two sources of expenditure on education.

Recognising that a good start or foundation is essential in strengthening higher education, India has made significant progress with the goal of 'education for all' over the years through various government policies and programmes. The public expenditure on education in India for 2013-2014 stands at 4.13 percent of GDP. According to the Ministry of Human Resource and Development (MHRD) 2016 educational statistics, the adult literacy rate in India has increased from 61percentto 69.5 percent during the period 2001-2011. The 71st round of National Sample Survey Office estimates the adult literacy rate at 70.5 percent for the year 2014. As of 2014-2015, in India the number of recognised schools, universities, colleges and stand-alone institutions stand at 1516865, 760, 38498 and 12276 respectively. The gross enrolment ratio (GER) is 101.4, 89.3, 62.5 and 23.0 for primary, lower secondary, higher secondary and tertiary education respectively. Despite the various measures taken by the governments, Indian educational system has not managed to increase the proportion of individuals from the higher secondary level.

The Table 6.1 presents the gender-wise distribution of students in various educational streams in India. It can be observed that majority of students are males and are in science and commerce courses. In technical education, the participation of female students is significantly relative to males; naturally only medicine including nursing has better proportion of female participation.

Table 6.1: Gender-wise Distribution of Students in Education in India (percent).

Education stream	*General education*		*Education stream*	*Technical/professional education*	
	Male	*Female*		*Male*	*Female*
Upto class 10th	54.2	45.8	Medicine	35.3	64.7
Humanities	49.9.	50.1	Engineering	75.2	24.8
Science	59.5	40.5	Management	62.3	37.7
Commerce	56.6	43.4	Law	63.9	36.2
Others	51.1	48.9	Vocational	82.8	17.2

Source: NSSO (2014): 71st round - Key Indicators of Social Consumption in India: Education.

The Table 6.2 presents the distribution of students by institutions and residence. It is observed that majority of the students, predominantly up to higher secondary levels, are in government institutions in rural areas in urban areas about 69 percent of students attend private (aided and unaided) institutions even at the primary level. This trend of private institutional dominance is followed at the higher secondary level also in comparison to the rural sector.

Table 6.2: Institution-wise Distribution of Students in Education in India (percent).

Institution	*Rural*	*Urban*	*Rural & urban*	*Rural*	*Urban*	*Rural & urban*
	Primary			*Upper primary*		
Government	73.2	30.9	62.0	75.8	38.0	66.0
Private aided	5.0	17.5	8.1	7.9	20.2	11.1
Private unaided	22.5	51.4	29.7	16.2	41.5	22.8
	Secondary & higher secondary			Graduation and above		
Government	63.5	37.5	55.8	47.9	38.0	43.5
Private aided	15.5	25.6	18.5	22.5	28.0	24.9
Private unaided	20.9	36.5	25.5	29.1	33.5	31.1
	Diploma and certificate					
Government	35.6	28.9	32.8			
Private aided	24.7	29.6	26.8			
Private unaided	39.3	40.5	39.8			

Source: NSSO (2014): 71st round - Key Indicators of Social Consumption in India: Education.

The lack of significant progress in the Indian education is widely explained in terms of financial constraints both public and private resources and by the opportunity cost of time of the households. Though household investments in education are influenced by a wide variety of factors, primarily households invest in education with the anticipation of economic and non-economic benefits from education. The economic benefits of education are measured familiarly in terms of internal rates of return to education. There are several other household characteristics such as income, religion, community, household size, parental education and occupation, place of residence, etc. There are also a host of social, cultural, demographic and other environmental factors that influence the quantum of expenditure that households make in education of their children. The supply side factors like nearness of educational institutions, type of institutions, type of courses pursued by the pupil, fee structure and placement facilities.

This paper aims to identify the determinants of household expenditure on education of children in India. In order to estimate the differential effects of the factors on the quantum of educational expenditure at different points of the conditional distribution, this paper follows the quantile regression method. The quantile regression estimation allows to look beyond the average effects and provides a description of the whole conditional distribution of household expenditure on education in terms of the determining variables. The pattern of household expenditure on children's education is analysed by gender, type of institution, type of courses and household characteristics. The cross section data of the 71st round (January-June 2014) NSSO survey is used in the empirical analysis.

6.2 A Brief Review of Recent Studies

Generally, at the household level, the private expenditure on education is influenced by a wide variety of socio-economic and demographic factors. It has been widely recognised that the household decision-making for investment in education can be understood at least partly in terms of economic factors. However, there is not much research on the extent of household expenditure on education and on determinants of household expenditure on education due to limited information on household expenditure, especially in developing countries including India.

Tilak (2002) investigate the determinants of family expenditure on education using the 1994 NCAER survey data on Human Development in rural India, supplemented by other sources. The elasticity of household expenditure on education to changes in household income on the one hand and the government expenditure on education on the other for different groups of population are calculated. The results show that household expenditures on education are sizeable and there is nothing like free education in India. Households from even lower socioeconomic strata, SC/ST, low income groups all spend considerable amounts on acquiring education. Also, households do not discriminate much against spending on girls' education. However, substantial differences exist in household expenditures between children attending government schools, government-aided schools and private schools. And among the determinants of household expenditure on education of children, household characteristics particularly household income and the education level of the head of the household are important. Further, the coefficients of elasticity show that government expenditure and household expenditure do not substitute each other, instead they complement each other.

Ota and Moffatt (2007), using micro data from a field survey of children in rural Andhra Pradesh, attempt to identify the key factors that influence the decision on schooling, a binary choice. The focus is on the effects of sibling competition within the household with a hypothesis that the child's position within the household is the key to capturing sibling rivalry. The many factors that affect the schooling decision are grouped into three sets of variables: characteristics of the child, characteristics of the household and features of the community in which the child lives. The probit estimates of the schooling decision show that of the child's characteristics, age and gender are the most important determinants of the schooling decision. The first-born children are less likely to attend school irrespective of gender, controlling for age. The presence of elder sisters increases the probability of schooling, whereas the presence of younger brothers decreases the probability of attending school. The boys compete within the same sex, while girls face double competition.

Motiram and Osberg (2012) analyse school attendance and total time spend in acquiring human capital (time in school plus travel time plus in-home instructional time) using the 1998-99 India time use survey and the 7th All India School Educational Survey. The estimated probit and selectivity bias correction regression estimates indicate that the inequality in human capital investment time in rural India can be explained more by the poor quality and availability of schooling to potential students than by parental education, income or barriers of SC/ST background.

Steinberg (2015) study the impact of NREGA, one of the largest workfare programs in the world introduced in 2008, on human capital outcomes of children aged 5-16. The paper uses the data of the NGO Pratham's survey on educational achievement of primary school children in India for cognitive testing, the Annual Status of Education Report (ASER) for 2005-2009 and the data from the NSSO rounds 60, 61, 62, 64 and 66 collected between 2004 and 2009. The results show that children score significantly low in mathematics and reading tests and more children are likely to drop out and less likely to both attend and be on track in school once the NREGA enters their district, primarily caused by increases in the opportunity cost of schooling for children. These results are primarily driven by children aged 13-17 which are precisely the age group that is most likely to enter the labour market. Though the results on human capital are similar for both boys and girls, girls are more likely to substitute for their mothers in domestic work, while boys are more likely to work outside the home for pay.

Bayar and Ilhan (2016) examine the determinants of education expenditure of Turkish households using the 2002, 2010 and 2013 Household Budget Survey of Turkey. The paper especially estimates the effects of different income groups on the education expenditure by Tobit method. The estimated results show that higher household income levels are associated with higher educational expenditure; higher income groups spend more on education and the poor spend less on education.

Also, parents with higher human capital spend more on their children's education; families whose household heads and mothers have higher education level are likely to invest more on education than the others. The paper observes that not only intergenerational educational mobility but also intergenerational income mobility is low in Turkey.

6.3 Data and Methodology

The data used to analyse the household expenditure on education is derived from the 71st round NSSO (January-June2014) data. The NSSO 71st round covers a sample of 36479 households from 4577 villages in rural India and 29447 households from 3720 blocks in urban India. The stratification of the households has been on the basis of having any student (aged 5-29 years) currently attending formal education at primary level or above. The NSSO data contains information on participation of individuals aged 5-29 years in pursuit of education in the country during the period January-June 2014, the extent of use of educational infrastructure, facilities and incentives provided by the government and private sectors and its impact on current attendance status of population in the educational institutions, the private expenditure incurred by households on education and the extent of educational wastage in terms of dropping-out and discontinuance and its causes. For each student in the survey household, the private expenditure on payment of course fees, including tuition fees, examination fees, purchase of books, stationery and uniforms, expenses on conveyance, private coaching, etc. is related to current academic session of study of a student for the basic course.

Quantile Regression Method

In the empirical estimation of the household expenditure on education, this paper follows the quantile regression method. The classical regression estimates only the conditional mean value E(y|x) for all levels of the outcome variable which does not capture the differential impact of determinants across different levels of the outcome variable. It restricts the effect exclusively on the specific location of the outcome variable conditional distribution. The quantile regression extends this approach allowing effects to differ at the conditional distribution of outcome variable at different locations. The quantiles are cut points where a sample is divided into equal sized, two or more subgroups. The 50thquantile is also the median value. The quantile regression estimates conditional quantile functions. In analogy with classical linear regression methods which is based on minimising sums of squared residuals and meant to estimate models for conditional mean functions, the quantile regression methods are based on minimising asymmetrically weighted absolute residuals and intend to estimate conditional median functions and a full range of other conditional quantile functions.

The quantile regression model, introduced by Koenker and Bassett (1978) as an extension from the notion of ordinary quantile, is a more general class of linear models in which the conditional quantiles have a linear form. The quantile regression model is specified as:

$$y_i = \beta_\theta x_i + u_{\theta i} \quad \theta \in (0,1) \tag{6.1}$$

Consider a real valued random variable y characterised by the distribution function:

$$f(y) = P(y \leq y_0) \tag{6.2}$$

Then, the θth quantile of y is defined as:

$$Q_\theta = \inf\,[y: f(y) \geq \theta] \tag{6.3}$$

Given the set of regressors, x_i, the quantile regression can be specified as:

$$f_\theta = (\theta - \beta_\theta x_i | x_i) = P(y_i < \theta | x_i) \tag{6.4}$$

which is essentially a different form of equation (6.1) where the distribution of the error term um is $u_{\theta i}$ is unspecified and the only constraint being the quantile restriction:

$$Q_\theta(u_{\theta i}|x_i) = 0 \tag{6.5}$$

The estimation of conditional mean function is specified as:

$$\hat{\beta} = \arg min_\beta \sum_{i=1}^{N} (y_i - \beta x_i)^2 \tag{6.6}$$

The linear conditional quantile function is specified as:

$$Q_y(\theta | x_i = x_0) = \beta_\theta x_i \tag{6.7}$$

can be estimated by solving the equivalent of expression (6.6):

$$\hat{\beta}_\theta = \arg min_\beta \sum_{i=1}^{N} \gamma_\theta (y_i - \beta x_i) \tag{6.8}$$

where γ_θ (u) is the so-called check function defined as:

$$\gamma_\theta(u) = \begin{Bmatrix} \theta u & if\ u \geq 0 \\ (\theta - 1)u & if\ u < 0 \end{Bmatrix} \tag{6.9}$$

The expanded version of the quantile regression is specified as:

$$min_\beta \left[\sum_{i:y_i \geq \beta x_i} \theta |y_i - \beta x_i| + \sum_{i:y_i < \beta x_i} (1-\theta) |y_i - \beta x_i|\right] \tag{6.10}$$

The quantile regression coefficient is interpreted as the marginal change at the jth conditional quantile of y with respect to one of the regressors.

6.4 Empirical Analysis

The quantile regression analysis of this paper is to capture the effects of the determinants of private household education expenditure at different quantiles along its distribution. The dependent variable is divided in five quantiles. The Table 6.3 presents the descriptive statistics of all variables used in the study.

Table 6.3: Descriptive Statistics of Variables in Household Education Expenditure Analysis.

Variable	*Description*	*Mean*	*Std. dev.*
lnHHEDExp	Per capita private household expenditure on education (Rs.)	8.476	1.713
lnPCE	Per capita consumption expenditure, proxy for household income (Rs.)	9.860	0.612
Age	Age (years)	13.80	5.06
MEducation	Mother's education (years)	7.09	5.08
Male	If male=1, 0 otherwise	0.56	0.49
Rural	If rural=1, 0 otherwise	0.57	0.49
FSelfEmp	If father is self-employment=1, 0 otherwise	0.53	0.49
Hindu	If Hindu=1, 0 otherwise	0.79	0.40
SC/ST	If SC/ST=1, 0 otherwise	0.30	0.46
School10	If attending upto class X=1, 0 otherwise	0.66	0.47
Commerce	If studying in commerce or humanities streams=1, 0 otherwise	0.13	0.33
Science	If studying in science streams =1, 0 otherwise	0.06	0.24
Professional	If studying in medicine or engineering streams=1, 0 otherwise	0.07	0.26
Vocational	If studying in vocational streams=1, 0 otherwise	0.03	0.18
GovtSchool	If studying in government institution=1, 0 otherwise	0.53	0.49
EngMedium	If English medium education=1, 0 otherwise	0.41	0.49
InsChange	If change of education institution=1, 0 otherwise	0.17	0.37
Scholarship	If receiving scholarship=1, 0 otherwise	0.18	0.38
Aid	If received books and stationery=1, 0 otherwise	0.03	0.18
Obs.	93446		

The Table 6.4 presents the average household expenditure on education for different levels of education and for different types of institutions. It is observed that with increase in level of current attendance, the expenditure on education increases. The rural-urban difference narrows down at higher levels of general education. At primary level, expenditure in urban areas is Rs.10083perstudent which is more than four times that in rural areas. At graduation and post-graduation levels, the average expenditure for female students are more than their male counterparts in rural areas. The average expenditure for different levels of study in different types of institutions shows substantial huge difference. At all levels of education, both in rural and urban areas, the household educational expenditure is invariably higher at private aided and unaided institutions than government institutions. Even at the primary level, the average educational expenditure is about six times higher even in private aided schools and seven times higher in private unaided institutions both in urban and rural sectors.

Table 6.4: Average Household Expenditure on Education in India (Rs. per student).

Education level	*Rural*			*Urban*		
	Male	*Female*	*Person*	*Male*	*Female*	*Person*
Primary	3061	2512	2811	10604	9489	10083
Upper primary	3603	2813	3242	11864	10940	11466
Secondary	5568	4534	5100	13781	13284	13547
Higher secondary	9820	8012	9031	21681	18442	20179
Graduate	11306	11813	11527	17480	16161	16771
Post graduate	13017	16715	14604	19090	16565	21249
Diploma	15209	10706	13422	23040	21249	21947
	Government	*Private aided*	*Private unaided*	*Government*	*Private aided*	*Private unaided*
Primary	965	6452	7907	2149	11881	14242
Upper primary	1605	6013	9514	3356	12074	18553
Secondary	3328	5896	11222	5540	14096	21565
Higher secondary	6056	10803	13988	9668	20066	30810
Graduate	8753	11730	17093	11560	16993	26380
Post graduate	11403	14224	25372	13580	20978	29661
Diploma	10603	14935	20976	12184	19059	46445

Source: NSSO (2014): 71st round - Key Indicators of Social Consumption in India: Education.

The Figure 6.1 shows the quantile regression plots. The graph shows that the distribution of the private/household expenditure on education varies at the tails of the expenditure distribution where the expenditure is at the extremes. This is the reason to use quantile regression to study the determinants of private expenditure on education across the entire distribution for a given set of regressors.

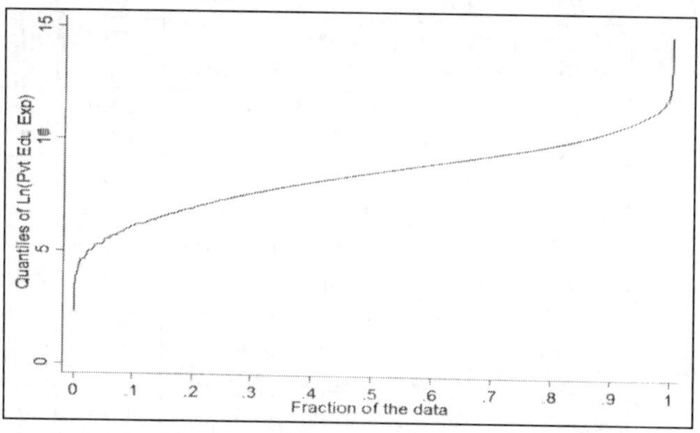

Figure 6.1: Quantile Plot of Household Expenditure on Education.

The empirical quantile regression equation for estimating the determinants of private household educational expenditure is specified as:

$$lnHHEDExp = \beta_0 + \beta_1 HHIncome + \beta_2 Age + \beta_3 Gender + \beta_4 MotherEducation + \beta_5 Residence + \beta_6 Community + \beta_7 Religion + \beta_8 Fatheroccupation + \beta_9 Coursestudying + \beta_{10} Educationinstitution + u_i \quad (6.11)$$

The Table 6.5 presents the OLS and the 10th, 25th, 50th, 75th, and 90th quantile regression estimates of household expenditure on education per student. The-R-square and Pseudo R-square values indicate better explanatory power of the included variables in explaining the variations in private education expenditure across households in India. It is also to be noted that almost all the regression coefficients are statistically significant and in the expected direction. The empirical estimates show that household income, age of the child, male child, mother's education, father's occupation, Hindu religion, English medium education, change of institution, and professional education have positive effects whereas below 10th education level, rural background, socially backward community, government educational institutions, science, commerce and vocational subjects and scholarships and aid in the form of books and stationeries have negative impact on household expenditure on education. In fact, the in-kind aid substantially reduces household expenditure on education of children than the financial aid and scholarships. Households spend significantly on medical and engineering education and for English medium institutions. Rural households and SC/ST groups spent less on education of children.

Table 6.5: OLS and Quantile Regression Estimates of Household Educational Expenditure in India.

Dependent variable: ln(HHEDExp)

Variable	*OLS*	*Q10*	*Q25*	*Q50*	*Q75*	*Q90*
lnPCE	0.601*** (0.006)	0.625*** (0.011)	0.631*** (0.009)	0.612*** (0.008)	0.573*** (0.007)	0.550*** (0.008)
Age	0.082*** (0.001)	0.082*** (0.002)	0.079*** (0.001)	0.074*** (0.001)	0.070*** (0.001)	0.068*** (0.001)
MEducation	0.024*** (0.0006)	0.024*** (0.001)	0.023*** (0.0008)	0.023*** (0.0008)	0.023*** (0.0008)	0.068*** (0.0009)
FSelfEmp	0.039*** (0.006)	0.045*** (0.011)	0.049*** (0.011)	0.039*** (0.007)	0.044*** (0.007)	0.036*** (0.008)
Male	0.069*** (0.006)	0.083*** (0.011)	0.077*** (0.009)	0.067*** (0.007)	0.062*** (0.007)	0.056*** (0.008)
Rural	-0.163*** (0.007)	-0.170*** (0.013)	-0.150*** (0.010)	-0.150*** (0.008)	-0.153*** (0.008)	-0.141*** (0.009)
Hindu	0.084*** (0.008)	0.108*** (0.014)	0.094*** (0.001)	0.091*** (0.009)	0.093*** (0.009)	0.110*** (0.010)

SC/ST	-0.135*** (0.007)	-0.180*** (0.013)	0.156*** (0.010)	-0.128*** (0.008)	-0.103*** (0.008)	-0.095*** (0.009)
School10	-0.591*** (0.018)	-0.290*** (0.033)	-0.455*** (0.023)	-0.654*** (0.021)	-0.772*** (0.021)	-0.872*** (0.024)
Commerce	-0.358*** (0.016)	-0.087*** (0.031)	-0.234*** (0.024)	-0.409*** (0.020)	-0.561*** (0.019)	-0.669*** (0.022)
Science	-0.259*** (0.018)	-0.059 (0.034)	-0.180*** (0.027)	-0.331*** (0.022)	-0.412*** (0.022)	-0.468*** (0.025)
Professional	0.413*** (0.017)	0.663*** (0.033)	0.482*** (0.026)	0.349*** (0.021)	0.284*** (0.021)	0.247*** (0.024)
Vocational	0.014*** (0.021)	0.230*** (0.040)	0.086*** (0.031)	-0.023*** (0.026)	-0.080*** (0.026)	-0.120*** (0.029)
GovtSchool	-0.971*** (0.007)	-1.291*** (0.013)	-1.161*** (0.010)	-0.954*** (0.008)	-0.772*** (0.008)	-0.678*** (0.009)
EngMedium	0.679*** (0.007)	0.801*** (0.014)	0.741*** (0.011)	0.695*** (0.009)	0.648*** (0.009)	0.611*** (0.010)
InsChange	0.051*** (0.008)	0.061*** (0.015)	0.051*** (0.012)	0.055*** (0.010)	0.037*** (0.009)	0.026*** (0.011)
Scholarship	-0.190*** (0.008)	-0.239*** (0.015)	-0.193*** (0.012)	-0.195*** (0.010)	-0.178*** (0.009)	-0.145*** (0.011)
Aid	-0.737*** (0.007)	-0.941*** (0.032)	-0.922*** (0.025)	-0.799*** (0.021)	-0.596*** (0.021)	-0.383*** (0.233)
Constant	1.069*** (0.068)	0.408*** (0.127)	1.062*** (0.101)	2.051*** (0.082)	3.092*** (0.081)	3.829*** (0.092)
Pseudo R-square	-	0.461	0.483	0.483	0.479	0.480
R-square	0.71					
F-value	12996.91					

Note: Standard errors in parentheses. *** significant at 1 percent level.

In the quantile regression estimates, which describe the effects at different quantiles of the educational expenditure distribution, a percentage increase in consumption expenditure monotonically decreases the education expenditure from 6.2 percent at the lower to 5.5 percent at the higher quantile. This shows that the proportion of household income spent on education is higher at the lower quantile and is decreasing at the higher quantiles, a result similar to the findings in Turkey by Bayar and Ilhan (2016). The OLS regression coefficient of per capita consumption expenditure is also 0.60 showing that on an average the households spend about 6 percent on education of children with one percent increase in the per capita household income.

The education of mother has positive and statistically significant effect on the household education expenditure and the effect is almost a constant 2 percent throughout the expenditure distribution, similar to the OLS result. The self-employment of father also has a similar positive effect on the higher education distribution. Irrespective of the quantiles, self-employed parents spend about 4 percent more relative to other occupations on the education of their children. Though households spend about 7 percent higher on the education of male children compared to female children the marginal effect declines throughout the education expenditure distribution. At the 10th and the 25th quantiles, the gender coefficients are 0.082 and 0.077 percent respectively and at the 75th and 90th quantiles the gender coefficients are 0.062 and 0.056 percent respectively. This shows that at the higher quantiles the gender bias in educational investments is significantly low than the lower quantiles. The religion has a positive effect on private education expenditure. The estimated coefficients suggest that households belong to Hindu religion tend to spend nearly 8-10 percent more on education of their children. The rural dummy has a negative sign and its impact is decreasing across the quantiles. The coefficients at 10th and the 90th quantiles have a significant difference - about 3 percent - in spending than the middle quantiles. This shows that households in rural areas spend about 16 percent less on education compared to urban households and households in the lower quantiles in rural areas also spend considerably less on education than the rural households at the higher quantiles.

The social group dummy (SC/ST) has a negative effect but a decreasing trend across the quantiles. The scheduled caste/tribe households spend less than other communities on education. The gap between the education expenditure of the two groups are narrow both at the higher quantiles compared to the lower quantiles, but at the middle quantiles the gap is slightly larger. The OLS estimate of -0.135 shows that the SC/ST groups spend on average 13 percent less than the non-SC/ST communities. These results imply that households at both ends of expenditure distribution are able to better utilise the benefits extended to the SC/ST students both at the lower and higher levels of education, especially the scholarships and tuition fees waiver schemes, especially in government institutions. These results are also confirmed by the negative coefficients of scholarship, aid provision, and government institution dummies. In fact, the effect of studying government institutions and getting free books and stationeries are larger at all quantiles than the 1-2 percent effect of scholarships on reducing the household educational expenditure.

Though scholarships are given to non-SC/ST communities also by many state governments, like backward class scholarships, the number of beneficiaries and the amount of benefit are low and are restricted to poor and within certain limits, compared to SC/ST scholarships for which all SC/ST students are eligible. The scholarship dummy shows a negative effect on private expenditure on education indicating the wards of households who have scholarship spend less on education expenditure. It has a decreasing effect across the quantiles, a significant difference between the 10th and 90th quantiles from 2.4 percent to 1.4 percent. Thus, the scholarship schemes of the governments have more effect on the lower quantile than at the higher quantiles. Similarly, the in-kind aid dummy, free books and stationary provisions, has negative effect on the private expenditure on education showing less need for purchase of education materials. There is a significant difference between the coefficients of the lower quantiles and the higher quantiles, from more than 90 percent at the 10th to about 80 percent at the median quantile to 38 percent at the 90th quantile. Similarly, the type of institution the student attends i.e. whether the student goes to a government or a private institution matter. The household expenditure is significantly higher when the student is enrolled in the private institution and less if enrolled in the government institution. The regression coefficient on the enrollment in government institution dummy is negative which has a decreasing impact across the quantiles. The OLS coefficient shows a significant 97 percent less expenditure in government institutions relative to enrollment in private educational institutions. At the 10th and 25th quantiles the effects are larger, the coefficients being-1.29 and -1.16 respectively and at the 75th and 90th quantiles -0.95, -0.77 and -0.68 respectively, which are considerably less compared to the lower quantiles. Also, the increase in the proportion of the education expenditure in the government institution as the level of education increases is lesser compared to the proportion of education expenditure in the private institutions. Hence, the students at the lower quantiles tend to enroll in government institutions and get the incentives and the students at the higher quantiles are likely to enroll mostly in private institutions and the incentives may not necessarily available in private institutions (Tilak, 2002).

Among the other education related variables, the English medium of instruction has a significantly positive effect on the private education expenditure compared to vernacular medium institutions and its effects are decreasing across the quantiles. The percentage amount spend is high in English medium institutions at the lower quantiles than at the higher quantiles, from 80 percent to 60 percent. Most of the English medium institutions are private educational institutions and hence they charge high fees and many of the government schemes for weaker sections are not available in these private institutions. However, at higher education levels, some benefits are available even to the meritorious poor students in the form of institutional concessions and the slightly better off households among the poor are able to tap these avenues. School education is less costly for households as its coefficients are negative - on average 60 percent -and increasing – from 30 percent to 80 percent - over the private education expenditure distribution. Obviously, such education expenditure pattern shows that thc students from the lower quantiles are mostly attending the government institutions and the students from the higher quantiles are most likely in the private institutions.

In addition, the estimated coefficients of commerce, humanities and science dummies show that the proportion of household education expenditure incurred for commerce or humanities courses are lesser than the professional courses like medicine or engineering. The coefficients are decreasing over the quantiles. On average, the household expenditures on these educational streams are lower by 25 to 35 percent. The professional education expenditure has a positive effect on the private expenditure on education. The students who pursue medicine or engineering spend more than 40 percent on education than others. The coefficients of the quantiles have a decreasing trend across the quantiles. The proportion of educational expenditure by the lower quantile households are almost 50 percent greater than the higher quantiles households. The vocational education dummy has a positive effect at the lower quantiles and a negative effect from the median quantile. This implies that a significant number of students from the lower quantiles pursue vocational studies than children at higher quantiles of private/household education al expenditure.

The Figure 6.2 plots the OLS and quantile regression coefficients of the determinants of private education expenditure across the distribution. The dotted lines are the OLS coefficients which is an average and constant across the distribution of private education expenditure. The quantile regression coefficient plots show that the effects of the determinants on educational expenditure of households are not the same across the distribution. Compared to the constant marginal effects of the OLS estimates, the plots of the marginal effects on expenditure on education show a continuous decline with an increase in income and age, and for medium of instruction, below 10th school, science, professional and vocation education streams of education. The plots of the effects of the social background, type of institution, scholarships and aid for books and stationeries show continuous rise in marginal effects and the plots of male child, mother's education, father's self-employment, rural background, and change of institution coefficients reflect differential effects at different quantiles, crossing over the OLS coefficients generally at the median values. The quantile plots also show the opposite effects at the extreme ends of the educational expenditure distribution for income, age, gender, social group, institution type, medium of instruction, change of institution, scholarships and aid, and courses of study compared to the average OLS effects throughout the distribution.

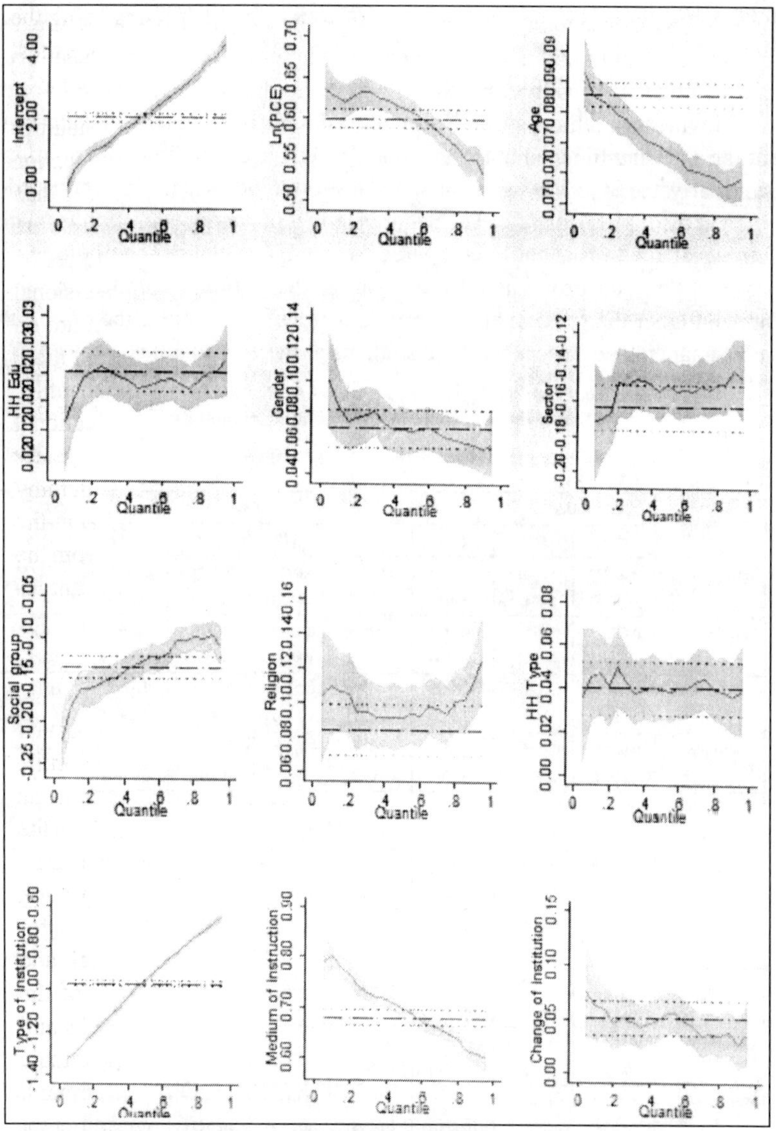

Figure 6.2: OLS and Quantile Regression Plots of the Determinants of Household Expenditure on Education in India.

To further investigate the gender and community differences in private expenditure on education in India, the quantile regression is estimated for male and female students and SC/ST and non-SC/ST communities separately. The Table 6.6 reports the estimates for 10th and 90th quantiles for each of the sub-samples. The effect of household income on educational expenditure of households is much higher at the lower quantiles compared to higher quantiles for both males and females as well as in SC/ST and non-SC/ST households. The self-employment of father has a significant negative effect in non-SC/ST households whereas its effect on educational expenditure is positive in SC/ST households. The non-SC/ST self-employment of fathers spend less, almost double the amount, on education at the 10th quantile than at the 90th quantile of the expenditure distribution. Similarly, the SC/ST households spend less on students at the lower quantile than at the higher quantile. The negative effect of school education is much strong at the 90th quantile compared to the 10th quantile. The household expenditures on professional education at the bottom quantiles are also much higher than that of at the upper quantiles. The same is the case with non-financial aid except for male students at the 10th quantile.

Table 6.6: Quantile Regression Estimates of Household Education Expenditure in India by Gender and Community.

Dependent variable: ln(HHEDExp)

Variable	*Males*		*Females*		*SC/ST*		*Non-SC/ST*	
	Q10	*Q90*	*Q10*	*Q90*	*Q10*	*Q90*	*Q10*	*Q90*
lnPCE	0.61*** (0.015)	0.53*** (0.011)	0.65*** (0.018)	0.57*** (0.012)	0.67*** (0.024)	0.57*** (0.017)	0.61*** (0.013)	0.54*** (0.010)
Age	0.08*** (0.001)	0.07*** (0.002)	0.08*** (0.003)	0.07*** (0.002)	0.10*** (0.003)	0.08*** (0.002)	0.076*** (0.002)	0.063*** (0.001)
MEducation	0.02*** (0.001)	0.024** (0.001)	0.02*** (0.002)	0.02*** (0.001)	0.02*** (0.022)	0.02*** (0.001)	0.02*** (0.001)	0.03*** (0.001)
FSelfEmp	0.06*** (0.014)	0.04*** (0.012)	0.03*** (0.021)	0.03*** (0.012)	0.02 (0.023)	0.05*** (0.016)	-1.30*** (0.015)	-0.64*** (0.010)
Male	-	-	-	-	0.07*** (0.022)	0.04*** (0.016)	0.08*** (0.013)	0.06*** (0.010)
Rural	-0.16*** (0.016)	-0.12*** (0.013)	-0.19*** (0.020)	-0.17*** (0.013)	-0.15*** (0.026)	-0.18*** (0.018)	-0.17*** (0.014)	-0.12*** (0.010)
Hindu	0.14*** (0.018)	0.11*** (0.014)	0.09*** (0.022)	0.09*** (0.015)	0.05*** (0.033)	0.17*** (0.023)	0.14*** (0.016)	0.08*** (0.012)
SC/ST	-0.18*** (0.017)	-0.10*** (0.013)	-0.17*** (0.020)	-0.10*** (0.013)	-	-	-	-
School10	-0.23*** (0.041)	-0.10*** (0.033)	-0.40*** (0.054)	-0.85*** (0.037)	-0.34*** (0.071)	-0.88*** (0.049)	-0.30*** (0.038)	-0.86*** (0.029)
Commerce	-0.03*** (0.038)	-0.68*** (0.030)	-0.20*** (0.050)	-0.64*** (0.033)	-0.01*** (0.067)	-0.65*** (0.047)	-0.13*** (0.035)	-0.70*** (0.029)

Science	-0.04*** (0.042)	-0.44 (0.033)	-0.20*** (0.056)	-0.49*** (0.037)	-0.47*** (0.078)	-0.44*** (0.054)	0.08*** (0.039)	-0.48*** (0.029)
Professional	0.72*** (0.034)	0.22*** (0.031)	0.55*** (0.059)	0.37*** (0.040)	0.66*** (0.077)	0.30*** (0.053)	0.67*** (0.037)	0.24*** (0.028)
Vocational	0.36*** (0.046)	-0.13*** (0.036)	-0.07*** (0.077)	-0.10*** (0.052)	-0.24*** (0.084)	-0.18*** (0.058)	0.22*** (0.046)	-0.09*** (0.035)
GovtSchool	-1.31*** (0.017)	-1.19*** (0.013)	-1.26*** (0.021)	-0.69*** (0.014)	-1.24*** (0.027)	-0.72*** (0.019)	-1.30*** (0.015)	-0.64*** (0.011)
EngMedium	0.79*** (0.018)	0.72*** (0.015)	0.81*** (0.022)	0.60*** (0.015)	0.72*** (0.031)	0.59*** (0.022)	0.82*** (0.016)	0.62*** (0.013)
InsChange	0.07*** (0.018)	0.04*** (0.015)	0.05*** (0.024)	0.002*** (0.017)	0.07** (0.034)	0.04* (0.024)	0.05*** (0.017)	0.03*** (0.013)
Scholarship	-0.22*** (0.020)	-0.15*** (0.015)	-0.25*** (0.023)	-0.15*** (0.016)	-0.19*** (0.025)	-0.11*** (0.017)	-0.30*** (0.021)	-0.21*** (0.015)
Aid	-0.74*** (0.007)	-0.94*** (0.032)	-0.86*** (0.049)	-0.31*** (0.031)	-0.90*** (0.052)	-0.42*** (0.036)	-0.96*** (0.042)	-0.33*** (0.032)
Constant	0.52*** (0.161)	4.06*** (0.127)	0.34*** (0.200)	3.57*** (0.134)	0.40*** (0.262)	3.33*** (0.183)	0.67*** (0.147)	3.99*** (0.111)
Pseudo R-square	0.47	0.48	0.44	0.47	0.40	0.47	0.47	0.48
Obs.	52239		41207		27832		65614	

Note: Standard errors in parentheses. ***significant at 1 percent level ** significant at 5 percent level * significant at 10 percent level.

6.5 Conclusion

Households spend substantial part of their income on education of their children in India. This private expenditure is increasing despite subsidised education system with substantial government spending and various financial aid programmes. Households incur expenditure on education as an investment with sizable returns for various levels of education. Apart from the private returns, human capital investments have social returns also. Hence, the overall benefit of investing in education is well recognised and therefore household expenditure on education is worthy. However, there exist other barriers to education such as availability, access and quality of education, and infrastructure and location of educational facilities. There are socioeconomic, demographic and regional issues in the provision and utilisation of educational services also. The aim of this paper is to identify the determinants of private household expenditure on education in India using the 2014 NSSO 71st round survey data and applying the quantile regression method. The paper focused on the socio-economic characteristics of the students currently attending educational institution. The quantile regression is used to capture the differential impacts across the distribution of the private education expenditure.

The quantile regression estimates show consumption expenditure (proxy for income), social group, type of institution, scholarship and in-kind incentives and courses the student is currently attending have significant effects on the private education expenditure. The proportion of income spend on education of children increases more in the lower quantiles than in the higher quantiles. In other words, lower quantile households are more sensitive to the changes in household income than the higher quantile households. The general observation of gender differences in educational expenditure by the households is not borne out in this study. The gender bias does exist only at the lower quantiles but is considerably less at the higher quantiles. From the social group perspectives, the SC/ST households spends less than the non-SC/ST groups at the lower quantiles and the difference gets reduced at the higher quantiles, probably due to the access to community specific scholarships and other incentives especially free education and tuition fees waiver schemes. Compared to scholarships, the provision of educational materials such as books and stationeries has higher impact on household expenditure on education. The type of the institution the student goes to and English medium of education are the important determinants of the private education expenditure. The proportion of expenditure spend on the government institution is lot lesser than the expenditure spend on the private institution. It holds true across the quantiles especially for the lower quantiles, since more students from the lower quantiles attend the government institution. In addition, substantial differences exist in private expenditure on education on students attending government institutions and private institutions. The students from the higher income groups tend to attend the private institutions. The results of this paper reveal that despite the government policies and programmes to provide educational facilities such as free education, scholarships and incentives to make education affordable, the lower income groups still spend a considerable amount of their income on education of children.

7

The Determinants of Earnings: 2SLS-IV Estimation of Returns to Education

7.1 Introduction

Human capital, especially the acquired skills, is one of the most important factors for economic growth in every modern economy (Schultz, 1961; 1962; Becker, 1964). Among the various forms and components of human capital, education is the single most factor that plays a vital role in the determination of earnings of workers in both formal and informal sectors in the labour markets. The role of education cannot be underestimated and as a component of human capital, it is needed to put human on a better position to ensure development. As Alfred Marshall puts it, "The most valuable of all capital is that invested in human beings Humans are seen as the regulators of all things and investing in them is a sure way of achieving a better use of other forms of capital. The role of education in modern development is strongly evident in various studies conducted across the world. Most empirical studies in different countries have confirmed that educated individuals earn higher wages and are in prestigious occupations. Psacharopoulos (1972; 1985; 1986; 1994) and Psacharopoulos and Patrinos (2018) find a strong positive relationship between education and earnings in almost all countries around the world, especially in middle and low income countries. Similarly, Card (1999) argues that education indeed is an investment in human capital which enhances productivity and pays off the forgone earnings with higher wages in future.

It has been proven that the higher the level of education attained the higher will be the returns. This shows that, the return to education depends on the qualification or diploma one has (Spence 1973). This is of the view that, the higher one's qualification, the greater his ability to think and make productive decisions. This has been the reason for higher level of education worldwide. Countries in Africa also have seen increasing number of undergraduate degrees in recent years, reducing the value of a first degree and compelling others to earn a postgraduate degree. Hauser et al. (2000) and Edgerton et al. (2012) find substantial evidence that postsecondary education puts one on a higher occupational position than sub-high school education. Krueger and Lindahl (2001) argue that, though primary education plays a role in ensuring development and growth for individuals and countries, much growth and development is seen with the attainment of higher level of education.

Most of the empirical works on education investments and returns there off have been using the theoretical frameworks of Schultz (1961; 1962), Becker (1962; 1964) and Mincer (1974). The earnings function approach of Mincer uses years of schooling and experience gained in computing the returns to an individual's investment in education i.e. earnings. Many studies worldwide have seen results identical to that of Mincer (Goldberg and Smith, 2008). Notwithstanding the achievement chalked by the Mincer model, many studies have augmented/extended the Mincerian equation to incorporate various factors in determining the returns to schooling (Griliches 1977; Glewwe, 1991; 2002; Card, 1999; 2001; Klein and Vella, 2010). For example, empirical studies frequently adjust returns to schooling to the quality of education and occupational choice. The standard of education in developed countries is higher than that in developing countries considering the availability of learning aid in the former countries. This definitely results in differences in the quality gained from the education between these countries (Hanushek and Wobmann, 2010).

The Ghanaian Education System

According to the Ghana Education Service, since 1987, the education system is made up 6 of years of primary education, 3 years of junior high education, 3 years of senior high education (which was increased to 4 years from 2007 to 2009 but later reverted back to the 3-year system) and 4 years of undergraduate education, which makes a total of 16 years of education. The chance of gaining admission into secondary school depends on a good grade in the common entrance examination. After 1997, the government of Ghana introduced a more generalised system of examination for the junior secondary and the senior secondary education. The West African Examination Council (WAEC) conducts the Basic Education Certificate Examination (BECE) for pupils in the third year of junior secondary (9 years of education) and West African Senior Secondary Certificate Examination (WASSCE) for the third year senior secondary (12 years of education) students. Post-secondary education includes university and vocational training institutions. Most of the vocational institutions like teaching and nursing have a 2-year training period which awards a diploma certificate. To earn more will require one to pursue a bachelor degree lasting for two years (16 years of education) which are mostly referred to as 'top-ups'. The increasing number of bachelor degrees at the universities for non-vocational courses have made it necessary to pursue mostly two more years of graduate studies to be qualified for employment. In recent years, the Ghana system of education has been reformed incorporating information and communication technology in the study curricular making pupils improve their skills right from an early age to the tertiary level. The Ghana government has also embarked on series of projects, capitation grant, school feeding programme, and distribution of laptops to schools which have ensured increased number in enrolment and possible development of skills (MOFEP, 2010-2014).

Marriage and Extra Earnings

Being married adds up one's earnings (Bartlett and Callahan, 1984; Fernandez, 2003; Aguilera, 2008). There is a premium attached to married workers as the assortative mating theory (Greenwood et al. 2014) has shown that marriage and the level of education of one's spouse are positively related. Different studies have attributed their findings to different views. The division of labour theory has it that when the work in the household is well divided between married couple, with woman set to do work in the house and man working more hours in an institution, there is bound to be higher earnings. This is because the man tends to work more hours and be more productive; when one gets married, he is deemed responsible and tasked with other responsibilities. This duty comes with it an increase in the earnings of such a person.

Other studies also have different perspective to explaining wage differences between among married and unmarried workers. Employers discriminate in favour of married workers and the former know married workers have families to support thereby giving them extra financial support which comes at extra work by the latter. The employers believe married workers will surely work harder and hence deserve an extra pay for their service. Others also have a social perspective as to why wage differentials exit among married and unmarried workers. Nock (1998) argues that the social group in which one is introduced into by a married partner has an influence on the kind of job he does and the wage he receives. Marriage provides people with social capital including access to family and friends and a large circle of opportunities.

Societies in Africa and Ghana deem marriages as a social prestige and the married people are 'respected' in society. Most married men and women are believed to be responsible and are put in respectable positions in their working environments. These positions are assumed to come with extra earnings. It is therefore necessary to factor this in one's earnings. Therefore, the question is: does marriage influence one's earnings? Parents play a major role in the education of their wards. The former's ability to read and write and also their earnings have a major role to play in determining the latter's education and earnings (Chen and Hamori, 2009; Chen and Feng, 2011). Therefore, it is important to understand whether parental education has a role to play in child's earnings, and hence the question is: do parents' education influence ward's earnings? Some studies have found that, in developing countries, the investment in human capital has no significant effect on workers (Psacharopoulos, 1985, World Bank, 1989). Studies using years of schooling as a measure of human capital consider the years spent in formal schooling. Therefore, the effects of human capital on one's earnings need to be examined in Ghana.

Therefore, the main objectives of this paper are to (i) know if certificates plays a role in the hiring and earnings of workers, (ii) examine the role of parents in determining the wages of their wards, (iii) identify the determinants worker choice between private and public sector job, (iv) estimate the rate of return to education in Ghana, and (v) analyse the link between marriage and earnings. The data for this study is taken from the Sixth Round of Ghana Living Standards Survey (GLSS) conducted from September 2012 to September 2013 in Ghana. The GLSS covers various aspects of demographic characteristics of the population, educational level, health, employment, migration, conditions of housing, agriculture and non- farming business activities. The First Ghana Living Standards Survey was carried out in 1987. The sixth Ghana Living Standards Survey sample covers each of the 10 regions of Ghana and a nationwide survey of 18,000 households. Empirically, instrumental variable (IV) method has been used to estimate the effect of education, marital status and experience on earnings addressing the issue of endogeneity among the variables.

7.2 A Brief Review of Recent Studies

This section briefly reviews the theoretical and available literature on education and earnings. Generally human capital is defined as the accumulated knowledge and skill of a worker, acquired either through formal schooling or through experience in the labour market that contributes to his or her productivity. The human capital is essentially made up of the health, formal education and training gained. An individual with a higher level of accumulated learning and training combined with innate ability like positive work attitude is believed to be highly productive and therefore receive a higher wage. However, workers with the same level of human capital - years of schooling, quality of education, training and attitude to work - may receive different wages in the labour market. Such wage differentials may arise due to personal productivity characteristics of the workers and/or differential treatment in the labour market such as discrimination by sex or race.

Schultz (1961; 1962) and Becker (1964) works on the concept of investment in human capital enriches the literature on human capital by stressing on the essence of training - general and specific - in determining wages and on influencing productivity. The essence of training is to improve old skills and be enriched with new ones. For the skilled worker, on-the-job training adds up to the worker's skills and further increase his productivity. As such skill acquisition through training comes with cost which must either be borne by the person if it is a general training or by the organisation if it's a specific training. With such training and experience, the workers are to be adequately compensated with an increase in wages paid. Hence, as one ages, the addition to skills and knowledge from training will decrease and hence the age-earning profile of the worker becomes steeper and concave. In fact, the training gained within the formal schooling improves their knowledge and skills just like a general or specific training, also tend to steepen the age-earnings profile.

The typical age-earning profile of a typical worker is depicted in Figure 7.1. The untrained worker earns a constant wage over his working life (UU). A trained worker will have his earnings profile like T'T', which is less than an untrained worker at the beginning as the worker spends a part of his earnings as the cost of his training. A worker's earnings rise steeply above the earnings of the untrained worker and moves steadily. An additional training will see the curve T'T' move up and steadily over his working years like TT.

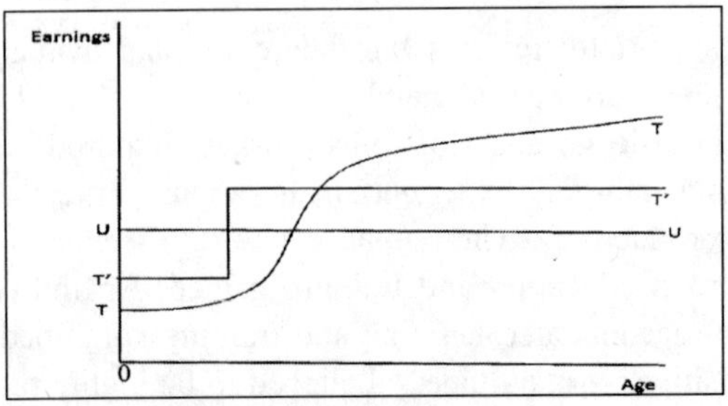

Figure 7.1: Age-Earning Profile.

Alternative views to the neoclassical view of investment in human capital, such as Spence's (1973) market signaling hypothesis hold the view that education does not augment any productive skills, but is simply used as a screening device by the employer or the holder of a certificate signals to the labour market his productivity (Glewwe, 1991). This credential/screening/signaling model argues that employers do not consider the ability of people before they employ them but rather consider their certificates and degrees. This means that, people are hired without any formal consideration of their level of productivity, firms make an uncertain investment knowing nothing about a potential employee's ability and capability. Firms consider education as an observable, alterable characteristic and attributes of potential employee (signals). The potential employees with the given set of signals and indices are faced with an offered wage corresponding to the expected marginal product of employers. The education signal is costly and potential employees will invest in education provided there is a higher return for it. So, if employers give a higher offer wage to highly educated workers, potential employees will invest a lot in education so as to be offered these wages. Education is not to be completely productive, but a signal to the potential employers.

In the empirical literature, Trostel (2002) estimate returns to education in 28 countries using data from the International Social Survey Programme for the period 1985 to 1995. The study employs both the Mincer's OLS model and the instrumental variable (IV) method in estimating the returns to education. They observe that workers outside the continental Europe earn slightly more; 19.0 percent rate of return to females in Netherlands as compared to 19.2 percent in Philippines. The results indicate that the heterogeneity in the returns was as a result of diminishing marginal returns to schooling, per capita income of the countries and relative spending on education. The pooled data analysis shows that the rate of return of education to men to be 4.8 percent as against 5.7 percent for women. When spousal education is used as instrument for education variable in the IV, the rate of return to education is biased downwards by 20 percent. The parental education instrument even has a 40 percent increase in the rate of return to education.

Chen and Hamori (2009) and Chen and Feng (2011) examine the impact of parental education on one's wage earnings in China in 2007 using the China Urban Household Supplemental Survey and employing the 2 SLS method. The study shows that the ability of workers depends on their education and parents' education. The father's education is shown to be correlated with the child's first job search and mother's education with the initial ability of the child. The results indicate that father's education has a positive effect on influencing one's first job in the state sector by 3.9 percent higher than mother's education. The father's education also influences the wages of those who never change job. The mother's education on the other hand has effect on those in coastal areas and in non-state jobs.

With respect to African countries, Mwabu and Schultz (1996) and Schultz (1999; 2003) estimate the returns to schooling for two African countries, Ghana and Cote d'Ivoire, using an extended Mincerian equation. For Ghana, the study uses the Ghana Living Standard Survey (GLSS) of 1987-88, 1988-89 and 1991-92 and the Cote d'Ivoire Living Standard Survey 1985/86 and 1986/87. The results for Ghana indicate that individuals with primary school education alone earned an average rate of return of 4 percent, with secondary school education earning an average of 11 percent and the university education gets an average rate of return of 16 percent. The study also finds that the distribution of earnings is in favour of the younger than the older generation since most of the former are university graduates. Also, those in the urban areas earn more on average than those in the rural areas. The estimates for Cote d'Ivoire show the average rate of returns to primary school education to be 11 percent, for secondary school an average rate return of 28 percent and for university graduate an average rate of return being 15 percent. The significant difference in returns to tertiary graduate and secondary school graduate is a result of the importance employers attach to the secondary school certificate holders who mostly have technical knowledge.

Twumasi Baffour (2013; 2015) analyse the determinants of earnings of the urban worker in Ghana and Tanzania using the Urban Household Worker Survey from 2004 to 2006. The study employs the Mincerian OLS method, the instrumental variable method and the multinomial logit method in estimating the role of education and individual household in facilitating entry into employment sectors. The OLS results show that the rate of return to education in Tanzania and Ghana are 11.3 percent and 7.9 percent respectively. The education-earnings relationship exhibits a convex relationship as one with higher level of education earning more than those with lower levels of education. The IV result shows a higher rate of return than the OLS estimates for Tanzania and Ghana to 12.5 percent and 10.9 percent respectively. This shows the endogeneity of education. In the multinomial logit estimates age and education have a higher probability of being employed in Tanzania and Ghana; having only a primary or secondary education reduces the probability of not-working by 7 percent. Secondary and tertiary educations increase the probability of being employed in the public sector but reduce that of being self-employed. Access to non-labour income increases the probability of not working in Tanzania, and in Ghana, access to non-labour income increases the likelihood of self-employment.

7.3 Data and Methodology

The source of data for the study is the 6th round of the Ghana Living Standard Survey (GLSS) conducted by the Ghana Statistical Service. The first round of GLSS was conducted in 1987/1988 with the subsequent rounds conducted on 1991/92, 1998/99, 2005/2006 and 2012/2013. The round 6 of the GLSS data has been collected from a nationally representative sample of 18000 households during September 2012 and September 2013. The part A of the GLSS survey contains information on demographic characteristics, education, health, marital status, fertility, migration, income, consumption and expenditure patterns, employment, experience, wages, child labour, etc. of Ghanaian households. Since the objective of the paper is to analyse the relationship between education and earnings, observations with age below 14 years and the unemployed has been taken out of the sample. Also, observations without at least a year of formal education have not been included in the data. Thus, the database for this study is 20214 observations.

Mincerian Earnings Function

Empirically, there exist a voluminous literature on the estimation of returns to education following the human capital approach of Schultz (1961; 1962) and Becker (1964) and the semi-logarithmic earnings function approach of Mincer (1974). The Mincerian earnings function is generally estimated by the OLS method with the log of earning specified as dependent on formal schooling, experience and experience square only:

$$lnEarnings = \beta_0 + \beta_1 Schooling + \beta_2 Experience + \beta_2 Experience^2 + u \tag{7.1}$$

The applied econometrics literature shows that a wrongly specified earnings model will result in bias and inconsistent estimates. Since its introduction, most studies have criticised the Mincer model of omitted variable bias and misspecification bias (Griliches, 1977; Ashenfelter et al. 1999). Studies have been employing techniques like proxy variable or instrumental variable in estimating returns to education. Griliches (1977) employs the IQ of individuals as a proxy to cater for the ability heterogeneity in education and earning. He argues that one's level of ability has a role to play in determining one's earnings and therefore ability is an endogenous variable. The estimation earnings function with proxy variables is specified as:

$$lnEarnings=\beta_0+\beta_1 Schooling+\beta_2 Experience+\beta_3 Experience^2+\beta_4 Ability+u \quad (7.2)$$

The unobserved ability is peroxide with intelligent quotient (IQ) which is specified as:

$$Ability=\alpha_0+\alpha_1 IQ+ v \quad (7.3)$$

where it is assumed that u and v are not correlated with the independent variables. It is also assumed that α_1 should be positive and significant so as to indicate the relevance of the proxy IQ for the ability variable. Griliches (1977) finds that the Mincer OLS model had the estimates biased upwards, and thus, the Mincer model predicted higher values for returns to education but after the inclusion of the ability proxy, the estimates were down.

However, the problems with the proxy method are the possibility of correlation between ability and education leading to the potential endogeneity bias and the difficulty in choosing a suitable proxy. Further, the explanatory variables are not always exogenous and independent; they may be correlated with the error term leading to the potential endogeneity bias, a result of omission of variables, measurement error and simultaneity. With the considerations of heterogeneity and endogeneity biases in the earnings function, various forms instrumental variables (IV) are introduced to augment the classical approaches of Mincer and Becker (Glewwe 1991; Card 1999; 2001). To use the IV method, one has to identify the endogenous variable and find a variable that is partially correlated with the endogenous also the same variable uncorrelated with the error term of the main regression model. Thus, the coefficient of the instrument should be non-zero and covariance between the variable and the error term should be zero.

With the instruments for correcting the endogeneity bias are more than one, the method of Two Stage Least Square (2SLS) is adopted. The condition for this approach is also the same as for the proxy variable approach.

In the empirical analysis, Trostel (2002) and Baffour (2013) use the 2SLS method to estimate the earnings function. The difference between IV and OLS estimates depends on the extent to which the instrument influences schooling decisions at different levels. If the instrument affects the decisions mostly at an early level of one's education, the IV estimator may be higher than the OLS estimator, this is because the instruments reflects the payoff to schooling at lower rather than higher schooling levels (Baffour, 2013). Also, the probability error in the completed level of education is unaffected by its measurement error when the IV model is used. This situation makes the IV estimates higher than the OLS.

Two Stage Least Squares-Instrumental Variable Method

In the 2SLS or IV estimation, a reduced form equation is the expression of an endogenous variable solely in terms of exogenous variables, taking out the presence of endogeneity bias from the estimating equation. The structural equations may be specified as:

$$y=\gamma z+\beta x+u \tag{7.4}$$

$$z=\delta IV+\varepsilon \tag{7.5}$$

where x is the set of exogenous variables and z is a set of endogenous variables, IV is a set of set of instruments. The assumption is that E(IV,ε)=0 ensuing that there is no correlation between the instruments and the error term. The equation (7.5) is first estimated using the OLS method and the estimates, $\hat{z}$, are obtained. This is then substituted in place of Z in equation (7.4) and using OLS $\hat{y}$ is obtained. The estimate $\hat{y}$ from equation (7.4) is therefore unbiased and consistent.

Many studies use parental education level as instruments for child schooling in the earnings function. The use of parental background as instruments is based on the fact that child schooling is highly correlated with their parental education. Schultz (1988), Chen and Feng (2011) and Baffour (2013) use parental background as a proxy for determining one's wages. Incorporating parental education level has seen a significant effect on wage determination. Chen and Feng (2011) assign different roles to parental education: while mother's education primarily serves as a proxy for unmeasured ability, father's education stands for family connections useful in finding a good first job. Mother's education also plays a major role in parenting and development of a child's ability since they spent more time with their children than fathers. The two stage estimating equations are specified as:

$$lnW=\beta_0+\beta_1 Edu+\beta_2 Exp+\beta_3 Exp^2+\beta_4 Married+u \tag{7.6}$$

$$Edu=\delta_0+\delta_1 FEdu+\delta_2 MEdu+\delta_3 Exp+\delta_4 Exp^2+\delta_5 MStatus+\varepsilon \quad (7.7)$$

where equation (7.6) is the regression model endogenous variable and equation (7.7) is the model with instruments, father and mother education, assuming that the error terms are uncorrelated with any of the independent variables. The equation (7.7) is first estimated by OLS and the estimate of schooling is then substituted into (7.6) and then the OLS regression of equation (7.6) is estimated. The final estimates of lnW will be unbiased and consistent and also solve the endogeneity problem posed by schooling.

However, in order to estimate such simultaneous equations, the identification problem associated with structural and IV equations need to be resolved. This problem is as to whether the parameters of equation (7.4) can be estimated from equation (7.5). If this is done, then the equation is said to be identified, if not it is unidentified or underidentified. The possibility of deriving the coefficients of equation (7.6) depends on whether the equation is identified i.e. whether the rank and order conditions of the equation are satisfied. The order condition is satisfied if the number of predetermined variables absent in an equation are equal or greater than one less of the number of endogenous variables in that equation. If it is equal, the equation is said to be just identified and if greater it is said to be overidentified.

The satisfaction of the order condition does not guarantee an equation to be identified or not, it only shows whether it is just identified or overidentified. The final conclusion depends on the rank condition of the equation. The method for finding the order condition is:

$$K - k \geq m - 1 \quad (7.8)$$

where K is the number of predetermined variables in the model, k is the number of predetermined variables in a given equation and m is the number of endogenous variables in the equation. The rank condition is satisfied if a non-zero determinant can be found from the coefficients of the variables excluded from an equation, but included in the other equation. This is the necessary and sufficient condition that must be satisfied in order to determine the identification of an equation.

To apply the 2SLS method in estimation, it is essential to test for the presence of simultaneity and endogeneity. Even if the test shows all the variables are exogenous, there may be endogeneity problem that results in the OLS being biased and inconsistent as a result of the correlation between the endogenous variable and the error term, i.e. $cov(z,u)\neq 0$. It is only when this is confirmed, the 2SLS method can be used. The Hausman specification test tests for the simultaneity problem (Hausman, 1978). To perform the test, the endogenous variable is ran on the explanatory variables

(7.9) using OLS and the residuals are saved (7.10) and these are then substituted (7.11) and estimated again (7.12). The final estimates (7.13) are tested for significance using the t test; if the coefficients of the residuals are statistically different from zero, the null hypothesis $\theta = 0$ (exogeneity) is rejected, and thus the variable is considered to be endogenous. The endogeneity test procedure is specified as:

$$z = \beta x + \varepsilon \tag{7.9}$$
$$\hat{\varepsilon} = z - \hat{z} \tag{7.10}$$
$$y = \gamma z + \beta x + u \tag{7.11}$$
$$y = \gamma z + \beta x + \theta\hat{\varepsilon} + u \tag{7.12}$$
$$\hat{y} = \hat{\gamma}\hat{z} + \hat{\beta}x + \hat{\theta}\hat{\varepsilon} \tag{7.13}$$

Further, it is also necessary to test for the strength of the instruments or weak exogeneity in the model. To find out, equation (7.15) is run and the first stage regression estimates of equation (7.16) are obtained. Its error term and the R-square are also computed. This is then substituted into equation (7.14) and an F-test computed with the R-square from the two regressions. The coefficient γ is tested using the t-test under the null hypothesis of weak instruments. If this test is rejected, it confirms that education is an endogenous variable and the instruments are strong. The partial R-square, the R-square from equation (7.15) satisfies the rank condition of the model. The instruments test procedure is specified as:

$$y = \gamma z + \beta x + u \tag{7.14}$$
$$z = \delta IV + \varepsilon \tag{7.15}$$
$$\hat{z} = \hat{\delta} IV \tag{7.16}$$
$$y = \gamma\hat{z} + \beta x + \hat{\varepsilon} + u \tag{7.17}$$
$$\hat{y} = \hat{\gamma}\hat{z} + \hat{\beta}x + \hat{\varepsilon} \tag{7.18}$$

To ensure the 2SLS method is appropriate in estimating earnings function, Sargan (1958) test of overidentification is to be conducted. Overidentification is the situation whereby the number of instruments is more than the endogenous variable in the equation. It is only when this condition is fulfilled the model be correctly specified. This test satisfies the order condition of the model. The Sargan (1958) test is specified as:

$$S_{\chi^2} = \frac{\hat{\theta}\varepsilon(\varepsilon'\varepsilon)^{-1}\widehat{\theta\varepsilon}}{\hat{\theta}'\hat{\theta}/n} \tag{7.19}$$

where $\hat{\theta}$ is the estimated error term from the 2SLS, ε is the residual from the IV estimation and n is the sample size in the estimation. This test follows the chi-square distribution with m-k degrees of freedom, m being the number of instruments and k being the number of endogenous variables. The null hypothesis of the test is that the instruments are uncorrelated with the error term and the instruments are valid or the model is correctly specified.

In the determination of earnings, the worker's decision to work and the occupation choice, after acquiring formal education, are crucial. Also, the sector of work - public, private, self-employment - is important to the wage earnings. Such decisions of workers are dependent on a host of household characteristics and reservation and potential/offer wage. The individual will choose the work status considering the utility or satisfaction they gain from the earnings or any other means (Baffour, 2013). One will choose to be in the labour market, if the offer wage is more than the reservation wage. The investment in one's human capital determines the offer wage and the household characteristics like age and marital status determines the reservation wage. Assume that u_{ij} is the utility an individual i gains from working either in the private or public sector (j) and suppose that this utility is decomposed into two parts, observable s_{ik} and unobservable stochastic process η_i, so that:

$$u_{ij} = s_{ik} + \eta_i \tag{7.20}$$

Then, the probability that the individual i will choose to work in the jth is given by:

$$P(u_{ij} > u_{iq})\ i \neq q \tag{7.21}$$

Since the choice of the sector of work is a decision variable, the logit regression model. The choice of labour market status is the dependent variable and the household characteristics like level of education attained, marital status, age, sex, residence and the monthly wages are the set of independent variables. The monthly wage is assumed to be same as the expected wage from the two sectors. The logit model is a nonlinear model and follows the logistic distribution. The logit regression is specified as:

$$y_i = \alpha_0 + \alpha_k s_k + \eta_i \tag{7.22}$$

where y_i=1 provided the respondents decides to work in the private sector and gains utility working there and y_i=0 if he decides to work in the public sector. The probability of working in the private sector is given by:

$$P_i = Prob(y_i = 1) = Prob(y_i > 0) \tag{7.23}$$

$$P_i = Prob(\alpha_0 + \alpha_k s_k + \eta_i > 0) = Prob(\eta_i > -\alpha_0 - \alpha_k s_k) \tag{7.24}$$

$$P_i = 1 - \Phi(-\alpha_0 - \alpha_k s_k) \tag{7.25}$$

where Φ is the cumulative distribution function of η. Since the logistic function is nonlinear, the maximum likelihood estimation is used in estimating the coefficients of the logistic model.

Logistic Regression Method

In the logistic model, each outcome y_i has a density function:

$$f(y) = P_i^{y_i} (1 - P_i)^{1-y_i} \tag{7.26}$$

Each y_i takes on either a value of 1 or 0 with probability f(1)=P_i and f(0)=(1-P_i). Therefore, the likelihood function is defined as:

$$L = f(y_1, y_2, \dots, y_n) = f(y_1) f(y_2) \dots f(y_n) \tag{7.27}$$
$$L = P_1^{y_1}(1 - P_1)^{1-y_1} P_2^{y_2}(1 - P_2)^{1-y_2} \dots P_n^{y_n}(1 - P_n)^{1-y_n} \tag{7.28}$$
$$L = \prod_{i=1}^{n} P_i^{y_i}(1 - P_i)^{1-y_i} \tag{7.29}$$

Taking log:

$$lnL = \sum_{i=1}^{n} y_i lnP_i + (1 - y_i)\, ln(1 - P_i) \tag{7.30}$$
$$lnL = \sum_{i=1}^{n} y_i ln\Phi(\alpha_0 + \alpha_k s_k) + (1 - y_i) \ln [1 - \Phi(\alpha_0 + \alpha_k s_k)] \tag{7.31}$$

The logit model therefore is specified as:

$$P(y = 1) = \Phi(\alpha_0 + \alpha_k s_k) = \frac{1}{1+e^{-(\alpha_0+\alpha_k s_k)}} \tag{7.32}$$
$$P(y_i = 1) \to 0 \; as \; (\alpha_0 + \alpha_k s_k) \to -\infty \tag{7.33}$$
$$P(y_i = 1) \to 1 \; as \; (\alpha_0 + \alpha_k s_k) \to \infty \tag{7.34}$$

The coefficients α_k determines only the direction of the influence of the independent variables to the choice of labour market status. The magnitude of the effect of covariates on the choice of sector of work is determined by their average partial effects. The marginal effects are computed as:

$$Marginal\,effect_k = \frac{\Phi(\alpha_0 + \alpha_k s_k)\alpha_k}{n} = \frac{\frac{e^{(\alpha_0+\alpha_k s_k)}}{\left[1+e^{(\alpha_0+\alpha_k s_k)}\right]^2}\alpha_k}{n} \tag{7.35}$$

The marginal effects are estimated for each independent variable and therefore the mean effect of each variable is estimated. The odds ratio of the logit model is also computed to measure the probability of choosing private sector to the public sector as:

$$\left[\frac{P}{1-P}\right] = e^{\alpha_0+\alpha_k s_k} \tag{7.36}$$

$$P = \frac{e^{(\alpha_0+\alpha_k s_k)}}{1+e^{(\alpha_0+\alpha_k s_k)}} \tag{7.37}$$

$$ln\left[\frac{P}{1-P}\right] = \alpha_0 + \alpha_k s_k \tag{7.38}$$

This shows the log odds of the logistic model is a linear outcome of the predictor variables.

7.4 Empirical Analysis

The Table 7.1 presents the definition and descriptive statistics of the variables used in the empirical analysis of the relationship between education and earnings in Ghana. The mean monthly wage is 470 Ghana cedis (Ghc) with a standard deviation of 27.14 Ghc which shows quite a large difference in the wages. The mean completed years of education in Ghana is 10.5 years showing that most workers have at least a basic level of education. The same can be said of the parents' levels of education as most have attained basic education with mean completed years of education being 12.8 and 13.1 years for mothers and fathers in Ghana. The mean working experience is 8.5 years and this shows a sizable working experience of workers. The 30.2 years of mean age of workers shows that the Ghanaian labour force is young.

Table 7.1: Descriptive Statistics of Variables in the Education-Earnings Relationship Analysis in Ghana.

Variable	*Description*	*Mean*	*Std. dev.*
Wages	Wages (Ghana cedis (Ghc) per month)	470.063	27.140
lnWages	Log of wages	3.849	0.058
Education	Number of years of formal education completed (years)	10.499	2.108
Experience	On the job experience computed as age – years of education (years)	8.535	4.609
Experience square	Square of experience	178.370	113.648
Age	Age (years)	30.152	3.065
Mother education	Education of mother (years)	12.887	2.610
Father education	Education of father (years)	13.080	2.598
Obs.		20214	

From Table 7.2, it can be observed that about 64.2 percent are married workers and 35.8 percent of unmarried workers in the Ghnanian work force. The mean monthly wage for these two groups is almost the same with the married workers earning 471 Ghc and the unmarried workers having 469 Ghc. Though there is not much of a difference in the monthly wages earned by unmarried and married workers, marital status is important for work status. On average, the monthly wages of the workers increase as they attain higher level of education. This is seen in the 4.18 percent increase in wage from a junior secondary certificate to a senior secondary certificate. It further increases by 6.93 percent and 11.48 percent when one gains a bachelor's degree and a post bachelor degree respectively. This shows that at every higher level of education, there is a possibility of wage increase.

Table 7.2 Average Monthly Wages of Workers in Ghana

Worker	*Observations*	*Percent*	*Mean*	*Std. dev.*
Public sector	9126	45.15	465.912	26.890
Private sector	11088	54.85	470.023	27.002
Unmarried	12978	64.20	469.351	27.523
Married	7236	35.80	471.340	26.391
Junior high certificate	1674	8.30	427.330	14.507
Senior high certificate	12240	60.50	445.186	13.162
Bachelor degree	5652	28.00	476.050	22.366
Post bachelor degree	648	3.20	530.686	16.133

The Table 7.3 shows the monthly wage with respect to the education level attained given the marital status and gender of the respondents. The married workers at every level of completed years of education earn mean monthly wage more than the unmarried workers, except for bachelor degree holders, where unmarried workers earning slightly more than married workers. The variation in the average monthly wages is high for workers with senior high certificate irrespective of whether they are married or not. It is also to be noted that, with the exception of post bachelor degree, males on average, earn more than females at every level of education attained.

Table 7.3 Mean Monthly Wages by Marital Status and Gender in Ghana

Education level	*Married*	*Unmarried*	*Males*	*Females*
Junior high certificate	429.34 (14.47)	426.32 (14.42)	427 (14.43)	427 (15.21)
Senior high certificate	463.10 (17.51)	461.30 (18.10)	463 (18.32)	461 (18.10)
Bachelor degree	493.48 (15.78)	494.53 (15.43)	495 (16.65)	494 (15.32)
Post bachelor degree	529.60 (16.20)	522.02 (14.45)	524 (15.91)	526 (15.43)

Note: Standard deviations in parentheses.

The empirical wage function, the Mincerian earnings equation, with education and experience is estimated by the OLS method. The Mincerian earnings function has been extended to capture the possibility of marriage influencing wages/earnings. Studies have shown that marriage to be significant in influencing one's wages. Becker (1973; 1974), Benham (1974) and Tiefenthaler (1997) have also shown the significance of marrying and a spouse's education playing a significant impact in one's earnings. The estimating extended Mincer equation is specified as:

$$lnW = \beta_0 + \beta_1 Edu + \beta_2 Exp + \beta_3 Exp^2 + \beta_4 Married + u \quad (7.39)$$

An alternative specification is the use of certificates gained in place of completed years of education:

$$lnW = \beta_0 + \beta_1 Primary + \beta_2 Junior + \beta_3 Senior + \beta_4 Bachelor + \beta_5 Post\ Bachelor + \beta_6 Exp + \beta_7 Exp^2 + \beta_8 Married + u \quad (7.40)$$

To consider the presence of endogeneity of the education variable, the instrumental variable method is used with parental education as IVs. The IV equation is specified as:

$$lnW = \beta_0 + \beta_1 Fathereducation + \beta_2 Mothereducation + \beta_3 Exp + \beta_4 Exp^2 + \beta_5 Married + u \quad (7.41)$$

The completed years of education is endogenous and because of this the estimates of the OLS may be biased downwards. To check this endogeneity problem and also identify the possible instruments influencing completed years of education, a series of test are conducted. The Table 7.4 presents the correlation coefficients between completed years of education and parents' education and the Table 7.5 presents the tests of endogeneity, weak instruments and overidentification. The estimated correlation coefficients show that there exists a strong positive relationship between one's years of completed education and that of their parents. This therefore affirms the use of parents' education as an instrument for completed years of education.

Table 7.4: Correlation between Individual's Education and Parent's Education.

Variable	*Father's education*	*Mother's education*
Individual's education	0.623	0.616
Father's education	-	0.434

The post estimation of the residual from the IV shows that education is an endogenous variable and the OLS estimation suffers from an omitted variable bias. The results presented in Table 7.5 shows that the Wu-Hausman F-test value is 35551.79 rejecting the null hypothesis of no endogeneity in the model. The result of the first stage regression gives a partial R-square value 0.74 and an F-test value of 29120.5, thus rejecting the null hypothesis of weak instruments. This shows the instruments used for education are strong and relevant and also satisfies the rank condition. The Sargan test for overidentification shows a chi-square value of 0.058 with a probability of 0.81, failing to reject the null hypothesis of correctly specified model and valid instruments. It shows that the conditions for using the IV model are valid and it is appropriate to use the IV model in estimating the rate of return to education. The results from the over identification test satisfies the order condition for using 2SLS.

Table 7.5: Endogeneity, Validity of Instruments and Overidentification Tests.

Test	*Endogeneity*	*Weak instruments*	*Over identification*
Null hypothesis	Variables are exogenous	Instruments are weak	Model is correctly specified
Wu-Hausman F-test	35551.79*** (0.00)	-	-
Durbin chi-square	3021.74*** (0.00)	-	-
Partial R-square	-	0.742	-
F-test	-	29120.5*** (0.00)	-
Sargan chi-square	-	-	0.0578 (0.81)

The estimated results of all these specifications are presented in Table 7.6. The OLS results confirm the a priori expectation and show that the effect of education on monthly wages is positive and statistically significant at 1 percent level. Holding all other variables constant, one additional year of completed formal education on average increases the monthly wage by 2.04 percent. The coefficient of experience has a significant positive sign implying that an additional year of working experience adds to one's monthly wages. As expected, the nonlinear relationship between experience (experience squared) and earnings is negative and statistically significant at 1 percent showing as one ages and gains experience, a time will come when the returns to experience declines due to non-investment in human capital. It can also be seen from the extended Mincer equation estimates that the average private returns to education increases by an additional 0.3 percent for married person. Though not high, the coefficient is highly significant at 1 percent level showing that there exists a marriage premium in the labour market of Ghana and confirms the belief that marriage influences the wages of workers either by increasing the hours worked or as a subjective measure from employers to give a marriage premium to their married employees.

In the estimates of rate of return to the certificates, all levels of educational attainment have positive and statistically significant coefficients. As compared to the basic education certificate, a secondary school certificate, on average, adds 4.1 percent to one's monthly earnings. Further, gaining a bachelor degree added 10.8 percent to one's earnings and a post bachelor degree added 21.7 percent to one's monthly earnings. This shows that there is an increasing trend in one's monthly wage as one moves up on the attainment of higher education. Thus, in line with the human capital investment theory, years of education and work experience play a significant role in explaining the rate of return to investments in human beings.

Table 7.6: OLS and 2SLS-IV Estimates of Wage Functions in Ghana.

Dependent variable: ln(Monthly wages)

Variable	*OLS*			*2SLS-IV*
Education	0.021*** (4.27)	0.024*** (5.95)	-	-
Senior high certificate	-	-	0.041*** (6.71)	-
Bachelor degree	-	-	0.107** (2.31)	-
Post bachelor degree	-	-	0.217** (1.98)	-
Father education	-	-	-	0.384*** (5.32)
Mother education	-	-	-	0.332*** (4.87)
Experience	0.0006*** (8.43)	0.0007*** (9.01)	0.0012*** (10.59)	0.0007*** (8.80)
Experience^2	-0.00002*** (8.81)	-0.00003*** (9.49)	-0.00005*** (10.43)	-0.00002*** (9.17)
Married	-	0.0014*** (7.75)	0.0026*** (9.76)	0.0018*** (10.03)
Constant	3.518*** (3.91)	3.462*** (4.37)	3.747*** (4.51)	3.462*** (4.38)
R-square	0.73	0.76	0.79	0.75
F-value	78803.45	8813.71	13999.92	-
Chi-square	-	-	-	30057.36

Note: Absolute t-values for OLS and z-values for 2SLS-IV estimates in parentheses.
***significant at 1 percent level **significant at 5 percent level *significant at 10 percent level.

The 2SLS-IV estimates presented in the last column of Table 7.6 show that there is, on average, an additional 0.36 percent rate of return to parents' education on the monthly wages of workers as compared to the OLS estimates. This shows a downward bias of the OLS model and shows that the absence of marriage and parents' influence on one's education will have his or her wages underestimated. The other reason is that, the instruments, parents' education, influence one's education at an early stage and hence affects one's earnings. The coefficients of the variables are highly significant at 1 percent level. The chi-square value for the IV is significant at 1 percent level showing that all the variables used in the estimation are jointly significant.

The logit estimates of the decision of an individual to be either in the private or public sector of the labour market are presented in Table 7.7.

The logit results show that all the independent variables make it more likely for one to be in the private sector and all are statistically significant. The monthly wage makes it more likely for one to be in the private sector as well as one's age. Irrespective of the educational level one has, he or she is more likely to participate in the private sector. It can also be seen that when one is in any urban city in Ghana, like Accra, Kumasi, Cape Coast and Takoradi, such a person is more likely to be in the private sector. This can be attributed to the increasing demand of people in such areas and the desire of others to indulge in anything to make a living with the increasing number of people around. Married people are also more likely to be in the private sector, their decision can be attributed to the difficulty in gaining access to public sector work and also their decision to contribute to the family upkeep. Males are more likely to be in the private sector than females but such an effect is not statistically significant.

Table 7.7: Logit Estimates of Sector of Work Employment in Ghana.

Dependent variable: Choice of private sector work

Variable	*Coefficient*	*Odds ratio*	*Marginal effect*
Monthly wages	0.0063*** (7.59)	0.9937	0.0016
Age	0.1255*** (2.70)	1.0126	0.0031
Senior high certificate	0.4963*** (8.29)	1.6426	0.1229
Bachelor degree	0.7609*** (9.62)	2.1401	0.1884
Post bachelor degree	0.8514*** (6.90)	2.3430	0.2108
Urban Ghana	0.1224*** (4.13)	1.1302	4.13
Married	0.0630** (2.13)	1.0651	2.13
Male	0.0555* (1.87)	1.0570	1.87
Constant	1.9689*** (7.10)	7.1631	-
Likelihood ratio	-13853		
LR chi-square	124.90		
Pseudo R-square	0.45		

Note: z-values in parentheses. *** significant at 1 percent level ** significant at 5 percent level * significant at 10 percent level.

The magnitude of the effects of each of the covariates, the average partial effects, are computed and presented in the last column of Table 7. An increase in one's monthly wage is 0.16 percent more likely to have the person partake in the private sector. An additional age of one is 0.3 percent more likely to influence one to be in the private sector than in the public sector. A senior high certificate holder is 12 percent more likely to be in the private sector than a basic education certificate holder. The percentage increases to 19 for one with a bachelor degree to be more likely to choose the private sector. A post bachelor degree holder is 21 percent more like to be in the private sector than the basic education certificate holder. This shows that as one attains higher level of education the likelihood of the person being in the private sector increases. Thus, there is an increasing desire for potential graduates to be in the private sector. The desire to be independent, have easy access to modem form of technology to work with and also work with a more dynamic team could be some of the reasons why most graduates desire to be in the private sector.

Those living in urban Ghana are 3 percent more likely to be in the private sector than those in rural Ghana. This shows increasing opportunities for people living in urban Ghana and also the reason for continual migration into these areas (Sackey, 2008). The demand for most services in rural areas are not provided by the state and it rests on individuals to provide such services to people thereby having majority of people go into the private sector work in the urban areas. Males are 1.4 percent more likely to be in the private sector than females. This may be attributed to the equal chance that either sexes have in choosing to be in the private sector showing effective affirmative action or lack of prejudice in the labour market of Ghana. One's ability to be in the private sector depends on his or her education level, accessibility to information to know the most appropriate working decision to take. Also, most females engage in trade and other small business to make ends meet. Married men and women are 2 percent more likely to be in the private sector than the unmarried persons. The chance of getting married to an educated partner makes it easier for one to be in the private sector.

The computed odds ratios show that the odds of being in the private sector is 0.994 times the odds of being in the public sector for a 1 Ghc increase in monthly wages. This shows there is the possibility for one to decide to be in the private sector when the potential wages of the sector increases. It is believed that private sector workers are fairly treated and well paid. The story is different with public sector workers where there are frequent industrial strikes and are largely unpaid wages and benefits. A senior high school certificate gives 1.6 times odds of being in the private sector than being in the public sector. The odds increase to 2.1 times the odds of the public sector and 2.3 times with a bachelor and post bachelor degrees. This shows that the private sector is a playing field for people with higher levels of education. This explains the reason why the government has undertaken the 'single spine pay policy' to poach most graduates into the public sector. But it can be seen that most people with higher levels of education moving to the private sectors are mostly there because of the conditions of service and other incentives which will ensure their personal and professional development. The opportunity to have in service training is mostly undertaken by private sector employers and the opportunity to advance in one's career is easily seen in the private sector than the public sector in Ghana.

The odds of being in the private sector is 1.01 times the odds of being in the public sector for an increase in the one's age. This result can be attributed to the no retirement age of most private sector work while the retirement age is 60 years in the public service. The odds of being in the private sector is 1.13 times the odds of being in the public sector when one is in the urban areas in Ghana. Most businesses and opportunities are in the nation's capital Accra and other major urban cities. The easiness to start a business and flourish in it will only be possible when one is in the urban areas. The most likely reason for this is the availability of modem technologies and accessibility to major inputs in running a business. Such facilities are not readily available in rural areas and the only job that an educated person can do in the rural area will be to be a public sector worker. The difficulties and harsh conditions of living in rural Ghana force a lot of people into the urban cities to find jobs and be engaged in private work.

The odds of being in the private sector is 1.07 times the odds of being in the public sector given one is married. Marriage serves to connect people from different backgrounds. The possibility of having a partner being introduced to people in a higher social class is high. Also, most employers in the private sector have special treatment for their married employees and such treatments entice potential workers to be in such working environment. The odds of being in the private sector is 1.05 times the odds of being in the public sector if one is a male. This possibility is statistically not significant at 5 percent indicating that, the choice of working environment either a man or woman wish to be in is not so much of an issue in Ghana. Women have equal chances of being in the private sector as males, provided they have the required skills and knowledge of the market. One's chance of getting into the private sector depends on the fulfillment of the necessary requirement desired.

7.5 Conclusion

This paper considers the human capital investment model of earnings determination in Ghana using the Sixth Round of Ghana Living Standards Survey (GLSS) conducted from September 2012 to September 2013 by the Ghana Statistical Service. Along with education and experience, marriage is also considered as an important influencing factor on the earnings of workers in Ghana labour market. The objectives of this paper are to estimate the rate of return to education, to know if school credentials play a role in determining one's earnings, to examine the parents' role in influencing one's earnings, to find out how one's marital status contributes to his or her earnings and lastly to know the decision of workers to choose between working in the private or public sector of the Ghana labour market. Employing an extended Mincerian earnings function, this paper shows that education and experience significantly influence the earnings of workers positively. This finding has been in line with those of other studies in Africa and the world at large. Further, there is a positive correlation between higher levels of learning and earnings, the longer one stays in school the higher the returns for such a person. Though the opportunity cost is high, the higher rate of return offsets the total cost of schooling. The study also finds that, though education is significant in the determination of one's wage, one's marital status should be considered too.

The OLS estimation of the wage model suffers from the omission of relevant variables which are actually influencing the years of education. The education variable is endogenous and not accounting for this endogeneity biases downward the rate of return. The omitted variables are parental education which influences the changes in the ability of wards at the initial stages of their education. To correct for this endogeneity problem and ensure there is no error in the estimation, the 2SLS-IVmodelhas been estimated with parents' education as instruments. The 2SLS estimates show that the effect of education has been biased downwards when estimated by the OLS method.

The decision of workers to choose either the private or public sector has been estimated using the logit regression model. The logit estimates show that gender does not matter much in choosing where to work in the Ghana labour market, but other covariates like age, education, wage, marital status and residence do influence the work decision to be in the private sector.

From the empirical analysis of the labour market of Ghana, this paper has arrived at the following main conclusions. The human capital investment theory of Schultz and Becker applies to the Ghanaian economy. The earnings function approach of Mincer is appropriate to estimate the returns to investment in education in Ghana. In Ghana, education is a positive investment whose returns are greater. Also, the credentialist model by Spence is seen to be operational in the Ghanaian labour market. Employers hire workers based on the certificate they have and their earnings reflect the level of education attained. It can also be concluded that, in the estimation of returns to education, the role of parents' education should be considered. This will ensure an unbiased and efficient estimate of returns to educational investments. One without a good start to education might not have a higher return. Education is productive and ensures one gains a high return for services provided. This return is seen not dependent solely on education but also on the inbuilt characteristics, nature of people and the benefits that comes with being married. Further, marriage also matters in the Ghanaian labour market.

Time Series Econometrics

8

The Causality between Financial Development and Economic Growth: ARDL Estimation of the Effect of Financial Development on Economic Growth

8.1 Introduction

The nexus relationship between financial development and economic growth dates back at least to Schumpeter (1911) who emphasised the positive role of financial development on economic growth. The subsequent debate centered around the issue whether the financial sector actually leads the real sector in the process of economic development or the reverse. There is no universal consensus to date on the causal link between financial development and economic growth. In the theoretical literature, there exists three different streams of views on the direction of the causality between economic growth and financial development. The first view is the "supply leading" notion a la Schumpeter (1911) and Patrick (1966) which states that financial development is a precondition for economic growth; The second view is the "demand-following" due to Robinson (1952) which advocates that real economic growth leads financial development; and the third view is the bidirectional causality between financial development and economic growth (Demetriades and Hussein, 1996; Greenwood and Smith, 1997).

The links between financial development and economic growth is amply demonstrated by the experience of India. Following the balance of payments crisis, India introduced financial sector reforms as a part of structural economic reforms programme in 1991. The adoption of liberalisation and globalisation policies and market reforms were designed to promote efficiency in the economy through promotion of competition.

The principal objective of financial sector reforms has been to improve allocative efficiency of resources, ensure financial stability and maintain confidence in the financial system by enhancing its soundness and efficiency. No doubt the economic and financial reforms have yielded significant results and the Indian economy has undergone tremendous transformation achieving higher growth rates and high investment rates especially foreign direct investments and foreign collabarations over the subsequent periods.

The patterns of growth rates of some of the financial indicators of India are presented in Table 8.1 and Figure 8.1. It is observed that domestic credit to private sector as a percentage of GDP has doubled during the period 1990 to 2016, increasing gradually over the years from 25 percent to almost 50 percent. The stock market turnover ratio increased from 37.59 in 1990 to 55.21 in 2016. The stock market turnover ratio increased sharply in 2009 due to steep rise in share prices from a very low level in 2008, as the global financial crisis heightened. Broad money as a share of GDP has increased steadily from 44.74 to 75.5 percent in 2016. The gross domestic savings as share of GDP has gradually increased from 24.91 to 31.85 percent in 2016. The credit to government owned enterprises increased from 12.25 percent to 19.64 percent since 1990s over 2016.

Table 8.1 Trend in Financial Development Indicators in India

Indicator	*1990s*	*2010s*
Domestic credit to private sector (percent of GDP)	25.01	49.78
Stock market turnover ratio	37.59	55.21
Broad money supply (percent of GDP)	47.90	77.80
Gross domestic savings (percent of GDP)	26.16	31.85
Credit to government owned enterprises (percent of GDP)	12.25	19.64

Source: World Bank (2017): Global Financial Development Database.

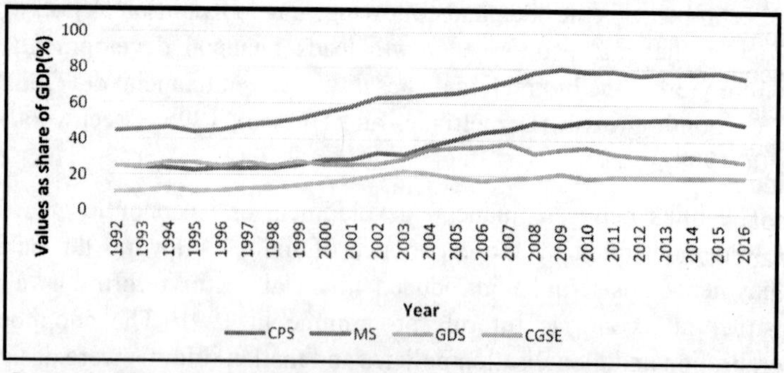

Source: World Bank (2017): Global Financial Development Database.

Figure 8.1 Trend in Financial Development Indicators in India.

The empirical evidences suggest that the strength and direction of the relationship between financial development and economic growth is sensitive to the variables used to measure financial development. In addition, the findings suggest that outcome between two sectors differs from country to country overtime. The elusive causal direction of the two seems from certain limitations of the existing literature on this issue: most studies are mainly cross-sectional, which cannot satisfactorily address the country-specific issues; and many studies are largely drawn from bivariate causality analysis and may therefore suffer from the omission of variables bias.

An appropriate measure of financial development plays an important role in analysing the causal relationship between financial development and economic growth. However, with wide diversification of financial services, construction of financial development indicators is not a simple task (Ang and McKibbin, 2007). In the literature, the most commonly used measures of financial development do not capture the actual development of financial system of a country, especially for developing countries. For example, the ratio of broad money (M2) to GDP is typically considered as a standard measure of financial development, it may not necessarily reflect financial depth as money is used as store of value in the absence of other more attractive alternatives (Khan and Senhadji, 2003). These indicators also overlook the financial openness of a country and ignore the utilisation angle of domestic financial system. Given the multi-dimensional nature of the financial system, it is to be noted that the deep financial systems do not necessarily provide high degrees of financial access and highly efficient systems are not necessarily more stable than the less efficient ones. To overcome these shortcomings, a more robust indicator that captures all aspects of the financial system is required.

The findings from the available literature do not clearly establish a harmony about the direction of causality between financial development and economic growth. And several studies have used different types of financial proxy variable for measuring financial development, which does not encompass all aspects of the financial sector and therefore fail to provide an efficient measure of financial development. Therefore, this paper attempts to construct a comprehensive index of financial development for India applying the principal component analysis on the financial data over the period 1992 to 2016 from the Global Financial Development Database of the World Bank. This paper also investigates the causal relationship between financial development and economic growth Applying the Autoregressive Distributed Lag (ARDL) model that examines the dynamic interaction of economic growth with financial development. The long-run and short-run relationships between them respectively are analysed by the cointegration and error correction models. This paper further takes into account the influence of economic reforms on economic growth and financial development, an important gap overlooked by most of the past Indian studies on this literature.

8.2 A Brief Review of Recent Studies

Ample literature, both theoretical and empirical, exists on the relationship between financial development and economic growth over the years. The theoretical contributions highlight the different services provided by the financial sector that can affect output and economic growth. However, the empirical relationship between economic growth and financial development has been controversial as the causality has remained an important issue of debate.

King and Levine (1993) use cross-country data to analyse four kinds of evidence to evaluate the theoretical predictions regarding the links between financial development and growth. First, an analysis of 80 countries over the period 1960-1989 using three-stage least squares (3SLS) estimation method show that the predictable components of financial depth - the relative importance of banks as opposed to central banks and the ratio of private credit to GDP - are positively and significantly related to each growth indicator and the sources of growth. Second, they evaluate five countries' experiences with financial sector reforms. Third, they review firm level evidence on the allocative effects of financial reforms. Finally, the success of general policy reforms on financial development is investigated. All the results indicate that the initial level of financial development is a good predictor of the subsequent rate of economic growth. The findings suggest that government policies toward financial systems may have an important causal effect on long-run growth.

Sinha and Macri (2001) examine the relationship between financial development and economic growth using time series data for eight Asian countries - India, Japan, Korea, Malaysia, Pakistan, Philippines, Sri Lanka and Thailand. The study uses multivariate vector autoregression model in Granger over the period 1950-1997. Two types of analyses are performed in this study: The estimated regression results for augmented production function show a positive and significant relationship between the income variables and financial variables for India, Malaysia, Pakistan and Sri Lanka. The multivariate causality tests show a two-way causal relationship between income and financial variables for India and Malaysia, one way causality from financial variables to income variables for Japan and Thailand and reverse causality for Korea, Pakistan and Philippines.

The empirical results do not support the general view of a clear and positive relationship between financial development and economic growth in Asian economies.

Rioja and Valev (2004) examine the relationship between financial development and economic growth by grouping countries a panel of 74 countries according to the levels of financial development and income levels. The study applies the Generalised Method of Moments (GMM) dynamic panel technique for the period 1961-1995averaging over 5-year intervals. The dynamic panel GMM results prove a consistent nonlinear relationship between financial development and economic growth. The differential effect of financial development is positive but diminishes as countries reach high region. The results also suggest that the effect of financial development on economic growth is uncertain for countries with low levels of financial development.

Halkos and Trigoni (2010) examine the direction of the causality between financial sector and economic growth of the 15 country European Union for the period 1975-2005 using VAR models. The growth of real sector is expressed by real GDP per capita growth, while the size of the financial system by the ratio of domestic credit to GDP. The deposit rate and inflation are used as indexes of monetary policy. The estimated VAR results show that in the short-run, the size of the financial system does not directly affect growth, although its increase leads to an increase in the deposit rate and consequently to a decrease in real GDP per capita. However, according to the estimated Vector Error Correction Mechanism (VECM) model, the significance of the error correction coefficients implies that there is a relationship between real sector, financial sector and monetary policy in the long-run.

In the Indian context, Bell and Rousseau (2001) examine whether financial intermediaries have played a leading role in influencing India's economic performance using the National Accounts Statistics during the post-independence era from 1951 to 1991.A set of vector autoregressive (VAR) and Vector Error Correction Models (VECM) are constructed to evaluate the strength and direction of the links between measures of formal intermediation and various economic aggregates. The estimated results show that the expansion of financial sector has played an enabling role in promoting capital accumulation and has been instrumental in promoting aggregate investment and output. However, financial development has not influenced the total factor productivity in the organised manufacturing sector. Thus, the activities of the financial sector have had an important impact on India's post-Independence economic performance.

Kar and Mandal (2014) study the impact of financial structure, financial deepening and measures of financial activity on the economic growth in India following the financial sector reforms. Particularly, the test whether the financial reforms facilitate the growth process operating through the stock market or the banking sector. They use monthly data for the post-reform Indian economy from April 1994 to March 2008 applying the modified Pantula principle associated with the VECM method. The variables considered are constant price Index of Industrial Production (IIP) as a proxy for growth and a set of alternative financial sector variables to capture stock market and banking sector, viz. size vs activity of financial sector and bank-based vs stock market-based financial structure. The estimated results show that financial deepening has a strong long-run impact on economic growth. In the banking sector, both the size and activity variables contribute independently to economic growth, while in the stock market, it is the size that contributes to the growth process. The activity level is much more significant for the banking sector but for the stock market it is only the size of the sector that is significant. The long-run coefficients of banking sector variables in the cointegrating relationships are significantly higher than those for the stock market. This indicates that even though stock market has become important after financial reforms, banks continue to play a dominant role in facilitating the growth process.

Chakrabarty (2010) examine the impact of the developments in the financial sector on economic growth in India in the post 1991 economic reforms period using quarterly data applying the techniques of cointegration and VECM. The cointegration results show that capital-output ratio and rate of growth of human capital have positive effect on real rate of growth of GDP, irrespective of the indicator of stock market development. An increase in the market capitalisation has a negative effect, whereas turnover has no significant effect on economic growth in India. On the other hand, the money market rate of interest has a positive effect on economic growth, which indicates that the banking system reforms have improved the growth rate of real GDP in the post-reform period in India. From the results of VECM, the error correction term relating to market capitalisation and inflation help to adjust short-run dynamics of economic growth when market capitalisation is used as an indicator of stock market development. On the other hand, while using turnover as the indicator of stock market development, the error correction term relating to turnover is not helping to adjust short-run dynamics of economic growth. Thus, the stock market development makes no significant contribution while the reforms in the banking sector, particularly those related to interest rate deregulation, play a significant role in economic growth. These findings imply that liberalisation of foreign portfolio flows in the Indian stock market since 1991 has not effectively interacted with the real sector of the Indian economy.

Nain and Kamaiah (2014) examine the relationship between financial development and economic growth in India in the non-linear Granger causality framework employing the Toda and Yamamoto test for the period 1990-2010. Separate indices are constructed to capture stability, access, depth and efficiency characteristics of the financial system of India. The Johansen cointegration test results show that there is no cointegration between economic growth and access, depth, efficiency characteristics of financial system and financial development as a whole, except between stability characteristic and economic growth. The estimated VECM show that the coefficients are insignificant, except that stability of financial system and economic growth tend to be in equilibrium. The non-linear Diks and Panchenko causality test shows that there is no non-linear causal relationship between financial development and economic growth.

Lenka (2015) and Lenka and Sharma (2017) use annual time series data for India for the period 1980-2011 to examine the relationship between economic growth and financial development. The study employs the autoregressive distributed lag (ARDL) bound testing approach to cointegration and Error Correction Model (ECM) to find the long-run and short-run causality between economic growth and financial development. The study uses principal component method to combine eleven selected measures of financial development into a single index. The result of the cointegration test based on ARDL bound test presents a strong evidence for long-run relationship among the variables suggesting that financial development is one of the long-run determinants of economic growth and not vice-versa. Diagnostic tests for the presence of serial correlation, heteroscedasticity and normality in the data are also performed before estimating the long-run and short-run relationships. The estimated error correction coefficient suggests that about 2 percent of the disequilibria in GDP growth of the previous year's shock adjust back to the long-run equilibrium in the current year.

Overall the literature reflects ambiguity about the impact of financial development on economic growth. One possible reason for the mixed empirical evidence is the choice of proxy for financial development. A number of different proxy measures for financial development across different sample periods coupled with different techniques might have led to different results. Hence, this paper attempts to construct a comprehensive index for financial development capturing various dimensions of financial development and evaluates its impact on economic growth in India.

8.3 Data and Methodology

The data used in this paper covers the period 1992 to 2016 from the Global Financial Development Indicators and World Development Indicators of the World Bank. In the empirical estimation of the effect of financial development on economic growth, besides financial development indicators and GDP per capita, other commonly used variables in the literature are government spending as share of GDP as an indicator of macroeconomic stability and volume of trade as share of GDP that captures the degree of openness. The estimating model in the log liner form is specified as:

$$lnGDPpc_t = \beta_0 + \beta_1 ln(FDI)_t + \beta_2 lnx_t + u_t \tag{8.1}$$

where y_t is GDP per capita at factor cost, FDI is an index of financial development, x_t is a vector of control variables - inflation, trade openness and government consumption expenditure and u_t is the error term. All variables are in natural logarithm.

Financial development encompasses the depth, size, access and efficiency of the financial system and the performance and activities of the financial markets, banks, bond markets and financial institutions. Inclusion of all indicators of financial development separately in the same estimation model may cause problems of multicollinearity and over-parameterisation. To comprehensively capture all these dimensions in a single measure, a composite index seems inevitable. To construct such an index, the financial development index, this paper uses the principal component analysis over several dimensions of financial indicators. Following Cihak et al. (2012), several measures of some important characteristics of financial systems are considered: (i) depth - size of financial institutions and markets, (ii) access - degree to which individuals can and do use financial institutions and markets, and (iii) efficiency - efficiency of financial institutions and markets in providing financial services. The Table 8.2 presents the indicators of financial markets that are used in the construction of the financial development index. The six selected measures of the depth, access and efficiency of the financial system viz. BMS, PCB, DCP, GDS, CGE and STR are combined to derive a single index of financial development using the Principal Component Analysis (PCA).

Table 8.2 Description of Financial Indicators

Indicator	*Description*	*Proxy measure*
BMS	Broad money supply (percent of GDP)	Financial institution depth
PCB	Private credit by banks (percent of GDP)	Financial institution depth
DCP	Domestic credit to private sector (percent of GDP)	Financial market depth
GDS	Gross domestic savings (percent of GDP)	Financial institution access
CGE	Credit to government owned enterprises (percent of GDP)	Financial institution efficiency
STR	Stock market turnover ratio	Financial market efficiency

Source: World Bank (2017): Global Financial Development Database.

The PCA captures the potentially high correlation among the different measures of financial development in the construction of the financial development index. The PCA retains all the variations in the data even though it reduces the dimensionality of it. It transforms the data into uncorrelated new variables i.e. principal components. The maximum variation of the original variables is contained in the first component. The second component accounts for the next largest amount of variability not accounted for by the first component, and so on. Thus, each principal component is basically a weighted average of the underlying variables. According to the PCA procedure, the jth factor can be expressed as:

$$F_j = w_{J1}z_1 + w_{J2}z_2 + \cdots\cdots\cdots + w_{JN}z_N \qquad j = 1,2,\cdots\cdots,N \qquad (8.2)$$

where F_j is the estimate of jth factor, w_j is the weight on factor score coefficient and N is the number of variables.

Auto Regressive Distributed Lag Model

In the econometric analysis, to estimate the long-run and short-run impact of financial development on economic growth, the Auto Regressive Distributed Lag (ARDL) method of Pesaran, Shin and Smith (2001) is employed. There are several advantages of using the ARDL method as it is adoptable irrespective of whether the underlying variables are I(0) or I(1) process and also it provides a unified framework for testing and estimation of cointegration relations in the context of a single equation. If the F-statistic (Wald test) establishes that there is a single long-run relationship and the sample data size is infinite, the ARDL error correction representation becomes relatively more efficient. The ARDL model can also be reparameterised into ECM to give the short-run dynamics and long-run relationship of the underlying variables.

Generally, time series data contain unit root and non-stationary. However, the time series is required to be stationary to avoid any inconsistencies in coefficient estimation. Therefore, it is critical to check the stationarity properties and to identify the integration order of each series. It is standard that a variable is said to be stationary if it has time-invariant mean, time-invariant variance and the value of the covariance between the two time periods depends only on the distance or gap or lag between the two time periods and not the actual time at which the covariance is computed. The standard Augmented Dickey-Fuller (ADF) unit-root test addresses the potential non-stationary concerns. The regression to be estimated for the application of ADF test is specified as:

$$\Delta y_t = \beta_1 + \beta_2 t + \delta y_{t-1} + \sum_{i=1}^{m} \alpha_i \Delta y_{t-i} + \varepsilon_t \quad (8.3)$$

where y_t is a variable at time t,ε_t is the disturbance term that is generated from a white noise process and is assumed to be independently and identically distributed with zero mean and constant variance. Sufficient lags of Δy_t must be included to ensure no autocorrelation in the error term. Hence, the Schwarz Information Criterion (SIC) test is utilised to confirm that autocorrelation is not present. The null hypothesis is that the series has a unit root ($\delta = 0$) meaning that the series is non-stationary against the alternative hypothesis of the series being stationary. If a unit root (non-stationarity) exists, then δ would not be statistically different from zero. If the p-value of the coefficient of y_{t-1} is less than 0.05 at 5 percent level of significance, the null hypothesis is rejected indicating that the series is stationary.

To empirically analyse the long-run relationship and dynamic interaction of economic growth with financial development, equation (8.1) has been estimated by the ARDL cointegration method. The procedure is adopted for four important reasons:

(a) The bound test is simple as opposed to other multivariate cointegration technique such as Johansen cointegration; it allows cointegrating relationship to be estimated by ordinary least squares (OLS) once the lag order is selected.

(b) The bound test procedure does not require the pre-testing of the variables included in the model for unit root unlike other techniques such as Engle and Granger and Johansen tests which require that all the variables to be integrated of the same order I(1). However, the ARDL technique is applicable irrespective of whether regressor in the model is I(0) or I(1).

(c) The test is relatively more efficient in small sample data sizes as is the case of this study.

(d) The error correction method integrates the short-run dynamics with long-run equilibrium without losing long-run information.

The unrestricted error correction model of ARDL model is used to examine the long-run and short-run relationship which takes the following form:

$$\Delta lnGDPpc = \gamma_0 + \gamma_1 lnGDPpc_{t-1} + \gamma_2 lnFD_{t-1} + \gamma_3 lnINF_{t-1} + \gamma_4 lnGEXP_{t-1} + \gamma_5 lnTROP_{t-1} + \sum_{i=1}^{q} \theta_i \Delta lnGDPpc_{t-i} + \sum_{i=1}^{q} \omega_i \Delta lnFD_{t-i} + \sum_{i=1}^{q} \eta_i \Delta lnINF_{t-i} + \sum_{i=1}^{q} \kappa_i \Delta lnGEXP_{t-i} + \sum_{i=1}^{q} \xi_t \Delta lnTROP_{t-i} + \varepsilon_t \quad (8.4)$$

where Δ is the difference operator and q is the lag length. The first part of the equation (8.4) with δ_2, δ_3, δ_4, and δ_5 refers to the long-run coefficients and the second part with θ, ω, η, κ and ξ refers to the short-run coefficients and ε_t is the error termassumed to be uncorrelated with the independent variables. The null hypothesis of no cointegrating relationship $H_0: \gamma_2 = \gamma_3 = \gamma_4 = \gamma_5 = 0$ is tested against the alternative hypothesis $H_1: \gamma_2 \neq \gamma_3 \neq \gamma_4 \neq \gamma_5 \neq 0$ which implies cointegrating relationship.

The ADRL bounds F-test procedure is about imposing restrictions on long-run parameters using the Wald coefficient restrictions check and obtaining the Wald F-statistics. There could be three probable outcomes in relation to cointegration amid the F-statistic is compared against the lower and upper band critical values. When the estimated F-statistic surpasses the upper band critical value, then the null proposition can be rejected. If the expected F-statistic is less than the lower band critical value, then the null hypothesis cannot be rejected. When the estimated F-statistic is in between the lower and upper band critical values, then the outcome is inconclusive. Narayan (2004) proposes critical values for small samples while the critical values of Pesaran, Shin and Smith (2001) is for large samples. Since this paper uses a small sample size, the estimated F-statistics are evaluated against the Narayan's critical values to ascertain the long-term relation between the series.

The first step in the ARDL test is to estimate equation (8.4) by OLS to test for existence of a long-run relationship among variables by conducting an F-test for the joint significance of the coefficients of the lagged levels of variables. When cointegration is established, the conditional ARDL long-run model for $LGDPpc_t$ can be estimated as:

$$\Delta lnGDPpc = \gamma_0 + \sum_{i=1}^{q} \gamma_1 \, lnGDPpc_{t-1} + \sum_{i=1}^{q} \gamma_2 \, lnFD_{t-1} + \sum_{i=1}^{q} \gamma_3 \, lnINF_{t-1} + \sum_{i=1}^{q} \gamma_4 \, lnGEXP_{t-1} + \sum_{i=1}^{q} \gamma_5 \, lnTROP_{t-1} + \varepsilon_t \quad (8.5)$$

In the final step, the short-run dynamic parameters are obtained by estimating an error correction model (ECM) with the long-run estimates.

The short-run error correction model is used to identify short-run dynamics and to verify the robustness of the estimated long-run coefficients with respect to equation (8.4). The estimating equation is specified as:

$$\Delta lnGDPpc = \mu_0 + \sum_{i=1}^{q} \theta_i \Delta lnGDPpc_{t-i} + \sum_{i=1}^{q} \omega_i \Delta lnFD_{t-i} + \sum_{i=1}^{q} \eta_i \Delta lnINF_{t-i} + \sum_{i=1}^{q} \kappa_i \Delta lnGEXP_{t-i} + \sum_{i=1}^{q} \xi_t \Delta lnTROP_{t-i} + \tau ECM_{t-1} + \varepsilon_t \quad (8.6)$$

where

where θ, ω, η, κ and ξ refer to the short-run dynamic coefficients to equilibrium and τ is the coefficient of speed of adjustment. To check the goodness of fit of the ARDL model, diagnostic tests to examine the serial correlation, functional form, normality and heteroscedasticity and stability tests are performed.

8.4 Empirical Analysis

This chapter presents the empirical estimates of the impact of financial development on economic growth in India. The PCA has been applied on the raw data to construct the financial development index. The first principal component explains the variation of the dependent variable better than any other linear combination of the indicators used. Therefore, the first principal component is considered as an appropriate measure of the characteristics of financial system as well financial sector development in each PCA performed. The component scores/loadings indicate the contributions of variables included in the PCA to the standardised variance of the first principal component. These contributions are the weights used to construct the financial index using the aggregation method.

The Table 8.3 presents the components score coefficient matrix. The eigen values in indicate that the first principal component explains about 74 percent of the standardised variance. Hence, the first principal component is the more relevant measure of financial development as it explains the variations of the dependent variable better that the linear combination of other explanatory variables. Therefore, only information related to the first principal component is considered to form the composite indicator. The factor score are obtained by the corresponding factor score coefficients using equation (8.2). Thus, a composite Financial Development Indicator (FDI) is constructed through PCA method.

Table 8.3: Components Score Coefficient Matrix.

Variable	*Eigen value*	*Component*	*Cumulative percentage*
lnDCP	9.938	0.462308	0.7420
lnCGE	0.460	0.430950	0.9253
lnPCB	0.266	0.462308	0.9789

(*Contd...*)

lnGDS	0.186	0.404854	0.9992
lnBMS	0.099	0.269501	0.9999
lnSTR	0.033	0.049861	1.0000

The Table 8.4 presents the descriptive statistics of the variables for the sample period 1992-2016. The average gross domestic product per capita is $1031.79 and the average GEXP is 11.05 percent of GDP. The average inflation rate is 7.43 percent and the mean of trade openness is 36.39 percent of GDP.

Table 8.4: Descriptive Statistics of Variables in Financial Development and Economic Growth Analysis.

Variable	*Description*	*Mean*	*Median*
GDPpc	Per capita GDP measured at factor cost (2010 U.S dollars) as proxy for economic growth	1031.789 (402.66)	902.906
FDI	Financial development index constructed over proxy measures for depth, access and efficiency of financial institutions and markets	3.674 (3.710)	3.026
GEXP	General government final consumption expenditure as share of GDP	11,058 (0.687)	11.084
TROPN	Sum of exports and imports as a share of GDP as a measure of trade openness	36.394 (12.962)	37.910
INF	Inflation measured by the consumer price index	7.434 (3.015)	6.649
Obs.		25	

Note: Standard deviation in parentheses.

As a first step in the time series econometric analysis of the relationship between financial development and economic growth, the ADF test is performed. Even though the ARDL model does not necessitate prior checking of the unit root issue, in the empirical analysis it is essential to ascertain that variables do not have a unit root problem and their integration order is not more than one. The ADF unit-root test results presented in Table 8.5 indicate that the null hypothesis that the series is non-stationary is rejected for FDI, GEXP and INF at levels for GDPpc and TROPN at first difference. At first difference all the variables are stationary. Further, the order of integration of all the variables is not greater than one i.e. I(1), which is important for long-term cointegration analysis.

Table 8.5: ADF Unit Root Test of Stationarity.

Variable	*At levels*		*At first difference*		*Order of integration*
	Constant	*Constant+ trend*	*Constant*	*Constant+ trend*	
lnFDI	0.027***	0.810	0.007***	0.017***	I(1)
lnGDPpc	1.855	0.785	0.004***	0.021***	I(1)
lnGEXP	0.115***	0.367	0.719	0.010***	I(1)
lnINF	0.016***	0.077***	0.005***	0.007***	I(1)
lnTROPN	0.414	0.997	0.000***	0.0002***	I(1)

Note: ***significant at 1 percent level.

The result of the estimated bounds F-test is reported in Table 8.6. For the equation (8.4) when GDP per capita is the dependent variable, the F-statistic of 10.96 is higher than the upper band critical value of 6.200 at 1 percent significance level. Hence, the null hypothesis of zero cointegration is rejected implying that there is a single cointegration. The bound test evidence confirms the long-run relationship because the calculated F-statistic is greater than the critical values of the upper level of the bound at 1 percent level of significance.

Table 8.6: Bounds Cointegration Test.

Level of significance	*Lower bound*	*Upper bound*	*F-statistic*
1 percent	4.760	6.200	10.96*
5 percent	3.470	4.630	

Thus, the series are cointegrated in the long-run. The estimates of the ARDL model of the relationship between per capita GDP and financial development and other control variables are reported in Table 8.7. The Table 8.7 also presents the results of a number of diagnostics checks conducted to assess the overall reliability of the estimated model. The diagnostic checks indicate that the model does not suffer from severe econometric problems. The ARDL estimates show that nearly 80 percent of the variation in GDPpc is explained by the chosen independent variables showing the ADRL model to be efficient. The LM test indicates that the serial correlation assumption should be rejected. The Ramsey test check for model specification and normality showed that the specification is correct and the errors are normally distributed. The Auto Regressive Conditional Heteroscedasticity (ARCH) test indicates that the regressors are independent and errors are homoscedastic. Thus, the estimated Auto Regressive Distributed Lag (ADRL) model is reliable.

Table 8.7: ARDL Estimates of the Effect of Financial Development on Economic Growth.

Variable	*Coefficient*
lnGDPpc(-1)	2.802** (23.23)
lnGDPpc(-2)	-1.560*** (9.61)
lnGDPpc(-3)	0.165** (2.37)
lnFDI	0.078*** (17.89)
lnFDI(-1)	0.0345*** (9.49)
lnFDI(-2)	-0.025*** (15.21)
lnFDI(-3)	0.029*** (8.02)
lnINF	-0.095*** (17.50)
lnINF(-1)	-0.078*** (14.80)
lnINF(-2)	-0.053*** (14.42)
lnINF(-3)	-0.013*** (2.30)
lnGEXP(-1)	0.179*** (6.57)
lnGEXP(-2)	-0.170*** (5.79)
lnGEXP(-3)	0.227*** (5.79)
lnTROPN	-0.356*** (18.75)
lnTROPN(-1)	-0.250*** (13.71)
lnTROPN(-2)	-0.292*** (21.54)
lnTROPN(-3)	-0.168*** (8.27)
Constant	-1.368*** (8.27)
R-square	0.795
DW statistic	1.884
Functional form	0.020(0.886)
Normality	1.320(0.517)
Heteroscedasticity	3.259(0.071)

Note: Absolute t-values in parentheses.
*** significant at 1 percent level** significant at 5 percent level.

The ADRL estimates for the long-run relation between economic growth and financial development are presented in Table 8.8. The estimates show that all the variables are as statistically significant. The positive coefficient of FDI implies that a 1 percent increase in financial development will lead to an increase of about a half point in real GDP per capita in the economy. The negative coefficient of TROPN shows that trade openness decreases real GDP per capita more than 1 percent. A negative sign for trade openness against the strategy of export led growth hypothesis. However, in a developing country like India, that is heavily dependent on raw material and agricultural exports and capital intensive imports, open trade may adversely affect economic growth. As expected, inflation is negatively related with GDP per capita, a 1 percent increase in inflation will reduce real GDP per capita by one-third of a point. Similarly, an increase in government expenditure reduces economic growth by one-fourth of a point. Over public expenditure causes high inflation which in turn may lead to underdeveloped financial systems in a developing country like India thereby reducing economic growth.

Table 8.8: ADRL Estimates of Long-Run Effects of Financial Development on Economic Growth.

Variable	*Coefficient*
lnFDI	0.492** (2.28)
lnINF	-0.330*** (3.25)
lnGEXP	-0.267** (2.27)
lnTROPN	-1.390*** (3.83)
Constant	3.359356

Note: Absolute t-values in parentheses. *** significant at 1 percent level** significant at 5 percent level.

The Table 8.9 presents the estimated short-run dynamics of the ARDL model. The statistical significance of the error correction term (ECM) implies there exists a long-run causality such that past equilibrium errors play a significant role in determining current outcomes. The negative sign of the ECM coefficient shows the short-run adjustment to shocks towards long-run values. The coefficient of ECM determines the speed of the correction towards the equilibrium relationship. The estimated ECM coefficient of -0.371shows that any divergence from the long-run relation in the current period should be adjusted by around 37 percent in the following period, which implies that the speed of adjustment is rather slow. This finding is consistent with the cointegration test results.

The estimated ARDL results further reveal that the short-run ΔFDI coefficient magnitude is less than that of the long-run. The coefficients of variables TROPN and FD index in current year are positive indicating that trade openness and financial development have positive impact on GDP per capita. The coefficients of INF and GEXP are negative reflecting that inflation rate and general government final consumption expenditure have negative impact on economic growth. The reliability checks validate that the estimated ECM equation does not have serious estimation issues.

Table 8.9: ADRL Estimates of Short-Run Dynamic Error Correction Model.

Variable	*Coefficient*
Δ(lnGDPpc(-1))	1.395*** (6.55)
Δ(lnGDPpc(-2))	-0.165*** (8.34)
Δ(lnFDI)	0.078*** (4.83)
Δ(lnFDI(-1))	0.076*** (5.17)
Δ(lnFDI(-2))	0.029 (1.43)
Δ(lnINF)	-0.095*** (3.64)
Δ(lnINF(-1))	0.039*** (6.12)
Δ(lnINF(-2))	-0.013 (1.61)
Δ(lnGEXP)	-0.127*** (2.62)
Δ(lnGEXP(-1))	-0.057*** (5.20)
Δ(lnGEXP(-2))	-0.227** (1.98)
Δ(lnTROPN)	0.356*** (2.80)
Δ(lnTROPN(-1))	0.460 (0.14)
Δ(lnTROPN(-2))	0.168 (1.55)
ECM (error correction)	-0.371** (2.48)
Adjusted R-square	0.690
AIC	-5.543
SIC	-4.495
Durbin-Watson statistic	2.066
F-statistic	46.581

Note: Absolute t-values in parentheses. *** significant at 1 percent level** significant at 5 percent level.

8.5 Conclusion

There exists a close association between financial development and economic development in an economy. Studies that explore this relationship have employed various measures of financial development indicators. This paper attempts to construct a single financial development index, applying the principal components analysis method over six indicators of the depth, access and efficiency of the financial system in India viz. broad money supply, domestic credit to private sector by banks, gross domestic savings and credit to government owned enterprises, all as percent of GDP, and stock market turnover ratio. The time period covered is the post liberalisation period from 1992 to 2016 and data is obtained from the 2017 World Development Indicators and Global Financial Development Indicators of the World Bank. The dependent variable is economic growth measured as GDP per capita and independent variable is Financial Development Index (FDI) along with certain macroeconomic variables inflation (INF), trade openness (TROPN) and general government final consumption expenditure (GEXP). In the empirical estimation, this paper follows the auto regressive distributed lag (ARDL) model, employing bound testing approach, to cointegration techniques and error correction model (ECM).

The ARDL bounds cointegration test supports the long-run relationship between financial development and economic growth. The estimated effect of financial development and economic growth is significantly a positive. In the long-run, trade openness has a significant negative impact on economic growth implying that import led growth is harmful for Indian economy. The inflation rate and government expenditure also significantly reduce long-run growth of the economy. The short-run error correction model suggests that financial development has significantly positive effect but the magnitude of the short-run effect is less than that of the long-run. The coefficients of trade openness in current year is positive indicating that trade openness and financial development have positive impact on GDP per capita in the short span. The estimated error correction coefficient (-0.371) indicates that any divergence from the long-run relation in the current period should be adjusted by around 37 percent in the following period. This indicates a slow pace of adjustment of the Indian economy to shocks. The financial system in India, comprising both the bank-based and market-based indicators of financial development, has played a significant positive role on India's post-Independence economic performance. Thus, financial development can promote long-run economic growth even in an environment in which financial activities are highly regulated.

9

The Causality between External and Domestic Markets: ARCH-GARCH Estimation of the Effect of Exchange Rate Volatility on Stock Market Return Volatility

9.1 Introduction

Globalisation has resulted in numerous global links throughout the world bringing every nation close to each other and in fact the modern world is seen as a single global village. This current wave of globalisation has not only expanded the markets for products and economic integration, but also resulted in a marked growth in interactions among international financial institutions and their markets. A byproduct of such global integration of financial markets is also that economies are highly vulnerable for the changes occurring in international financial markets (Karunanayake, Valadkhani and O'Brien, 2010). Just like that growth of an economy is strongly related to its domestic financial system where the national stock market plays a vital role in providing capital for investments, the global financial system with which the domestic financial markets are linked through FIIs, also plays a critical role in achieving such economic growth (Muktadir-Al-Mukit, 2012).

The changes in global financial markets also influence the exchange rates, the fluctuations of which have repercussions to economies throughout the world. Karoui (2006) observes that emerging market countries are attempting to adjust their currencies around certain powerful global currencies such as US dollars, by adopting free floating rates or managed floating exchange rates so that fluctuations in exchange rates in such currencies become too small compared to others. In this context, Joseph (2002) notes that the exchange rate directly affects international competitiveness of the firms based on the price levels of inputs and outputs of such firms. This instability in international markets and volatility of exchange rates affects the stock prices as well as returns in the domestic stock markets and causes stock price volatility. The volatility in stock returns is frequently used as a measure of risk and such volatility in stock returns is widely used for hedging, asset pricing, portfolio selection, etc. (Jegajeevan, 2012). Peiris and Peiris (2011) demonstrate that people tend to believe volatility as a signal of market disruption where the capital markets are not functioning at the expected level together with presence of mispriced securities. Thus, volatility in stock returns is perceived critical so that understanding the volatility of the stock returns has long been a topic of considerable interest.

Especially an investor holding foreign equities is naturally exposed to exchange rate fluctuations. Both portfolio performance and the decision regarding whether to hedge foreign exchange risk depends, amongst other things, on the relationship between equity and currency returns. Policymakers care about this relation as valuation changes induced by foreign exchange and equity returns generate significant swings in international investment positions. However, while there is a vast literature on the link between interest rate differentials and exchange rates across countries, little is known about the relation between exchange rates and international equity returns. From asset pricing viewpoint, the correlation between exchange rates and equity returns depends on the covariance between returns and currency and stock market risks. Hau and Rey (2006) suggest that foreign exchange and equity market returns should be negatively correlated because of portfolio rebalancing. To see the mechanism, consider a portfolio manager of a country with money invested in another country. When the stock market of that foreign country rises relative to the home country, the manager is overweight with foreign country equities and, to return to a neutral position, sells foreign country stocks and then sells the foreign currency proceeds for local currency. The sale of foreign currency for local currency causes the foreign currency to depreciate at the same time the foreign stock market is outperforming.

The nature and magnitude of the interdependence between stock prices and exchange rates have implications for a number of crucial domestic issues as well as for international finance. The relationship between a country's stock market and its foreign exchange market, especially in the volatility of them, has been a subject of theoretical and empirical investigation for long. However, the empirical evidence on the influence of exchange rate volatility on the volatility of stock returns is inconsistent (Mishra, 2004; Solnik, 1987; Zubair, 2013). The existence of a positive association between exchange rate and share market volatilities is also contrasted with evidence for a negative association between them.

Since the mid-1980s international equity has been increasing at a rate of 34 percent per annum which reflects a pattern of rapidly increasing international equity investment. An increased cross-border equity flows create a higher demand for and supply of currencies in which international equity prices are denominated leading to some degree of interdependence between stock market and exchange rate changes. Further, the positive and significant spillover of volatility may increase the nonsystematic residual international portfolio risk faced by international investors, hence reducing the gains from the international portfolio diversification.

The Asian crisis of 1997-98 and the global financial crisis of 2007 have made a strong pitch for dynamic linkage between stock prices and exchange rates. During the crisis period, the emerging markets have collapsed due to substantial depreciation of exchange rates (in terms of US$) as well as dramatic fall in the stock prices. This has become important again from the view point of large cross-border movement of funds due to portfolio investment and not due to actual trade flows, though trade flows have some impact on stock prices of the companies whose main sources of revenue comes from foreign exchange. Therefore, it is important to understand the interlink between financial markets and exchange rates.

The purpose of this paper is to empirically investigate the impact of exchange rate volatility on stock market return volatility in India. The paper uses daily market values of BSE SENSEX and the daily exchange rate values of US dollar-rupee, euro-rupee and pound-rupee exchange rates for a period of six years from January 5, 2010 to December 31, 2015. The data on daily market values of BSE SENSEX are obtained from the Bombay Stock Exchange and the exchange rates are obtained from the Reserve Bank of India websites. The standard methods of time series data analysis are carried out. The Augmented Dickey-Fuller (ADF) test is done for stationarity. Empirically, the standard Ordinary Least Squares (OLS), Auto regressive Conditional Heteroscedasticity (ARCH) and Generalised Auto regressive Conditional Heteroscedasticity (GARCH) models are estimated on the effect of exchange rate volatility on stock market return volatility.

9.2 A Brief Review of Recent Studies

Theoretically, the relationship between exchange rate market and stock market has been explained by two alternative models: the good market or flow-oriented model and the portfolio balance or stock-oriented model. The former theory argues that causality runs from exchange market to stock market while the latter theory describes that changes in the stock market affects the exchange market (Khan and Ali, 2015). The flow-oriented model states that changes in exchange rate affect international competitiveness and trade balances, thereby influencing real income and output. And stock prices, generally interpreted as the present values of future cash flows of firms, react to exchange rate changes and form the link among future income, interest rate innovations, current investment and consumption decisions (Dornbusch and Fischer, 1980). The stock-oriented model views exchange rates as equating the supply and demand for assets such as stocks. Since the values of financial assets are determined by the present values of their future cash flows, expectations of relative currency values play a considerable role in their price movements. Therefore, stock price innovations may affect, or be affected by, exchange rate dynamics (Branson, 1983; Frankel, 1983; Zhao, 2010).

The goods market hypothesis suggests that changes in exchange rates affect the competitiveness of multinational firms and hence their earnings and stock prices. A depreciation of the local currency makes exporting goods cheaper and may lead to an increase in foreign demand and sales. Consequently, the value of an exporting firm would benefit from a depreciation of its local currency. On the other hand, because of the decrease in foreign demand of an exporting firm's products when the local currency appreciates, the firm's profit will decline and so does its stock prices. In contrast, for importing firms the sensitivity of firm value to exchange rate changes is just the opposite. An appreciation (depreciation) of the local currency leads to an increase (decrease) in the firm value of importing firms. Additionally, variations in exchange rates affect a firm's transaction exposure, i.e. exchange rate movement affects a firm's future payables (or receivables) denominated in foreign currency. For an exporter, an appreciation of the local currency reduces profits, while a depreciation of the local currency increases profits. Further, stock prices could be affected by exchange rate movements because such movements will induce equity flows.

According to the portfolio balance approach, exchange rates, like all commodities, are determined by market mechanism. A blooming stock market would attract capital flows from foreign investors and hence causes an increase in the demand of a country's currency and vice versa. As a result, rising (declining) stock prices are related to an appreciation (depreciation) in exchange rates. Moreover, foreign investment in a country's equity securities could increase over time due to the benefits of international diversification that foreign investors would gain. In addition to returns, capital flows can be induced by less risky investment climate of a country. An improvement in a country's investment climate such as stable political system, a fair legal system, financial openness and liberalisation will lead to capital inflows and a currency appreciation. Further, movements in stock prices may influence exchange rates since investors' wealth and money demand may depend on the performance of the stock market. For example, during the time of a crisis, a sudden dislocation of asset demands may incur because of the herding behaviour of investors or the loss of confidence in economic and political stability. This dislocation usually results in a shift of portfolio preference from domestic assets to assets denominated in other currencies, implying a decrease in the demand of money. This will lead to a decrease in the domestic interest rate and in turn lead to capital outflows causing the currency to depreciate (Pan et al. 2007).

Empirically, Shapiro (1975), Levi (1994) and Marston (2001) show a positive association between exchange rate and stock market volatilities in the US. It is also shown that the competitiveness and the market values of the firms are directly affected by the exchange rate. Aggarwal (1981) and Agrawal et al. (2010) also report a positive association between exchange rate and stock market volatilities. But, Branson and Henderson (1985) and Frankel (1983), using the portfolio balanced model, demonstrate that the connection between the movements of exchange rate and US stock market has a negative relationship. They further depict that at the macro level the domestic wealth falls as a result of fall in the stock prices and thereby a capital outflow would occur as a result of drop in the interest rates which creates a reduction in demand for domestic money so that domestic currency gets depreciated. However, Jorion (1990) and Bartov and Bodnar (1994) fail to find a significant contemporaneous relation between US dollar movements and stock returns for US firms. Thus, despite the theoretical association between exchange rate and stock market volatilities, early empirical studies have not produced convincing evidence to support the relationship between exchange rate and stock market movements (Jorion, 1991).

Najang and Seifert (1992) report that the absolute difference in the stock returns have positive impact on the exchange rate volatility for US dollar movement and stock return for US firms. Sekmen (2011), using

ARIMA models on stock returns for the US, observe that exchange rate volatility negatively affects stock returns. Even the availability of hedging instruments could not lessen the negative impact of exchange rate volatility on the volume of trade. Ajayi and Mougoue (1996) and Ajayi et al. (1998) provide evidence for unidirectional causality from stock market to currency markets for advanced economies and no consistent causal relations in emerging markets.

Donnelly and Sheehy (1996) observe a significant contemporaneous relation between exchange rate and the market value of large UK exporters. Maysami and Koh (2000) argue that interest rate and exchange rate should also be considered as determinants of UK stock prices and obtain a positive association between the UK stock prices and exchange rate. Zhao (2010) empirically examine the dynamic relationship between Renminbi (RMB) real effective exchange rate and stock price in China with VAR and multivariate GARCH models for the period January 1991 to June 2009. The results show that there is not a stable long-term equilibrium relationship between RMB real effective exchange rate and stock price. There are also not mean spillovers between the foreign exchange and stock markets. Furthermore, the paper examines the cross-volatility effects between foreign exchange and stock markets using likelihood ratio statistic. There exist the bidirectional volatility spillovers effects between the two markets, indicating the past innovations in stock market have the great effect on future volatility in foreign exchange market, and vice versa.

Among the stock market studies on Asian countries, Ramasamy and Yeung (2002) examine the links between foreign exchange and stock markets and their implications for capital controls in six Asian countries (Bangladesh, Japan, Philippines, Vietnam, china, Indonesia) over the period 1995-2001.They find inconsistent results for bivariate causality between stock prices and exchange rates . Chiang and Yang (2003) show that stock returns and currency values are positively related for six Asian markets (Bangladesh, Japan, Philippines, Vietnam, china, Indonesia). Adjasi and Biekpe (2005) report that relative currency movements influence stock price volatility for six Asian markets (Bangladesh, Japan, Philippines, Vietnam, china, Indonesia). Pan et al. (2007) examine dynamic linkages between exchange rates and stock prices for six East Asian countries (Bangladesh, Japan, Philippines, Vietnam, china, Indonesia). Yau and Nieh (2009) investigate the exchange rate effects of the Taiwan Dollar against the Japanese Yenon stock prices in Japan and Taiwan and find a long-term equilibrium and asymmetric causal relationships.

As far as studies on stock market in India, Bahmani-Oskooee and Sohrabian (1992) show bidirectional causality between stock prices measured by the S&P500 index and effective exchange rates of dollar. Apte (2002), using the E-GARCH specification proposed by Nelson (1991), examine whether changes in the volatility of the stock market affects volatility in the foreign exchange market and vice versa in India. The model specification incorporates asymmetric effects of positive and negative return surprises on volatility both within the market as well as spillovers across the two markets. Empirical analysis with one of the major stock market indices supports the hypothesis of such volatility linkages while for the other index there appears to be a spillover from the foreign exchange market to the stock market but not the other way round.

Thus, the exchange rate market and the stock market have both positive and negative association. Some studies show that the stock market affects the foreign exchange rate while others have also observed that foreign exchange rate affect the stock market. Hence, the causality between the volatility of exchange and stock markets is inconclusive and needs further investigation.

9.3 Data and Methodology

In order to study the relationship between exchange rate volatility and stock market volatility, this paper uses the daily closing data on the stock market index BSE30 (SENSEX) and the daily closing US dollar-rupee exchange rate, euros-rupee exchange rate and British pound-rupee exchange rate for six years from January 5, 2010 to December 31 2015 with 1440 observations, The stock market data are obtained from the BSE exchange and the historical exchange rate data are taken from Reserve Bank of India websites.

Generalised Auto Regressive Conditional Heteroscedasticity Model

Empirically, this paper follows the generalised autoregressive conditionally heteroskedasticity (GARCH) model. The GARCH (q,p) process can be modeled as:

$$\varepsilon_t = \sigma_t x_t \tag{9.1}$$

where x_t is a sequence of a i.i.d. random variable and σ_t is a nonnegative process such that:

$$\sigma_t^2 = \alpha_0 + \alpha_1 \varepsilon_{t-1}^2 + \cdots + \alpha_q x_{t-q}^2 + \beta_1 \sigma_{t-1}^2 + \cdots + \beta_p \sigma_{t-p}^2 \tag{9.2}$$

and

$$\alpha_0 > 0\,,\ \ \alpha_1 \geq 0\,,\ \ i = 1, \ldots, q,\ \ \beta_j \geq 0,\ \ j = 1, \ldots, p \tag{9.3}$$

The conditions on parameters ensure strong positivity of the conditional variance in equation (9.2). Writing equation (9.2) in terms of a lag-operator B:

$$\sigma_t^2 = \alpha_0 + \alpha(B)\varepsilon_t^2 + \beta(B)\sigma_t^2 \quad (9.4)$$

where $\alpha(B) = \alpha_1 B + \alpha_2 B^2 + \cdots + \alpha_q B^q$ and $\beta(B) = \beta_1 B + \beta_2 B^2 + \cdots + \alpha_p B^p$ (9.5)

If the roots of the characteristic equation i.e.:

$$1 - \beta_1 x - \beta_2 x^2 - \cdots \beta_p x^p = 0 \quad (9.6)$$

lie outside the unit circle and the process (x_t) is stationary, then equation (9.2) can be written as:

$$\sigma_t^2 = \frac{\alpha_0}{1-\beta(1)} + \frac{\alpha(B)\varepsilon_t^2}{1-\beta(B)} = \alpha_0^* + \sum_{t=i}^{\infty} \delta_i \varepsilon_{t-i}^2 \quad (9.7)$$

where $\alpha_0^* = \frac{\alpha_0}{1-\beta(1)}$ and δ_i are coefficients of B^i in the expansion of $\alpha(B)[1-\beta(B)]^{-1}$. The expression (9.7) shows that the GARCH (q,p) process is an ARCH process of infinite order with a fractional structure of the coefficients. From equation (9.1), the GARCH (1,1) process is stationary if the process (σ_t^2) is stationary.

As the data is time series, the presence of unit root and stationarity of the series using the Augmented Dickey-Fuller (ADF) test is to be performed in order to avoid constructing spurious regressions when working with non-stationary time series data. The null hypothesis is that a unit root is present in a time series sample and the alternative hypothesis says that the series doesn't have a unit root. The unit root specification is:

$$\Delta y_t = \alpha + \beta_t + \gamma y_{t-1} + \delta_1 \Delta y_{t-1} + \cdots + \delta_{p-1} \Delta y_{t-p-1} + \varepsilon_t \quad (9.8)$$

where α is a constant and β_t is the coefficient on time trend and p is the lag order of the autoregressive process. The unit root test is then carried out under the null hypothesis $y = 0$ against the alternative hypothesis $y < 0$.

Empirically, the impact of exchange rate volatility on stock market volatility is analysed first by the OLS method:

$$r_t = \beta_0 + \beta_1(USD\_INR)_t + \beta_2(EURO\_INR)_t + \beta_3(GBP\_INR)_t + \varepsilon_t \quad (9.9)$$

where r_t is the daily stock returns calculated as the natural logarithm of the daily closing price relative to previous day i.e. $SENSEX_t = \ln[(\text{stock price}_t/(\text{stock price}_{t-1})]$, $(USD\_INR)_t$ is the logarithm of daily exchange rate i.e. $(USD\_INR)_t = \ln[(USD\_INR_t/(USD\_INR_{t-1})]$, GBP_INR_t is the natural logarithm of daily exchange rate i.e. $(GBP\_INR)_t = \ln[(GBP\_INR_t/(GBP\_INR_{t-1})]$, $EURO\_INR_t$ is the natural logarithm of daily exchange rate i.e.

$EURO\_INR_t = \ln[(EURO\_INR_t/(EURO\_INR_{t-1})]$ β_0, β_1, β_2, and β_3 are the coefficients of the parameters, and u_t is the white noise error term.

The auto regressive conditional heteroscedasticity (ARCH) model describes the variance of the current error term or innovation as a function of the actual sizes of the previous time period error, terms often the variance is related to the squares of the previous innovations. Let, $\varepsilon_t = x_t\, \sigma_t$ where ε_t is the error term (return residuals, with respect to a mean process). The ε_t is split into a stochastic piece x_t and a time-dependent standard deviation σ_t characterising the typical size of the term. The null hypothesis is that, in the absence of ARCH components, $\Upsilon_i = 0$ for all i=1, 2,...p. The alternative hypothesis is that, in the presence of ARCH components, at least one of the estimated Υ_i coefficients must be significant. The suitability of the estimated OLS model is then tested with the ARCH test. The ARCH process is specified as follows:

$$r_t = \gamma_0 + \gamma_1(USD\_INR)_t + \gamma_2(EURO\_INR)_t + \gamma_3(GBP\_INR)_t + \varepsilon_t \tag{9.10}$$
$$\varepsilon_t^2 = \alpha_0 + \alpha_1\varepsilon_{t-1}^2 + \cdots + \alpha_p\varepsilon_{t-p}^2 \tag{9.11}$$

The generalised autoregressive conditional heteroscedasticity GARCH (p, q) process (where p is the order of the ARCH term ε^2 and q is the order of the GARCH terms σ^2) is specified as:

$$r_t = \gamma_0 + \gamma_1(USD\_INR)_t + \gamma_2(EURO\_INR)_t + \gamma_3(GBP\_INR)_t + \varepsilon_t \tag{9.12}$$
$$\varepsilon_t^2 = \alpha_0 + \alpha_1\varepsilon_{t-1}^2 + \cdots + \alpha_p\varepsilon_{t-p}^2 + \delta_1\sigma_{t-1}^2 + \cdots + \delta_q\sigma_{t-q}^2 \tag{9.13}$$

where the parameter γ_0, is the intercept, γ_1, γ_2, and γ_3 are the coefficients of the estimated parameters of the mean equation, σ_t^2 is the conditional variance, $\alpha_1\varepsilon_{t-1}^2$ is the news about volatility from the previous period, measured as the lag of the squared residual from the mean equation which is defined as ARCH term, and $\delta_1\sigma_{t-1}^2$ is the last period's forecast variance which is defined as the GARCH term.

The GARCH specification requires that in the conditional variance equation, parameters, α_0, α_1 and α_2 to be non-negative and the sum of α_1 and α_2 to be less than one to secure the covariance stationarity of the conditional variance:

$$r_t = \phi_t + \varepsilon_t \tag{9.14}$$

$$\sigma_t^2 = \phi_0 + \theta_1\varepsilon_t^2 + \theta_2\sigma_t^2 + \eta_1 v(USD\_INR)_t + \eta_2 v(EURO\_INR)_t + \eta_3(GBP\_INR)_t \tag{9.15}$$

where v represents the volatility of the exchange rates calculated through a GARCH (1,1) process to capture impact of exchange rate volatilities on stock return volatilities.

9.4 Empirical Analysis

The Figures 9.1 to 9.3 presents the trend exchange rates of Indian rupee with the US dollar, euro and British pound for the period January 5 2010 to December 31 2015. All the three exchange rate movements show upward trend from 2012 and peaking at the beginning of 2014. There is also significant volatility in all the three exchange rates.

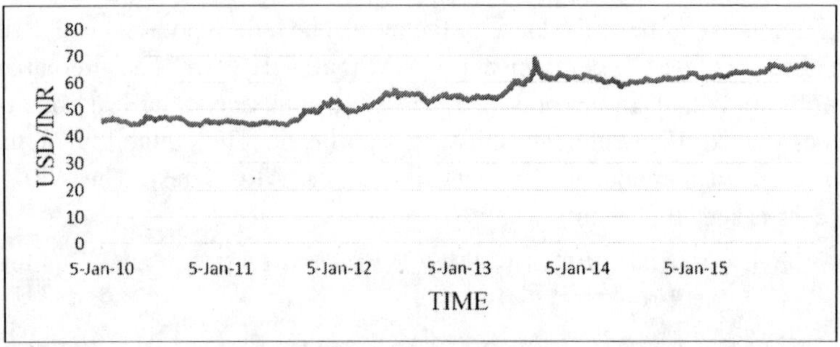

Figure 9.1: Trend in US Dollar-Indian Rupee Exchange Rate.

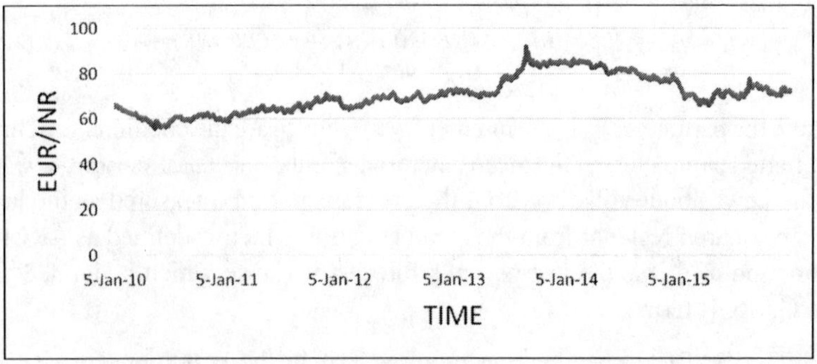

Figure 9.2: Trend in Euros-Indian Rupee Exchange Rate.

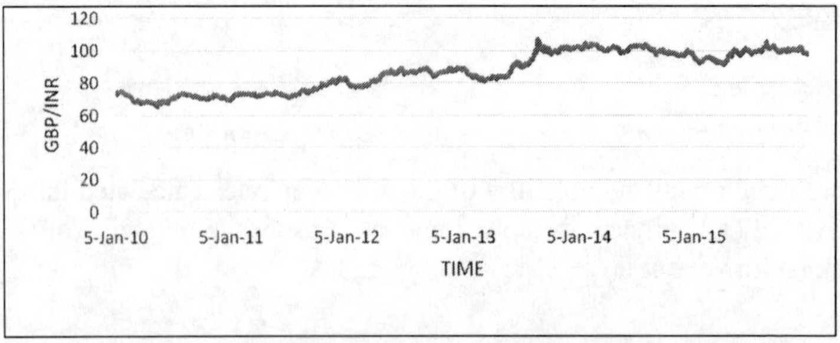

Figure 9.3: Trend in British Pound-Indian Rupee Exchange Rate.

The Table 9.1 presents the variability of the variables in the empirical analysis if the causal relationship between stock prices and exchange rates in India. The skewness is to be 0 and kurtosis to be equal to 3 in order to indicate that the variables are normally distributed. The data are tested for the normality through Jarque-Bera test which shows that the JB test has passed and all variables have normal distribution.

Table 9.1: Descriptive Statistics of Stock Market Index and Foreign Exchange Rates.

Statistic	*BSE SENSEX*	*USD_INR*	*GBP_INR*	*EURO_INR*
Std. dev.	0.00798	0.0021	0.0038	0.0044
Skewness	0.10956	0.9642	0.1749	0.0183
Kurtosis	3.00204	3.5162	3.3233	3.6751
Jarque-Bera test	1276.26	26235.24	331.889	168.783
Obs.	1440			

The ADF test for stationarity of the variables presented in Table 9.2 rejects the null hypothesis of unit root in the levels form as the probability values are less than 0.05. Therefore, all the variables are stationary at levels.

Table 9.2: ADF Unit Root Test of Stationarity.

Variable at levels	*t-statistic*	*Prob.*
BSE SENSEX RETURN	-30.765**	0.000
USD/INR	-17.392**	0.000
GBP/INR	-17.335**	0.000
EUR/INR	-17.573**	0.000

The Table 9.3 presents OLS and GARCH estimates of the effect of exchange rates on the BSE SENSSEX returns. In the OLS results, both US dollar-rupee exchange rate and euro-rupee exchange rates have a negative association with the BSE SENSEX returns whereas the nexus between British pound-rupee exchange rate and BSE SENSEX returns are positive. However, only the US dollar-rupee exchange rate has a significant impact on the BSE SENSEX returns while the British pound-rupee and euro-rupee exchange rates are insignificant in determining the BSE SENSEX returns. The suitability of the regression OLS estimation is tested with the ARCH test if the squared residuals of OLS equation (9.9) contain autocorrelation or heteroscedasticity. The results of the ARCH test reject the null hypothesis at 1 percent significant level indicating that classical OLS estimated coefficients are not effectively estimated so that inferences based on such coefficients are unreliable.

Table 9.3: OLS and GARCH Estimates of the Effect of Volatility in Exchange Rates on Stock Market Returns in India.

Variable	*OLS*	*GARCH*	
	BSE SENSEXreturn	*Mean BSE SENSEXreturn*	*Volatility of BSE SENSEXreturn*
USD	-0.334*** (0.114)	-0.111 (0.097)	-
GBP	0.092 (0.080)	0.108** (0.050)	-
EURO	-0.056 (0.064)	-0.113*** (0.038)	-
Constant	0.0005** (0.0002)	0.0005*** (0.0001)	-
R-square	0.007	-	-
Adj. R-square	0.005	-	-
Durbin-Watson statistic	1.598	-	-
F-statistic	0.020	78.795*** (0.000)	-
Obs*R-square		74.811*** (0.000)	
Variance equation			
RESID $(-1)^2$	-	0.162*** (0.017)	0.150*** (0.016)
GARCH (-1)	-	0.826*** (0.016)	0.819*** (0.017)
v(USD_INR)	-	-	-0.027 (0.015)
v(GBP_INR)	-	-	-0.052 (0.040)
v(EURO_INR)	-	-	0.106*** (0.026)
Constant	-	1.41E-06*** (3.15E-07)	1.14E-06 (4.43E-07)

Note: Standard errors in parentheses. *** significant at 1 percent level ** significant at 5 percent level * significant at 10 percent level.

In contrast to the OLS estimates, the estimated mean BSE SENSEX returns GARCH (1,1) process show that the US dollar-rupee exchange rate has an insignificant impact on BSE SENSEX returns while British pound-rupee and euro-rupee exchange rates have a significant impact on BSE SENSEX returns. However, there is no deviation from the OLS estimates with regard to sign of the relationship between foreign exchange rates and market returns as the GARCH (1,1) model also produces a positive association between British pound-rupee exchange rate and BSE SENSEX stock market returns while a negative association with other two currencies. The results further reveal that the magnitude of the coefficients are high for US dollar-rupee exchange rate and euro-rupee exchange rate compared to British pound-rupee exchange rate indicating that those currencies are having a relatively strong link with the stock market returns compared to British pound-rupee exchange rate. The intercept term is positive and statistically significant which indicates that there is significant time invariant component in the return generating process.

Both the ARCH and GARCH parameters are satisfying the non-negativity condition while both parameters are significant at 1 percent significant level. The GARCH parameter is significantly greater than the ARCH term illustrating that the volatility of stock returns is more sensitive to its own lagged values than to its new surprises. Consequently, the effect of previous period's forecast variance is more persistent. In addition, the summation of GARCH and ARCH parameters closer to unity indicates that the shocks to the BSE SENSEX stock returns have high persistent effects and the response to volatility decays at a slower rate.

The estimated exchange rate volatilities of US dollar-rupee, British pound-rupee and euro-rupee on the volatility of BSE SENSEX returns by GARCH (1,1) model indicate a lower and significant ARCH parameter. This shows a weak support for the presence of last period's shocks on stock market return volatility whereas relatively large and statistically significant GARCH parameter provides strong evidence for the presence of previous surprises. Despite the inclusion of exchange rate volatilities, the sum of ARCH and GARCH parameters as a measure of volatility presence is still approximately closer to unity indicating a weak impact on exchange rate volatilities on the stock market return volatilities irrespective of the currency.

The empirical results on the relationship between the volatilities in stock market index and foreign exchange rates show that the effect of euro-rupee exchange rate volatility is positive and statistically significant on the stock market return volatility. An increase in euro-rupee exchange rate volatility increases volatility of stock returns of BSE SENSEX by about 10 percent. This is expected as the globalisation as well as open market economic policies, Indian capital market has become a potential destination for foreign investors to park their investments which creates a severe exposure to the foreign currency risk. As an emerging market economy, India still lacks a developed market for hedging instruments to mitigate potential exchange rate risk exposures. This can be a potential reason behind the positive association between euro-rupee exchange rate volatility and stock market return volatility. The empirical results further reveal that volatilities of US dollar-rupee and British pound-rupee exchange rates negatively influence the stock return volatilities but the effects are statistically insignificant.

Diagnostic tests of correlogram of squared residual test and heteroscedasticity test are performed in order to assess the suitability and reliability of the ARCH and GARCH estimation models. The estimated results of the tests are presented in Table 9.4. In the correlogram test, all Q statistics at all lags under normal GARCH model are statistically insignificant at 1 percent level indicating no significant serial correlation among the residuals. On the other hand, in the heteroscedasticity test, the p-value of the Obs*R-square is insignificant indicating the non-existence of ARCH effect.

Table 9.4: Correlogram of Squared Residual and Heteroscedasticity Tests.

Lag	*AC*	*PAC*	*Q-statistics*	*Prob.*
1	0.036	0.036	1.8548	0.173
2	-0.004	-0.006	1.8814	0.39
3	-0.03	-0.03	3.2117	0.36
4	-0.026	-0.023	4.1591	0.385
5	-0.009	-0.008	4.2898	0.508
6	-0.003	-0.004	4.3037	0.636
7	-0.014	-0.016	4.6086	0.708
8	-0.005	-0.005	4.6387	0.795
9	0.036	0.036	6.5348	0.685
10	-0.025	-0.029	7.4414	0.683
11	-0.017	-0.015	7.8387	0.728
12	0.012	0.015	8.044	0.782
13	0.012	0.011	8.2421	0.827
14	0.019	0.017	8.773	0.845
15	-0.033	-0.035	10.379	0.795
16	0.001	0.006	10.382	0.846
17	0.029	0.03	11.625	0.822
18	-0.027	-0.033	12.217	0.808
19	-0.027	-0.024	13.806	0.795
20	-0.024	-0.02	14.62	0.79
F-statistic	1.850	Prob.		0.174
Obs*R-square	1.850	Prob. Chi-square		0.174

9.5 Conclusion

With globalisation of capital markets and liberalisation the capital account, global investors diversify their portfolios across currencies and national stock markets. Since exchange rate risk and its association with the local stock market is an important component of the overall portfolio risk, this trend can be expected to link the stock market and the forex market more closely. This paper empirically investigates the effect of exchange rate volatility on stock market return volatility from India's perspective. The daily time series data for BSE SENSEX stock market index and exchange rates of US dollar/rupee, British pound/rupee, Euros/rupee over a period of six years from January 2010 to December 2015 is used in the empirical analysis. In the estimation, this paper applies the ARCH and GARCH models in order to estimate the effect of exchange rate volatility on stock market return volatility. The empirical results of the study reveal that the volatility of Euro/rupee exchange rate has a positive and significant impact on BSE SENSEX return volatility whilst the effect of volatility of US dollar/rupee and British pound/rupee exchange rates are insignificantly negative. It is observed that the GARCH parameter is significantly greater than the ARCH term illustrating that the volatility of stock returns is more sensitive to its own lagged values than to its new surprises. The shocks to the BSE SENSEX stock returns have highly persistent effects and the response to volatility decays at a slower rate.

10

The Causality between Capital Market and Economic Growth: VECM Estimation of the Effect of Stock Market Performance on Economic Growth

10.1 Introduction

Economic growth is generally understood to indicate the level of development of a society. Among the various measures of economic growth, the performance of capital market is the single most indicator of the health of an economy, especially the industrial and financial growth. The capital or stock market also plays a significant role in resource mobilisation and integration with the global economy. In fact, the development of the stock market of an economy and its performance is considered as the basis for industrialisation of an economy. The stock market acts not only as a measure of economic development, but also contributes to the acceleration of economic growth. That is why governments of most nations tend to have keen interest in the performance of stock markets. Adjasi and Yartey (2007) argue that the capital (stock) market accelerates economic growth by providing a boost to domestic savings and increasing the quantity and quality of investment. The development of capital market transforms a country from a simple saver to an investor (Ewah et al. 2009). The capital market therefore positively influences economic growth through encouraging savings among individuals and providing avenues for firm financing.

The capital market, where buyers and sellers engage in trade of financial securities like bonds, stocks, etc., consists of primary markets which deal with trade of new issues of stocks and other securities, and secondary markets where the exchange of existing or previously-issued securities are traded. The performance of capital market in an economy can be understood by parameters like market size, market capitalisation - the market value of a company's outstanding shares, market liquidity - the ratio of total value of shares traded to GDP, market turnover - the total value of shares traded in relation to the size of the market, market volatility - the rate and magnitude of changes in stock prices, and market efficiency. The stock market in India is under the strong regulatory mechanism and a more modernised market infrastructure and has a significant watch of the Reserve Bank of India. However, with the global financial crisis that originated from the US sub-prime mortgage market, the capital market of India delivered a sluggish performance. While the stock market suffered from volatility and weak form inefficiency, the market at the same time showed a strong potential for greater market size, more liquidity and reasonable market turnover ratio (Mishra et al. 2010).

This paper attempts to investigate the static and dynamic relationship between capital market and economic growth in India. The main objective of this paper is to examine the long and short-run causal relationship among the components of capital market performance and economic growth of India. This study considers real GDP as the measure of economic growth and market capitalisation, sensex, nifty50 and the value of shares traded as measures of capital market performance, along with other macroeconomic variables like rate of inflation (WPI) and interest rate (call money rate). The macro data are collected from the Reserve Bank of India (RBI), and the daily data on stock market are collected from the Bombay Stock Exchange (BSE) and the National Stock Exchange (NSE) for seventeen years from January 2000 to December 2016 consisting of 6210 observations. In the empirical analysis, the unit root test addresses the stationarity of the time series data and the graphical representation of it is explained by the correlogram. The Vector Error Correction Model (VECM) is employed to analyse the long-run and short-run causal relationship between the capital market performance and economic growth in India during the study period.

10.2 A Brief Review of Recent Studies

Maysami et al. (2004) examine the relation among macroeconomic variables and sector stock performance in Singapore. The macroeconomic variables include interest rate, inflation, exchange rate, industrial production and money supply. The stock market indices used are the SES All-S

Equities Finance Index, SES All-S Equities Property Index and SES All-S Equities Hotel Index as well as Singapore Composite Index. The vector error correction model results show that the Singapore stock market and the SES All-S Equities Property Index have significant relationship with all macroeconomic variables identified, while the SES All-S Equities Finance Index and SES All-S Equities Hotel Index have significant relationship with only few variables.

Schneider et al. (2008) study the long-run relationship between macroeconomic variables in Germany over the period 1991Q1-2005Q4. These long-run relations are based on production, arbitrage, solvency and portfolio balance conditions, together with stock-flow and accounting identities. The underlying economic theory provides five long-run relations or equilibrium conditions among the nine variables of the macro-model. The long-run relationships are embedded in an unrestricted VECM model with nine variables. The estimated VECM model, subject to the theoretical restrictions on the long-run coefficients, identifies five long-run relationships.

Ewah et al. (2009) investigate the impact of stock market performance on economic growth in Nigeria for the time series data from 1980-2002 using market capitalisation, value of shares traded, all share index, average prime lending rate, inflation rate, national savings and gross domestic product. The Error Correction Mechanism (ECM) is employed to determine the short-run and long-run effects of stock market performance on economic growth. The OLS estimates show that the stock market has positive and significant effect on economic growth in Nigeria. It also revealed that market capitalisation has a negative but significant relationship with gross domestic product.

Kehinde et al. (2013) examine the impact of capital market on economic growth in the log-run in Nigeria using annual data from 1981 to 2010 using an ordinary least square and vector auto regression methods. The Johansen cointegration technique identifies three co-integrating equation and the vector auto regression suggest the existence of long-run relationship between stock market and real GDP.

Ozurumba and Chigbu (2013) study the direction of causality between capital market performance and economic development and the transmission mechanism between capital market performance and economic development in Nigeria. The Johansen cointegration test shows that the variables are cointegrated implying that there is a long-run equilibrium relationship between capital market and economic development in Nigeria.

The Granger causality test shows the direction of causality is from capital market to economic development. The regression results show a significant impact of capital market on economic development in Nigeria.

Wild and Lebdaoui (2014) examine the relationship between stock market development and economic growth in Morocco for the period from 2000 to 2013 on quarterly basis. The proxies for stock market development are Morocco All Shares Index (MASI), market liquidity, market capitalisation and a principal component analysis-based stock market development index. After testing for cointegration, the dynamic interactions between real GDP growth and stock market development are investigated using both vector error correction model and Granger causality techniques. The results show that there exists long-run association between stock market development and economic growth and unidirectional Granger-causalities running from MASI, traded volume and stock market index to the real GDP, but no evidence of Granger causality from market capitalisation to real GDP.

In India, Mishra et al. (2010) analyse the key market parameters such as market size, market liquidity, market turnover ratio, market volatility and market efficiency of the Indian capital market over a period from 2002 to 2009 in order to assess the performance of the two leading stock markets of India, the Bombay Stock Exchange and NSE India. Application of time series econometrics shows evidence of greater volatility and weak form inefficiency of the Indian stock market. However, the market shows strong potential for greater market size, more liquidity and reasonable market turnover ratio.

Pal and Mittal (2011) investigate the long-run relationship between the Indian capital market and key macroeconomic variables employing a quarterly time series data spanning the period from January 1995 to December 2008. The capital market variables considered are stock market indices, value of shares traded and market capitalisation and the macro variables are money stock, interest rate and inflation rates. The Error Correction Mechanism analysis shows no significant impact of gross domestic savings of India on the Indian capital market.

Makwana (2012) provides an overview on various aspects of the Indian capital market which includes concept, meaning, nature, and scope of the capital market and origin, history, development of the Indian capital market. The paper also shows the trends of Indian stock market and capital market at time of global crisis. Analysing many factors that influence Indian capital market, such as macro-economic factors, global stock market performance, foreign investments, government and politic interferences, behavior of investors, etc., the paper concludes that the future of Indian stock exchange is undoubtedly very bright.

Mohanamani and Sivagnanasithi (2014) investigate the impact of macroeconomic variables on the behavior of Indian stock market using the monthly data for the period 2006 to 2013. The macro-economic variables considered are BSE sensex, call money rate, exchange rate between Indian rupees and US dollar, foreign institutional investment, industrial productivity, money supply and whole sale price index. The analysis reveals that the Indian stock market is positively related with whole sale price index, money supply and industrial productivity. The exchange rate and inflow of foreign institutional investment are insignificant to the Indian stock market. In the Granger causality sense, whole sale price index and industrial productivity influence the stock market to a great extent.

Muhammed Juman and Irshad (2015) also presents an overview of Indian capital market, reviewing the process of growth of capital markets, their evolving structure and their functioning through stock exchanges in India. The paper also discusses the evolution of regulatory mechanism for capital markets in India. The paper reveals that during the first and second five-year plans in India the public sector undertakings were healthier than the private undertakings, but shares of these were not listed in the stock exchange and the capital markets were not well organised. With economic reforms of India, the capital markets in India are well developed, especially after the introduction of SEBI.

Jency (2017) looks into the trends in capital market in India with reference to primary markets, mutual fund industry, FII, secondary markets and derivative markets between 2011 and 2016. The major observations of the study are that the market capitalisation of BSE has increased throughout 2011-15, but decreased by 7.11 percent in 2015-16, the total resources mobilised through issuance of equity declines continuously for 3 years from 2011-12 to 2014 15 and the cumulative net assets under management by all mutual funds increased by 27 percent during 2015-16. The paper concludes that on almost all the operational and systematic risk management parameters, settlement system, disclosures, accounting standards, the Indian capital market is at par with the global standards.

10.3 Data and Methodology

The daily data on stock market performance used in this study is for seventeen years from January 1st 2000 to December 31st 2016 resulting in 6210 observations and the variables are market capitalisation, value of shares traded, sensex, nifty, real GDP, wholesale price index (WPI) and interest rates. The sources of the secondary data are the official websites of Bombay Stock Exchange (BSE) and National Stock Exchange (NSE) and the Reserve Bank of India (RBI). The stock indices are collected from the historical indices column and the other variables are collected from the RBI Handbook of Statistics published by RBI.

Vector Error Correction Model

The empirical analysis of the VECM proceeds with checking for changes over time by time plots and correlogram or autocorrelation function (ACF) plot, a summary of correlation at different periods of time. The stability or stationarity of the data series is tested by the Augmented Dicky-Fuller (ADF) unit root test. The testing equation is specified as:

$$\Delta Y_t = \alpha + \beta t + \gamma Y_{t-1} + \delta \Delta Y_{t-1} + \delta_{p-1} \Delta y_{t-p+1} + \varepsilon_t \qquad (10.1)$$

where α is a constant, β is the coefficient on a time trend and p the lag order of the autoregressive process. The unit root test is then carried out under the null hypothesis (H_0): $\gamma=0$ and alternative hypothesis (H_1): $\gamma<0$. If the test statistic is less than the critical value, then the null hypothesis of $\gamma = 0$ is rejected and no unit root is present.

To test the long-run equilibrium between non-stationary time series, the trace and maximum eigen value Johansen cointegration test is used. The trace test examines the number of linear combinations (i.e. K) to be equal to a given value (K_0), and the alternative hypothesis for K to be greater than *C*, H_0:$K = K_0$ *and* $H_1: K > K_0$. If the null hypothesis is rejected, then there is at least one cointegrating relationship. For the maximum eigen value test $H_0: K = K_0$ and $H_1: K = K_0 + 1$. Rejection of the null hypothesis implies that there is only one possible combination of the non-stationary variables to yield a stationary process. In the presence of cointegration, an error correction mechanism captures the long-run adjustment of cointegrating variables i.e. the derivation from long-run equilibrium is corrected gradually through a series of partial short-run adjustments (Engel and Granger, 1987). Causality exists in at least one direction of variables contain cointegrating vector and in this case the direction of causal relationship is detected through VECM. Apart from identifying the direction of causality, the incorporation of the error correction term in the VEC model helps to analyse the long-term relationship between the variables. The number of lags for cointegrating relations is identified by the lag length selection criteria.

The causal inferences in the multivariate framework are made by estimating the parameters of the VECM equations of different models.

In this paper, the VECM approach has provided the following seven equations:

Model 1: $\Delta lnRGDP_t = \sum_{j=1}^{\rho-1} \beta_{I1}\, \Delta lnRGDP_{t-j} + \sum_{j=1}^{\rho-1} \beta_{I2}\, \Delta lnCAP_{t-j} + \sum_{j=1}^{\rho-1} \beta_{I1}\, \Delta lnSENSEX_{t-j} + \sum_{j=1}^{\rho-1} \beta_{I1}\, \Delta lnNIFTY_{t-j} + \sum_{j=1}^{\rho-1} \beta_{I1}\, \Delta lnVST_{t-j} + \sum_{j=1}^{\rho-1} \beta_{I1}\, \Delta lnINT_{t-j} + \sum_{j=1}^{\rho-1} \beta_{I1}\, \Delta lnWPI_{t-j} + \alpha_I ECT_{t-1} + \varepsilon_t$ (10.2)

Model 2: $\Delta lnCAP_t = \sum_{j=1}^{\rho-1} \beta_{I1}\, \Delta lnRGDP_{t-j} + \sum_{j=1}^{\rho-1} \beta_{I2}\, \Delta lnCAP_{t-j} + \sum_{j=1}^{\rho-1} \beta_{I1}\, \Delta lnSENSEX_{t-j} + \sum_{j=1}^{\rho-1} \beta_{I1}\, \Delta lnNIFTY_{t-j} + \sum_{j=1}^{\rho-1} \beta_{I1}\, \Delta lnVST_{t-j} + \sum_{j=1}^{\rho-1} \beta_{I1}\, \Delta lnINT_{t-j} + \sum_{j=1}^{\rho-1} \beta_{I1}\, \Delta lnWPI_{t-j} + \alpha_I ECT_{t-1} + \varepsilon_t$ (10.3)

Model 3: $\Delta lnSENSEX_t = \sum_{j=1}^{\rho-1} \beta_{I1}\, \Delta lnRGDP_{t-j} + \sum_{j=1}^{\rho-1} \beta_{I2}\, \Delta lnCAP_{t-j} + \sum_{j=1}^{\rho-1} \beta_{I1}\, \Delta lnSENSEX_{t-j} + \sum_{j=1}^{\rho-1} \beta_{I1}\, \Delta lnNIFTY_{t-j} + \sum_{j=1}^{\rho-1} \beta_{I1}\, \Delta lnVST_{t-j} + \sum_{j=1}^{\rho-1} \beta_{I1}\, \Delta lnINT_{t-j} + \sum_{j=1}^{\rho-1} \beta_{I1}\, \Delta lnWPI_{t-j} + \alpha_I ECT_{t-1} + \varepsilon_t$ (10.4)

Model 4: $\Delta lnNIFTY_t = \sum_{j=1}^{\rho-1} \beta_{I1}\, \Delta LnRGDP_{t-j} + \sum_{j=1}^{\rho-1} \beta_{I2}\, \Delta LnCAP_{t-j} + \sum_{j=1}^{\rho-1} \beta_{I1}\, \Delta lnSENSEX_{t-j} + \sum_{j=1}^{\rho-1} \beta_{I1}\, \Delta lnNIFTY_{t-j} + \sum_{j=1}^{\rho-1} \beta_{I1}\, \Delta lnVST_{t-j} + \sum_{j=1}^{\rho-1} \beta_{I1}\, \Delta lnINT_{t-j} + \sum_{j=1}^{\rho-1} \beta_{I1}\, \Delta lnWPI_{t-j} + \alpha_I ECT_{t-1} + \varepsilon_t$ (10.5)

Model 5: $\Delta lnVST_t = \sum_{j=1}^{\rho-1} \beta_{I1}\, \Delta lnRGDP_{t-j} + \sum_{j=1}^{\rho-1} \beta_{I2}\, \Delta lnCAP_{t-j} + \sum_{j=1}^{\rho-1} \beta_{I1}\, \Delta lnSENSEX_{t-j} + \sum_{j=1}^{\rho-1} \beta_{I1}\, \Delta lnNIFTY_{t-j} + \sum_{j=1}^{\rho-1} \beta_{I1}\, \Delta lnVST_{t-j} + \sum_{j=1}^{\rho-1} \beta_{I1}\, \Delta lnINT_{t-j} + \sum_{j=1}^{\rho-1} \beta_{I1}\, \Delta lnWPI_{t-j} + \alpha_I ECT_{t-1} + \varepsilon_t$ (10.6)

Model 6: $\Delta lnINT_t = \sum_{j=1}^{\rho-1} \beta_{I1}\, \Delta lnRGDP_{t-j} + \sum_{j=1}^{\rho-1} \beta_{I2}\, \Delta lnCAP_{t-j} + \sum_{j=1}^{\rho-1} \beta_{I1}\, \Delta lnSENSEX_{t-j} + \sum_{j=1}^{\rho-1} \beta_{I1}\, \Delta lnNIFTY_{t-j} + \sum_{j=1}^{\rho-1} \beta_{I1}\, \Delta lnVST_{t-j} + \sum_{j=1}^{\rho-1} \beta_{I1}\, \Delta lnINT_{t-j} + \sum_{j=1}^{\rho-1} \beta_{I1}\, \Delta lnWPI_{t-j} + \alpha_I ECT_{t-1} + \varepsilon_t$ (10.8)

Model 7: $\Delta lnWPI_t = \sum_{j=1}^{\rho-1} \beta_{I1}\, \Delta lnRGDP_{t-j} + \sum_{j=1}^{\rho-1} \beta_{I2}\, \Delta lnCAP_{t-j} + \sum_{j=1}^{\rho-1} \beta_{I1}\, \Delta lnSENSEX_{t-j} + \sum_{j=1}^{\rho-1} \beta_{I1}\, \Delta lnNIFTY_{t-j} + \sum_{j=1}^{\rho-1} \beta_{I1}\, \Delta lnVST_{t-j} + \sum_{j=1}^{\rho-1} \beta_{I1}\, \Delta lnINT_{t-j} + \sum_{j=1}^{\rho-1} \beta_{I1}\, \Delta lnWPI_{t-j} + \alpha_I ECT_{t-1} + \varepsilon_t$ (10.9)

where Λ is the first difference operator, ε_t is white noise error term, ECT is the error correction term, ρ is the order of VECM model which is translated to lag ρ-1 in the ECM and the pace of adjustment is represented by α_1 after the variables lnRGDP, lnCAP, lnSENSEX, lnNIFTY, lnVST, lnINT, lnWPI deviate from the long-run equilibrium in period t-1.

Then, specify the coefficient diagnostics i.e. Granger causality using VEC Wald tests, residual diagnostics, i.e. serial correlation using VEC LM Test, VEC residual normality test using Jarque-Bera test, VEC residual heteroscedasticity test using ARCH test and then finally stability diagnostics using CUSUM test. The Wald chi-square test is a way to find out if explanatory variables in a model are significant. The VEC Breusch-

Godfrey LM serial correlation test is a test for autocorrelation in the errors in a regression model. The VEC Jarque-Bera test is a normality test to check the distribution of the model. The Auto Regressive Conditional Heteroskedasticity (ARCH) test is a test of volatility clustering i.e. whether the variance of the current error term is related to the size of the previous periods' error terms. The CUSUM stability test is to ensure the reliability of the coefficients of the normalised cointegration model for the long-run and vector error correction model for the short-run. The estimated model is stable if all roots have modulus less than one and lie inside the red line from the graph.

10.4 Empirical Analysis

The descriptive statistics of the variables used in the empirical analysis are presented in Table 10.1. There are 6210 observations in the daily data for the period January 1, 2000 to December 31, 2016. The Jarque-Bera test measures the difference of skewness and kurtosis of a series with those from the normal distribution. The Jarque-Bera statistic rejects the null hypothesis of non-normal distribution for all the variables since their probability values are lesser than 0.05.

Table 10.1: Descriptive Statistics of the Variables in the Stock Market Performance and Economic Growth Analysis.

Variable	*Description*	*Mean*	*Median*	*Jarque-Bera*
Real GDP	Proxy for economic growth; quarterly data converted to daily data (Rs.)	1492005 (810542.8)	1128335	825.451
Market capitalisation	Market value of outstanding shares of a company; multiplying stock price by total number of shares outstanding (Rs.).	5293647 (9932960.1)	4432596	1766285
Sensex	S&P BSE 30 index of Bombay Stock Exchange; market-weighted stock market index of 30 well-established and financially sound companies	13824.28 (8066.264)	14770.83	389.1699
Nifty50	Nifty50 of National Stock Exchange	4176.52 (2417.713)	4371.925	382.3110
VST	Total number of shares traded multiplied by their respective matching prices (Rs.)	1.29E+08 (7.4E+08)	1.23E+08	3496.774
Interest rate	Call money rate; interest rate on short-term loan that banks give to brokers who in turn lend the money to investors to fund margin accounts	6.73 (2.41)	6.82	1532672.0

(*Contd...*)

WPI	Inflation rate; Wholesale price index	108.28 (16.42)	109.42	72.14
No. of obs.		6210		

Note: Standard deviations in parentheses.

In the graphical analysis, the time series plots of all the seven variables are presented in Figure 10.1. The plots show that the variables lnRGDP, lnCAP, lnSENSEX and lnNIFTY are showing upward trend and are constantly increasing over the period. The variables lnWPI, lnVST and lnINT show seasonal elements implying that these variables are not stationary which are to be further checked for unit root before carrying the analysis.

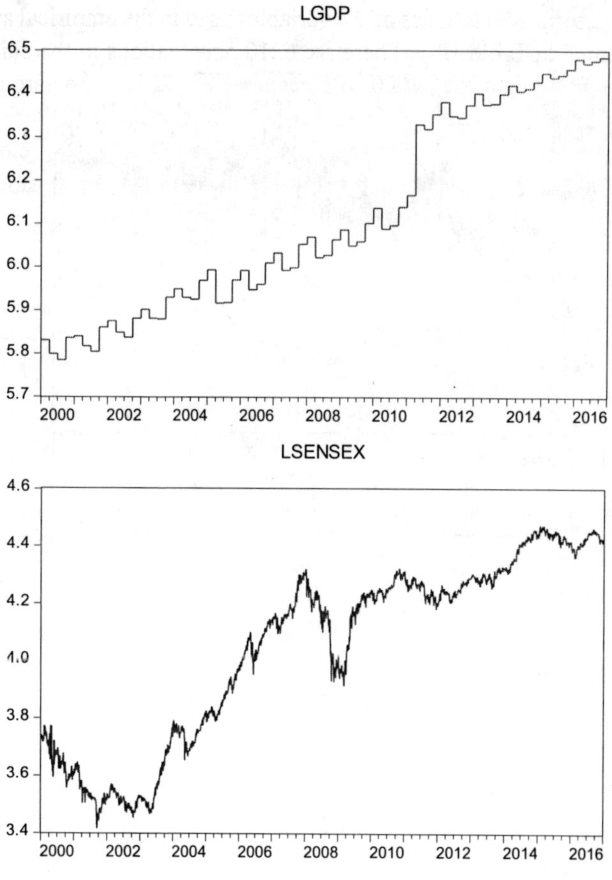

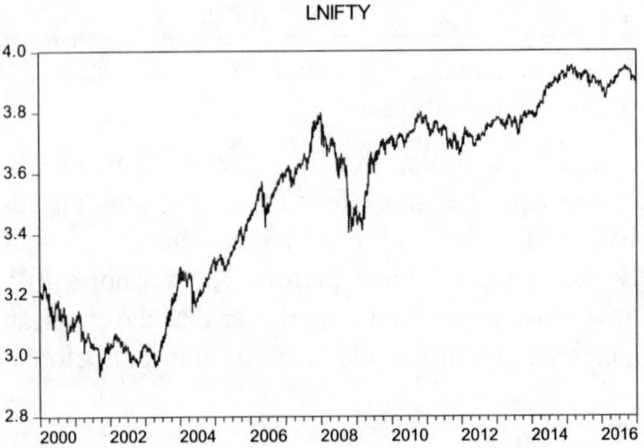
LNIFTY
4.0
3.8
3.6
3.4
3.2
3.0
2.8
2000
2002
2004
2006
2008
2010
2012
2014
2016

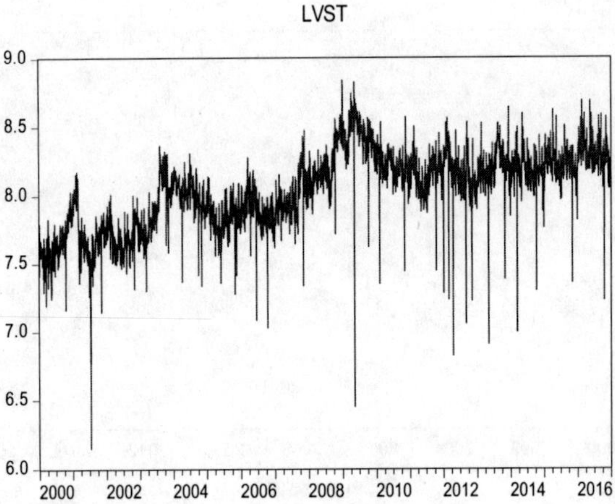
LVST
9.0
8.5
8.0
7.5
7.0
6.5
6.0
2000
2002
2004
2006
2008
2010
2012
2014
2016

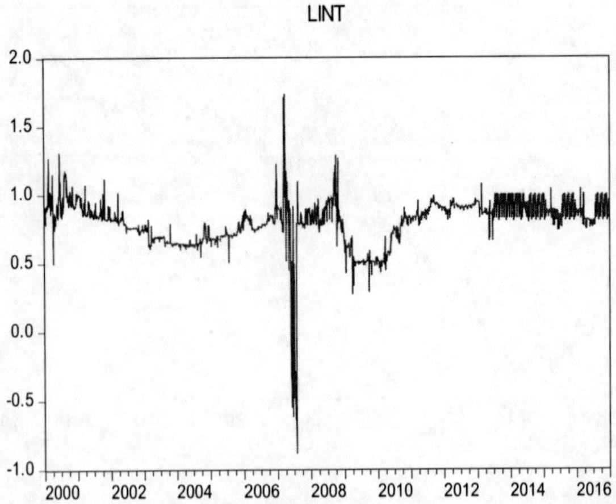
LINT
2.0
1.5
1.0
0.5
0.0
-0.5
-1.0
2000
2002
2004
2006
2008
2010
2012
2014
2016

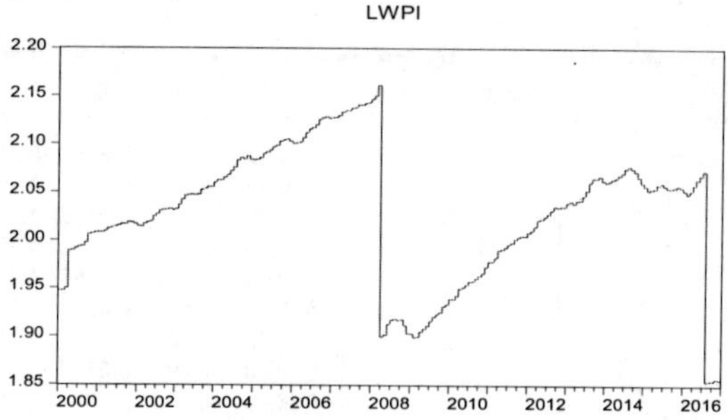

Figure 10.1: Time Series Plots of the Variables.

The correlogram or the autocorrelation plots against lag k (24 lags) for all the seven variables are presented in Figure 10.2. The dotted lines in the plots of the ACF are the approximate two standard error bounds The ACF plots enable to find quickly whether the plot follows stationarity or not. If the series contains a trend, the trend should be removed first and the first difference enables to check whether the non-stationarity is removed or not. All the variables are made stationary in its first difference, and hence all the variables are integrated of order 1 i.e. I(1). In the correlogram at level, the autocorrelation coefficients of the variables show no trend. In the correlogram of first difference, it is clear that the series have become stationary. The autocorrelation coefficients of all the seven variables at levels are very high even up to 24 lags showing typical non-stationary time-series. The correlogram for first difference of the variables show that the value of autocorrelation coefficients is 0.00 at all the lagged periods implying that the series have attained stationarity at first difference.

Autocorrelation	Partial Correlation		AC	PAC	Q-Stat	Prob
		1	1.000	1.000	6207.2	0.000
		2	0.999	-0.00...	12410.	0.000
		3	0.999	-0.00...	18607.	0.000
		4	0.998	-0.00...	24800.	0.000
		5	0.998	-0.00...	30988.	0.000
		6	0.997	0.00...	37171.	0.000
		7	0.997	-0.00...	43349.	0.000
		8	0.996	-0.00...	49523.	0.000
		9	0.996	-0.00...	55692.	0.000
		1...	0.995	-0.00...	61856.	0.000
		1...	0.995	-0.00...	68015.	0.000
		1...	0.994	-0.00...	74169.	0.000
		1...	0.994	-0.00...	80319.	0.000
		1...	0.993	-0.00...	86464.	0.000
		1...	0.993	-0.00...	92604.	0.000
		1...	0.993	-0.00...	98739.	0.000
		1...	0.992	-0.00...	10486...	0.000
		1...	0.992	-0.00...	11099...	0.000
		1...	0.991	-0.00...	11711...	0.000
		2...	0.991	-0.00...	12323...	0.000
		2...	0.990	-0.00...	12934...	0.000
		2...	0.990	-0.00...	13545...	0.000
		2...	0.989	-0.00...	14155...	0.000
		2...	0.989	-0.00...	14764...	0.000

Autocorrelation	Partial Correlation		AC	PAC	Q-Stat	Prob
		1	-0.00...	-0.00...	0.0041	0.949
		2	-0.00...	-0.00...	0.0082	0.996
		3	-0.00...	-0.00...	0.0123	1.000
		4	-0.00...	-0.00...	0.0164	1.000
		5	-0.00...	-0.00...	0.0205	1.000
		6	-0.00...	-0.00...	0.0246	1.000
		7	-0.00...	-0.00...	0.0287	1.000
		8	-0.00...	-0.00...	0.0328	1.000
		9	-0.00...	-0.00...	0.0369	1.000
		1...	-0.00...	-0.00...	0.0410	1.000
		1...	-0.00...	-0.00...	0.0451	1.000
		1...	-0.00...	-0.00...	0.0493	1.000
		1...	-0.00...	-0.00...	0.0534	1.000
		1...	-0.00...	-0.00...	0.0575	1.000
		1...	-0.00...	-0.00...	0.0616	1.000
		1...	-0.00...	-0.00...	0.0657	1.000
		1...	-0.00...	-0.00...	0.0699	1.000
		1...	-0.00...	-0.00...	0.0740	1.000
		1...	-0.00...	-0.00...	0.0781	1.000
		2...	-0.00...	-0.00...	0.0822	1.000
		2...	-0.00...	-0.00...	0.0864	1.000
		2...	-0.00...	-0.00...	0.0905	1.000
		2...	-0.00...	-0.00...	0.0947	1.000
		2...	-0.00...	-0.00...	0.0988	1.000

Figure 10.2a: ACF of lnRGDP at Level and at First Difference.

Autocorrelation	Partial Correlation		AC	PAC	Q-Stat	Prob
		1	0.999	0.999	6199.1	0.000
		2	0.998	-0.00...	12385.	0.000
		3	0.997	-0.00...	18558.	0.000
		4	0.996	-0.00...	24719.	0.000
		5	0.994	-0.00...	30866.	0.000
		6	0.993	-0.00...	37000.	0.000
		7	0.992	-0.00...	43122.	0.000
		8	0.991	-0.00...	49231.	0.000
		9	0.990	-0.00...	55327.	0.000
		1...	0.989	-0.00...	61410.	0.000
		1...	0.988	-0.00...	67480.	0.000
		1...	0.987	-0.00...	73537.	0.000
		1...	0.985	-0.00...	79582.	0.000
		1...	0.984	-0.00...	85614.	0.000
		1...	0.983	-0.00...	91633.	0.000
		1...	0.982	-0.00...	97639.	0.000
		1...	0.981	-0.00...	10363...	0.000
		1...	0.980	-0.00...	10961...	0.000
		1...	0.979	-0.00...	11558...	0.000
		2...	0.978	-0.00...	12153...	0.000
		2...	0.976	-0.00...	12747...	0.000
		2...	0.975	-0.00...	13340...	0.000
		2...	0.974	-0.00...	13932...	0.000
		2...	0.973	-0.00...	14523...	0.000

Autocorrelation	Partial Correlation		AC	PAC	Q-Stat	Prob
		1	-0.00...	-0.00...	4.E-05	0.995
		2	-0.00...	-0.00...	7.E-05	1.000
		3	-0.00...	-0.00...	0.0001	1.000
		4	-0.00...	-0.00...	0.0001	1.000
		5	-0.00...	-0.00...	0.0002	1.000
		6	-0.00...	-0.00...	0.0002	1.000
		7	-0.00...	-0.00...	0.0002	1.000
		8	-0.00...	-0.00...	0.0003	1.000
		9	-0.00...	-0.00...	0.0003	1.000
		1...	-0.00...	-0.00...	0.0004	1.000
		1...	-0.00...	-0.00...	0.0004	1.000
		1...	-0.00...	-0.00...	0.0004	1.000
		1...	-0.00...	-0.00...	0.0005	1.000
		1...	-0.00...	-0.00...	0.0005	1.000
		1...	-0.00...	-0.00...	0.0005	1.000
		1...	-0.00...	-0.00...	0.0006	1.000
		1...	-0.00...	-0.00...	0.0006	1.000
		1...	-0.00...	-0.00...	0.0006	1.000
		1...	-0.00...	-0.00...	0.0007	1.000
		2...	-0.00...	-0.00...	0.0007	1.000
		2...	-0.00...	-0.00...	0.0008	1.000
		2...	-0.00...	-0.00...	0.0008	1.000
		2...	-0.00...	-0.00...	0.0008	1.000
		2...	-0.00...	-0.00...	0.0009	1.000

Figure 10.2b: ACF of lnCAP at Level and at First Difference.

Autocorrelation	Partial Correlation		AC	PAC	Q-Stat	Prob
		1	1.000	1.000	6207.3	0.000
		2	0.999	-0.00...	12410.	0.000
		3	0.999	0.013	18608.	0.000
		4	0.998	0.007	24802.	0.000
		5	0.998	0.014	30991.	0.000
		6	0.997	0.018	37176.	0.000
		7	0.997	0.015	43357.	0.000
		8	0.997	0.009	49535.	0.000
		9	0.996	0.006	55708.	0.000
		1...	0.996	0.046	61878.	0.000
		1...	0.996	0.030	68046.	0.000
		1...	0.995	0.044	74211.	0.000
		1...	0.995	0.041	80374.	0.000
		1...	0.995	0.004	86534.	0.000
		1...	0.994	-0.00...	92693.	0.000
		1...	0.994	0.002	98850.	0.000
		1...	0.994	-0.00...	10500...	0.000
		1...	0.994	-0.00...	11115...	0.000
		1...	0.993	-0.00...	11730...	0.000
		2...	0.993	0.000	12345...	0.000
		2...	0.993	-0.00...	12959...	0.000
		2...	0.993	-0.02...	13573...	0.000
		2...	0.992	0.009	14187...	0.000
		2...	0.992	-0.00...	14801...	0.000

Autocorrelation	Partial Correlation		AC	PAC	Q-Stat	Prob
		1	0.015	0.015	1.3295	0.249
		2	-0.03...	-0.03...	7.8750	0.019
		3	-0.00...	-0.00...	8.2181	0.042
		4	-0.02...	-0.02...	12.164	0.016
		5	-0.02...	-0.02...	15.837	0.007
		6	-0.04...	-0.04...	27.276	0.000
		7	-0.00...	-0.00...	27.283	0.000
		8	-0.01...	-0.01...	28.286	0.000
		9	-0.08...	-0.08...	68.765	0.000
		1...	-0.05...	-0.05...	84.651	0.000
		1...	-0.06...	-0.07...	110.74	0.000
		1...	-0.06...	-0.07...	137.71	0.000
		1...	-0.00...	-0.01...	137.72	0.000
		1...	0.022	0.005	140.68	0.000
		1...	0.008	-0.01...	141.04	0.000
		1...	-0.00...	-0.01...	141.09	0.000
		1...	0.019	0.005	143.27	0.000
		1...	0.007	-0.00...	143.61	0.000
		1...	-0.00...	-0.01...	143.94	0.000
		2...	0.038	0.023	153.10	0.000
		2...	0.048	0.029	167.54	0.000
		2...	-0.01...	-0.02...	168.46	0.000
		2...	0.020	0.017	170.88	0.000
		2...	0.035	0.032	178.32	0.000

Figure 10.2c: ACF of lnSENSEX at Level and at First Difference.

Autocorrelation	Partial Correlation		AC	PAC	Q-Stat	Prob
		1	1.000	1.000	6207.2	0.000
		2	0.999	-0.00...	12410.	0.000
		3	0.999	0.013	18608.	0.000
		4	0.998	0.007	24801.	0.000
		5	0.998	0.016	30990.	0.000
		6	0.997	0.011	37175.	0.000
		7	0.997	0.016	43355.	0.000
		8	0.997	0.012	49532.	0.000
		9	0.996	0.009	55705.	0.000
		1...	0.996	0.027	61875.	0.000
		1...	0.995	0.033	68041.	0.000
		1...	0.995	0.039	74205.	0.000
		1...	0.995	0.026	80366.	0.000
		1...	0.995	0.009	86525.	0.000
		1...	0.994	0.004	92682.	0.000
		1...	0.994	-0.00...	98836.	0.000
		1...	0.994	-0.01...	10498...	0.000
		1...	0.993	-0.00...	11113...	0.000
		1...	0.993	-0.00...	11728...	0.000
		2...	0.993	-0.00...	12342...	0.000
		2...	0.993	-0.00...	12956...	0.000
		2...	0.992	-0.02...	13570...	0.000
		2...	0.992	-0.00...	14183...	0.000
		2...	0.991	-0.01...	14796...	0.000

Autocorrelation	Partial Correlation		AC	PAC	Q-Stat	Prob
		1	0.014	0.014	1.1934	0.275
		2	-0.03...	-0.03...	10.038	0.007
		3	-0.00...	-0.00...	10.346	0.016
		4	-0.03...	-0.03...	16.557	0.002
		5	-0.01...	-0.01...	17.939	0.003
		6	-0.04...	-0.05...	32.235	0.000
		7	-0.00...	-0.00...	32.468	0.000
		8	-0.01...	-0.02...	34.388	0.000
		9	-0.05...	-0.05...	52.270	0.000
		1...	-0.05...	-0.06...	72.834	0.000
		1...	-0.06...	-0.07...	99.652	0.000
		1...	-0.03...	-0.04...	107.18	0.000
		1...	-0.01...	-0.02...	108.05	0.000
		1...	-0.00...	-0.01...	108.06	0.000
		1...	0.016	0.000	109.75	0.000
		1...	0.016	0.002	111.43	0.000
		1...	0.011	-0.00...	112.16	0.000
		1...	0.019	0.008	114.39	0.000
		1...	-0.00...	-0.02...	114.77	0.000
		2...	0.037	0.026	123.42	0.000
		2...	0.049	0.037	138.39	0.000
		2...	0.013	0.007	139.44	0.000
		2...	0.034	0.033	146.68	0.000
		2...	0.039	0.043	156.35	0.000

Figure 10.2d: ACF of lnNIFTY at Level and at First Difference.

Autocorrelation	Partial Correlation		AC	PAC	Q-Stat	Prob
		1	0.890	0.890	4916.9	0.000
		2	0.870	0.378	9622.3	0.000
		3	0.861	0.240	14226.	0.000
		4	0.859	0.203	18815.	0.000
		5	0.858	0.164	23393.	0.000
		6	0.849	0.083	27872.	0.000
		7	0.845	0.086	32315.	0.000
		8	0.840	0.059	36704.	0.000
		9	0.838	0.060	41069.	0.000
		1...	0.840	0.086	45459.	0.000
		1...	0.836	0.051	49810.	0.000
		1...	0.835	0.054	54149.	0.000
		1...	0.834	0.055	58480.	0.000
		1...	0.831	0.036	62783.	0.000
		1...	0.832	0.052	67099.	0.000
		1...	0.828	0.018	71365.	0.000
		1...	0.825	0.018	75604.	0.000
		1...	0.824	0.030	79839.	0.000
		1...	0.825	0.038	84080.	0.000
		2...	0.824	0.029	88311.	0.000
		2...	0.820	0.013	92505.	0.000
		2...	0.820	0.026	96697.	0.000
		2...	0.818	0.018	10087...	0.000
		2...	0.818	0.025	10505...	0.000

Autocorrelation	Partial Correlation		AC	PAC	Q-Stat	Prob
		1	-0.41...	-0.41...	1057.7	0.000
		2	-0.04...	-0.25...	1069.5	0.000
		3	-0.03...	-0.21...	1078.4	0.000
		4	-0.00...	-0.17...	1078.4	0.000
		5	0.037	-0.09...	1086.9	0.000
		6	-0.02...	-0.09...	1091.6	0.000
		7	0.008	-0.06...	1092.0	0.000
		8	-0.01...	-0.06...	1093.0	0.000
		9	-0.02...	-0.09...	1096.0	0.000
		1...	0.028	-0.05...	1100.9	0.000
		1...	-0.01...	-0.05...	1101.8	0.000
		1...	-0.00...	-0.05...	1101.8	0.000
		1...	0.009	-0.03...	1102.3	0.000
		1...	-0.01...	-0.05...	1104.3	0.000
		1...	0.027	-0.02...	1108.8	0.000
		1...	-0.01...	-0.02...	1109.4	0.000
		1...	-0.00...	-0.03...	1110.0	0.000
		1...	-0.00...	-0.04...	1110.1	0.000
		1...	0.006	-0.03...	1110.3	0.000
		2...	0.013	-0.01...	1111.4	0.000
		2...	-0.01...	-0.02...	1112.9	0.000
		2...	0.006	-0.02...	1113.0	0.000
		2...	-0.00...	-0.02...	1113.3	0.000
		2...	0.010	-0.01...	1113.9	0.000

Figure 10.2e: ACF of lnVST at Level and at First Difference.

Autocorrelation	Partial Correlation		AC	PAC	Q-Stat	Prob
		1	0.959	0.959	5715.6	0.000
		2	0.921	0.009	10983.	0.000
		3	0.887	0.043	15876.	0.000
		4	0.861	0.078	20487.	0.000
		5	0.834	-0.01...	24814.	0.000
		6	0.812	0.051	28910.	0.000
		7	0.789	0.002	32784.	0.000
		8	0.774	0.089	36514.	0.000
		9	0.764	0.061	40141.	0.000
		1...	0.755	0.035	43683.	0.000
		1...	0.743	-0.00...	47118.	0.000
		1...	0.738	0.096	50510.	0.000
		1...	0.738	0.077	53898.	0.000
		1...	0.735	-0.00...	57260.	0.000
		1...	0.712	-0.21...	60420.	0.000
		1...	0.690	-0.01...	63384.	0.000
		1...	0.674	0.066	66213.	0.000
		1...	0.667	0.086	68983.	0.000
		1...	0.663	0.072	71721.	0.000
		2...	0.656	-0.02...	74404.	0.000
		2...	0.647	-0.01...	77013.	0.000
		2...	0.639	-0.01...	79560.	0.000
		2...	0.630	-0.03...	82037.	0.000
		2...	0.626	0.074	84480.	0.000

Autocorrelation	Partial Correlation		AC	PAC	Q-Stat	Prob
		1	-0.02...	-0.02...	4.9306	0.026
		2	-0.06...	-0.06...	28.741	0.000
		3	-0.09...	-0.09...	79.040	0.000
		4	0.012	0.002	79.867	0.000
		5	-0.05...	-0.06...	97.731	0.000
		6	-0.00...	-0.01...	97.806	0.000
		7	-0.09...	-0.10...	150.74	0.000
		8	-0.04...	-0.07...	165.84	0.000
		9	-0.02...	-0.04...	169.00	0.000
		1...	0.032	-0.00...	175.28	0.000
		1...	-0.08...	-0.10...	218.09	0.000
		1...	-0.05...	-0.08...	236.51	0.000
		1...	0.033	0.002	243.26	0.000
		1...	0.237	0.202	592.06	0.000
		1...	0.002	0.002	592.09	0.000
		1...	-0.08...	-0.07...	633.42	0.000
		1...	-0.10...	-0.09...	703.29	0.000
		1...	-0.04...	-0.07...	714.33	0.000
		1...	0.037	0.016	722.95	0.000
		2...	0.028	0.003	727.81	0.000
		2...	-0.01...	0.008	729.27	0.000
		2...	0.012	0.026	730.22	0.000
		2...	-0.05...	-0.08...	749.26	0.000
		2...	-0.02...	-0.06...	752.45	0.000

Figure 10.2f: ACF of lnINT at Level and at First Difference.

Autocorrelation	Partial Correlation		AC	PAC	Q-Stat	Prob
		1	0.997	0.997	6179.5	0.000
		2	0.995	-0.00...	12327.	0.000
		3	0.992	-0.00...	18441.	0.000
		4	0.989	-0.00...	24524.	0.000
		5	0.987	-0.00...	30574.	0.000
		6	0.984	-0.00...	36593.	0.000
		7	0.981	-0.00...	42579.	0.000
		8	0.978	-0.00...	48533.	0.000
		9	0.976	-0.00...	54456.	0.000
		1...	0.973	-0.00...	60347.	0.000
		1...	0.970	-0.00...	66206.	0.000
		1...	0.968	-0.00...	72033.	0.000
		1...	0.965	-0.00...	77829.	0.000
		1...	0.962	-0.00...	83594.	0.000
		1...	0.960	-0.00...	89327.	0.000
		1...	0.957	-0.00...	95029.	0.000
		1...	0.954	-0.00...	10069...	0.000
		1...	0.951	-0.00...	10633...	0.000
		1...	0.949	-0.00...	11194...	0.000
		2...	0.946	-0.00...	11752...	0.000
		2...	0.943	-0.00...	12307...	0.000
		2...	0.941	-0.00...	12858...	0.000
		2...	0.938	-0.00...	13407...	0.000
		2...	0.935	-0.00...	13952...	0.000

Autocorrelation	Partial Correlation		AC	PAC	Q-Stat	Prob
		1	-0.00...	-0.00...	8.E-07	0.999
		2	-0.00...	-0.00...	2.E-06	1.000
		3	-0.00...	-0.00...	2.E-06	1.000
		4	-0.00...	-0.00...	3.E-06	1.000
		5	-0.00...	-0.00...	4.E-06	1.000
		6	-0.00...	-0.00...	5.E-06	1.000
		7	-0.00...	-0.00...	5.E-06	1.000
		8	-0.00...	-0.00...	6.E-06	1.000
		9	-0.00...	-0.00...	7.E-06	1.000
		1...	-0.00...	-0.00...	8.E-06	1.000
		1...	-0.00...	-0.00...	9.E-06	1.000
		1...	-0.00...	-0.00...	9.E-06	1.000
		1...	-0.00...	-0.00...	1.E-05	1.000
		1...	-0.00...	-0.00...	1.E-05	1.000
		1...	-0.00...	-0.00...	1.E-05	1.000
		1...	-0.00...	-0.00...	1.E-05	1.000
		1...	-0.00...	-0.00...	1.E-05	1.000
		1...	-0.00...	-0.00...	1.E-05	1.000
		1...	-0.00...	-0.00...	1.E-05	1.000
		2...	-0.00...	-0.00...	2.E-05	1.000
		2...	-0.00...	-0.00...	2.E-05	1.000
		2...	-0.00...	-0.00...	2.E-05	1.000
		2...	-0.00...	-0.00...	2.E-05	1.000
		2...	-0.00...	-0.00...	2.E-05	1.000

Figure 10.2g: ACF of lnWPI at Level and at First Difference.

The results of the ADF test for the stationarity of the variables are presented in Table 10.2. The results show that all the variables are non-stationary in level form since their ADF values are less than the critical values except the variable lnINT which is stationary at the level and is integrated of order I(0). However, the null hypothesis of no unit root was accepted for all other variables but was rejected in first difference. Thus, all the variables are integrated of order one i.e. I(1).

Table 10.2: ADF Unit Root Test of Stationarity.

Variable	*At level*	*Prob.*	*First difference*	*Prob.*
lnRGDP	-0.1870	0.937	-78.843	0.0001
lnCAP	-1.663	0.450	-78.78	0.0001
lnSENSEX	-0.384	0.909	-30.475	0.00
lnNIFTY	-0.39	0.908	-29.45	0.00
lnVST	-3.555	0.007	-.32.253	0.00
lnINT	-4.824	0.00	-19.841	0.00
lnWPI	-2.041	0.270	-78.77	0.0001

Note: Critical values for significance at 1 percent level are 3.43 and for 5 percent level 2.86.

Since the variables are integrated of the same order, their cointegrating relationship has to be examined using the Johansen co-integration procedure. Before the Johansen test to be carried the lag length should be selected. The optimum lag length selection criteria used in the paper are the sequential modified Likelihood Ratio (LR) test, Final Prediction Error (FPE), Akaike Information Criterion (AIC), Schwarz Information Criterion (SIC) and Hannan-Quin Information Criterion (HQ). The results are presented in Table 10.3. As various criteria show different results, the AIC lag selection criterion is used. The AIC identifies the lag length of 5 and hence for the cointegration test, the lag length of 4 (5-1) is used in this paper.

Table 10.3: Lag Length Selection Criteria.

Lag	*lnLR*	*LR*	*FPE*	*AIC*	*SC*	*HQ*
0	42020.97	-	3.02e-15	-13.568	-13.561	-13.565
1	130906.2	177540.7	1.05e-27	-42.257	-42.196	-42.236
2	131261.7	709.3898	9.50e-28	-42.356	-42.242*	-42.317
3	131420.7	316.8470	9.16e-28	-42.391	-42.224	-42.334
4	131557.1	271.6003	8.91e-28	-42.420	-42.199	-42.343*
5	131645.3	175.3427	8.80e-28*	-42.433*	-42.159	-42.338
6	131678.5	65.94527	8.84e-28	-42.428	-42.106	-42.314
7	131714.5	71.29254	8.88e-28	-42.423	-42.043	-42.292
8	131764.6	99.38401*	8.88e-28	-42.424	-41.990	-42.273

The Table 10.4 presents the results of Johansen cointegration test. A necessary but not sufficient condition for cointegrating test is that each of the variables be integrated of the same order. The Johansen cointegration test uses two statistics: the trace test and the likelihood eigen value test.

Table 10.4: Johansen Cointegration Test.

Hypothesised no. of CEs	*Eigen value*	*Trace statistic*	*0.05 critical value*	*Prob.*
None *	0.02891	514.9071	125.6154	0.0001
At most 1 *	0.026129	337.0015	95.75366	0.0000
At most 2 *	0.013511	172.8732	69.81889	0.0000
At most 3 *	0.012115	88.54613	47.85613	0.0000
At most 4	0.001232	12.98823	29.79707	0.8921
At most 5	0.000820	5.344109	15.49471	0.7712
At most 6	4.15E-05	0.257535	3.841466	0.6118
Hypothesised no. of CEs	***Eigen value***	***Max-eigen statistic***	***0.05 critical value***	***Prob.***
None *	0.028291	177.9057	46.23142	0.0000
At most 1 *	0.026129	164.1282	40.07757	0.0001

(Contd...)

At most 2 *	0.013511	84.32709	33.87687	0.0000
At most 3 *	0.012115	75.55790	27.58434	0.0000
At most 4	0.001232	7.644121	21.13162	0.9241
At most 5	0.000820	5.086574	14.26460	0.7308
At most 6	4.15E-05	0.257535	3.841466	0.6118

The trace and the eigen value tests in Table 10.4 suggest that there are three cointegrating equations at 5 percent significance level among the gross domestic product, market capitalisation, sensex, nifty50, value of shares traded, interest rate and whole sale price index. Therefore, the null hypothesis that there is no co-integration among the variables is rejected. Since the long-run cointegrating relationship is found among the variables, an estimation of cointegrating vectors is employed. Since all the variables are stationary with I(1) except lnINT which is of order I(0), and there is evidence of cointegration, the Granger causality is performed in the VECM, which allows a distinction to be made between short-run and long-run causality.

The cointegrating equations include an Error Correction Term (ECT) and the residual of cointegrating equations derived is called as speed of adjustment towards long-run equilibrium. The error correction term must be significantly negative showing the long-run Granger causality; insignificance of ECT implies that there is no long-run causality from the independent variable(s) to the dependent variable. The estimated results of the VECM models are presented in Table 10.5 for the causal relationship between the variables, along with diagnostic checks of the model. The diagnostic tests are the Wald test for short-run causality, Breusch-Godfrey LM test for residual serial correlation, Jarque-Bera residual normality test and the ARCH residual heteroscedasticity test. For brevity, only the coefficient of lagged variables with their t-values and probability are indicated along with the coefficients.

Table 10.5: VECM Estimates of Stock Market Performance and Economic Growth in India.

Variable	*lnGDP*	*lnCAP*	*lnSENSEX*	*lnNIFTY*	*lnVST*	*lnINT*	*lnWPI*
ECT	-6.52E-05 (0.51	-0.0004 (0.59)	-0.0003 (1.43)	-0.0003 (1.36)	0.059 (1.56)	0.014 (8.13)	0.0002 (1.01)
D[lnGDP(-1)]	-0.0002 (0.02)	-0.016 (0.24)	0.010 (0.39)	0.015 (0.62)	0.335 (0.99)	-0.039 (0.23)	0.0001 (0.007)
D[lnGDP(-2)]	-0.001 (0.08)	-0.0008 (0.01)	-0.012 (0.46)	-0.004 (0.16)	0.334 (0.99)	0.294 (1.74)	-0.0003 (021)
D[lnCAP(-1)]	-0.0001 (0.04)	0.0003 (0.02)	0.008 (1.56)	0.008 (1.69)	0.033 (0.46)	-0.002 (0.07)	-3.13E-05 (0.01)

(Contd...)

D[lnCAP(-2)]	-4.89E-06 (0,002)	2.01E-05 (0.002)	0.004 (0.89)	0.005 (0.98)	-0.035 (0.50)	0.011 (0.35)	3.63E-05 (0.01)
D[lnSENSEX (-1)]	-0.0030 (0.18)	-0.0019 (0.02)	0.010 (0.28)	0.041 (1.28)	-0.072 (0.14)	-0.105 (0.47)	0.0004 (0.02)
D[lnSENSEX (-2)]	-0.002 (0.09)	-9.32E-06 (0.0001)	-0.031 (0.92)	-0.031 (0.98)	-0.125 (0.25)	-0.135 (0.60)	0.0004 (0.02)
D[lnNIFTY (-1)]	0.003 (0.17)	-0.0002 (0.002)	0.006 (0.17)	-0.026 (0.76)	0.420 (0.79)	0.030 (0.12)	-0.0004 (0.02)
D[lnNIFTY(-2)]	0.0012 (0.07)	9.19E-05 (0.001)	-0.002 (0.07)	-0.008 (0.23)	0.465 (0.88)	0.137 (0.57)	-0.0004 (0.02)
D[lnVST(-1)]	-9.33E-05 (0.20)	-0.0006 (0.26)	-0.0005 (0.57)	-0.0002 (0.21)	-0.434 (3.27)	0.022 (3.74)	0.0002 (0.38)
D[lnVST(-2)]	-5.30E-05 (0.12)	-0.0004 (0.16)	-0.001 (0.55)	-0.0009 (1.10)	-0.210 (1.69)	0.009 (1.74)	0.0001 (0.21)
D[lnINT(-1)]	-0.0015 (0.61)	0.0049 (0.97)	-0.002 (0.99)	-0.002 (1.04)	0.104 (3.72)	-0.020 (1.54)	0.001 (1.26)
D[lnINT(-2)]	0.0006 (0.66)	-0.0006 (0.11)	0.002 (0.85)	0.0005 (0.30)	0.061 (2.17)	-0.053 (4.17)	0.002 (1.37)
D[lnWPI(-1)]	-0.0002 (0.02)	0.0014 (0.02)	-0.013 (0.60)	-0.007 (0.37)	0.192 (0.61)	0.023 (0.16)	3.86E-05 (0.003)
D[lnWPI(-2)]	0.0001 (0,01)	-0.0004 (0.006)	0.006 (0.26)	0.004 (0.21)	0.034 (0.11)	-0.190 (1.34))	0.0004 (0.03)
Constant	0.0001 (2.24)	0.0002 (0.69)	0.0001 (1.18)	0.0001 (1.27)	-5.29E-05 (0.04)	-4.20E-05 (0.07)	-1.47E-05 (0.26)
Wald test	0.9942	1.0000	0.2651	0.1132	0.000	0.000	0.9989
Breusch-Godfrey LM test	0.6245	0.6123	0.5552	0.6341	0.000	0.000	0.1478
Jarque-Bera test	1310	1620	3307	44089.93	6739	6659	2320
ARCH test	0.9122	0.9749	0.0543	0.000	0.000	0.000	0.9791

Note: Absolute t-values in parentheses.

In Table 10.5, the estimated VECM results of lnRGDP shows that during the study period the process has converged in as the ECT is -6.52E-05 and the probability values are more than 0.05 showing that they are not significant. The Wald test does not indicate short-run causality from lnRGDP to the independent variables. The chi-square statistics accepts the null hypothesis that lnRGDP cannot affect other variables in the short-run because the corresponding p-value is not significant (0.9942). The LM test does not reject the null hypothesis that there is no serial correlation as the p-value is greater than 0.05 (0.6245). And there is no evidence of heteroscedasticity as the chi-square value is greater than 0.05 (0.9122). The model residual is normally distributed as the Jarque-Bera test value is greater than 0.05 and accepts the null hypothesis.

The estimated VECM results of lnCAP show that during the study period the process has converged in as the ECT is -0.00039 and the probability values are more than 0.05 showing that they are not significant.

The Wald test does not indicate short-run causality from lnCAP to the independent variables. The chi-square statistics accepts the null hypothesis that lnCAP cannot affect other variables in the short-run because the corresponding p-value is not significant (1.0000). The LM test does not reject the null hypothesis that there is no serial correlation as the p-value is greater than 0.05 (0.6123). And there is no evidence of heteroscedasticity as the chi-square value is greater than 0.05 (0.9749). The model residual is normally distributed as the Jarque-Bera test value is greater than 0.05 and accepts the null hypothesis.

The estimated VECM results of lnSENSEX show that during the study period the process has converged in as the ECT is -0.00364 and the probability values are more than 0.05 showing that they are not significant. The Wald test does not indicate short-run causality from lnSENSEX to the independent variables. The chi-square statistics accepts the null hypothesis that lnSENSEX cannot affect other variables in the short-run because the corresponding p-value is not significant (0.2651). The LM test does not reject the null hypothesis that there is no serial correlation as the p-value is greater than 0.05 (0.5552). And there is no evidence of heteroscedasticity as the chi-square value is greater than 0.05 (0.0543). The model residual is normally distributed as the Jarque-Bera test value is greater than 0.05 and accepts the null hypothesis.

The estimated VECM results of lnNIFTY show that during the study period the process has converged in as the ECT is -0.000327 and the probability values are more than 0.05 showing that they are not significant. The Wald test does not indicate short-run causality from lnSENSEX to the independent variables. The chi-square statistics accepts the null hypothesis that lnSENSEX cannot affect other variables in the short-run because the corresponding p-value is not significant (0.1132). The LM test does not reject the null hypothesis that there is no serial correlation as the p-value is greater than 0.05 (0.6341). And there is evidence of heteroscedasticity as the chi-square value is almost zero (0.0000). The model residual is normally distributed as the Jarque-Bera test value is greater than 0.05 and accepts the null hypothesis.

The estimated VECM results of lnVST show that during the study period the process has not converged in as the ECT is a positive 0.05863 and the probability values are more than 0.05 showing that they are not significant. The lagged variables of lnVST and lnINT are significant as the probabilities are lesser than 0.05. The Wald test does not indicate short-run causality from lnVST to the independent variables. The chi-square statistics accepts the null hypothesis that lnVST affects other variables in the short-run because the corresponding p-value is significant (0.0000). The LM test rejects the null hypothesis that there is no serial correlation as the p-value is lesser than 0.05 (0.0000). And there is evidence of heteroscedasticity as the chi-square value is almost zero (0.0000). The model residual is normally distributed as the Jarque-Bera test value is greater than 0.05 and accepts the null hypothesis.

The estimated VECM results of lnINT shows that during the study period the process has not converged in as the ECT is a positive 0.01380 and the probability values are more than 0.05 showing that they are not significant. The lagged variables of lnVST(-1) are significant as the probabilities are lesser than 0.05. The Wald test indicates short-run causality from lnINT to the independent variables. The chi-square statistics accepts the null hypothesis that lnINT affects other variables in the short-run because the corresponding p-value is significant (0.0000). The LM test rejects the null hypothesis that there is no serial correlation as the p-value is lesser than 0.05 (0.0000). And there is evidence of heteroscedasticity as the chi-square value is almost zero (0.0000). The model residual is normally distributed as the Jarque-Bera test value is greater than 0.05 and accepts the null hypothesis.

The estimated VECM results of lnWPI shows that during the study period the process has not converged in as the ECT is a positive 0.000155and the probability values are more than 0.05 showing that they are not significant. The lagged variables of lnVST(-1) are significant as the probabilities are lesser than 0.05. The Wald test does not indicate short-run causality from lnWPI to the independent variables. The chi-square statistics accepts the null hypothesis that lnWPI does not affect other variables in the short-run because the corresponding p-value is not significant (0.9989). The LM test does not reject the null hypothesis that there is no serial correlation as the p-value is greater than 0.05 (0.1478). And there is no evidence of heteroscedasticity as the chi-square value is almost zero (0.9791). The model residual is normally distributed as the Jarque-Bera test value is greater than 0.05 and accepts the null hypothesis.

The stability test presented in Figure 10.3 shows that all the models are dynamically stable as the trend lines lies within the boundaries.

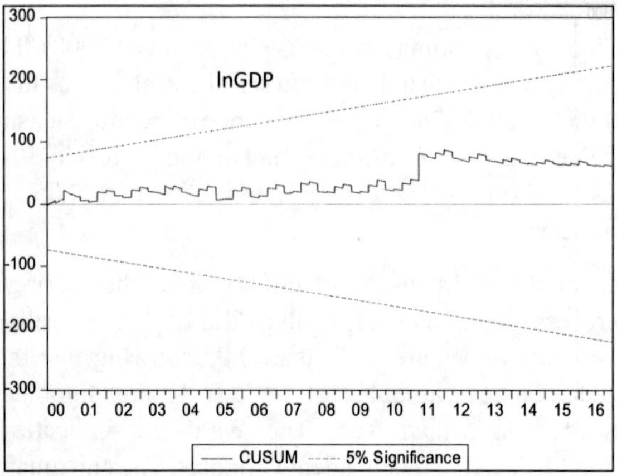
lnGDP
300
200
100
0
-100
-200
-300
00 01 02 03 04 05 06 07 08 09 10 11 12 13 14 15 16
CUSUM
5% Significance

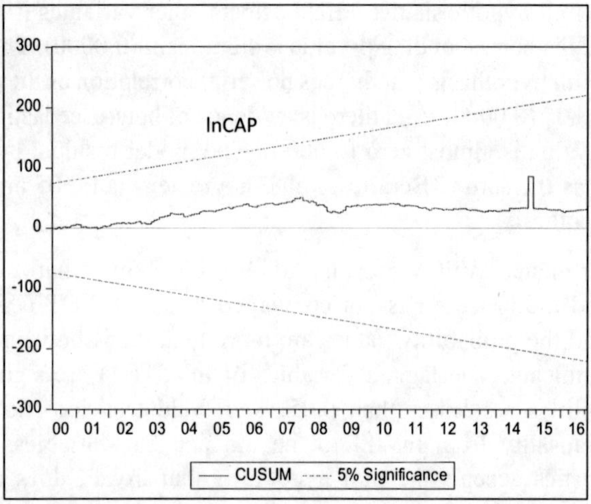
lnCAP
300
200
100
0
-100
-200
-300
00 01 02 03 04 05 06 07 08 09 10 11 12 13 14 15 16
CUSUM
5% Significance

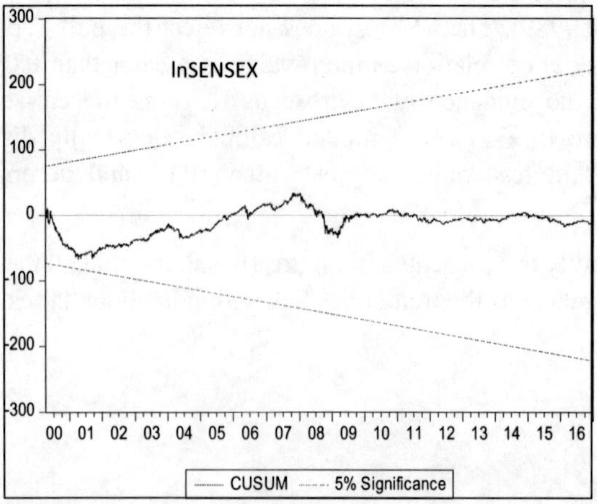
lnSENSEX
300
200
100
0
-100
-200
-300
00 01 02 03 04 05 06 07 08 09 10 11 12 13 14 15 16
CUSUM
5% Significance

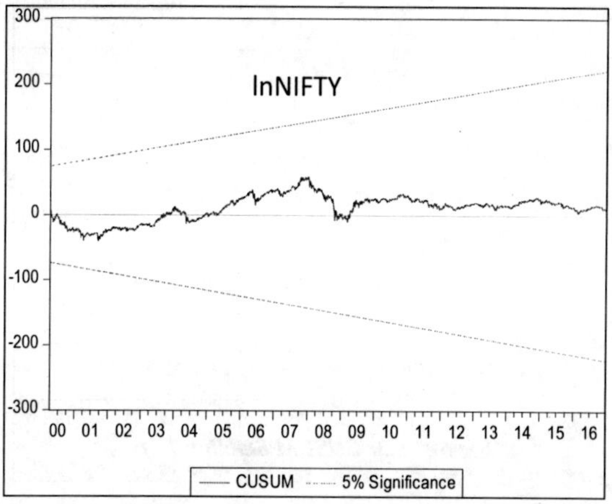
lnNIFTY
300
200
100
0
-100
-200
-300
00 01 02 03 04 05 06 07 08 09 10 11 12 13 14 15 16
CUSUM 5% Significance

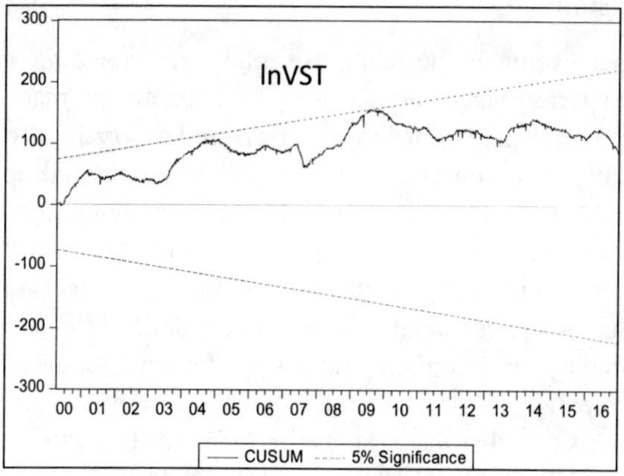
lnVST
300
200
100
0
-100
-200
-300
00 01 02 03 04 05 06 07 08 09 10 11 12 13 14 15 16
CUSUM 5% Significance

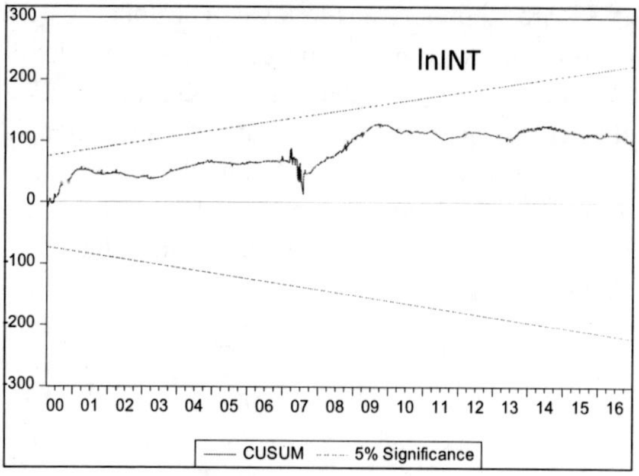
lnINT
300
200
100
0
100
200
300
00 01 02 03 04 05 06 07 08 09 10 11 12 13 14 15 16
CUSUM 5% Significance

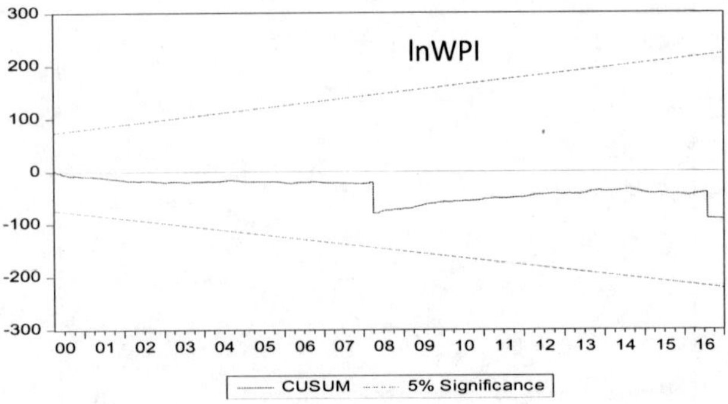

Figure 10.3: CUSUM Stability Test.

10.5 Conclusion

This paper examines the relationship between economic growth and capital market performance in India along with other major macroeconomic variables for a period of seventeen spanning from January 2000 to December 2016 with daily data consisting of 6210 observations and applying the vector error correction model (VECM). The variables considered are real gross domestic product, the measure of economic growth, and the measures of capital market performance are market capitalisation, sensex, nifty and value of shares traded. The macroeconomic variables are interest rates, measured by the call money rate, and inflation rate, measured by the wholesale price index. The ADF unit root test the graphical representation of correlogram show that the data are stationary at first difference for the variables lnRGDP, lnCAP, lnSENSEX, lnNIFTY, lnWPI, and the variables lnINT and lnVST are stationary at the level. The Johansen cointegration test results identified three cointegrating equations in the long-run. Since all the variables showed the existence of cointegration among them, the VECM model is used to analyse the long-run causality among these seven variables. Each of these variables is individually modeled as dependent variables and their relations with the rest of the variables are estimated using the VECM approach. The stability tests exhibit that the models are dynamically stable in all cases.

11

The Causality between Public Expenditure and Economic Growth: VECM Estimation of the Effect of Government Expenditure on Economic Growth

11.1 Introduction

Public expenditure plays a significant role in the functioning of an economy. The relationship between public expenditure and economic growth is obvious and has been extensively studied both theoretically and empirically. The theoretical foundation of this relationship can be traced as far back as Wagner (1883) in his famous Wagner's Law. Wagner advanced his 'law of rising public expenditures' analysing trends in the growth of public expenditure and in the size of public sector. Wagner's law postulates that: (i) the extension of the functions of the states leads to an increase in public expenditure on administration and regulation of the economy; (ii) the development of modern industrial society would give rise to increasing political pressure for social progress and call for increased allowance for social consideration in the conduct of industry; and (iii) the rise in public expenditure will be more than proportional increase in the national income and thus result in a relative expansion of the public sector. Musgrave and Musgrave (1973), in support of Wagner's law, argue that as progressive nations industrialise, the share of the public sector continue to grow in the national economy.

The role of public expenditure in the economy is now well grounded in the macroeconomic theory after the Keynesian revolution. The macroeconomic theory establishes credit for public expenditure not only in the determination of level of income but also its distribution. Keynesian macroeconomics provides a theoretical basis for the developments in public expenditure programmes in developed economies. However, empirical studies on the relationship between government expenditure and economic growth arrive at different and even conflicting results. The direction of causality between public expenditure and economic growth is not always clearly established. Whether public expenditure causes economic growth or whether economic growth necessitates more government expenditure is the moot question. Some studies suggest that increase in government expenditure on socio-economic and physical infrastructure impact long-run growth rate of the economy. For instance, government expenditure on health and education raises that productivity of labour and increase the growth of national output. Similarly, public expenditure on infrastructure such as road, power etc. reduces production costs, increase private sector investment and profitability of firms, thus ensuring economic growth (Barro, 1990; Barro and Salai-i-Martin, 1992). There is also overwhelming evidence that fast growing economies has heavily expanded their public investments. Even some studies suggest bi-directional causality between government expenditure and economic growth.

The main objective of this paper is to establish the direction of the casual relation between public expenditure and economic growth. Specifically, this paper aims to analyse whether the level of government expenditure has been properly managed to accelerate the economic growth or whether the government expenditure has been used excessively which may hurt the domestic economy because of increased taxes and/or high government borrowing. This paper assesses the relative impacts of different components of public expenditure on economic growth. Empirically, this paper examines the relationship and the direction of causality among GDP, total government expenditure, inflation and total revenue as a percentage of GDP in India. The annual time series data for 30 years during 1983 and 2013 for India from the World Bank Indicators is used in the empirical analysis. Econometrically, the Augmented Dickey-Fuller (ADF) and Philips-Perron (PP) tests for unit root, Granger causality test for the direction of causality, Johansen's cointegration test for cointegration, and Vector Error Correction Model (VECM) for testing the long and short-run relationship between the variables are employed.

11.2 A Brief Review of Recent Studies

Bagdigen and Cetintas (2004) examine the Wagner's Law of long-run relationship between public expenditure and GDP for Turkey over the period 1965-2000. The hypothesised relationship is that public expenditure is the outcome, not cause, of growth in GDP. Therefore, the causality is from GDP to public expenditure. Using cointegration and Granger causality tests, they empirically find no causality in both directions. Thus, neither Wagner's Law nor Keynes hypothesis is valid for Turkey.

Chude and Chude (2013) investigate the long and short-run effects of public expenditure in education on economic growth in Nigeria over a period from 1977 to 2012 using the error correction model. The results of the study indicate that total expenditure on education is statistically highly significant and has a positive effect on economic growth in Nigeria in the long run. Thus, it is concluded that economic growth is clearly impacted by factors both exogenous and endogenous to the public expenditure in Nigeria.

Odo et al. (2016) study the long-run causal relationship between public expenditure and economic growth in South Africa from 1980 to 2014 employing cointegration test, vector error correction mechanism and Granger causality test. The estimated results show an insignificant negative relationship between total government expenditure and economic growth, a significant positive relationship between economic growth and total revenue, and significant positive relationship between inflation and economic growth. The pair-wise Granger causality shows a one way causality running from national income to total government expenditure that seems to support the Wagner's theory. Thus, the study concludes that a stable long-run relationship exists between public expenditure and economic growth in South Africa and that the growth in national income leads to increase in government expenditure as implied by Wagner's hypothesis in South Africa.

In India, Gangal and Gupta (2013) analyse the impact of public expenditure on economic growth between 1998 and 2012 using the annual data of total public expenditure and GDP per capita from World Economic Outlook and IMF. The study employs the ADF unit root, cointegration, and Granger causality tests. The econometric results reveal that there is a positive impact of total public expenditure on economic growth and there is a unidirectional relationship, from total public expenditure to GDP in India.

Lhoungu et al. (2016) study the causal relationship between public expenditure and economic growth in India for 30 years from 1980-81 to 2009-10 employing the Granger causality, ADF and cointegration tests as well as the ECM model. Empirically, the causality from GSDP to public expenditure is shown to be weak while the causality from public expenditure to GSDP is strong. The ECM also reveals that there is strong bi-directional causality only between growth (GSDP) and public expenditure on social services in the long-run.

11.3 Data and Methodology

In the empirical analysis, this paper uses annual time series data for 30 years from 1983-2013 from World Bank Indicators (WBI) for India. The variables are GDP, total government expenditure, inflation and total revenue as a percentage of GDP expressed in 2010 US$. The GDP is measured in constant price, general government final consumption expenditure includes all government current expenditures for purchases of goods and services including national defense and security, inflation is measured by the consumer price index that reflects the annual percentage change in the cost to the average consumer of acquiring a basket of goods and services, and the revenue is measured by the cash receipts from taxes, social contributions, and other revenues such as fines, fees, rent, and income from property or sales. The econometric tests and models used in the analysis include unit root test, Johansen cointegration test, Granger causality test and VEC model. The Johansen's (1988) cointegration approach and VECM have employed in this paper to investigate the casual relationship between public expenditure and economic growth in India. Before this, the stationarity of the time series and the co-relationship between the two series need to be checked.

Unit Root Test: The unit root test is to test the stationarity of the time series. There are two ways to test for stationarity using unit root test in the time series: the ADF and PP unit root tests.

Augmented Dickey-Fuller Test: A variable is said to be stationary if it has time-invariant mean, time-invariant variance and the value of the covariance between the two time periods depends only on the distance or gap or lag between the two time periods and not the actual time at which the covariance is computed. The regression to be estimated for the application of ADF test is:

$$\Delta y_t = \beta_1 + \beta_2 t + \delta y_{t-1} + \sum_{i=1}^{n} \alpha_i \Delta y_{t-i} + u_t \tag{11.1}$$

where y_t is the stationary series, Δy indicates the first difference of y_t, β_2 is trend of time and u_t is the error term. The null hypothesis is that the series has a unit root ($\delta = 0$) meaning that the series is non-stationary against the alternative hypothesis of the series being stationary. If a unit root (non-stationarity) exists, then δ would not be statistically different from zero. If the p-value of the coefficient of y_{t-1} is less than 0.05 at 5 percent level of significance, the null hypothesis is rejected indicating that the series is stationary.

Phillips-Perron Test: The Phillips-Perron (PP) unit root tests differ from the ADF tests mainly in how they deal with serial correlation and heteroskedasticity in the errors.

Cointegration Test: If two time series data are non-stationary, there is a possibility that there exists a linear combination of the two variables, such that the error term is stationary. The two variables are said to be cointegrated if they have a long term or equilibrium relationship between them. Therefore, the cointegration between the variables is to be tested using the eigen value and trace statistic:

Trace statistic: $Trace = -T\sum_{t=r+1,.....,\lambda_p^1}\sum Log(1-\lambda_t^1)$ (11.2)

where $\lambda_{r+1}^1, \ldots \ldots, \lambda_p^1$ are (p-r) number of estimated eigen values.

Maximum eigen value statistic: $\lambda_{max}(r, r+1) = -TLog(1-\lambda_{r+1}^1)$ (11.3)

H_0: No cointegration (r=0) and H_1: presence of cointegration (r>0)

where 'r' implies cointegrating relation. If the absolute value of the computed trace and computed eigen value statistics are greater than their respective critical values, then the null hypothesis is rejected at 5 percent level of significance concluding that there exists at least one cointegrating relation between the variables. Then, the test for cointegration is:

H_0: presence of one cointegrating relation (r=1)

H_1: presence of more than one cointegrating relation among the variables (r>1).

Based on the value of the computed trace statistic and the eigen value, null hypothesis is either accepted or rejected.

If the both the time series are cointegrated, then the direction of causality between them needs to be tested. The existence of a relationship between the variables does not show the direction of influence. The causal relationship between them may be short-run or long-run. The short-run causality is established by the analysis of the joint significance of the lagged explanatory variable and movements of the deviations from the long-run path are explained by long-run causality.

Granger Causality Test: The Granger causality approach allows determining the direction of the short-run relations between the variables. This model is expressed in two equations as:

$$y_t = \alpha_0 + \sum_{i=1}^{n}\alpha_i\, y_{t-1} + \sum_{j=1}^{n}\beta_j\, x_{t-1} + u_{1t} \quad (11.4)$$

$$x_t = \mu_o + \sum_{i=1}^{n} \alpha_i \, y_{t-1} + \sum_{j=1}^{n} \delta_j \, x_{t-1} + u_{2t} \qquad (11.5)$$

The null hypothesis is that one variable does not Granger cause the other against the alternative hypothesis which states that the variable Granger causes the other. The coefficients are jointly tested for their significance. If their p-value exceeds 0.05 at 5 percent level of significance, the null hypothesis is rejected indicating causality between the two variables and no causality otherwise.

Vector Error Correction Model: Causality exists in at least one direction if the variables contain cointegrating vector and the direction of a causal relationship is detected through vector error correction model (VECM). Engel and Granger (1987) show that in the presence of cointegration, there always exist a subsequent error correction representation, captured by the error-correction term which captures the long-run adjustment of cointegration variables. The VEC has cointegration relations built into specification so that it restricts the long-run behavior of the endogenous variables to converge to their cointegrating relationships while allowing for short-run adjustment dynamics. The cointegrating term is the Error Correction Mechanism (ECM) since the deviation from long-run equilibrium is corrected gradually through a series of partial short-run adjustments. The error correction term needs to be significant at 0.05 level for long-run causality, otherwise there is no long-run causality from the independent variable(s) to the dependent variable. Apart from identifying the direction of causality, the incorporation of the error correction term in the VECM model helps to analyse the long-term relationship between the variables. The error correction model is specified as:

$$\Delta lnRGDP_t = \sum_{j=1}^{p-1} \beta_1 \, \Delta lnRGDP_{t-j} + \sum_{j=1}^{p-1} \beta_2 \, \Delta lnGEXP_{t-1} + \sum_{j=1}^{p-1} \beta_3 \Delta lnREV_{t-1} + \sum_{j=1}^{p-1} \beta_4 \Delta lnINF_{t-1} + \alpha_1 ECT_{t-1} + u_t \qquad (11.6)$$

where the first difference operator is represented as Δ and u_t is the white noise error term and j is the lag length. The error correction term is denoted by ECT and the order of the VECM model is presented by p which is translated to p-1 in the ECM. The term α_1 represents the pace of adjustment after the lnRGDP, lnGEXP, lnREV and lnINF deviate from the long-run equilibrium in period t-1.

11.4 Empirical Analysis

In the empirical analysis, the econometric model to be estimated is specified as:

$$\text{lnRGDP}_t = \beta_0 + \beta_1 \text{lnGEXP}_{t-1} + \beta_2 \text{lnREV}_{t-1} + \beta_3 \text{lnINF}_{t-1} + u_t \qquad (11.7)$$

where RGDP represents real gross domestic product, GEXP is the total government expenditure, REV refers to total revenue as percentage of gross domestic product, INF refers to inflation, and u_t is the error term and $\alpha_0 \ldots \alpha_3$ are the parameters. The Table 11.1 presents the descriptive statistics of variables to analyse the causal relationship between public expenditure and economic growth in India. All variables are expressed in US$ at current prices during the period 1983 to 2013. The GDP averages US$ 27.333 and varies between 26.491 and 28.315 USD with a standard deviation of 0.560. INF averages 1.996 and ranges from 1.182 to 2.630; GEXP averages 25.191 USD and varies from 24.304 to 26.0186 USD. The mean of REV is USD 2.518 and its variation is from 2.410 to 2.683.

Table 11.1: Descriptive Statistics of Variables in the Public Expenditure and Economic Growth Analysis.

	ln(RGDP)	*ln(INF)*	*ln(GEXP)*	*ln(REV)*
Mean	27.333	1.996	25.191	2.518
Median	27.289	2.167	25.229	2.518
Maximum	28.315	2.623	26.018	2.683
Minimum	26.491	1.183	24.304	2.411
Std. Dev.	0.560	0.432	0.5141	0.065

The Table 11.2 reports the results of the Augmented Dickey-Fuller test (ADF) and Phillips-Perron (PP) unit root tests on the natural logarithms of the levels and first differenced forms of the variables. The guideline for testing the significance of the variable is that the t-statistic reported by the test should be less than the critical value at 5 percent and the corresponding probability (*p*) values should be greater than 0.05 (or 5 percent). If the p-value is less than 0.05 then the null hypothesis is rejected and the alternative hypothesis is accepted.

Table 11.2: ADF and Phillips-Perron Unit Root Tests of Stationarity.

Variable	*ADF test*		*PP test*	
	At level	*At first difference*	*At level*	*At first difference*
ln(RGDP)	2.149	-4.435*	4.204	-4.412*
ln(INF)	-3.132*	-6.928*	-3.132*	-11.88*
ln(GEXP)	0.726	4.511*	-0.674	-2.983*
ln(REV)	-3.600*	-7.345*	-3.660*	-7.345*
Order of integration	I(1)		I(1)	

The Johansen cointegration test results are presented in Table 11.3. The trace and maximum eigen statistics for the variables ln(RGDP) ln(REV), ln(GEX) and ln(INF) show that there are two statistically significant cointegrating vectors. In other words, the trace test indicates one cointegrating equation at the 0.05 level of significance and the max-eigen value test also indicates one cointegrating equation.

Table 11.3: Johansen Cointegration Test.

Hypothesised no. of CE(s)	*Trace test*			*Maximum eigen value*		
	Eigen value	*Trace statistic*	*Critical value*	*Eigen value*	*Max-Eigen statistic*	*Critical value*
None*	0.847	97.648	47.856	0.847	48.838	27.584
At most 1	0.464	31.811	29.797	0.464	17.672	16.132
At most 2	0.396	13.138	15.495	0.396	6.121	8.265
At most 3	0.0006	0.0170	3.841	0.0006	0.017	3.841
	Trace test indicates 1 cointegrating equation(s) at the 0.05 level			Max-eigen value test indicates 1 cointegrating equation(s) at the 0.05 level		
	*denotes rejection of the hypothesis at the 0.05 level			* denotes rejection of the hypothesis at the 0.05 level		

The result of the error correction model from normalised cointegration equation presented in Table 11.4 indicates a long-run significant positive relationship between total revenue as percentage of GDP and economic growth showing as expected that increase in government revenue leads to increase in the growth of the economy.

Table 11.4: ECM Estimates of Normalised Cointegration Equation.

lnRGDP	*lnGEXP*	*lnREV*	*lnINF*
1.000000	-0.841406	7.18E+09	2.85E+09

The Table 11.5 presents VECM estimation for lnGDP=f (lnREV, lnGEXP, lnINF). The Johansen cointegration test reveals 2 cointegrating equations for lnGDP, lnREV, lnGEXP, lnINF, which has been specified while estimating vector error correction model. The coefficient of ECM (-1) is -0.0029 and its p-value of 0.030 is less than the 5 percent (0.05) level of significance. If there is a long-term relationship between two or more variables, Granger causality test is applied to detect the direction of the casual relationship (unidirectional or bi-directional). The null hypothesis is β_i=0, under the null hypothesis x does not Granger-cause y; if the null hypothesis is rejected, it can be said that x Granger cause y. Similarly, whether y Granger cause x can be tested. However, Granger test is sensitive to lag selection, and hence four lag lengths are selected considering the length of the time series.

Table 11.5: Vector Error Correction Model Estimates of Economic Growth in India.

Error Correction	*Coefficient*	*Std. error*	*t-statistics*	*p-value*
ECT(-1)	-0.002903	0.001251	-2.320264	0.0300
D(lnRGDP(-1)) = C(2)	0.093701	0.483703	0.193716	0.8482
D (lnGEXP (-1)) = C(4)	0.105203	0.285151	0.368936	0.7157
D (lnREV(-1)) = C(6)	4.97E+08	7.16E+09	0.069428	0.9453
D (lnINF (-1)) = C(8)	-6.85E=09	3.78E+09	-1.813052	0.0835
C = C(10)	4.62E+10	1.87E+10	2.475108	0.0215
Adj. R-square	0.618715	F-statistics		3.226

The Table 11.6 presents the results of the pair-wise Granger causality tests. The p-values are greater than 0.05 and thus the null hypothesis that there is no causality between the variables for various lag lengths cannot be rejected. The pair-wise granger causality test of the variables indicates one way causality moving from gross domestic product to total government expenditure. The causality from gross domestic product to government revenue also exists showing that the growth of the economy leads to increase in government revenue. Further, causality from inflation to gross domestic product is there showing that inflation can lead to the growth of the economy in both long and short runs.

Table 11.6: Pair-wise Granger Causality Test.

Null hypothesis	*F-statistic*	*Prob.*
GEXP does not Granger cause RGDP	2.98817	0.0666
RGDP does not Granger cause GEXP	5.45824	0.0100
REV does not Granger cause RGDP	0.22833	0.7973
RGDP does not Granger cause REV	5.67526	0.0085
INF does not Granger cause RGDP	10.0500	0.0005
RGDP does not Granger cause INF	2.53160	0.0976
REV does not Granger cause GEXP	0.01076	0.9893
GEXP does not Granger cause REV	5.91778	0.0072
INF does not Granger cause GEXP	5.40372	0.0104
GEXP does not Granger cause INF	1.17228	0.3244
INF does not Granger cause REV	6.28792	0.0056
REV does not Granger cause INF	4.00496	0.0295
No. of observations	30	

11.5 Conclusion

The main objectives of the paper are to examine the casual relationship among GDP, total government expenditure, inflation and total revenue as a percentage of GDP in India. The paper uses annual time series data for 30 years from 1983 to2013 collected from the World Bank and applies econometric methods of Augmented Dickey-Fuller (ADF) and Philips-Perron (PP) tests for unit root, Granger causality test for the direction of causality, Johansen's cointegration test for cointegration, and Vector Error Correction Model (VECM) for testing the long and short-run relationship between the variables. The unit root tests show that the variables are stationary after first difference and Johansen cointegration test reveals one cointegrating vector suggesting that there exists stable long-run equilibrium relationship between public expenditure and covariates. The direction of causality is detected using the Granger causality test. The vector error correction models also used to analyse the long run relationship in the economy. The error correction coefficient is negative and statistically significant indicating that the speed of adjustment between the short-run dynamics and the long-run equilibrium is about 0.03 percent. The pair-wise Granger causality test indicates one way causality moving from gross domestic product to total government expenditure and from gross domestic product to government revenue showing that the growth of the economy leads to increase in both government revenue and expenditure. Thus, the results of this paper show a stable long-run relationship between public expenditure and economic growth in India.

12

The Causality between Money Supply, Inflation and Economic Growth: VECM Estimation of the Effect of Broad Money and Price Level on Economic Growth

12.1 Introduction

Economic growth, money supply and inflation are important macroeconomic parameters that play crucial role in an economy. An understanding of the nexus between the macroeconomic variables is important for to the policymaking in ensuring effective macroeconomic stabilisation policies. Over the past few decades, policy makers have become more aware of the socioeconomic costs of inflation, and thus, more concerned with the price level stability. Price stability is desirable because a rise in price level creates uncertainty in the economy and lowers economic growth (Fischer, 1993). However, the nature of the causal relationship between money supply and inflation is still an unsettled issue. In the macroeconomics literature, the classical economics says that an increase in money supply does not influence real output, but there will be proportionate increase in prices. Among the Keynesian and Monetarists schools, one of the most debated issues is the casual relationship between money supply, price level and GDP growth rate (Rami, 2010). The Monetarists claim that money plays an important role in the economy and that the stock of money supply leads to changes in nominal income and prices. An increase in money supply will affect output changes in the short-run whereas only in the long-.run prices will increase proportionately The Keynesians, on the other hand, maintain that money supply does not play any active role in changing the income and prices. Instead, the GDP and price changes are mainly caused by changes aggregate demand and aggregate supply.

Numerous studies have been carried out to ascertain the impact of money supply on economic growth and inflation in developing and developed countries with mixed and varying results. Some empirical studies examine the causal relationship between money supply, GDP and prices in India (Rangarajan and Arif, 1990; Das, 2003; Rami, 2010). Das (2003) finds that money has a positive effect on price and there is a feedback between money and price and also between output and price in India.

The available few Indian empirical studies on the relationship between money supply, inflation and growth use short periods and weak empirical methods and are outdated. Therefore, this paper aims to provide an updated empirical evidence on the nature of causal relationship between growth rate, price level and money supply using the latest data and more rigorous empirical methodology. The main objectives of this paper are to examine the causal relationship among output (GDP) and broad money (M_3) and consumer price index (CPI) in India and to analyse the long-run relationship between GDP, CPI and M_3) in India. This paper covers a long period, 56 years from 1960 to 2016 for India. The annual data on the variables are collected from the RBI and World Bank databases. Empirically, this paper applies the causality test, cointegration test, and vector error correction mechanism (VECM) techniques.

12.2 A Brief Review of Recent Studies

Apart from theoretical literature, a lot of empirical work has been done by the researchers on the association among these macroeconomic variables in India. Monetary economics focuses on the behavior of prices, monetary aggregates, interest rates, and output. Classical economists say that an increase in money supply does not influence output and there will be proportionate increase in prices while monetarists were of the view that an increase in the money supply will effect the output in the short run whereas in the long run only prices will increase proportionately. The empirical literature broadly shows causal relationship among GDP, inflation and money supply in many countries and also in India.

Malik and Khawaja (2006) investigate the causality of inflation, output gap and real money in Pakistan for the period 1975-2003 using the Near-VAR approach. The Granger causality test is applied to test the direction of causality between inflation, and reserve money and real GDP. It is observed that inflation is caused by reserve money and inflation responds positively to monetary shocks whereas reserve money is caused neither by output gap nor by inflation. Similarly, reserve money does not cause output gap. The results show that effect of monetary policy transmits into inflation with a lag of half a year and another year to reach to the peak. The reserve money does not respond to lagged values of both inflation and output gap. The paper therefore argues that in deciding the stock of money each year, the central bank need not consider the past state of the economy.

Ahmed and Suliman (2011) examine the long-run relationships among real GDP, money supply and price level for Sudan using annual data over the period 1960 to 2005 employing the unit root test, cointegration test and Granger causality test. The unit root test results indicate that GDP and CPI are trend-stationary. The Granger causality test shows that there is unidirectional causation between money and prices in Sudan, the direction running from money supply from money supply to price. There is no reverse causation from price movements to money supply and also from prices to national income. The study also observes no causation between real GDP and money supply.

Hussain (2014) aims to assess the relative effectiveness of monetary and fiscal policy on aggregate output in the five SAARC countries (Bangladesh, India, Nepal, Pakistan and Sri Lanka). The standard unrestricted VAR model over the period of 1974-2007 to examine the relationship between fiscal-monetary policies and output. The results reveal that money supply, government expenditure, the real exchange rate and foreign interest rate are cointegrated in all the countries. The findings of the study show that the effectiveness of fiscal and monetary policy differs from country to country, depending upon the nature and the structure of the institutional factors in each country.

In India, Rangarajan and Arif (1990) examine the relationship between money supply, output and prices covering the period of 1961-62 to 1984-85, focusing on the determination of money supply and its link with fiscal operations. The study observes that an increase in credit leads to monetary expansion which gives rise to inflationary tendencies and this inflationary impact of monetary expansion is neutralised by additional output via transmission mechanism with partial adjustment over time.

Das (2003) study the nature of the relationship between price, money supply and output in India, using the annual data for the years 1992-2000 and employing the time series models of Vector Auto Regression (VAR) and Vector Auto Regression moving average (VARMA) model. The VARMA model is also used to determine the nature of causality i.e. unidirectional or bidirectional relationship. The cointegration test suggests that money, price and output are not cointegrated i.e. no long-run relationship among these three variables for the period under consideration, a result that is against the general belief of the existence of long-run equilibrium relationship. The analysis suggests that money has a positive causal effect on price and price has a causal effect on money, while both money and price affect output. There is also feedback between money and price and also between output and price.

Rami (2010) analyse the causality among narrow money (M_1) and broad money (M_3), price level (WPI) and output (GDP at factor cost) in India over the period covering 1951-2005 using the Granger causality test. The pairwise Granger causality test shows that money supply does not Granger cause WPI, WPI does not Granger cause money supply, money supply does not Granger cause output (GDP) and output (GDP) does not Granger cause money supply. The study observes that monetary policy, especially with regard to money supply, has limited implication for controlling inflation, and in fact, increasing money supply in India is due to the increase in the rate of inflation in India. Hence, money supply affects both output and inflation.

12.3 Data and Methodology

As the main objective of this paper is to understand the nature of long-run causal relationship among output, money supply and inflation in India, the a long period, 56 years from 1960 to 2016The annual time series data have been collected from the Reserve Bank of India and World Bank Indicators websites on the variables considered are GDP, broad money (M3) and Consumer Price Index (CPI).

When using the OLS estimation with such a long time series data, the problem of spurious regression between totally unrelated variables occurs due to the non-stationary process. Further, if the variables are cointegrated, there will be some linear combination of variables in the model. Therefore, the series has to be tested for stationarity and cointegration. The Augmented Dickey-Fuller (ADF) test examines the stationarity of the time series for unit root. If all the variables are stationary at the first difference I(1), then the long-run relationship is tested using the Johansen cointegration test and then estimated by the Vector Error Correction Mechanmism (VECM). The direction of causality between the variables is tested by the Granger causality test. The variance decomposition method is used to evaluate the proportion of forecast error variance.

Augmented Dickey-Fuller (ADF) Test: The ADF test for stationarity of the variables takes the following forms:

With constant term: $\Delta y_t = \beta_0 + \alpha y_{t-1} + \sum_{i=1}^{n} y_{t-i} + u_t$ (12.1)

With constant and trend: $\Delta y_t = \beta_0 + \beta_1 t + \alpha y_{t-1} + \sum_{i=1}^{n} y_{t-i} + u_t$ (12.2)

With no constant and trend: $\Delta y_t = \alpha y_{t-1} + \sum_{i=1}^{n} y_{t-i} + u_t$ (12.3)

The null hypothesis and alternative hypothesis of the ADF test are: H_0: α=1 and H_1: α< 1. The null hypothesis states the presence of unit root that is, the series is non-stationary against the alternative hypothesis that the series is stationary. If the p-value is less than 0.05 at 5 percent levels of significance, the null hypothesis is rejected indicating that the series is stationary.

Cointegration Test: The time series that must be differenced in order to render them stationary are referred to as integrated or stochastically trending series. Typically, linear combination of integrated process is also integrated. The residual from a regression of the two variables will be stationary. However, if a group of integrated variables share a common stochastic trend the linear combination will be non-integrated. The phenomenon of the elimination of a stochastic trend by an appropriate linear function is known as cointegration. Engle and Granger (1987) introduced the notion of cointegration and tied it closely to the VAR model. Johansen (1988) developed a cointegration test of VAR approach based on the of maximum likelihood method. If the test indicates that the variables are cointegrated, Vector Error Correction Mechanism (VECM) is done to obtain the rate of adjustment by the variables in the short run to achieve equilibrium in the long run. However, if the variables are not cointegrated, Vector Auto Regressive (VAR) model is used to capture the contemporaneous affect among the variables.

According to the Johansen cointegration test, a p-dimensional VAR model, involving k-lags, can be specific as:

$$z_t = \pi_1 z_{t-1} + \cdots + \pi_k z_{t-k} + \varepsilon_t \quad (12.4)$$

where z_t is (p x1) vector of p potential endogenous variables and each of π_t (pxp) is a matrix of parameters and ε_t is the white noise term. The equation (12.4) can be formed in an error correction model (ECM) form:

$$\Delta z_t = \pi_1 z_{t-k} + \sum_{i=1}^{k-1} \gamma_i z_{t-i} + \varepsilon_t \quad (12.5)$$

where Δ is the first difference operator, π and γ are (pxp) matrices of unknown parameters and k is the order of the VAR translated into a log of k-1 in the ECM and ε_t is the white noise term. Johansen and Juselius (1990) show that the rank of r of π is equal to the no of cointegrating vectors in the system. When the rank of π is reduced, even if all the variables are individually I(1), the level based long-run component would be stationary. In this case, there are (p-1) cointegrating vectors and vector error correction model (VECM) methodology is to be used.

Johansen and Juselius (1990) have developed two likelihood ratio tests. The likelihood ratio test based on the trace test tests the null hypothesis of 'r' cointegrating vector(s) against the alternative hypothesis of more than 'r' cointegrating vectors. The Trace statistic is specified as:

$$\text{Trace statistic: } \lambda_{Trace\,(r)} = -T\sum_{i=r+1}^{k} \ln[1-\lambda] \quad (12.6)$$

$$\text{Maximum eigen value statistic: } \lambda_{max}\,(r, r+1) = -Tln(1-\lambda) \quad (12.7)$$

H_0: No cointegration(r=0) and H_1: presence of cointegration(r>0)

where $\lambda^1_{r+1}, \ldots, \lambda^1_k$ are (k-r) number of estimated eigen values. The null hypothesis is that there is no cointegration against the alternative hypothesis of cointegration between the variables.

Granger Causality Test: If the two variables are I(1) and cointegrated, the Granger causality test is applied in the framework of the error correction mechanism (ECM). The Granger causality is based on the concept of causal ordering and is in the prediction sense rather than in a structural sense. As Granger (1969) puts it, "the future cannot cause the past"; if event y occurs after event x, then y cannot Granger cause x. The two variables may be contemporaneously correlated by chance but is unlikely that the past values of x will be useful in predicting y, given all the past values of y, unless x does actually cause y. A variable x is said to Granger cause another variable y if past values of x help predict the current level of y given all other appropriate information. Similarly, if y in fact causes x, then given the past history of y, it is unlikely that information on x will help predict y. The Granger causality test requires estimating the following pair of regression equations:

$$y_t = \sum_{i=1}^{p} \beta_{1i} x_{t-i} + \sum_{j=1}^{p} \beta_{2p+j} y_{t-j} + \varepsilon_{1t} \quad (12.8)$$

$$x_t = \sum_{i=1}^{p} \gamma_{1i} x_{t-i} + \sum_{j=1}^{p} \gamma_{2p+j} y_{t-j} + \varepsilon_{2t} \quad (12.9)$$

where p is the number of lags that adequately models the dynamic and the error terms are white noise. The error terms may, however, be correlated across equations. If the p parameters β_{2p+j} are jointly significant, then the null that x does not Granger cause y can be rejected. Similarly, if the parameters β_{1i} are jointly significant then the null that y does not Granger cause x can be rejected.

If the sets of x and y coefficients are not statistically significant in both the regressions, then the test suggests independence of the variables.

Conversely, unidirectional causality from x to y is indicated if the estimated coefficients on the lagged x are statistically different from zero as a group i.e. $\Sigma\beta_{1i} \neq 0$) and the set of estimated coefficients on the lagged y is not statistically different from zero i.e. $\Sigma\beta_{2j+p} = 0$. On the other hand, unidirectional causality from y to x exists if the set of lagged x coefficients is not statistically different from zero i.e. $\Sigma\gamma_{1i} = 0$) and the set of the lagged y coefficients is statistically different from zero i.e. $\gamma_{2j+p} \neq 0$.

Optimal Lag Length: The determination of optimal lag length of variables for further analysis like cointegration test, VAR and are to be chosen on the basis of any one of the criteria like the Akaike Information Criterion (AIC), Schwarz Information Criterion (SIC) and Hannan-Quinn Information Criterion (HQIC).

Akaike's Information Criterion: The AIC compares the quality of a set of statistical models ranking them from best to worst. The best model will be the one that neither under-fits nor over-fits. The AIC is calculated as:

$$AIC = -2(log\text{-}likelihood) + 2K \qquad (12.10)$$

where K is the number of model parameters. The log-likelihood is a measure of model fit.

Schwarz Information Criterion: The SIC (also SBC, SBIC) is a criterion for model selection among a finite set of models where the likelihood increases by adding parameters. The SIC is given by:

$$SIC = kln(n) - 2(\hat{L}) \qquad (12.11)$$

where the likelihood $\hat{L} = p(x|\hat{\theta}, M)$ where M is the model, x are the data, and $\hat{\theta}$ are the to-be-inferred parameters of the model.

Vector Error Correction Mechanism: If cointegration is found to exist between the variables, then error correction mechanism to the model dynamics is required as a third step to indicate the speed of adjustment from the short-run equilibrium to the long-run equilibrium state. A vector error correction model (VECM) is a restricted VAR for using with non-stationary series that are known to be cointegrated. VECM explains the adjustments in each time period towards its long-run equilibrium state when the equilibrium conditions are enforced. The error correction term derived from the cointegrating vector points out an independent direction where a stable meaningful long-run equilibrium state exists. The VECM has cointegration error correction relationship while allowing for short-run adjustment dynamics. The cointegrating term is the error correction term because of the deviation from the long-run equilibrium corrected progressively through a series of partial short-run adjustments. The speed of adjustment of any disequilibrium in the direction of a long-run equilibrium state is given by the size of the error correction term.

The general VECM can be specified as:

$$\Delta M3_t = \alpha_1 + \delta_1 ECT_{t-1} + \gamma_{1i}\sum_{i=1}^{n}\Delta M3_{t-1} + \varphi_{1i}\sum_{i=1}^{n}\Delta GDP_{t-1} + \omega_{1i}\sum_{i=1}^{n}\Delta CPI_{t-1} + \nu_t \quad (12.12)$$

$$\Delta GDP_t = \alpha_2 + \delta_2 ECT_{t-1} + \gamma_{2i}\sum_{i=1}^{n}\Delta GDP_{t-1} + \varphi_{2i}\sum_{i=1}^{n}\Delta M3_{t-1} + \omega_{2i}\sum_{i=1}^{n}\Delta CPI_{t-1} + \nu_t \quad (12.13)$$

$$\Delta CPI_t = \alpha_3 + \delta_3 ECT_{t-1} + \gamma_{3i}\sum_{i=1}^{n}\Delta CPI_{t-1} + \varphi_{3i}\sum_{i=1}^{n}\Delta M3_{t-1} + \omega_{3i}\sum_{i=1}^{n}\Delta GDP_{t-1} + \nu_t \quad (12.14)$$

where Δ represents the first difference operator. The term ECT_{t-1} is the error correction term which stands for the long-run relationship. The long-run causal relationship is pointed out by the negative and significant coefficient of the error correction term. When both the coefficients are significant, it implies bidirectional causality. When only one coefficient δ_1 is negative and significant, it evokes a unidirectional causality from x to y indicating that x drives y in the direction of long-run equilibrium but on in the opposite direction, and correspondingly, when only δ_2 is negative and significant, it points out a unidirectional causality from y to x implying that y drives x in the direction of long-run equilibrium but not in the opposite direction. Further, the short-run cause and effect relationship between two variables is pointed out by the lagged terms of Δy and Δx as explanatory variables. Hence, it is meant that x causes y only when the lagged coefficients, Δy, become significant in the regression of Δx.

Variance Decomposition: Variance decomposition is used to evaluate the proportion of forecast error variance in one variable elucidated by innovations in itself and that of other variables. The result helps to isolate the variation in y into two parts, the part of variation that is explained by the changes of x (independent variables) and another part that is completely due to chance i.e. unexplained.

12.4 Empirical Analysis

The Table 12.1 presents the definition and descriptive statistics of the variables used in the causal relationship among money supply, growth and inflation in India. All variables are measured in logarithm form. The mean of lnM3 is 28.23, lnCPI is 2.99, lnGDP is 30.86.

Table 12.1: Descriptive Statistics of Variables in the Relationship between Money Supply, Inflation and Economic growth Analysis

Variable	*Definition*	*Mean*	*Std. dev.*
lnGDP	Gross domestic product (Rs.)	30.86	0.86
lnM3	Broad money (Rs.)	28.23	2.53
lnCPI	Consumer price index	2.99	1.25

The variables are tested for stationarity using the Augmented Dickey-Fuller (ADF) unit root test at levels and at first difference. The Table 12.2 presents the results of ADF unit root test showing that lnM3, lnCPI and lnGDP are non-stationary at levels as their probability values exceed 0.05 leading to the acceptance of the null hypothesis that the series are non-stationary. However, they become stationary after taking the first difference and therefore, are integrated of order 1, that is the variables are I(1).

Table 12.2: ADF Unit Root Test of Stationarity.

Variable	*At levels*	*At first difference*		
	With intercept	*With intercept*	*With trend and intercept*	*None*
M3	-2.915 (0.92)	-2.915* (0.00)	-3.817* (0.00)	-0.430 (0.67)
CPI	-2.916 (0.901)	-2.916* (0.00)	-5.822* (0.00)	-2.395* (0.02)
GDP	-2.914 (1.00)	-2.915* (0.00)	-8.331 (0.00)	-0.726 (0.47)

Note: p-values in parentheses. * Rejection of null hypothesis at 5 percent level.

The existence of long-run relationships among the variables GDP, broad money and consumer price index are tested with the Johansen cointegration test. The Table 12.3 presents the test results of trace statistic, eigen value statistic and the probability values to determine the number of cointegrating equations. The trace test points out that the existence of one cointegrating equation at 5 percent level of significance. The maximum eigen value test also confirms this result. Therefore, there exists a long-run equilibrium relationship among the three variables and in the short-run there may exist likely deviations from this equilibrium.

Table 12.3: Johansen Cointegration Test.

Hypothesised no. of cointegration equations	*Trace statistic*			*Eigen value statistic*		
	Trace statistic	*0.05 critical value*	*Prob.*	*Maximum eigen statistic*	*0.05 critical value*	*Prob.*
None	53.995*	29.798	0.000	39.105	21.131	0.0001
At most 1	14.890	15.495	0.061	11.096	14.265	0.149
At most2	3.7954	3.841	0.051	3.795	3.841	0.051

Note: * Significance at 5percent level.

The Table12.4 shows the optimal lag length is 4 as indicated by LR, FPE, AIC criteria. This suggests that in the VAR estimation, each variable is lagged by 4 periods and the equation for each endogenous variable is regressed on 4 lags of itself and other endogenous variables in the system.

Table 12.4: Optimum Lag Order Selection.

Lag	*lnL*	*LR*	*FPE*	*AIC*	*SC*	*HQ*
0.	-13.915	-	0.0004	0.651	0.763	0.694
1.	326.366	628.211	1.13E-09	-12.091	-11.641*	-11.918
2.	342.628	28.147	8.56E-10	-12.370	-11.582	-12.068*
3.	350.604	12.883	8.99E-10	-12.331	-11.205	-11.899
4.	364.602	20.998*	7.55E-10*	-12.523*	-11.060	-11.962
5.	369.174	6.331	9.22E-10	-12.353	-10.552	-11.662

Note: * indicates lag order selected by the criterion at 5 percent level.

Therefore, there is a need to verify whether the disequilibrium relationship meets the long-run equilibrium or not with short-run adjustments. The estimated cointegration equation is:

$$lnM3(-1) = -\,5.115 - 0.614lnGDP(-1) - 0.419lnCPI(-1) \quad (12.15)$$
$$\qquad\qquad (2.83) \qquad\qquad (9.46)$$

(**Note:** Absolute t-values in parentheses. Both variables are significant at 5 percent level).

The cointegration regression shows that there exists a long-run relation between money supply and its determinants. If there is any deviation from long-run relation, within a short period of time, the system has a tendency to come back to the original level. That is, if there is a change in inflation as a result of these variables, inflation will adjust in the next period - this percentage of correction is called the error correction model. Therefore, the VAR model is estimated including the Error Correction Term (ECT) and with the lag length of four, which is determined by the AIC, for each variable in the system. The VECM estimates are presented in Table 12.5.

Table 12.5: VECM Estimates of Broad Money, CPI and GDP.

Variable	*D(lnM3)*	*D(lnCPI)*	*D(lnGDP)*
ECT	-0.053** (2.52)	0.084*** (2.58)	0.093*** (4.39)
D(lnM3 (-1))	0.309** (1.99)	0.479** (1.98)	-0.042 (0.26)
D(lnM3(-2))	0.515*** (3.33)	-0.146 (0.61)	0.190 (1.23)
D(lnM3(-3))	0.132 (0.86)	-0.382 (1.60)	-0.368** (2.38)
D(lnCPI(-1))	-0.197** (2.12)	0.372*** (2.58)	0.091 (0.97)
D(lnCPI(-2))	0.115 (1.19)	-0.135 (0.89)	0.014 (0.14)
D(lnCPI(-3))	-0.060 (0.73)	-0.029 (0.23)	0.285*** (3.50)

D(lnGDP(-1))	0.213* (1.74)	-0.699*** (3.66)	-0.082 (0.66)
D(lnGDP(-2))	0.056 (0.40)	-0.340 (1.56)	-0.240* (1.70)
D(lnGDP(-3))	0.193 (1.37)	-0.073 (0.33)	-0.133 (0.94)
Constant	-0.007 (0.24)	0.124*** (2.76)	0.078*** (2.69)
Adj. R-square	0.416	0.312	0.354
F-value	4.701	3.362	3.849
AIC	-4.399	-3.514	-4.381
SIC	-3.990	-3.105	-3.972

Note: Absolute t-values in parentheses. *** significant at 1 percent level ** significant at 5 percent level * significant at 10 percent level.

The estimated coefficient of the error correction term (ECT) in the money supply equation is negative and statistically significant indicating the existence of long-run relationship between the variables. The relative value of -0.053 shows the speed of adjustment of any short-run disequilibrium in money supply towards long-run equilibrium is 5.3 percent per year. That is, about 5.3 percent in deviations is corrected each year. However, in the CPI and GDP estimates, the estimated coefficients of the error correction term are significantly positive, showing that the error correction term contributes to changes in general price level and output.

In addition, the existence of Granger causality at least in one direction is implied by the existence of cointegration. The results show that there exists unidirectional causality from money supply to output and money supply to general price level in the long-run. The coefficient of the first difference of the CPI lagged by one period in money supply equation is statistically significant indicating the existence of short-run causality from price to money supply. The coefficient of GDP lagged by one period in CPI equation is statistically significant implying the existence of short-run causality from output to price level. The coefficient of the first difference of the money supply lagged by three period in GDP equation is statistically significant indicating the existence of short-run causality from money supply to output.

The Table 12.6 presents the results of Granger causality test among the macroeconomic variables, showing that the null hypothesis of lnGDP does not Granger cause lnM3 and lnM3 does not Granger cause lnGDP are rejected. Hence in the short-run, a bidirectional causality exists between money and output. The null hypothesis of lnCPI does not Granger cause lnM3 and lnCPI does not Granger cause lnGDP are rejected, showing unidirectional causation between price level and money supply and between money supply and output.

Table 12.6: Pair-wise Granger Causality Test.

Null Hypothesis	*F-statistic*	*Probability*	*Decision*
lnCPI does not Granger cause lnM3	2.069	0.117	Accept null hypothesis
lnM3 does not Granger cause lnCPI	4.119*	0.011	Reject null hypothesis
lnGDP does not Granger cause lnM3	2.116	0.111	Accept null hypothesis
lnM3 does not Granger cause lnGDP	0.776	0.513	Accept null hypothesis
lnGDP does not Granger cause lnCPI	2.932*	0.043	Reject null hypothesis
lnCPI does not Granger cause lnGDP	0.533	0.662	Accept null hypothesis

Note: * indicates significance at 5 percent level.

The variance decomposition is used in the study to evaluate the proportion of forecast error variance in one variable elucidated by innovations in itself and that of other variables. The variance decomposition presented in Table 12.7 shows that the shocks in money supply in year 1 accounted for 100 percent variation in itself, the shocks in fifth year lag accounts for 93.5 percent of variance in money supply, 0.6 percent of the variance in price level and 5.77 percent of variance in output. In the tenth lag period 92.83 percent of shocks in money supply has been explained by itself, by 1.9 percent of variance in price level and 5.2 percent of variance in output. For the price level, the first year shock to itself account for 98 percent variation in itself while shocks to money supply accounts for 1.8 variation, and in 10th year, 85 percent of variation is observed in itself, while shocks money supply accounts for 3 percent of variation in CPI. In output growth variation, in first year 87 percent of variation is due to itself, in the 10th year, a shock in money supply accounts to 20 percent of variation in GDP and a shock to CPI accounts to 31 percent variation in economic growth.

Table 12.7: Variance Decomposition on Money Supply, CPI and GDI in India.

Period	*Standard error*	*lnM3*	*lnCPI*	*lnGDP*
Variance decomposition of lnM3				
1.	0.0245	100.000	0.000	0.000
2.	0.0415	95.661	2.453	1.886
3.	0.062	94.748	1.467	3.786
4.	0.085	93.605	1.016	5.379
5.	0.108	93.595	0.629	5.775
6.	0.131	93.666	0.538	5.796
7.	0.154	93.559	0.743	5.697
8.	0.176	93.422	1.079	5.498
9.	0.198	93.194	1.460	5.345
10.	0.218	92.839	1.921	5.240

Variance decomposition of lnCPI				
1.	0.038	1.802	98.197	0.000
2.	0.068	1.011	92.4212	6.567
3.	0.087	1.675	85.885	12.439
4.	0.098	1.345	85.520	13.134
5.	0.105	1.619	85.867	12.514
6.	0.109	2.428	85.517	12.055
7.	0.114	2.836	85.653	11.511
8.	0.120	3.166	86.019	10.814
9.	0.128	3.607	85.987	10.406
10.	0.135	3.995	85.763	10.243
Variance decomposition of lnGDP				
1.	0.45	2.406	9.809	87.785
2.	0.033	3.411	11.615	84.973
3.	0.039	10.228	16.371	73.400
4.	0.0433	9.046	16.054	74.900
5.	0.047	10.692	14.964	74.344
6.	0.052	14.192	18.869	66.939
7.	0.059	14.969	24.088	60.943
8.	0.068	16.275	27.535	56.190
9.	0.078	18.513	30.063	51.424
10.	0.0873	20.982	31.558	47.460

12.5 Conclusion

This paper examines the causal relationship among money supply, inflation and price level in India using a long series from 1960 to 2016. The study uses econometric methodology such as the ADF unit root test, Johansen cointegration, Granger causality test and vector error correction techniques to investigate the long-run and short-run causality among the macroeconomic variables in India. The ADF test results show that the variables are non-stationary at levels but stationary at first difference without trend. The Johansen cointegration test shows cointegration among the variables. Therefore, this paper estimates the VECM model to analyse the long-run causality among the variables. The direction of causality is detected using the Granger causality test. The Granger causality test reveals that a directional causality exists between money and output, and unidirectional causation between inflation and output. The estimated empirical results of cointegration show that there is one cointegrating equation at 5 percent level of significance meaning that there is long-term stable relationship among the three variables -price level, output and inflation. The VECM results show short-run causality from money supply to price level. The speed of adjustment or correction of any short-run disequilibrium in money supply towards long-run equilibrium is 5.3 percent per year.

13

The Causality between Carbon Emissions and Public Health Expenditure: VECM Estimation of the Effect of Carbon Dioxide Emissions on Public Health Expenditure

13.1 Introduction

The world is growing at an unprecedented rate as a response to the new inventions and the fast innovations in technology. The upturn in economic activities in most countries goes along with an increase in energy consumption which eventually leads to increase in environmental pollution that pose danger to human health. The term environment is a multifaceted concept that comprises of land, air, water pollutions. The rapid developments in the manufacturing process and the consequential environmental impacts are extensively debated issues. Environmental pollution is a negative consequence of the development process, and many countries are grappling with this phenomenon. Most importantly, the emission of harmful gases into the environment due to the colossal expansion of the industrial sector is also increasing in an increasing pace. These gases are having adverse impact not only on the environment but also on human health. The increasing deterioration in environmental quality across the world is posing serious challenge to healthy living through the increasing threat of global warming. Poor environmental quality is responsible for many health damages and air, water and soil pollution increase the risks of illness. Among various environmental pollutions, air pollution has both chronic and acute effects on human health and contributes to increase in morbidity and hospital admissions. There are many evidences to show that mortality and morbidity are associated with air pollution. With increasing pollution, the health expenditure is also increasing. A healthy society is viewed as one of the important forms of wealth that is regarded as human capital both for the individual and the nation. Good health important also for increasing levels of productivity.

Concern for health has traditionally been much of the political priority compared to environmental issues across the world. The increasing damages to environment by carbon emissions, coupled with the increasing health and illness burden, is the immediate cause for the increasing share of government spending on healthcare in almost every country. Among all forms of environmental pollutions, air pollution is the main environmental risk to health (WHO, 2003). The air pollution is caused by air pollutants such as carbon monoxide emissions, sulfur, nitrous and carbon dioxide emissions of human activities especially the manufacturing sector of the economy and the air pollution related ill-health like various respiratory ailments increase the costs of healthcare. Improvement in the air quality will decrease global burden of air-borne diseases which will consequently lead to a reduction in both individual and aggregate health expenditures. It has been observed that counties with higher pollution output tend to have higher per capita healthcare expenditure, while those that spend more on defending environmental quality have lower expenditure on health care.

The main air pollutant, carbon dioxide (CO_2) is a colorless, odorless, non-combustible greenhouse-gas that contributes to global warming. Formed by complete combustion of fossil fuels (coal, charcoal, natural gas, petroleum) and carbon containing products (such as wood), it is released also through respiration by living organisms and by the gradual oxidation of organic matter in soil. Although relatively non-hazardous, it can create lethal oxygen-deficient environments in high concentrations, especially in congested spaces. It is one of the greenhouse gases and, since over the last 200 years its concentration in upper atmosphere has increased from 270 Parts Per Million (PPM) to 350 ppm is said to be the main cause of changes in global climatic patterns.

In India also, public expenditure on health is sizable. The expenditure on health is incurred by both the government and the household. The public expenditure on health is incurred by three tiers of the government: central government, state governments and local bodies. The Figure 13.1 shows the trend in public health expenditure, gross domestic product, carbon dioxide emission, infant mortality rate, total fertility rate in India during1980-2015. The gross domestic product, carbon dioxide emission and public health expenditure are showing an increasing trend while the infant mortality rate and total fertility rate are showing an increasing trend. An interesting point to note is that with increasing pace of output (GDP), the emission is also increasing and so do the public health expenditure in India. Studies by Boachie et al. (2014), Fattahi (2015), Fattahi et al. 2013), Jie (2008) and Mohammadzadeh et al. (2015) show that air pollution is one of the most fundamental management challenges and has a significant positive impact on health expenditure in developed and developing countries all around the world. With the increasing development of communities, air pollution is also increasing and has become a serious threat to individuals' health in most countries.

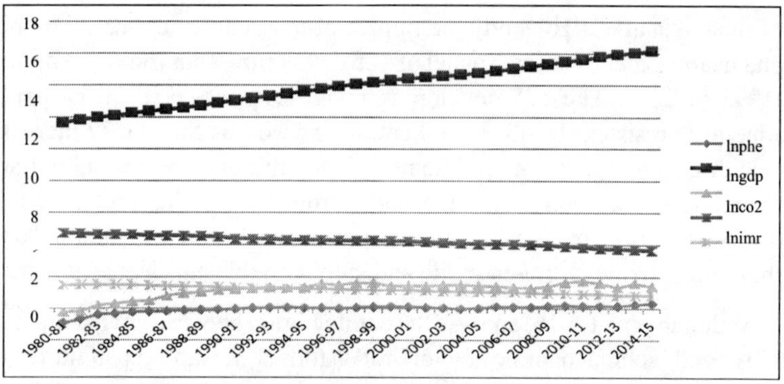

Figure 13.1: Trend in Public Health Expenditure, Gross Domestic Product, Carbon Dioxide Emission, Infant Mortality Rate, Total Fertility Rate in India.

The main objective of this paper is to estimate the effect of increasing carbon dioxide emissions on public health expenditure in India. This paper also analyses the short-run and long-run relationship among gross domestic product, carbon dioxide emission, infant mortality rate, total fertility rate and public health expenditure. In the empirical estimation this paper uses a time series data collected from the World Bank, Reserve Bank of India and NITI Aayog website for 34 years from 1980-81 to 2014-15. The variables considered are public health expenditure, gross domestic product at factor cost, carbon dioxide, infant mortality rate and total fertility rate. Since the data are time series, the usual stationarity test, cointegration test and error correction mechanism are performed. The graphical method and Augmented Dickey-Fuller (ADF) test are used to test stationarity and correlogram is applied to check the autocorrelation of the variables. The cointegration test is performed to check if there exists a long-run relationship between the variables, followed by the error correction mechanism (ECM) to check the adjustment or correction taking place in the disequilibrium.

13.2 A Brief Review of Recent Studies

Jerrett et al. (2003) explore the relation between healthcare expenditure and quality of environment, represented by air pollutants and government spending for protecting the environment in Ontario, Canada using two stage regression analysis. The unit root test is used to test the stationarity and cointegration test is used to find the long-run relationship between the variables. The results show that air pollution has a direct and statistically significant impact on child hospitalisation as a result of Asthma. After controlling for other variables that influence health expenditure, both total toxic pollution output and per capita municipal environmental expenditure have significant association with healthcare expenditure.

Yahaya et al. (2016) study the impact of environmental quality on per capita health expenditure in a panel of 125 developing countries for a period of 1995 to 2012. The 125 developing countries considered in the paper are having persistent health complications as well as the steady increase in health expenditures. The pollutants of the environment considered are carbon dioxide, carbon monoxide and nitrous oxide. The unit root test shows a long-run relationship among per capita health expenditure and carbon mono oxide, nitrogen oxide and sulphur oxide emissions.

Abdullah et al. (2016) analyse the cointegration between environmental quality and socioeconomic factor for national health expenditure in Malaysian from 1970 to 2014 using the auto regressive distributed lag (ARDL) model. The ADF unit root test rejects the null hypothesis of non-stationarity showing that most of the variables considered are stationary at first difference. The ARDL results show that GDP, carbon dioxide, nitrogen dioxide and sulphur dioxide emissions have a long-run relationship with health expenditure in Malaysia.

Yazdi and Khanalizadeh (2017) examine the role of environmental quality and economic growth in the determination of health expenditure in the Middle East and North Africa region (MENA - Algeria, Djibouti Egypt, Iran, Iraq, Jordan, Lebanon Libya, Morocco, Syrian and Tunisia) for the period 1995-2014. The CO_2 emissions per capita and PM10 emissions (micrograms per cubic meter) are used as measures of environmental quality. Empirically, the paper uses unit root test for stationarity, multivariate cointegration test and error-correction mechanism. To analyse the existence of long-run relationship, the autoregressive distributed lag (ARDL) model is applied. A comparison of the ratio of health expenditure to GDP in the MENA shows that the health expenditure/GDP ratio increased in most countries. The cross sectional analysis of certain periods show quite differences in the healthcare expenditure of MENA countries with similar levels of economic development. In the long-run, regardless of medical levels, expenditures on health care in the MENA countries are increasing.

Raeissi et al. (2018) analyse the short-run and long-run impact of air pollution on private and public health expenditure in Iran applying time series methods for the period 1972-2014. To explore the impact of environmental quality on health expenditure, the paper uses CO_2 emissions as an indicator of environmental quality. The Dickey-Fuller test has been used to determine the stationarity of the variables and the Wald test has been used to explore the long-term relationships among the variables. With cointegration among the variables, the SBC has been used to determine the optimal lag and third-rank and first rank lags have been identified as optimal for models. The estimated results show that the coefficient of CO_2 on health expenditure is significantly positive.

In the Indian context, Ghosh, (2010) probes cointegration and causality between carbon dioxide emissions and economic growth the auto regressive distributed lag (ARDL) bounds testing approach, complemented by the Johansen-Juselius maximum likelihood procedure in a multivariate framework by incorporating energy supply, investment and employment for the time span 1971-2006. The study fails to establish long-run equilibrium relationship and long-term causality between carbon emissions and economic growth. However, there exists a bidirectional short-run causality between the emission and growth. Hence, in the short-run, any effort to reduce carbon emissions could lead to a fall in the national income. The paper also finds a unidirectional short-run causality running from economic growth to energy supply and energy supply to carbon emissions. The absence of causality running from energy supply to economic growth implies that in India, energy conservation and energy efficiency measures can be implemented to minimise the wastage of energy across the value chain. Absence of long-run causality between carbon emissions and economic growth implies that in the long-run focus should be on harnessing energy from clean sources to curb carbon emissions, which would not impair economic growth.

Thus, there is ample evidence that carbon dioxide emission causes greater damage to the environment and health of humans and healthcare expenditure is huge and increasing in almost all countries. Almost all studies used similar variables and approach and conclude that there is long-run relationship between carbon dioxide emission and public health expenditure. All studies have shown that there is disequilibrium in the model and VECM is used but the quantum of correction made each period is not expressed clearly.

13.3 Data and Methodology

As the main objective of this paper is to analyse the impact of air pollution on public health expenditure in India, this paper considers variables like public health expenditure, carbon dioxide emission, infant mortality rate, total fertility rate and gross domestic product for empirical analysis. In this paper, carbon dioxide emission is taken as the measure of air pollution. The data are collected from the Reserve Bank of India, World Bank and NITI Aayog from for 34 years from 1980-81 to 2014-15. Since the data are time series, the usual tests time series analysis like graphical method, Augmented Dickey Fuller test, correlogram, determination of optimal lag length, cointegration and VECM analysis are performed.

Stationarity test: A time series data stationary if and only if its mean and variance are constant over time, and the value of covariance between two time periods depends only on the distance between the two time periods and not the actual time at which the covariance is computed. Therefore, it is advisable to check the unit root in the data before estimation. The usual method of checking for non-stationarity of a series is the Augmented Dicky-Fuller test.

Augmented Dicky-Fuller Test: In this method, the autocorrelation in the time series is checked for statistical significance. The ADF equation is specified as:

$$y_t = \rho y_{t-1} + u_t \tag{13.1}$$

where u_t is a white noise error term. If ρ=1, that is, in case of the unit root, the model becomes a random walk model without drift as there is no intercept in the equation, implying that y_t is dependent on its own lag term only, which is a non-stationary stochastic process. The presence of unit root is checked in three alternative ways:

y_t is a random walk: $\Delta y_t = \delta y_{t-1} + u_t$ (13.2)

y_t is a random walk with drift: $\Delta y_t = \beta_0 + \delta y_{t-1} + u_t$ (13.3)

y_t is a random walk with drift around a deterministic trend:

$$\Delta y_t = \beta_0 + \beta_1 t + \delta y_{t-1} + u_t \tag{13.4}$$

In each case, the hypotheses are:

H_0: δ=0 i.e. there is a unit root or the time series is non-stationary.

H_1: δ<0 i.e. the time series is stationary.

The ADF test is conducted augmenting the three equations by adding the lagged values of the dependent variable Δy_t. The ADF test is specified as:

$$\Delta y_t = \beta_0 + \beta_1 t + \delta y_{t-1} + \sum_{i=1}^{m} \alpha_i y_{t-i} + \varepsilon_t \tag{13.5}$$

If τ (tau) statistic is greater than the critical value, then the null hypothesis is rejected meaning the data is stationary. In the unit root tests, each variable in the data set is checked for stationary at levels, and if it is not, then the data is made stationary by finding the first difference and so on, or the variables are transformed, till all the variables are made stationary.

Correlogram and Auto-Correlation Function (ACF): The correlogram is commonly used to check randomness of the data set by computing autocorrelations at varying time lags. When data are random, the autocorrelations should be near zero for any and all time-lag separations. If non-random, then one or more of the autocorrelations will be significantly non-zero. A correlogram depicts the autocorrelation function (ACF), the correlation between values in a series and past values. The ACF at lag k, is denoted by ρ_k, $-1<\rho_k<+1$, is defined as:

$$\rho_k = r_k/r_0 = \textit{Covariance/Variance} \tag{13.6}$$

The plot of ρ_k against k is the correlogram. If the ACF shows a declining trend from the first lag, it implies that the variable is not stationary.

Optimal Lag Length: The determination of optimal lag for the variables is very essential in further econometric analysis like cointegration test, vector auto regressive (VAR) and vector error correction mechanism (VECM) estimations. The usual criteria are the Akaike Information Criterion (AIC), Schwarz Information Criterion (SIC) and Hannan-Quinn Information Criterion (HQIC). The AIC compares the quality of a set of statistical models to each other, ranking them from best to worst and chooses the 'best' one that neither under-fits nor over-fits. With n number of observations and k number of parameters, the AIC is computed as:

$$AIC = -2(\log - likelihood) + 2k \tag{13.7}$$

where k is the number of model parameters.

The SIC criterion for model selection is based on the likelihood function:

$$SIC = kLn(n)\text{-}2Ln(\hat{L}) \qquad (13.8)$$

where $\hat{L} = p(x|\hat{\theta}, M)$, M is the model, x are data and $\hat{\theta}$ are the to-be-inferred parameters of the model. The HQIC is a criterion is given as:

$$HQIC = -\ 2L_{max} + 2kLn[\ln(n)] \qquad (13.9)$$

where L_{max} is the log-likelihood. The final prediction error criterion (FPE) estimates the model-fitting error. For the FPE, an optimal model is the one that minimises:

$$FPE = V_n\left(1 + \frac{2p}{n-p}\right) \qquad (13.10)$$

where n is the number of data points, $V_n$is an index related to the prediction error, and p defines the number of parameters in the model.

Cointegration Test: The cointegration analysis is applied when all the variables are non-stationary at base level and are integrated of order one, i.e. I(1), which implies that they are stationary. Two or more variables are said to be cointegrated if they have a long-term or equilibrium relationship between them. It is possible for two (or more) variables to be I (1) (integrated of order 1 at the first difference level) individually, and yet a certain linear combination of those variable to be I (0) (integrated at order 0). This means, even though individually they attain stationarity at first difference, together they are stationary at base level, that is, they are cointegrated. If two or more I (1) variables are cointegrated, they must obey an equilibrium relationship in the long-run, although they may diverge substantially from that equilibrium in the short-run. Therefore, instead of individually checking for unit root for each variable in time series data, the cointegration test checks the long-run relation between the variables:

$$y_t = \alpha + \beta x_t + u_t \text{ and } u_t = (y_t - \beta_0 - \beta_1 x_t) \qquad (13.11)$$

If u_t is subjected to unit root analysis and is stationary i.e. I(0), although y_t and x_t are individually I(1) i.e. they have stochastic trends, their linear combination is I(0) so to say the linear combination cancels out the stochastic trends in the two series. The regression equation (13.11) is the cointegration equation and the slope parameter β is known as the cointegrating parameter. The Johansen (1988) cointegration test allows for more than one cointegrating relationships, unlike the Engel-Granger test for cointegration. There are two methods for testing the hypothesis under Johansen test. They are: trace test and the maximum eigen value test.

Trace Test: The trace is the sum of diagonal elements of a diagonal matrix. The null hypothesis states that the cointegration rank is equal to r, against the alternative that the cointegration rank is equal to m, which implies that the data is trend stationary. The test is, therefore, at most r cointegration relations as against m cointegration relations where r= 0,1,2…,m-1. The trace test examines the number of linear combinations (i.e. k) to be equal to a given value k_0 vs and the alternative hypothesis for k to be greater than k_0, H_0: k = k_0 vs H_1: k> k_0.

Maximum Eigen Value Test: The maximum eigen value test is similar to the trace test with a difference in the alternate hypothesis: H_0: k = k_0 vs H_1: k = k_0+1. Starting with k_0=0 and rejecting the null hypothesis implies that there is only one possible combination of the non-stationary variables to yield a stationary process.

Vector Error Correction Mechanism: The vector error correction mechanism (VECM) first used by Sargan (1975) and later popularised by Engle and Granger (1978) corrects for disequilibrium in the long-run. If two variables y and x are cointegrated, the VECM model helps to establish long and short-run equilibrium relationships between the variables. The model is fit to the first differences of the non-stationary variables adding a lagged error- correction term to the relationship. In the case of two variables, this term is the lagged residual from the cointegrating equation of one of the series on the other in levels. It expresses the prior disequilibrium from the long-run relationship, in which that residual would be zero. In the case of multiple variables, there is a vector of error-correction terms, of length equal to the number of cointegrating vectors i.e. cointegrating relationships among the series.

The Error Correction Mechanism (ECM) for cointegrated series is specified as:

$$\Delta y_t = \beta_0 + \textstyle\sum_{i=1}^{n} \beta_1 \Delta y_{t-i} + \sum_{i=1}^{n} \delta_i \Delta x_{t-i} + \gamma z_{t-1} + u_t \qquad (13.12)$$

$$z_{t-1} = y_{t-1} - \hat{\beta}_0 - \hat{\beta}_1 x_{t-1} \qquad (13.13)$$

where z is the error correction term (ECT) which shows how the last period deviation from long-run equilibrium influences the short-run dynamics of the dependent variable. Thus, the coefficient of the ECT, γ, is the speed of adjustment as it measures the speed at which y returns to equilibrium after a change in x.

13.4 Empirical Analysis

In the empirical analysis, all variables have been transformed into natural logarithmic form and the first difference of natural logarithm are taken to obtain more robust results. The Table 13.1 presents the descriptive statistics and definition of variables used in the analysis.

Table 13.1: Descriptive Statistics of Variables in the Carbon Emissions and Public Health Expenditure Analysis.

Variable	*Definition*	*Mean*	*Std. dev.*
lnPHE	Public expenditure on health and health related expenditures (percent of GDP)	-0.019	0.248
lnGDP	Gross domestic product (Rs. At constant prices)	13.95	1.341
$lnCO_2$	Carbon dioxide emissions (metric tons per capita)	1.189	0.513
lnIMR	Number of deaths per 1000 live births of children under one year of age	4.248	0.302
lnTFR	Number of children that would be born to each woman if she were to live to the end of her child bearing years and give birth to children in alignment with the prevailing age-specific fertility rate	1.195	0.212

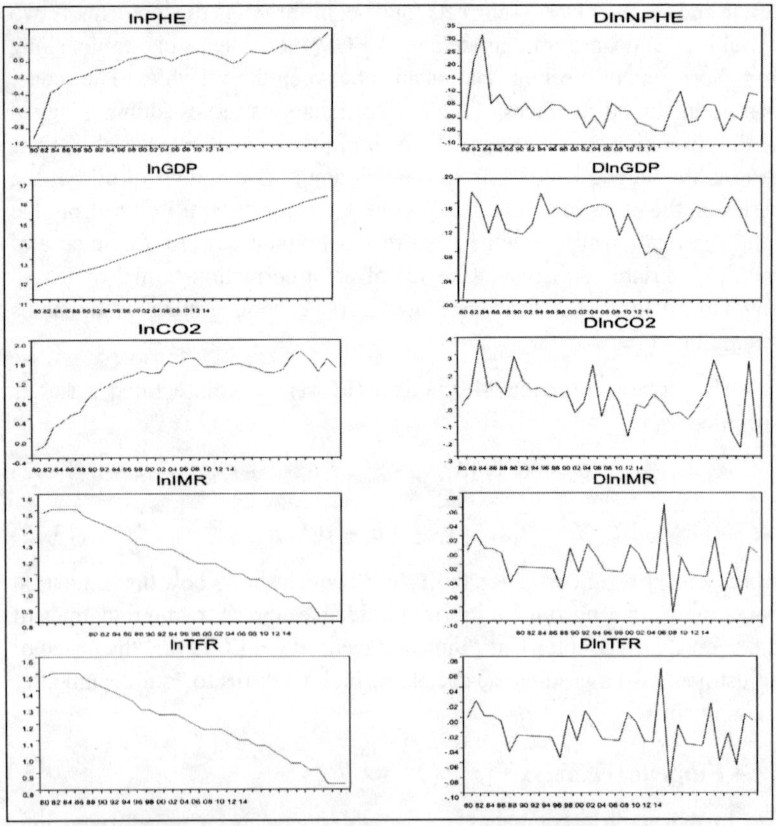

Figure 13.2: Stationarity of Variables at Level and at First Difference.

Augmented Dicky Fuller Test: The ADF to check for stationary i.e. the series does not contain unit root is performed for all variables. The test hypotheses for ADF test are:

H_0: The data contains unit root i.e. it is not stationary

H_1: The data does not contain unit root

The ADF test results at level and first difference results are presented in Table 13.2. For all the variables at levels, except infant mortality rate and GDP, the computed t-value is lesser than the critical t-value and therefore, the null hypothesis is accepted i.e. they are not stationary. On the other hand, after the first difference of the variables is taken, it is seen that the computed t-value is greater than the critical t-value for all the variables. Hence, the null hypothesis is rejected implying that the variables become stationary at the first difference. All of the first differenced variables are statistically significant at 5 percent level.

Table 13.2: ADF Test of Stationarity.

Variable	*Method*	*At level*		*At first difference*	
		ADF statistic	*p-value*	*ADF statistic*	*p-value*
lnPHE	With drift	-6.081	0.000	-3.949	0.046
	With drift and trend	-5.251	0.0008	-3.754	0.0323
	Without drift	-5.696	0.000	-3.679	0.006
lnGDP	With drift	-0.256	0.921	-3.335	0.021
	With drift and trend	-2.107	0.5227	-3.273	0.002
	Without drift	2.721	0.997	-1.036	0.020
$lnCO_2$	With drift	-3.800	0.006	-4.989	0.0003
	With drift and trend	-2.183	0.483	-6.338	0.000
	Without drift	0.552	0.830	-4.608	0.000
lnIMR	With drift	1.122	0.996	-4.740	0.000
	With drift and trend	-0.913	0.942	-4.914	0.002
	Without drift	-7.289	0.000	-0.688	0.041
lnTFR	With drift	0.620	0.988	-8.264	0.000
	With drift and trend	-3.967	0.019	-8.270	0.000
	Without drift	-4.513	0.000	-2.312	0.022

Note: At first difference all variables are significant at 5 percent level.

Correlogram and Auto-Correlation function: All of the five correlogram Tables 13.3a to 13.3e depict the correlogram for the variables lnPHE, lnGDP, lnCO2, lnIMR, lnTFR respectively at the levels. For all variables, the autocorrelation function starts at a very high value at lag 1

and declines slowly as the number of lags increases and the variables are autoregressive as there is a sudden cutoff in Partial Auto Correlation (PAC).

Table 13.3a: Correlogram of Public Health Expenditure in India (at level).

<table>
<tr><th>AC</th><th>PAC</th><th>Lags</th><th>AC</th><th>PAC</th><th>Q-statistic</th><th>Prob.</th></tr>
<tr><td>. |***** |</td><td>. |***** |</td><td>1</td><td>0.722</td><td>0.722</td><td>19.881</td><td>0.000</td></tr>
<tr><td>. |**** |</td><td>.|. |</td><td>2</td><td>0.500</td><td>-0.045</td><td>29.710</td><td>0.000</td></tr>
<tr><td>. |*** |</td><td>.|*. |</td><td>3</td><td>0.409</td><td>0.134</td><td>36.494</td><td>0.000</td></tr>
<tr><td>.|** |</td><td>.|. |</td><td>4</td><td>0.326</td><td>-0.020</td><td>40.931</td><td>0.000</td></tr>
<tr><td>. |** |</td><td>.|. |</td><td>5</td><td>0.272</td><td>0.051</td><td>44.119</td><td>0.000</td></tr>
<tr><td>.|*. |</td><td>.|. |</td><td>6</td><td>0.211</td><td>-0.038</td><td>46.099</td><td>0.000</td></tr>
<tr><td>.|*. |</td><td>.|. |</td><td>7</td><td>0.154</td><td>-0.008</td><td>47.191</td><td>0.000</td></tr>
<tr><td>.|*. |</td><td>.|. |</td><td>8</td><td>0.119</td><td>0.001</td><td>47.869</td><td>0.000</td></tr>
<tr><td>.|. |</td><td>.|. |</td><td>9</td><td>0.068</td><td>-0.054</td><td>48.098</td><td>0.000</td></tr>
<tr><td>.|. |</td><td>.|. |</td><td>10</td><td>0.004</td><td>-0.063</td><td>48.099</td><td>0.000</td></tr>
<tr><td>.|. |</td><td>.|. |</td><td>11</td><td>-0.027</td><td>-0.003</td><td>48.138</td><td>0.000</td></tr>
<tr><td>.|. |</td><td>.|. |</td><td>12</td><td>-0.030</td><td>0.016</td><td>48.189</td><td>0.000</td></tr>
<tr><td>.|. |</td><td>.|. |</td><td>13</td><td>-0.027</td><td>0.01</td><td>48.233</td><td>0.000</td></tr>
<tr><td>.|. |</td><td>.|. |</td><td>14</td><td>-0.016</td><td>0.027</td><td>48.249</td><td>0.000</td></tr>
<tr><td>.|. |</td><td>.|. |</td><td>15</td><td>-0.027</td><td>-0.03</td><td>48.297</td><td>0.000</td></tr>
<tr><td>.|. |</td><td>.|. |</td><td>16</td><td>-0.045</td><td>-0.021</td><td>48.435</td><td>0.000</td></tr>
</table>

Table 13.3b: Correlogram of Gross Domestic Product in India (at level).

<table>
<tr><th>AC</th><th>PAC</th><th>Lags</th><th>AC</th><th>PAC</th><th>Q-statistic</th><th>Prob.</th></tr>
<tr><td>.|*******|</td><td>. |*******|</td><td>1</td><td>0.912</td><td>0.912</td><td>31.647</td><td>0.000</td></tr>
<tr><td>.|******|</td><td>.|.</td><td>2</td><td>0.824</td><td>-0.040</td><td>58.297</td><td>0.000</td></tr>
<tr><td>.|***** |</td><td>.|. |</td><td>3</td><td>0.737</td><td>-0.044</td><td>80.297</td><td>0.000</td></tr>
<tr><td>.|*****|</td><td>.|. |</td><td>4</td><td>0.651</td><td>-0.047</td><td>98.005</td><td>0.000</td></tr>
<tr><td>.|****|</td><td>.|. |</td><td>5</td><td>0.568</td><td>-0.030</td><td>111.960</td><td>0.000</td></tr>
<tr><td>.|****|</td><td>.|. |</td><td>6</td><td>0.487</td><td>-0.045</td><td>122.560</td><td>0.000</td></tr>
<tr><td>.|*** |</td><td>.|. |</td><td>7</td><td>0.408</td><td>-0.044</td><td>130.240</td><td>0.000</td></tr>
<tr><td>.|**|</td><td>.|. |</td><td>8</td><td>0.330</td><td>-0.045</td><td>135.470</td><td>0.000</td></tr>
<tr><td>.|**|</td><td>.|. |</td><td>9</td><td>0.255</td><td>-0.040</td><td>138.710</td><td>0.000</td></tr>
<tr><td>.|*. |</td><td>.|. |</td><td>10</td><td>0.185</td><td>-0.032</td><td>140.490</td><td>0.000</td></tr>
<tr><td>.|*. |</td><td>.|. |</td><td>11</td><td>0.118</td><td>-0.040</td><td>141.240</td><td>0.000</td></tr>
</table>

.|. |	.|. |	12	0.055	-0.040	141.410	0.000
.|. |	.|. |	13	-0.007	-0.050	141.410	0.000
.*|. |	.|. |	14	-0.066	-0.050	141.680	0.000
.*|. |	.|. |	15	-0.123	-0.051	142.660	0.000
.*|. |	.|. |	16	-0.176	-0.043	144.770	0.000

Table 13.3c: Correlogram of Carbon Dioxide Emissions in India (at level).

AC	*PAC*	*Lags*	*AC*	*PAC*	*Q-statistic*	*Prob.*
. |******|	. |******|	1	0.843	0.843	27.073	0.000
. |***** |	.*|. |	2	0.679	-0.11	45.161	0.000
. |**** |	.|*. |	3	0.571	0.100	58.357	0.000
. |***|	.*|. |	4	0.460	-0.094	67.197	0.000
.|** |	.|. |	5	0.350	-0.040	72.497	0.000
.|** |	.*|. |	6	0.238	-0.099	75.033	0.000
.|*. |	.|. |	7	0.164	0.052	76.273	0.000
.|*. |	.|. |	8	0.103	-0.041	76.779	0.000
.|. |	.|. |	9	0.044	-0.017	76.877	0.000
.|. |	.|. |	10	-0.003	-0.024	76.878	0.000
.|. |	.|. |	11	-0.038	-0.012	76.957	0.000
.*| . |	.|. |	12	-0.071	-0.043	77.243	0.000
.*| . |	.|. |	13	-0.094	0.003	77.767	0.000
.*| . |	.*|. |	14	-0.135	-0.110	78.89	0.000
.*| . |	.|. |	15	-0.171	-0.018	80.774	0.000
.*| . |	.|. |	16	-0.175	0.034	82.85	0.000

Table 13.3d: Correlogram of Infant Mortality Rate in India (at level).

AC	*PAC*	*Lags*	*AC*	*PAC*	*Q-statistic*	*Prob.*
. |******|	. |******|	1	0.897	0.897	30.665	0.000
. |******|	.|. |	2	0.799	-0.032	55.711	0.000
. |***** |	.|. |	3	0.704	-0.036	75.771	0.000
. |**** |	.*|. |	4	0.606	-0.070	91.124	0.000
. |**** |	.|. |	5	0.514	-0.034	102.52	0.000
. |*** |	.|. |	6	0.436	0.014	110.99	0.000
. |*** |	.|. |	7	0.364	-0.021	117.11	0.000

.|** |	.|. |	8	0.293	-0.046	121.22	0.000
.|** |	.|. |	9	0.222	-0.057	123.67	0.000
.|*. |	.|. |	10	0.152	-0.052	124.87	0.000
. |*. |	.|. |	11	0.096	0.015	125.37	0.000
.|. |	.|. |	12	0.039	-0.054	125.45	0.000
.|. |	.|. |	13	-0.013	-0.029	125.46	0.000
.|. |	.|. |	14	-0.050	0.015	125.62	0.000
.*| . |	.|. |	15	-0.087	-0.044	126.11	0.000
.*| .|	.|. |	16	-0.123	-0.036	127.14	0.000

Table 13.3e: Correlogram of Total Fertility Rate in India (at level).

AC	*PAC*	*Lags*	*AC*	*PAC*	*Q-statistic*	*Prob.*
. |*******	. |*******	1	0.922	0.922	32.355	0.000
. |******|	*|. |	2	0.832	-0.113	59.545	0.000
. |***** |	*|. |	3	0.733	-0.110	81.307	0.000
. |***** |	.|. |	4	0.647	0.040	98.817	0.000
. |**** |	.*|. |	5	0.553	-0.116	112.04	0.000
. |*** |	.|. |	6	0.469	0.003	121.86	0.000
. |*** |	.*| . |	7	0.38	-0.082	128.55	0.000
.|** |	.|. |	8	0.301	-0.010	132.9	0.000
. |** |	.|. |	9	0.229	-0.006	135.52	0.000
. |*. |	.|. |	10	0.166	-0.023	136.94	0.000
. |*. |	.|. |	11	0.102	-0.059	137.5	0.000
.|. |	.|. |	12	0.048	0.007	137.63	0.000
.|. |	*|. |	13	-0.008	-0.081	137.63	0.000
.|. |	.|. |	14	-0.057	-0.011	137.83	0.000
.*|. |	.|. |	15	-0.102	-0.028	138.51	0.000
.*|. |	.*| .|	16	-0.152	-0.114	140.09	0.000

Since at the levels none of the variables are stationary, their first difference is taken and the correlogram of the first difference of all are presented in Tables 13.4a to 13.4d and 4e respectively.

Table 13.4a: Correlogram of Public Health Expenditure in India (at first difference).

<table>
<tr><th>AC</th><th>PAC</th><th>Lags</th><th>AC</th><th>PAC</th><th>Q-statistic</th><th>Prob.</th></tr>
<tr><td>. |*** |</td><td>. |*** |</td><td>1</td><td>0.44</td><td>0.44</td><td>7.182</td><td>0.007</td></tr>
<tr><td>. |*. |</td><td>. *| .|</td><td>2</td><td>0.133</td><td>-0.075</td><td>7.859</td><td>0.02</td></tr>
<tr><td>.|. |</td><td>.|. |</td><td>3</td><td>0.071</td><td>0.052</td><td>8.060</td><td>0.045</td></tr>
<tr><td>.*|. |</td><td>.|. |</td><td>4</td><td>0.041</td><td>-0.003</td><td>8.130</td><td>0.087</td></tr>
<tr><td>.|. |</td><td>.|. |</td><td>5</td><td>0.047</td><td>0.035</td><td>8.221</td><td>0.144</td></tr>
<tr><td>.|. |</td><td>.|. |</td><td>6</td><td>0.06</td><td>0.031</td><td>8.378</td><td>0.212</td></tr>
<tr><td>.|. |</td><td>.|. |</td><td>7</td><td>0.039</td><td>-0.003</td><td>8.448</td><td>0.295</td></tr>
<tr><td>. |*. |</td><td>. |*. |</td><td>8</td><td>0.126</td><td>0.134</td><td>9.197</td><td>0.326</td></tr>
<tr><td>. |*. |</td><td>.|. |</td><td>9</td><td>0.106</td><td>-0.009</td><td>9.743</td><td>0.372</td></tr>
<tr><td>.|. |</td><td>.|. |</td><td>10</td><td>0.007</td><td>-0.056</td><td>9.746</td><td>0.463</td></tr>
<tr><td>.*|. |</td><td>.*|. |</td><td>11</td><td>-0.071</td><td>-0.073</td><td>10.016</td><td>0.529</td></tr>
<tr><td>.*| . |</td><td>.*|. |</td><td>12</td><td>-0.158</td><td>-0.128</td><td>11.408</td><td>0.494</td></tr>
<tr><td>.*| . |</td><td>.|. |</td><td>13</td><td>-0.152</td><td>-0.042</td><td>12.758</td><td>0.467</td></tr>
<tr><td>.*| . |</td><td>.|. |</td><td>14</td><td>-0.111</td><td>-0.041</td><td>13.508</td><td>0.487</td></tr>
<tr><td>.|. |</td><td>.|. |</td><td>15</td><td>-0.03</td><td>0.053</td><td>13.567</td><td>0.559</td></tr>
<tr><td>.|. |</td><td>.|. |</td><td>16</td><td>0.027</td><td>0.031</td><td>13.618</td><td>0.627</td></tr>
</table>

Table 13.4b: Correlogram of Gross Domestic Product in India (at first difference).

<table>
<tr><th>AC</th><th>PAC</th><th>Lags</th><th>AC</th><th>PAC</th><th>Q-statistic</th><th>Prob.</th></tr>
<tr><td>. |*. |</td><td>.|*. |</td><td>1</td><td>0.144</td><td>0.144</td><td>0.793</td><td>0.373</td></tr>
<tr><td>. |*. |</td><td>.|. |</td><td>2</td><td>0.079</td><td>0.059</td><td>1.038</td><td>0.595</td></tr>
<tr><td>. |*. |</td><td>.|*. |</td><td>3</td><td>0.152</td><td>0.136</td><td>1.977</td><td>0.577</td></tr>
<tr><td>.*|. |</td><td>.*|. |</td><td>4</td><td>-0.146</td><td>-0.197</td><td>2.867</td><td>0.58</td></tr>
<tr><td>.|. |</td><td>.|. |</td><td>5</td><td>-0.039</td><td>-0.009</td><td>2.931</td><td>0.711</td></tr>
<tr><td>.*|. |</td><td>.*|. |</td><td>6</td><td>-0.161</td><td>-0.17</td><td>4.092</td><td>0.664</td></tr>
<tr><td>.*|. |</td><td>.|. |</td><td>7</td><td>0.095</td><td>0.011</td><td>4.507</td><td>0.720</td></tr>
<tr><td>.*|. |</td><td>.*|. |</td><td>8</td><td>-0.116</td><td>-0.122</td><td>5.149</td><td>0.741</td></tr>
<tr><td>***|. |</td><td>**|. |</td><td>9</td><td>-0.349</td><td>-0.297</td><td>11.213</td><td>0.261</td></tr>
<tr><td>.*|. |</td><td>.*|. |</td><td>10</td><td>-0.122</td><td>-0.089</td><td>11.987</td><td>0.286</td></tr>
<tr><td>.*|. |</td><td>.*|. |</td><td>11</td><td>-0.121</td><td>-0.087</td><td>12.777</td><td>0.308</td></tr>
<tr><td>.|. |</td><td>.|. |</td><td>12</td><td>-0.047</td><td>0.018</td><td>12.901</td><td>0.376</td></tr>
<tr><td>.|. |</td><td>.*|. |</td><td>13</td><td>0.019</td><td>-0.094</td><td>12.922</td><td>0.454</td></tr>
<tr><td>.|. |</td><td>.*|. |</td><td>14</td><td>-0.022</td><td>-0.092</td><td>12.952</td><td>0.530</td></tr>
<tr><td>. |*. |</td><td>.|. |</td><td>15</td><td>0.097</td><td>-0.042</td><td>13.563</td><td>0.559</td></tr>
<tr><td>.|. |</td><td>.|. |</td><td>16</td><td>0.032</td><td>-0.052</td><td>13.631</td><td>0.626</td></tr>
</table>

Table 13.4c: Correlogram of Carbon Dioxide Emissions in India (at first difference).

<table>
<tr><th>AC</th><th>PAC</th><th>Lags</th><th>AC</th><th>PAC</th><th>Q-statistic</th><th>Prob.</th></tr>
<tr><td>.|. |</td><td>.|. |</td><td>1</td><td>0.055</td><td>0.055</td><td>0.114</td><td>0.735</td></tr>
<tr><td>.|. |</td><td>.|. |</td><td>2</td><td>0.044</td><td>0.041</td><td>0.189</td><td>0.91</td></tr>
<tr><td>. |*. |</td><td>.|. |</td><td>3</td><td>0.076</td><td>0.072</td><td>0.424</td><td>0.935</td></tr>
<tr><td>. |*. |</td><td>. |*. |</td><td>4</td><td>0.099</td><td>0.091</td><td>0.836</td><td>0.934</td></tr>
<tr><td>. |*. |</td><td>. |*. |</td><td>5</td><td>0.100</td><td>0.087</td><td>1.271</td><td>0.938</td></tr>
<tr><td>. |*. |</td><td>. |*. |</td><td>6</td><td>0.130</td><td>0.113</td><td>2.028</td><td>0.917</td></tr>
<tr><td>. |*. |</td><td>.|. |</td><td>7</td><td>0.098</td><td>0.074</td><td>2.471</td><td>0.929</td></tr>
<tr><td>. |*. |</td><td>. |*. |</td><td>8</td><td>0.114</td><td>0.086</td><td>3.095</td><td>0.928</td></tr>
<tr><td>.|. |</td><td>.|. |</td><td>9</td><td>-0.014</td><td>-0.056</td><td>3.105</td><td>0.96</td></tr>
<tr><td>.*|. |</td><td>.*|. |</td><td>10</td><td>-0.086</td><td>-0.134</td><td>3.488</td><td>0.967</td></tr>
<tr><td>.|. |</td><td>.|. |</td><td>11</td><td>-0.011</td><td>-0.059</td><td>3.495</td><td>0.982</td></tr>
<tr><td>.|. |</td><td>.|. |</td><td>12</td><td>0.000</td><td>-0.043</td><td>3.495</td><td>0.991</td></tr>
<tr><td>. |*. |</td><td>. |*. |</td><td>13</td><td>0.118</td><td>0.107</td><td>4.313</td><td>0.987</td></tr>
<tr><td>.*|. |</td><td>.*|. |</td><td>14</td><td>-0.092</td><td>-0.101</td><td>4.833</td><td>0.988</td></tr>
<tr><td>.|. |</td><td>.|. |</td><td>15</td><td>0.025</td><td>0.05</td><td>4.873</td><td>0.993</td></tr>
<tr><td>.|. |</td><td>.|. |</td><td>16</td><td>-0.061</td><td>-0.043</td><td>5.124</td><td>0.995</td></tr>
</table>

Table 13.4d: Correlogram of Infant Mortality Rate in India (at first difference).

<table>
<tr><th>AC</th><th>PAC</th><th>Lags</th><th>AC</th><th>PAC</th><th>Q-statistic</th><th>Prob.</th></tr>
<tr><td>. |*. |</td><td>. |*|</td><td>1</td><td>0.135</td><td>0.135</td><td>0.697</td><td>0.404</td></tr>
<tr><td>.*|. |</td><td>.*|. |</td><td>2</td><td>-0.142</td><td>-0.163</td><td>1.486</td><td>0.476</td></tr>
<tr><td>. |** |</td><td>. |** |</td><td>3</td><td>0.24</td><td>0.297</td><td>3.814</td><td>0.282</td></tr>
<tr><td>.|. |</td><td>**|. |</td><td>4</td><td>-0.061</td><td>-0.208</td><td>3.972</td><td>0.410</td></tr>
<tr><td>.*|. |</td><td>.|. |</td><td>5</td><td>-0.189</td><td>-0.043</td><td>5.521</td><td>0.356</td></tr>
<tr><td>.|. |</td><td>.*|. |</td><td>6</td><td>-0.062</td><td>-0.155</td><td>5.692</td><td>0.458</td></tr>
<tr><td>.|. |</td><td>.|. |</td><td>7</td><td>-0.04</td><td>0.030</td><td>5.766</td><td>0.567</td></tr>
<tr><td>. |*. |</td><td>. |*. |</td><td>8</td><td>0.08</td><td>0.128</td><td>6.076</td><td>0.639</td></tr>
<tr><td>.|. |</td><td>.|. |</td><td>9</td><td>0.028</td><td>-0.010</td><td>6.115</td><td>0.728</td></tr>
<tr><td>*|. |</td><td>.*|. |</td><td>10</td><td>-0.096</td><td>-0.096</td><td>6.597</td><td>0.763</td></tr>
<tr><td>. |*. |</td><td>.|. |</td><td>11</td><td>0.09</td><td>0.053</td><td>7.031</td><td>0.797</td></tr>
<tr><td>.|. |</td><td>.|. |</td><td>12</td><td>0.025</td><td>-0.049</td><td>7.068</td><td>0.853</td></tr>
</table>

.*|. |	.*|. |	13	-0.184	-0.082	9.066	0.768
.|. |	.|. |	14	-0.045	-0.041	9.192	0.819
.*|. |	.*|. |	15	-0.102	-0.168	9.860	0.828
.*|. |	.*|. |	16	-0.185	-0.086	12.200	0.73

Table 13.4e: Correlogram of Total Fertility Rate in India (at first difference).

AC	*PAC*	*Lags*	*AC*	*PAC*	*Q-statistic*	*Prob.*
**|. |	**|. |	1	-0.307	-0.307	3.593	0.058
. |*. |	.|. |	2	0.149	0.060	4.461	0.107
.*|. |	.|. |	3	-0.074	-0.014	4.680	0.197
. |*. |	.|. |	4	0.076	0.047	4.920	0.296
.*|. |	.*|. |	5	-0.201	-0.179	6.668	0.246
. |** |	. |*. |	6	0.247	0.153	9.397	0.152
**|. |	.*|. |	7	-0.250	-0.131	12.294	0.091
. |*. |	.|. |	8	0.095	-0.045	12.725	0.122
.*|. |	.*|. |	9	-0.186	-0.155	14.449	0.107
.|. |	**|. |	10	-0.053	-0.207	14.593	0.148
. |*. |	. |** |	11	0.169	0.240	16.129	0.136
.*|. |	**|. |	12	-0.192	-0.241	18.213	0.109
.|. |	.|. |	13	0.062	0.039	18.438	0.142
.|. |	.|. |	14	0.031	-0.015	18.498	0.185
.|. |	.|. |	15	0.037	0.066	18.587	0.233
.|. |	.|. |	16	-0.040	0.050	18.695	0.285

Optimal Lag Length: The Table 13.5 shows the optimal lag length for all variables used for cointegration and VECM analysis. The conditions used for determining optimal lag length are sequential modified LR test, Final Prediction Error (FPM), Akaike Information Criterion (AIC), Schwarz Information Criterion (SIC) and Hannan-Quinn Information Criterion (HQ). Almost all the variables have optimal lag length as 1. The optimal lag length is used for further analysis in tests like cointegration and VECM.

Table 13.5: Optimal Lag Length Selection.

Variable	*Optimal lag*	*LL*	*LR*	*FPE*	*AIC*	*HQIC*	*SIC*
lnPHE	1	57.209	73.005*	0.0018*	-3.450*	-3.359*	-3.420*
lnGDP	2	79.181	9.369*	0.0005*	-4.617*	-4.480*	-4.571*
$lnCO_2$	1	25.961	77.517*	0.0137*	-1.452*	-1.361*	-1.421*
lnIMR	1	71.659	144.321*	0.0008*	-4.221*	-4.131*	-4.191*
lnTFR	1	81.844	142.663*	0.0004*	-4.839*	-4.748*	-4.808*

Note: * lag order selected by the criterion. All results are significant at 5 percent level.

Cointegration Test: The cointegration test is used to determine whether the variables have a long run relationship using the trace and max eigen value statistics. The hypotheses are:

H_0: The variables are not cointegrated

H_1: The variables are cointegrated

For the null hypothesis (H_0) to be rejected, the computed trace statistic and the max-eigen value statistic should be greater than the critical value and statistically significant at least at 5 percent level of significance. The trace and max eigen value statistics presented in Table 13.6 rejects the null hypothesis showing that the variables are cointegrated and have one cointegrating equation at 5 percent level of significance.

Table 13.6: Trace and Max Eigen Value Tests of Cointegration.

Hypothesised no. of CE(s)	*At level*				*At first difference*			
	Eigen value	*Trace statistic*	*Critical value*	*Prob.*	*Eigen value*	*Trace statistic*	*Critical value*	*Prob.*@
None *	0.753	91.983	69.818	0.003	0.753	46.215	33.876	0.001
At most 1	0.522	45.767	47.856	0.077	0.522	24.374	27.584	0.122
At most 2	0.356	21.393	29.797	0.333	0.356	14.566	21.131	0.320
At most 3	0.185	6.826	15.494	0.597	0.185	6.753	14.264	0.518
At most 4	0.002	0.073	3.841	0.787	0.002	0.0730	3.841	0.787

Note: Trace test indicates 1 cointegrating eqn(s) at the 0.05 level * rejection of the hypothesis at the 0.05 level @ MacKinnon-Haug-Michelis (1999) p-values.

The presence of cointegration in the series implies that there is a long-term relationship in the variables. The cointegration equation is:

$$ECT_{t-1} = 1.000 lnPHE_{t-1} + 0.490 lnGDP_{t-1} + 0.002 lnCO2_{t-1} - 0.559 lnIMR_{t-1} + 4.341 lnTFR_{t-1} - 9.67. \quad (13.14)$$

Hence, the Vector Error Correction Mechanism (VECM) analysis is to be used and the Error Correction Term (ECT) shows the speed with which the short-run fluctuations return to the long-run equilibrium values following an exogenous shock. The ECM should be negatively signed, indicating a move back towards equilibrium; a positive sign indicated movement away from equilibrium. The coefficient should lie between 0 and 1, 0 suggesting no adjustment one time period later, 1 indicating full adjustment. The Table 13.7 presents the estimated VECM results. The estimated error correction coefficient is negative and statistically significant showing that about 36.4 percent of the departure from long-run equilibrium is corrected every year.

Table 13.7: VECM Estimates of Causal Relationship between Carbon Emissions and Public Health Expenditure in India.

lnPHE(-1)	1				
lnGDP(-1)	0.490 (-0.124) [3.938]				
lnCO2(-1)	-0.002 (-0.062) [-0.040]				
lnIMR(-1)	-0.559 (-0.464) [-1.203]				
lnTFR(-1)	4.341 (-0.868) [5.000]				
C	-9.674				
Variable	D(lnPHE)	D(lnGDP)	DlLnCO2)	D(lnIMR)	D(lnTFR)
Coint. eq1	-0.364	-0.048	-0.557	0.032	-0.082
	(5.80)	(1.39)	2.78)	(0.86)	(2.23)
D(lnPHE(-1))	-0.020	-0.162	-0.370	0.160	0.009
	(0.13)	(1.95)	(0.77)	(1.77)	(0.10)
D(lnGDP(-1))	0.068	0.571	0.277	-0.244	-0.233
	(0.223)	(3.44)	(0.29)	(1.35)	(1.32)
D(lnCO2(-1))	-0.059	0.028	0.049	-0.049	0.003
	(0.90)	(0.77)	(0.23)	(1.25)	(0.07)
D(lnIMR(-1))	-0.072	0.031	-0.151	0.071	0.198
	(0.68)	(0.46)	(0.21)	(0.82)	(1.24)
D(lnTFR(-1))	0.550	0.068	0.604	-0.139	-0.321
	(1.92)	(0.43)	(0.66)	(0.81)	(1.91)
Constant	0.044	0.063	0.027	0.000	0.011
	(1.05)	(2.77)	(0.20)	(0.006)	(0.45)
Adj. R-squared	0.619	0.229	0.126	-0.023	0.223
F- statistic	9.677	2.584	1.766	0.880	2.527
Log-likelihood	61.895	81.553	23.602	78.757	79.584
AIC	-3.327	-4.518	-1.006	-4.349	-4.399
SIC	-3.010	-4.201	-0.689	-4.031	-4.082

Note: Absolute t-values in parentheses.

To find the long-term causality, the systems of equation for each variable are estimated with lags with the corresponding p-values. The estimated VECM with PHE as target variable is:

$$\Delta \ln PHE_t = -0.364ECT_{t-1} - 0.020\ln PHE_{t-1} + 0.067\ln GDP_{t-1} - 0.058\ln CO2_{t-1} - 0.058\ln CO2_{t-1} + 0.207\ln IMR_{t-1} + 0.549\ln TFR_{t-1} + 0.043 \quad (13.15)$$

To find the statistical significance of the coefficient of cointegrating equation the following estimated equation is used and the results are presented in Table 13.8:

D(lnPHE)=C(1)*[lnPHE(-1)+ 0.490*lnGDP(-1) - 0.002*lnCO2(-1)
-0.559*lnIMR(-1)+4.341*lnTFR(-1)-9.674]+C(2)*D(lnPHE(-1))
+C(3)*D(lnGDP(-1))+C(4)*D(lnCO2(-1))+C(5)*D(lnIMR(-1))
+C(6)*D(lnTFR(-1))+C(7) (13.16)

Table 13.8: Statistical Significance of Coefficients of Cointegrating Equation.

Variable	*Coefficient*	*Std. error*	*p-value*
C(1)	-0.364	0.062	0.000
C(2)	-0.020	0.150	0.894
C(3)	0.067	0.301	0.823
C(4)	-0.058	0.065	0.376
C(5)	0.207	0.306	0.504
C(6)	0.549	0.286	0.066
C(7)	0.043	0.041	0.302

In Table 13.8, C(1) is the coefficient of the cointegrating equation. The coefficient value of error correction term [C(1)] is negative and significant showing that there is a long run relationship in variables. C(7) is the constant term, C(2) is the coefficient of lagged dependent variable, C(3), C(4), C(5) and C(6) are the short-run coefficients that tell whether there is short-run relationship or not.

The short-run relationships are tested with the Wald test and the results are presented in Table 13.9. The test hypotheses are:

H_0: There is no short-run causality in the variables

H_1: There is short run-causality in the variables

In Table 13.9, it can be seen that the chi-square probability value is greater than 0.05 and null hypothesis can not be rejected. Hence, there is an evidence of short-run causality running from independent variables to the dependent variable.

Table 13.9: Wald Test for Short-Run Causality.

Test statistic	*Test value*	*Prob.*
F-Statistic	1.253	0.313
Chi-square	5.01	0.285
Null hypothesis	C(3)=C(4)=C(5)=C(6)=0	
Normalised restriction (= 0)	Value	Std. error
C(3)	0.067	0.301
C(4)	-0.058	0.065
C(5)	0.207	0.306
C(6)	0.549	0.286

The presence of serial correlation is tested with the Breusch-Godfrey serial correlation LM test. The test hypotheses are:

H_0 = There is no serial correlation

H_1 = There is serial correlation

As the Breusch-Godfrey serial correlation LM test results presented in Table 13.10 shows the probability of chi-square is greater than 0.05, and hence the null hypothesis could not be rejected meaning that there is no serial correlation.

Table 13.10: Breusch-Godfrey Serial Correlation LM Test for Serial Correlation.

F-statistic	*0.271*	*Prob.*		*0.606*
Obs*R-squared	0.354	Prob. chi-square		0.551
Variable	Coefficient	Std. error	t-statistic	Prob.
C(1)	-0.028	0.083	-0.339	0.737
C(2)	-0.104	0.252	-0.414	0.681
C(3)	0.022	0.308	0.073	0.942
C(4)	0.008	0.068	0.118	0.906
C(5)	-0.049	0.325	-0.150	0.881
C(6)	0.155	0.416	0.372	0.712
C(7)	0.002	0.042	0.050	0.960
RESID(-1)	0.199	0.382	0.521	0.606
R-squared	0.010	Mean dependent variable		1.08E-16
Adjusted R-square	-0.266	Std. dev. dependent variable		0.037
S.E. of regression	0.042	AIC		-3.277
Sum squared residual	0.044	SIC		-2.914
Log-likelihood	62.073	HQIC		-3.155
F-statistic	0.038	Durbin-Watson statistics		1.816
Prob.(F-statistic)	0.999			

The dynamic stability of the model is presented in Figure 13.3. As the stability line of the model is within the range, the model is dynamically stable.

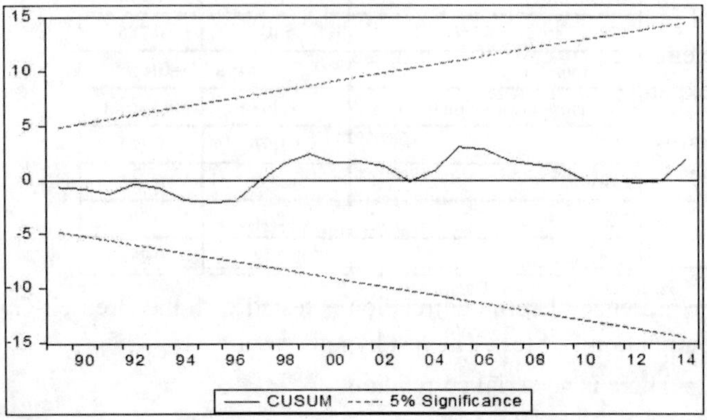

Figure 13.3: Dynamic Stability of the Model.

13.5 Conclusion

Health is central to the wellbeing of the citizens. Noting that the air pollution and the consequent environmental degradation has cascading effects on health and as a result health expenditure. It is in this light that, this paper looks at the effects of pollution on government spending on health. This paper analysed the effect of carbon dioxide emissions on public health expenditure in India. In the empirical analysis, this paper used a time series data collected from the World Bank, Reserve Bank of India and NITI Aayog website for 34 years from 1980-81 to 2014-15. This paper also analysed the short-run and long-run relationship among gross domestic product, carbon dioxide emission, infant mortality rate, total fertility rate and public health expenditure. The study commenced with testing the stationarity of the variables using the Augmented Dickey Fuller test. The ADF test finds that at level some variables are stationary but not all and at first difference all variables are stationary. For determining the optimal lag length AIC, SIC, HQC and FPE criteria are used. Considering all the criteria, the lag length is 1. The cointegration test is used to find the presence of long-run relationship among the variables. On the basis of trace test and maximum eigen value statistic, one cointegrating equation is obtained. Then the Vector Error Correction Mechanism (VECM) is used to correct the disequilibrium. The VECM results show that approximately 36,4 percent of the departure from long-run equilibrium is corrected every year. The dynamic stability check shows that the model is stable. This study finds that with 1 percent increase in carbon emissions, the public health expenditure is increasing by 0.36 percent. With 1 percent increase in GDP and TFR, the public health expenditure in increasing by 0.02 percent and 0.98 percent respectively. Based on the findings of this study, it is clear that the emission of CO2 is having a significant positive impact on public health expenditure in India.

Appendix 13

Table 13A: OLS Estimates of the Effect of Carbon emissions on Public Health Expenditure in India.

Dependent variable: lnPHE

Variable	*Coefficient*	*Std. error*	*t-statistic*	*Prob.*
lnGDP	0.018	0.113	0.160	0.873
lnCO2	0.361	0.055	6.522	0.000
lnIMR	-0.788	0.424	-1.858	0.073
lnTFR	0.981	0.667	1.470	0.151
Constant	1.472	2.977	0.494	0.624
R-squared	0.886	Mean of dependent variable		-0.019
Adjusted R-square	0.870	Std. dev. of dependent variable		0.248
Std. error of regression	0.089	AIC		-1.862
Sum squared residuals	0.239	SIC		-1.639
Log-likelihood	37.588	HQIC		-1.785
F-statistic	58.159	Durbin-Watson statistic		0.771
Prob(F-statistic)	0.000			

14

The Causality between International Private Transfers and Macro Variables: VECM Estimation of the Effects of Domestic, Host Country and Global Variables on Private Remittances and Transfers

14.1 Introduction

The volume of private transfers from people working abroad to the home country is substantial and has been increasing over time. With liberalisation and globalisation and free movements of labour across countries, the private transfers to the developing countries is a significant factor in the international flow of funds and is a source of capital investment for the capital scarce and labour surplus economies. The size of private transfers varies from one fifth to half of the economy for different developing countries. Addison (2004) argues that private remittances can create a positive impact on the economy through various channels. The remittances can impact savings, investments, growth, consumption, and poverty and income distribution. Private remittances help in raising the national income by providing foreign exchange and raising national savings and investments as well by providing hard currency to finance essential imports thereby curtailing any BOP crisis. Remittances also carry some positive effects on investments in developing countries, particularly raising enough and cheap capital to finance investment activities. The remittances are used to finance several social projects including school buildings, clinics and other infrastructure. International migration and private remittances significantly reduce the level, depth and severity of poverty in the developing world.

Adams and Page (2005) find a significant impact of international migration and remittances on poverty in many developing countries.

The private cash transfers are important source of income for many households in various developing countries. At the household level, the two principle motives of the private transfers are altruism and self-interested exchange (Cox, Hansen and Jimenez, 2004). The amounts received are large especially in poor households. Such large private transfers influence the poor households and boost their well-being and living standards. Private transfers are also of household economic status, education of children and better health seeking of poor families in developing countries. The private transfers are important for policy also as they also provide social and economic benefits similar to those of public programmes. The private transfers could crowd out public transfers in many ways.

India is the highest recipient of world private transfers, which is growing at an average of 15 percent every year. Much of India's private transfers come from the Indian migrants of skilled labour to countries like USA and Middle East countries in search of high earnings. Private transfers arise due to many factors ranging from cash transferred through 'formal' institutions like banks, non-bank financial institutions and money transfer operators. Gold and silver bought through baggage and gifts towards persons in India are gauged under current account of private transfers as they represent one side transfers. The Figure 14.1 presents the size and growth of private transfers to India during the period 1975-2015. With sizable private transfers to India, the private transfers, migration, economic growth and some of the macroeconomic variables of not only India but also the destination of the migrant Indians are interlinked.

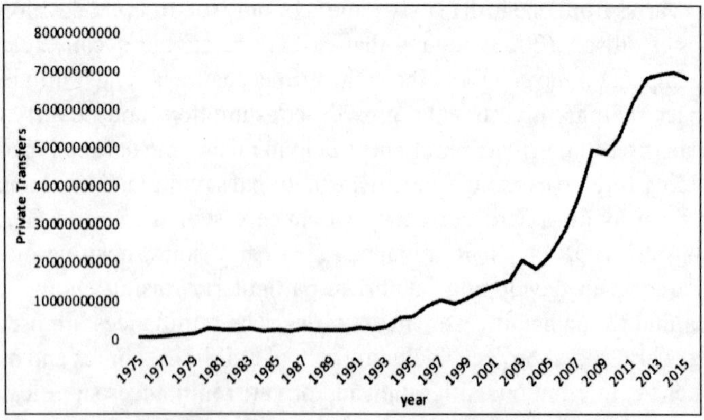

Figure 14.1: Private Transfers to India, 1975-2015.

This paper aims to identify the macroeconomic determinants of private transfers to India, not only that of India but also those of host countries. Specifically, this paper analyses the relationship between private transfers to India, gross domestic products of India and the US, exchange rate, inflation, crude oil price. Further, this paper also examines the short and long-run nature of relationship between the private transfers and these macroeconomic variables. For this purpose, the paper uses a time series data for 30 years from 1975 to 2015. In the empirical analysis, the time series methodologies of stationarity test, cointegration test and vector error correction model are applied.

14.2 A Brief Review of Recent Studies

Cox, Hansen and Jimenez (2004) argues that private transfers are widespread in developing countries and are highly important for household resources. The private transfers at the household level are consistent with altruistic behavior and there exists a strong transfer derivative in poor household. In an attempt to understand the inference between private transfers and public transfers, the authours check for the crowding out hypothesis i.e. whether private transfers reduce public transfers. The spline regression results of changes in private transfers on changes that have occurred in public transfers suggest that the potential for the crowding out is large for the public transfers targeted towards those in lower reaches of the income distribution.

Eozenov (2008) analyse the determinants of private transfers in rural Vietnam using the Vietnam Living Standards Survey applying parametric and semi-parametric methods of estimation of LPM and logit models. The estimated empirical results show that private transfers helped in income smoothing over the life cycle. Among other factors, age and gender of the household head are the major determinants of transfer inflows and outflows. The pre-transfer income is positively related to the net donor and negatively related with net recipient status especially for low levels of income. This result suggests that the private transfers just crowd out the redistributive public transfers targeted towards the rural poor at the family level.

In India, Trivedi and Panda (2014) examines the behaviour of private transfers to India. He notes that private transfers to India is significantly influenced by both home and host country macroeconomic factors, especially the oil price hikes. The private transfers to India have become a major source for reducing the magnitude of current account deficits and is used for consumption and investment purposes. The relationship between private transfers and the macroeconomic variables is examined with unit root test and cointegration tests and the vector error correction model is estimated.

14.3 Data and Methodology

In order to examine the relationship between private transfers and macroeconomic variables in India, this paper considers a time series data for 30 years from 1975 to 2015 for six variables viz. private transfers, GDP, consumer price index, exchange rate of India, GDP of the US and international crude oil price. The data on private transfers to India have been collected from the Reserve Bank of India Handbook of Statistics, and the data on GDP of India and US, consumer price index of India, international crude oil price and exchange rate of India have been collected from the World Bank sources. The GDP of India and consumer price index are taken as proxies for home country macroeconomic factors while the GDP of US and international crude oil price are used as host country macroeconomic variables as more than 65 percent of migrant workers of India work in USA and the Middle East. The exchange rate weighs up the valuation of Indian rupee with respect to the US dollars in the given span of time. All the monetary variables are expressed in terms of US for the ease of comparison. The Table 14.1 presents the definition and descriptive statistics of the variables used in the empirical analysis of private transfers to India and macroeconomic determinants.

Table 14.1: Descriptive Statistics of Variables in the International Private Transfers Analysis.

Variable	*Description*	*Mean*	*Std. dev.*
$lnPTS_{IN}$	All current transfers and remittances in cash or in kind received from all non-resident individuals by residents of India and total remittances and transfers to non-profit institutions (US$)	22.730	1.456
$lnGDP_{IN}$	Gross domestic product of India (US$)	26.803	0.872
$lnCPI_{IN}$	Consumer price index of India at 2010 constant price	3.520	0.902
$lnER_{INR}$	The price for which US dollars are exchanged for Indian rupee (US$)	3.203	0.725
$lnGDP_{US}$	Gross domestic product of US (US$)	29.583	0.688
$lnCOP_{IT}$	OPEC crude oil price per barrel (US$)	3.405	0.685

Vector Error Correction Model

The estimating equation of international private transfers to India is specified as:

$$lnPTS_t = \beta_0 + \beta_1 GDP_{INt} + \beta_2 CPI_{INt} + \beta_3 ER_{INt} + \beta_4 GDP_{USt} + \beta_5 COP_{ITt} + u_t \quad (14.1)$$

As the data used is time-series, the stationarity test, cointegration between the variables and existence of long-run equilibrium in the macroeconomic variables are to be checked. The stationarity is the state where the mean, variance and covariance are constant over a period of time; the alternate condition is the non-stationarity of the series. Hypothesis for testing the stationarity is the presence of unit root in the system. If there is a unit root in the system, spurious regression may result in wrong results. The Augmented Dickey-Fuller test for stationarity of the series is specified as:

$$\Delta y_t = \beta_0 + \delta y_{t-1} + \sum_{i=1}^{P} \alpha_i \Delta x_{t-i} + u_t \quad (14.2)$$

where u is a pure white noise error term and the order of auto regression is determined by the Schwarz information criterion to optimal lag length.

The Johansen cointegration test is used to check for the cointegration among the variables with possible combinations among the data in the given model. The cointegrating equation can be specified as:

$$u_{t-1} = y_{t-1} + \beta_0 + \beta_1 x_{t-1} \quad (14.3)$$

The Johansen test approaches the testing for cointegration examining the number of linearly independent combinations (k) for an (m) time series variables. The number of independent linear combinations (k) is related to the assumed number of non-stationary underlying autoregressive process (p): p=m-k. There are three possible outcomes: (i) if k=0, p=m, implying that the time series variables are not cointegrated, (ii) if $0<k<m$, $1<p<m$, implying that the time series variables are cointegrated, and (iii) if k=m, p=0, implying that all the time-series variables are stationary.

The Johansen test has two forms, trace test and maximum eigen value test. The trace test tests the hypothesis that the number of linear combinations i.e. k to be equal to a given value (k^0) and the alternative hypothesis that $k>k^0$: H_0: $k=k^0$, H_1: $k>k^0$ To test for the existence of cointegration using the trace test, k^0 is set to equal to 0 i.e. no cointegration, and if the null hypothesis is rejected, then there is at least one cointegration relationship. The difference of the maximum eigen value is the alternate hypothesis: H_0: $k=k^0$, H_1: $k=k^0+1$. Hence, starting with $k^0=0$ and rejecting the null hypothesis implies that there is only one possible combination of the nonstationary variables to yield a stationary process.

If there is cointegration in the non-stationary time series data, the Vector Error Correction Model (VECM) examines the long-run behaviour of the series by including the cointegration term as an Error Correction

Mechanism (ECM), which allows for long-run equilibrium relationship of cointegrating variables by partially correcting for the short-run adjustments. The VECM can be specified as:

$$\Delta y_t = \alpha_0 + \alpha_1 \Delta x_t + \alpha_2 u_{t-1} + \varepsilon_t \tag{14.4}$$

$$\Delta y_t = \alpha_0 + \alpha_1 \Delta x_t + \alpha_2 (y_{t-1} + \beta_0 + \beta_1 x_{t-1}) + \varepsilon_t \tag{14.5}$$

where Δy_t is the short-run effect. The equation (14.5) explains the relationship between the cointegration equation and the vector error correction mechanism. If the coefficient value of α_2 is negative and statistically significant, then the long-run equilibrium is possible. The negative and significant coefficient of the error correction term indicates that any short-term fluctuations between the independent variables and the dependent variable will be adjusted and give rise to a stable long-run relationship between the variables. If cointegration is detected between the series then there exists a long-term relationship between the variables.

14.4 Empirical Analysis

The Augmented Dickey-Fuller test results for unit root at levels and at first difference are presented in Table 14.2. The test hypothesis is: Ho: presence of unit root, and H_1:no unit root. At levels, the calculated test value is lesser than the critical value at 95 percent confidence interval, and hence the null hypothesis that there is a unit root in the system is accepted. At first difference, the estimated values are greater than the critical values, and hence the null hypothesis is rejected and the alternative hypothesis that there is no unit root in the system is accepted.

Table 14.2: ADF Unit Root Test of Stationarity.

Variable	*Model with*	*At level*		*At first difference*	
		τ-value	*p-value*	*τ-value*	*p-value*
Private transfers	Intercept	-1.401	00572	-6.706	0.000
	Intercept and trend	-2.374	0,386	-6.675	0.000
	None	4.161	0.000	-2.151	0.032
GDP of India	Intercept	0.084	0.960	-5.700	0.000
	Intercept and trend	-1.199	0,897	-5.620	0.000
	None	6.268	0.000	-2.100	0.044
Exchange rate of rupee	Intercept	-0.651	0.847	-4.200	0.002
	Intercept and trend	-1.350	0.857	-4.154	0.011
	None	2.147	0.991	-1.989	0.045
CPI of India	Intercept	-1.150	0.685	-6.600	0.000
	Intercept and trend	-1.719	0,723	-6.438	0.000
	None	4.092	0.000	-1.690	0.085

GDP of US	Intercept	-8.088	0.000	-2.962	0.048
	Intercept and trend	-2.870	0.182	-4.700	0.002
	None	2.318	0.994	-1.533	0.115
International crude oil price	Intercept	-1.563	0.491	-5.604	0.000
	Intercept and trend	-1.836	0.667	-5.515	0.000
	None	0.530	0.826	-5.597	0.000

The Johansen cointegration test results for the existence of number of cointegration relationships between the macroeconomic variables are presented in Table 14.3. The test hypothesis is: Ho: no cointegration, and H_1: there exists cointegration. The Johansen test rejects the null hypothesis of no cointegration between the variables. The trace statistic and the maximum eigen value statistic values are greater than critical values showing cointegration between the variables.

Table 14.3: Johansen Cointegration Test.

Hypothesised no. of CEs	*Trace statistic*	*p-value*	*Maximum eigen value*	*p-value*
None*	154.525	0.000	49.952	0.002
At most 1*	104.573	0.000	36.430	0.024
At most 2*	68.113	0.012	29.932	0.024
At most 3*	38.130	0.004	26.029	0.009
At most 4	12.150	0.149	10.828	0.163
At most 5	1.321	0.250	1.321	0.250

Note: * Rejection of null hypothesis at 5 percent level.

Since the variables are cointegrated the vector error correction model can be estimated. The cointegration equation gives the basis of the cointegration among the variables. The estimated cointegrating equation is presented in Table14.4.

Table 14.4: Cointegrating Equation of International Private Transfers to India.

Dependent variable: $\ln PTS_{IN}$

Variable	*Coefficient*	*t-value*
$\ln PTS_{IN}(-1)$	1.000	-
$\ln GDP_{IN}(-1)$	0.604	0.521
$\ln CPI_{IN}(-1)$	-2.810	-1.373
$\ln ER_{INR}(-1)$	-2.053	-1.506
$\ln GDP_{US}(-1)$	4.474***	7.428
$\ln COP_{IT}(-1)$	-0.949***	-4.525
Constant	-15.168	-

Note: *** significant at 1 percent level.

The cointegration result shows that there is a negative relationship between private transfers and exchange rate, crude oil price and consumer price index. The economic growth of India and the US, measured by their GDP, are positively associated with private transfers to India. An increase in the GDP of US will increase the private transfers to India by 4.5 percent whereas an increase in the international crude oil price will decrease the private transfers to India by almost 1 percent, both of which are statistically highly significant. Though not statistically significant, an increase in GDP of India will boost private transfers to India, whereas an increase in inflation and exchange rate will dampen the private transfers to India.

The vector error correction model (VECM) is applied to find if there is any long-run equilibrium condition in the model. The lag length of 2 has been identified by the Schwarz Information Criterion (SIC). The estimated vector error correction results are presented in Table 14.5. In the estimated VECM, the error correction term is negative and statistically significant showing that 23.3 percent of variation in the short-run deviations of private transfers is adjusted to attain the long-run equilibrium value. The there exists a long-run causality between private transfers and the macroeconomic variables.

Table 14.5: VECM Estimates of International Private Transfers to India.

Variable	*Coefficient*	*Absolute t-value*	*p-value*
ECT	-0.233***	2.60	0.013
$D(\ln PTS_{IN}(-1))$	-0.484**	2.522	0.018
$D(\ln PTS_{IN}(-2))$	0.086	0.411	0.684
$D(\ln GDP_{IN}(-1))$	1.785*	1.840	0.078
$D(\ln GDP_{IN}(-2))$	1.934**	2.200	0.037
$D(\ln CPI_{IN}(-1))$	-1.482	1.115	0.275
$D(\ln CPI_{IN}(-2))$	-0.821	-0.878	0.388
$D(\ln ER_{INR}(-1))$	1.161	0.986	0.333
$D(\ln ER_{INR}(-2))$	0.898	0.958	0.347
$D(\ln GDP_{US}(-1))$	-4.016**	2.300	0.030
$D(\ln GDP_{US}(-2))$	1.394	0.898	0.378
$D(\ln COP_{IT}(-1))$	0.157	1.197	0.243
$D(\ln COP_{IT}(-2))$	-0.063	0.470	0.643
Constant	0.088	0.462	0.647
R-square	0.456		
F-value	4.62		

Note: *** significant at 1 percent level ** significant at 5 percent level
* significant at 10 percent level.

The long-run equilibrium condition is thus:

$D(\ln PTS_{IN})$: $-0.233*[(\ln PTS_{IN}(-1))+0.604*(\ln GDP_{IN}(-1))-2.810*(\ln CPI_{IN}(-1))$
$-2.053*(\ln ER_{INR}(-1))+4.474*(\ln GDP_{US}(-1))-0.949*(\ln COP_{IT}(-1))-15.168]$
$-0.484*[D(\ln PTS_{IN}(-1))]+0.086*[D(\ln PTS_{IN}(-2)]+1.785*[D(\ln GDP_{IN}(-1))]$
$+1.934*[D(\ln GDP_{IN}(-2))]+1.161*[D(\ln ER_{INR}(-1))]+0.898*[D(\ln ER_{INR}(-2))]$
$-1.482*[D(\ln CPI_{IN}(-1))]-0.821*[D(\ln CPI_{IN}(-2))]-4.016)*[D(\ln GDP_{US}($-
$1))]+1.394*[D(\ln GDP_{US}(-2))]+0.157*[D(\ln COP_{IT}(-1))]-0.063*[D(\ln COP_{IT}(-2))]+0.088.$

14.5 Conclusion

The international private transfers to India have been the highest compared among the transfer receiving countries in the world. Moreover, it is growing at an annual rate of 15 percent over the years. Most of these private transfers come from the US and the Middle East, largely as remittances sent by migrants for family maintenance in India. Such private transfers also help in reducing poverty, investments, and to some extent crowd out public transfers. The private transfers have also a strong causal relationship with macroeconomic variables and international variables. Especially the size of transfers in influenced by the GDP of host countries and international prices such as oil price and exchange rates. To examine the long-run relationship between private transfers to India and other such macro variables, this paper has considered six variables over 30 years period from 1975 to 2015. As the data used is time series, various tests of data and relations among the variables are checked and the appropriate model is estimated. The explanatory variables considered are the GDP of India and the US, exchange rate, consumer price index of India, and international crude oil price.

The ADF stationarity test shows that there is no unit root at the first difference of the time series data. The Johansen cointegration test shows the presence of cointegrating equations in the system. The estimated vector error correction model shows that the GDP of US has significantly high impact on private transfers to India. An increase in the GDP of US increases private transfers to India by 4.5 percent whereas an increase in international crude oil price decrease private transfers to India by almost 1 percent, both of which are statistically highly significant. The increase in GDP of India influences private transfers to India positively, while an increase in consumer price index and exchange rate reduces the private transfers to India. The error correction term is statistically significant and negative showing that 23.3 percent of short-run deviations in private transfers to India are adjusted in the long-run equilibrium. Given the size and significance of international private transfers to India, efficient policy measures are needed to channel the private transfers to India for development and infrastructure building of the country which could also contribute to build social overheads and reduce poverty and unemployment problem in India.

Panel Data Econometrics

15

The Determinants of International Migration: Panel Data Analysis

15.1 Introduction

Migration of labour is a key driver in economic development as well as individual development and is one of the high-priority issues for both developing and developed countries. Human migration is defined as the movement by people (as individuals, family units or large groups) from one place to another with the intentions of settling, permanently or temporarily in a new location. Demographers classify migration generally into two types: (i) internal migration - a change of residence within national boundaries, such as between states, provinces, cities, or municipalities or from rural to rural, rural to urban, urban to rural and urban to urban localities, and (ii) international migration - a change of residence over national boundaries, moving to another and stay in the host country for some minimum length of time. Weinstein and Pillai (2001) refer to a third type of migration - forced migration when a person is moved against wish (slaves) or when the move is initiated because of external factors (natural disaster or civil war), as refugee or displaced. Both international and internal migration - permanent, temporary, forced - have everlasting and significant demographic and cultural impacts on the economies and societies of the chosen destination and the place of origin.

There are several reasons and motives, push and pull factors, that cause migration. International migrants leave their origin countries in search of economic opportunities in another country or to rejoin family members who have migrated earlier for jobs or some political issues. Among the individual factors, education is the single most reason for international migration, as students for studies abroad or for employment. Other push factors which impel people to relocate are poor medical care, unavailability of jobs, fewer opportunities, primitive conditions, political fear and religious discrimination, natural disasters and lower odds of finding courtship. The pull factors may include higher chances of employment, better living standards, education, health facilities, security, family ties and marriage, lower crime rate, etc.

The migrants do not move to any one place or a country, they are dispersed across regions and countries around the world, with most having moved from middle-income to high-income regions or countries. In 2015, 244 million people, or 3.3 percent of the world's population lived outside their country of origin. According to the UN 2015 Report, the total number of emigrants from Germany has been 4.045 million, followed by the U.S (3.023 million), Italy (2.9 million), Portugal (2.306 million) and France (2.145 million). Among destination countries, the US records the largest number of international migrants (46.6 million), the other top destination countries being Germany (12.0 million) and United Kingdom (8.5 million). The recent Pew Research Center research on Origins and Destinations of World's migrants highlights the differences in number of outgoing migrants from a country. From the Tables15.1 to 15.3, it is evident that for most of the selected origin countries, the migrant flows have increased over the years, their population have increased between 2001 and 2015, and the unemployment rates have decreased till 2007 and then increased upto 2013 and started declining thereafter. The Figure 15.1 portrays that GDP of all 11 selected countries has an upward linear trend over the span 2000 to 2017.

Table 15.1: Total Number of Migrants in 11 Selected OECD Countries, 2000-2017.

(000s)

Country	*2000*	*2010*	*2017*	*Country*	*2000*	*2010*	*2017*
Australia	380	480	540	Portugal	2000	1940	2270
Canada	1150	1270	1360	Spain	1300	1100	1350
France	1530	1950	2210	Sweden	260	300	350
Germany	3350	3850	4210	United Kingdom	3870	4460	4920
Italy	3120	2610	3030	United States	1990	2650	3020
New Zealand	490	660	830				

Table 15.2: Trend in Population in 11 Selected OECD Countries, 2001-2015.

(000s)

Country	*2000*	*2005*	*2010*	*2015*	*Country*	*2000*	*2005*	*2010*	*2015*
Australia	19269	20239	22120	23800	Portugal	10399	10566	10652	10418
Canada	31025	32288	34169	35950	Spain	41392	44043	46789	46398
France	59911	61234	63027	64457	Sweden	8898	9039	9390	9764
Germany	81536	81671	80895	81708	United Kingdom	59149	60287	63307	65397
Italy	57506	58808	59730	59504	United States	284852	295130	308641	319929
New Zealand	3908	4135	4370	4615					

Table 15.3: Trend in Unemployment Rates in 11 Selected OECD Countries, 2001-2015.

(percent)

Country	*2000*	*2007*	*2013*	*2015*	*Country*	*2000*	*2007*	*2013*	*2015*
Australia	6.7	4.4	5.7	6.1	Portugal	3.8	8.0	16.3	12.4
Canada	7.2	6.0	7.1	6.9	Spain	10.4	8.2	26.1	22.1
France	8.6	7.7	9.9	10.4	Sweden	4.7	6.2	8.1	7.4
Germany	7.8	8.7	5.2	4.6	United Kingdom	4.7	5.3	7.5	5.3
Italy	9.6	6.1	12.2	11.9	United States	4.7	4.6	7.4	5.3
New Zealand	5.4	3.7	6.3	5.4					

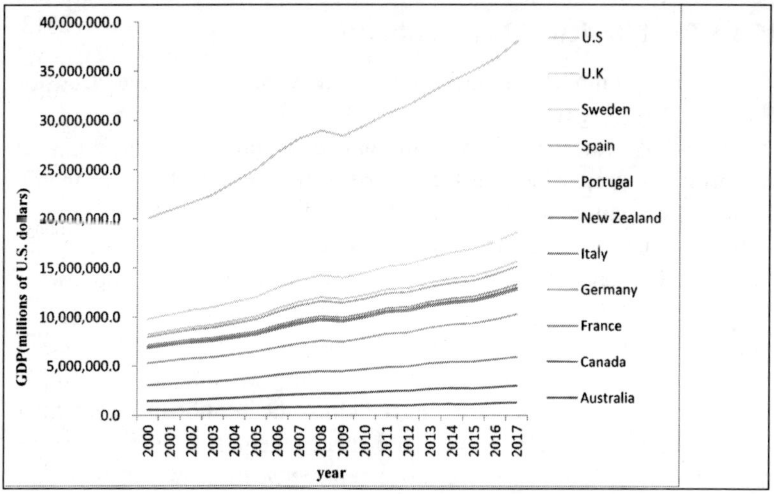

(US$ million)

Figure 15.1: Trend in GDP in 11 Selected OECD Countries, 2000-2017.

Given that these 11 select OECD countries enjoy positive growth rates and high standards of living, as well as low unemployment rates, a moot question is why so many people of these countries migrate to other countries. This paper tries to identify the determinants of international migration and to measure the impact of these determinants on international migration of these select 11 OECD countries, namely Australia, Canada, France, Germany, Italy, New Zealand, Portugal, Spain, Sweden, United Kingdom and United States. The data for this study is for 15 years from 2002 to 2016 collected from various sources. With 15 years data for 11 countries, the total number of observations is 1650. Empirically, this paper follows the panel data regression methods. In this paper, the number of migrants is the response variable. The determinants of international migration are time-invariant factor such as the distance between the countries and the explanatory variables such as population, population, unemployment rate, gross domestic product of origin and destination countries. The empirical analysis distinguishes between the role played by the same explanatory variable in the sending region (push factor) and in the destination region (pull factor). The estimates derived using panel techniques such as pooled ordinary least squares, fixed effects between-group, fixed effects within-group, fixed effects least squares dummy variable method and random effects generalised least squares are computed and compared. Thereafter Hausman test and Breusch-Pagan test are implemented to realise the better estimation technique.

15.2 A Brief Review of Recent Studies

The earliest model of migration, the gravity model, is derived from the Newton's law of gravity, which states that "any two bodies attract one another with a force that is proportional to the product of their masses and inversely proportional to the square of the distance between them". In case of migration, the gravity model is utilised to predict the degree of migration interaction between two places. When used geographically, the words 'bodies' and 'masses' are replaced by 'locations' and 'importance' respectively, where importance can be measured in terms of exogenous (economic and non-economic) variables like population, gross domestic product or other appropriate variables. Thus, the gravity model of migration implies that as the importance of one or both of the location increases, there will also be an increase in movement between them. However, the farther apart the two locations are, the movement between them will be less, a phenomenon known as distance decay. Greenwood (1985) argues that the omission of distance or spatial structure in general may seriously affect empirical studies on migration because distance is a proxy that captures all costs that cannot be measured but surely affects migration flows.

Ravenstein (1885) is the earliest migration theory based on the observation of migration patterns in Great Britain, and later the United States. He proposed that although most migrants travel short distances, longer-distance migrants prefer to go to centers of commerce or industry. Each stream of migration produces a counter-stream at the destination. Large towns owe more of their growth to migration than to natural development and the volume of migration increases with the development of industry and commerce and as transportation improves; most migration is from agricultural areas to urban centers and the main cause of migration is economic. These observations motivated an abundance of quantitative models of migration flows and the aggregate variables that affect those flows.

The Ravenstein as well as Newton based gravity models posit that migration between origin place i and destination place j, m_{ij}, is a positive function of repulsive forces or push factors at i (R_i) and attractive forces or pull factors at j (A_j) and is inversely related to the 'friction' or distance between i and j (D_{ij}):

$$m_{ij} = f(R_i, A_j)/g(D_{ij}) \tag{15.1}$$

In practice, most formulations of the gravity model simply assume that migration between i and j is directly proportional to the product of the two places' populations and inversely proportional to the intervening distance:

$$m_{ij} = (P_i P_j)/D_{ij} \tag{15.2}$$

Population and distance represent the standard gravity variables and population size of both origin and destination countries affect positively the migration while distance, a proxy to costs of migration, discourages migration.

Stouffer (1940) argues that there is no necessary relationship between mobility and distance. Stouffer extends the Ravenstein gravity model by introducing the notion of intervening opportunities. He proposed that migration over a given distance is held to be directly proportional to the number of opportunities at that distance and inversely proportional to the number of intervening opportunities or possible alternative migration destinations between i and j. In other words, the number of persons going a given distance is directly proportional to the percentage increase in opportunities at that distance. In this approach, the nature of particular place may be more important than distance in determining where migrant goes, as generally migrant's base migration decisions on the characteristics, social and economic conditions of the origin and destination.

Lee (1966) summarises the factors which enter into the decision to migrate and the process of migration as: (i) factors associated with the area of origin, (ii) factors associated with the area of destination, (iii) intervening obstacles, and (iv) personal factors. Lee hypotheses that both the destination and the origin have characteristics that attract or repel migrants and that perceptions of these characteristics differ between migrants. Lee notes that not only the actual factors at origin and destination result in migration, but also the perception of these factors leads to migration. Thus, the pull and push factors of migration depend on the evaluation of the situation at origin and knowledge of the situation at the destination.

Lowry (1966) introduces wages and unemployment rates so as to assess for the role played by the economic variables. The basic form of the Lowry model is:

$$m_{ij} = g\left(\frac{u_i}{u_j}, \frac{w_i}{w_j}, \frac{L_i L_j}{D_{ij}}\right) e_{ij} \tag{15.3}$$

where m_{ij} measures the flows of migrants from region i to region j, g is a gravitational constant, u is the unemployment rate, w is the hourly wage in manufacturing sector, L is the labour force, D is the (airline) distance between the two regions and e is the error term. In this formulation, the unemployment rate and the wage level play two different roles. An increase (decrease) in the value of one of these variables in the region of origin or destination relative to the value of the same variable in the destination or origin region can discourage (encourage) migration. That is, they may act as push factors when their value encourages people to leave their country of origin or they may act as pull factors in the destination region when they attract people from other regions.

Mukhopadhyay (1980) compare the aggregate 1961 and 1971 Indian censuses data on birth place migration streams to assess the quantitative magnitudes of various rates of migration for both genders between rural and urban sectors. The analysis shows that the rural migrants in general are deterred by distance (as per gravitational theories of migration), whereas urban migrants in general have a higher propensity to travel long distance.

Anjomani (2002) analyse US interstate migration by groups of determinants: (i) previous gross migration as a proxy for social networks or availability of information, (ii) economic variables like regional income, employment rate, unemployment rate, local income tax, (iii) amenity variables such as population density, mean temperature, welfare benefits, criminality rate, and (iv) demographic variables population size or growth, mean educational level, median population age.

van Wissen et al. (2008) classify the determinants of migration into 6 types of exogenous variables: (i) gravity variables like population size, with positive influence, and physical distance, with negative influence; (ii) economic variables like gross domestic product per capita, newly created businesses, wages, etc., which attract migration, (iii) labour market variables like levels and/or rates of employment and unemployment, changes in working conditions, etc., (iv) real estate variables or housing market variables, possibly high prices of houses and low vacancy rates deterring migration unless anticipated by potential migration, (v) environment variables such as terrain conditions, population density, degree of urbanisation, social behaviour of local inhabitants, climatic conditions, leisure and entertainment activities, which affect quality of life both on short and long-term, and (vi) policy variables like governmental subsidies, local taxes, defense spending, educational offer, urban area plan, or direct measures such as migration incentives and policies also act as a pull factor for migration.

van Leuvensteijn and Parikh (2002) study interregional migration in 16 regions of Germany in order to identify the factors involved, using a panel data and allying the Least Square Dummy Variable (LSDV) and Generalised Method of moments (GMM) estimations. The variables include differential unemployment rate, wage differential for blue-collar and white-collar workers, differentials in hospital and hotel beds per inhabitant, differential in per capita rented or owned housing, differential in rental price per square km, distance between the main cities and differential in cost of living index.

Kumar and Aggarwal (2003) examine migration in Assam by pooling of the 1901 to 1991 Indian census data for 10 major states from where people migrated to Assam. The census data provides total migration from other states and other countries along with the distribution of Assam population by language, sex composition, workers versus non-workers, rural-urban migration and district-wise migration in Assam. They also consider unemployment rate at destination sector and per capita income and urbanisation rates at the destination and origin regions. The study shows that distance and urbanisation are very significant factors for domestic migration, while prospects of higher earnings is the big attraction for foreign migrants, and for female migration, the family related reasons is the main cause.

Andrienko and Guriev (2004) study the determinants of internal migration in Russia using a panel data on gross region-to-region migration flows during 1992-1999 by estimating the effects of economic, political and social factors. The study shows that people relocate from poorer and job scarce regions with worse public good provision to ones that are richer and more prospering both in terms of employment prospects and public goods.

van Wissen et al. (2008) analyse out-migration and in-migration in Sweden, Netherlands and United Kingdom, and in Spain to validate the models. For both out-migration and in-migration, the explanatory variables used in the study are population size, employment, regional mass, unemployment, gross domestic product, accessibility and population density. Internal migration has been modeled as a two-stage process with out-migration followed by destination choice, conditional on out-migration. The internal migration model is estimated as Poisson regression model for the period 1991-1995, and using the estimated model coefficients, the model is validated by predicting the flows for 1996-1998.

Ghatak, Mulhern, and Watson (2008) analyse interregional migration in Poland using the Seemingly Unrelated Regression Equations (SURE) method. The variables considered are GDP per capita, unemployment rate, number of dwellings per 1,000 inhabitants, number of students per 1,000 inhabitants, road distance between capital cities, density of road length, and rate of infant mortality. Though, the Polish regional migration is low by international standards, which is a feature of transitional economies, the migration pattern followed economic patterns being influenced by relative regional economic opportunities and costs. The analysis shows that asymmetry in unemployment and GDP per capita in the origin and destination provinces have strong effect on internal migration. The GDP per capita in the donor province had a stronger influence than in the destination province. Unemployment has a stronger impact on migration in destination rather than donor provinces. Further, provincial migration has been influenced by distance, regional facilities like road infrastructure, human capital and housing.

Etzo (2011) investigate the determinants of interregional migration flows in Italy after the upsurge of 1996, after two decades of decreasing internal migration rates. The fixed effects vector decomposition estimator (FEVD) and the generalised method of moments (GMM) are applied to a gravity model on bilateral migration flows for the period 1996-2005 using population size, distance between main cities, GDP per capita, unemployment rate, infrastructure index and crime rate in both origin and destination regions. The study shows that GDP per capita and unemployment rate are the key determinants whose changes push migrants out from their regions and direct them to prosperous destinations. The distance is also an important determinant and that migrants respond differently to the same variable in the region of origin rather than in the destination one.

Bunea (2012) examine the potential determinants of internal migration in Romania using county data for the period 2004-2008 applying panel data methodologies. From a static point of view, the fixed effects Least Square Dummy Variable regression (LSDV) estimates show significant impacts of population size, real gross product per capita, amenity index, road density and crime rate, and from a dynamic point of view the two step generalised method of moments (GMM) estimates show significant effects of previous migration ratio, population size and amenity index.

15.3 Data and Methodology

This paper uses panel data on international migration between 11 OECD countries for 15 years from 2002 to 2016, a total of 1650 observations. The countries considered are Australia, Canada, France, Germany, Italy, New Zealand, Portugal, Spain, Sweden, United Kingdom and United States. In the empirical analysis, the number of migrants is the response variable and the independent variables are population, unemployment rate, gross domestic product of origin and destination countries, which act as pull and push factors of migration. In the panel context, the time invariant variable is the distance between the two countries.

The data on the dependent variable is assembled from the OECD International Migration database, which gives the number of migrants from country i to country j in thousand units. The distance between two countries is taken from the distance table of distance calculator in the website globefeed.com. The country-wise unemployment rate data is extracted from the ILOSTAT website, where the variable is defined as the number of unemployed persons as a percentage of the total number of employed and unemployed persons (labour force). The statistics on gross domestic product is collected from the IMF World Economic Outlook database, which is measured in US$ millions. The yearly data on population (in thousand units) is derived from the United Nations Population Division database.

In the empirical formulation of the gravity model (Lowry 1966), the number of people moving from region i to region j, m_{ij} depends positively to the population size in each region P_i, P_j and negatively to the distance between the two regions D_{ij}. The basic gravity model is specified as:

$$m_{ij} = g\frac{P_i^{\alpha} P_j^{\beta}}{D_{ij}^{\gamma}} \quad (15.4)$$

where g is a constant. Generalising to include all the possible push and pull factors, an extended version of the gravity model is specified as:

$$m_{ij} = g^{\alpha_0} \frac{P_i^{\alpha 1} P_j^{\alpha 2}}{D_{ij}^{\alpha 3}} \prod_{s=1}^{n} \frac{x_{sj}^{\gamma}}{y_{si}^{\delta}} \qquad (15.5)$$

where y_{si} includes all the possible exogenous variables in the origin region *i* that acts as push factors of migration while X_{sj} include all the exogenous variables that can attract (pull) migrants to the destination *j* (Andrienko and Guriev, 2004).

In logarithmic form, the linear specification of the gravity model is expressed as:

$$lnm_{ij} = \alpha_0 lng + \alpha_1 lnP_i + \alpha_2 lnP_j + \alpha_3 lnD_{ij} + \sum_{s=1}^{n}(\gamma_s lnx_{sj} - \delta_s lnx_{si}) \qquad (15.6)$$

The bilateral migration flows together with distance and the identification of push and pull factors make the logarithmic equation a spatial interaction model.

Panel Data Method

In the econometric estimation, the panel data model is specified as:

$$y_{it} = \alpha + \beta x_{it} + \lambda_i + \gamma_t + u_{it} \qquad (15.7)$$

where γ_t is the solely time dependent variables that does not vary across cross-sections (individual heterogeneity), λ_i is the time invariant solely cross-section dependent variables (country fixed effects), and u_{it} the idiosyncratic error term which satisfy the usual ordinary least square assumptions.

The pooled OLS regression of panel estimation is specified as:

$$y_{it} = \alpha + \beta x_{it} + \lambda_i + u_{it} \qquad (15.8)$$

The pooled regression of y_{it} on x_{it} using all the data together assumes that there is no correlation across individuals or across time periods for any individual. If λ_i contains only a constant term, then estimation by OLS provides consistent and efficient estimates of the intercept α and the slope vector β.

The fixed effects within group regression of panel estimation method removes the effect of those time-invariant characteristics, which are assumed to be unique to the individual and fixed over time, so that the net effect of the predictors on the outcome variable can be obtained. The fixed effects within group panel regression model is specified as:

$$y_{it} = \beta x_{it} + \alpha_i i + u_{it} \qquad (15.9)$$

Taking deviations from the group means:

$$(y_{it} - \bar{y}_i) = \beta(x_{it} - \bar{x}_i) + (u_{it} - \bar{u}_i) \qquad (15.10)$$

Then, the regression parameters are estimated using the within group averages as:

$$\hat{\beta}_W = \frac{\sum_{i=1}^{n}\sum_{t=1}^{T}(x_{it} - \bar{x}_i)(y_{it} - \bar{y}_i)}{\sum_{i=1}^{n}\sum_{t=1}^{T}(x_{it} - \bar{x}_i)^2} \qquad (15.11)$$

The fixed effects between group panel regression of estimation method uses the variation of the group means around the overall mean:

$$(\bar{y}_i - \bar{y}) = \beta(\bar{x}_i - \bar{x}) + (\bar{u}_i - \bar{u}) \qquad (15.12)$$

The parameters of the fixed effects between group panel regression is estimated as:

$$\hat{\beta}_B = \frac{\sum_{i=1}^{n}\sum_{t=1}^{T}\bar{x}_i - \bar{x})(\bar{y}_i - \bar{y})}{\sum_{i=1}^{n}\sum_{t=1}^{T}\bar{x}_i - \bar{x})^2} \qquad (15.13)$$

The fixed effects least squares dummy variable (LSDV) panel regression estimation method specifies a set of dummy variables for each cross-section:

$$y_{it} = \beta x_{it} + d\lambda_i + u_{it} \qquad (15.14)$$

The random effects generalised least squares panel regression estimation method assumes that the variations across observations are random, and hence the time invariant variables can be included in the estimating equation. The random effects panel regression model is specified as:

$$y_{it} = \alpha + \beta x_{it} + \varepsilon_{it} \qquad (15.15)$$

where ε_{it} =(λ_i+u_{it}) is the composite error term. In the estimation, as there is serial correlation in errors i.e. $Cov(u_{it},u_{is})=\sigma^2\#0$, the OLS is inefficient. Therefore, to obtain consistent estimates, the generalised least squares (GLS) method of estimation is to be used.

The pooling of cross section and time series in a panel regression can be tested with the F-test:

H_0: fixed effects intercepts are zero i.e. pooled OLS is applicable.

H_1: fixed effects intercepts are non-zero i.e. fixed effects method is applicable.

The Breusch Pagan Lagrangian Multiplier test for random effects model is based on the OLS residuals. The null hypothesis in the LM test is that variance of errors from a regression is dependent on the values of the independent variable i.e. presence of heteroscedasticity or there is no significant difference across units i.e. no panel effect, which means that pooled OLS can be applicable.

H_0: $\sigma_u^2 = 0$ or correlation between ε_{it} and $\varepsilon_{is} = 0$ or pooled OLS method is applicable.

H_1: $\sigma_u^2 \neq 0$ or random effects method is applicable.

LM is distributed as a chi-squared distribution.

The Hausman specification test is used to choose between fixed or random effects. The Hausman test compares the random and fixed effects estimators which should be approximately the same if the zero-correlation OLS assumption [$Cov(\lambda_i, x_{it})=0$] holds, but different if the assumption is false:

H_0: the preferred model is random effects
H_1: the fixed effect model.

The Hausman test is specified as:

$$H = (\hat{\beta}_{RE} - \hat{\beta}_{FE})'\Omega^{-1}(\hat{\beta}_{RE} - \hat{\beta}_{FE}) \sim \chi_k^2 \qquad (15.16)$$

where Ω^{-1} is the variance-covariance matrix and the statistic is distributed as chi square.

15.4 Empirical Analysis

The determinants of migration considered in this paper are previous year (one year lag) population size, unemployment rates and gross domestic products for both origin and destination countries. The time-invariant factor affecting migration is the distance between the two countries. Some country-specific variables are language, temperature, etc. which may be termed as unobserved heterogeneity and controlled by the panel. With 11 countries and 15 years, for each country, the migration to the remaining 10 countries are considered. The Table 15.4 presents the definition and Table 15.5 presents the descriptive statistics of variables used in the empirical analysis. The United Kingdom has the highest average number of outgoing migrants in thousands (10459.09), whereas Sweden has the lowest (865.46). The migrants from New Zealand travel the highest average distance (16116.68kms), while for German migrants, the average distance traveled is the lowest (5502.041kms). The highest mean recorded for previous year origin population size is 302942.763 thousand of the United States, while New Zealand has the lowest average population size (4272.320 thousand) over the years. In case of unemployment rate of the previous year, Spain has the highest average (15.853), whereas New Zealand has lowest mean (5.247). The highest mean for previous year origin gross domestic product is US$14327509 million for United States, whereas New Zealand has the lowest mean (US$127375.025 millions).

Table 15.4: Definition of Variables in International Migration Analysis.

Variable	*Definition*
Migrants	Number of migrants in the current time period (t) leaving out of their origin or birth country *i* to go to their destination countries of choice *j* (thousands of persons).
Distance	Distance between countries is the straight line distance (flying or air distance) between the two countries based on their center latitudes and longitudes (kilometers).
OPop	Total number of people residing in the origin country (thousands).
DPop	Total number of people residing in the destination country (thousands).
OUnemp	Origin country unemployment rate - ratio of number of unemployed workers to total labour force.
DUnemp	Destination country unemployment rate - ratio of number of unemployed workers to total labour force.
OGDP	Origin country gross domestic product at constant prices (US$ millions).
DGDP	Destination country gross domestic product at constant prices (US$ millions).

Table 15.5: Descriptive Statistics of Variables in International Migration Analysis.

Country	*Migrants*	*Distance*	*OGDP*	*DGDP*	*OUnemp*	*DUnemp*	*OPop*	*DPop*
Australia	3055.285 (5735.95)	13841.05 (3311.628)	855536.4 (185017.1)	2712457 (4062779)	5.45 (0.69)	8.28 (3.92)	21405.1 (1475.6)	67038.04 (82847.79)
Canada	2978.56 (4711.28)	7676.9 (3303.60)	1290574 (214976.1)	2668953 (4080032)	7.13 (0.65)	8.11 (4.0)	33432.57 (1559.56)	65835.29 (83415.94)
France	5085.94 (5208.14)	5553.04 (6369.77)	2196240 (337918.3)	2578386 (4098827)	8.85 (0.86)	7.94 (4.0)	62263.72 (1447.49)	62952.17 (83989.87)
Germany	5146.22 (4479.74)	5502.04 (6033.41)	3064541 (501258)	2491556 (4095118)	7.68 (1.11)	8.05 (3.96)	81370.67 (294.74)	61041.48 (83765.86)
Italy	6522.43 (10142.63)	5799.47 (6037.60)	1954614 (223026.1)	2602549 (4096556)	9.0 (2.0)	7.92 (3.96)	59085.16 (734.51)	63270.03 (83981.51)
New Zealand	3887.48 (9153.23)	16116.68 (4696.63)	127375 (26578.41)	2785273 (4022259)	5.25 (1.08)	8.30 (3.91)	4272.32 (215.37)	68751.31 (81694.87)
Portugal	2688.09 (4315.04)	6012.24 (6419.6)	262392.7 (33122.96)	2771771 (4030975)	9.51 (3.79)	7.87 (3.8)	10549.58 (86.48)	68123.59 (82165.6)
Spain	3901.49 (6298.31)	5910.10 (6492.31)	1360869 (221568)	2661923 (4082320)	15.85 (6.45)	7.23 (2.28)	45079.39 (1868.13)	64670.61 (83779.92)
Sweden	865.46 (862.78)	5713.0 (5392.0)	366119.1 (66378.44)	2761398 (4037282)	7.02 (1.2)	8.12 (3.99)	9271.61 (284.15)	68251.38 (82074.25)
UK	10459.09 (9452.79)	5513.86 (6019.77)	2174332 (320951.7)	2580577 (4098751)	6.02 (1.028)	8.22 (3.94)	62112.57 (2139.44)	62967.29 (83988.25)
US	5660.63 (6041.25)	7671.42 (3954.07)	14327509 (2275331)	1365259 (964572.9)	6.47 (1.7)	8.17 (3.99)	302942.8 (11036.85)	38884.27 (25710.3)

Note: Standard deviations in parentheses.

In the econometric estimation of the determinants of migration, the first task is to identify the appropriate method of estimation, and the second task is to measure the effect of the factors that influence migration. There are various methods of estimating a panel data model, the pooled OLS regression, fixed effects within-group, between-group and least squares dummy variable, and random effects generalised least square methods. Empirically, the estimating extended gravity model is expressed as:

$$lnm_{ijt} = \beta_0 + \beta_1 lnDis_{ij} + \beta_2 lnOGDP_{it-1} + \beta_3 lnDGDP_{jt-1} + \beta_4 lnOUnemp_{it-1} + \beta_5 lnDUnemp_{jt-1} + \beta_6 lnOPop_{it-1} + \beta_7 lnDPop_{jt-1} + \lambda_i + u_{ijt} \quad (15.17)$$

where the prefixes O and D stand for origin and destination countries respectively. The least squares dummy variables (LSDV) is specified as:

$$lnm_{ijt} = \beta_0 + \beta_1 lnDis_{ij} + \beta_2 lnOGDP_{it-1} + \beta_3 lnDGDP_{jt-1} + \beta_4 lnOUnemp_{it-1} + \beta_5 lnDUnemp_{jt-1} + \beta_6 lnOPop_{it-1} + \beta_7 lnDPop_{jt-1} + \beta_8 d2003 + \beta_9 d2004 + \cdots + \beta_{21} d2016 + \lambda_i + u_{ijt} \quad (15.18)$$

with time dummies for the years 2003 to 2016 respectively. The application of fixed effects and random effects methods lie with the question of where to include the time-invariant and individual heterogeneity factors before running the regression.

The empirical results of the panel data estimates are presented in Table 15.6. The coefficient estimates of distance of migration from pooled OLS, fixed effects between-group and random effects GLS methods have statistically significant negative effect on migration at 1 percent level. The estimates of these three methods indicate that for one percentage increase in distance between two countries, there will be 0.52 to 0.76 percent decrease in the number of outgoing migrants respectively. Thus, it is evident that distance between two countries affects the migration negatively, the greater the distance, the lesser will be number of migrants willing to leave their home country. In fixed effects within-group and least square dummy variable estimates, the coefficient of distance variable has been omitted due to collinearity problem.

Table 15.6: Pooled OLS, Fixed Effects LSDV, Within-Group and Between-Group, and Random Effects GLS Estimates of Migration in 11 Select OECD Countries.

Dependent Variable: ln(Outgoing migration)

Variable	*Pooled OLS*	*Fixed effects within-group*	*Fixed effects between-group*	*Fixed effects LSDV*	*Random effects GLS*
lnDist	-0.633*** (20.26)	-	-0.761*** (6.36)	-	-0.515*** (4.97)
lnOGDP	0.075 (0.37)	-1.209*** (39.34)	-1.615 (1.53)	-0.937*** (29.81)	-1.602*** (7.53)
lnDGDP	1.482*** (7.33)	2.445*** (78.53)	0.011 (0.01)	2.338*** (70.75)	2.479*** (11.65)

lnOUemp	-0.540*** (5.82)	0.245*** (49.62)	-2.038*** (3.81)	0.269*** (54.72)	0.234*** (6.38)
lnDUemp	-0.693*** (7.46)	-0.115*** (23.3)	-1.913*** (3.57)	-0.227*** (39.41)	-0.108*** (2.93)
lnOPop	0.536** (2.40)	-0.427*** (5.54)	2.411** (2.07)	-0.661*** (8.74)	2.213*** (8.61)
lnDPop	-1.026*** (4.59)	-1.819*** (27.19)	0.598 (0.51)	-1.986*** (23.14)	-2.080*** (8.09)
Constant	-1.592** (2.16)	13.435*** (16.88)	12.597** (2.35)	15.462*** (16.92)	-2.303 (1.21)
σ_u	-	3.148	-	3.014	1.134
σ_ε	-	0.319	-	0.315	0.319
ρ	-	0.990	-	0.989	0.926
R-square	0.514	0.034	0.3523	0.0512	0.439
F-value/ χ^2	248.91	6476.57	21.23	2916.36	763.18

Note: Absolute t-values for pooled OLS, fixed effects for within-group, between-group and LSDV regressions, and z-values for random effects GLS regression are in parentheses. **** significant at 1 percent level ** significant at 5 percent level * significant at 10 percent level.

The gross domestic product of origin countries discourages migration, whereas the GDP of destination countries encourage migration significantly. The coefficient estimates are significant at 1 percent level in fixed effects within-group, LSDV and random effects methods of estimation. With growing economy, people have more opportunities, and hence no need to migrate. The discouragement effect of home GDP ranges between 1 to 1.6 percent. The random effects GLS estimate for the coefficient of destination GDP shows the maximum effect on the migration. It has a positive and relatively elastic value of 2.48 and thus implies that with one percent increase in the destination GDP, the number of migrants will increase by about 2.5 percent. This shows that migrants prefer to go to a country with better economic growth and living standards acting as a pull factor for migration.

The unemployment rate of previous year at the origin country encourages migration significantly according to fixed effects within-group, LSDV and random effects estimates whereas pooled OLS and fixed effects between group estimates indicate discouragement in the migration. Fixed effects between-group estimate is more elastic and other estimates are inelastic. From the results, it can be inferred that origin unemployment rate acts as a push factor of migration. This is because high unemployment rate origin country means many people are unable to find any work and will have the incentive to migrate to countries which are having higher options of employment. Thus, origin unemployment rate directly influences migration from the home country. In contrast, the coefficient estimates of unemployment rate in the previous year of the destination countries across all methods of estimation are negative and statistically significant at 1 percent level. The coefficient estimates show that for one percent increase in the unemployment rate in the destination country, the outward migration from home country will decrease by 0.10 to 1.9 percent. Thus, it is evident that unemployment rate in the destination country discourages people to leave their origin country as high unemployment rates in the destination country means long spells of search and wait and less probability of finding a suitable job there.

The pooled OLS and fixed effects between-group and random effects coefficient estimates of previous year origin population are significantly positive, whereas fixed effects within-group and LSDV estimates are significantly positive. A one percentage increase in population of origin country increases migration by 2.2 to 2.4 percent, acting as push factor in migration from the origin country. This may be because a large origin population implies lower chances of employment or receiving better opportunities. Compared to the positive effects, the reduction in migration due to home country population increase is rather less, 0.42 to 0.66 percent only. The coefficient estimates of population size of destination countries from all the methods (except insignificant positive fixed effects between-group estimates) are negative and significant at 1 percent level. The estimates indicate that a one percentage increase in the size of the destination population reduces the migration by 1 to 2. Thus, higher the population in the destination country, lower will be the number of people willing to move from their birth or place i.e. a populated country does not attract migration.

The variance of within-group residuals (σ_u) of the random effects GLS estimation (1.13) is much lower than the fixed effects within-group variance (3.13) showing that much of the variations in international migration in the 11 OECD countries are due to time effects rather than country effects. This is also seen from the constant variance of overall error residuals (σ_ε) across estimation methods. The intra-class correlation (ρ) between 0.92 and 0.99 by the panel estimates show that 92.6 to 99 percent of the variations in migration is due to differences across the panels. The R^2 values are in the range of 0.03 of fixed effects within-group estimation to 0.51 of pooled regression and fixed effects LSDV estimations, with 0.44 of random effects GLS estimation. The F-values, indicating whether all the coefficients in the model are different from zero, show that model is correctly specified for pooled OLS and all three fixed effects within-group, between-group and LSDV estimation methods, and by the Wald χ^2 value for the random effects

GLS model. All the test statistics have p-values less than 0.05 showing significance of the fitted model for estimation.

Given the five estimation methodologies of the migration model, the appropriate estimation method is to be identified. The F-test value for pooled OLS vs fixed effects within-group estimation is 6476.57, strongly rejects the null hypothesis that all the coefficients in the model excluding the constant are zero and hence the pooled OLS is not applicable. The Breusch Pagan LM test for pooled OLS vs random effects GLS estimation rejects the null hypothesis of homoscedasticity and hence the pooled OLS method is not applicable. Since the alternative hypothesis of heteroscedasticity is to be accepted, the random effects GLS method may be a suitable method of estimation for the model. The Breusch Pagan LM test model is specified as $lnm_{it} = \beta x_{it} + u_i + \varepsilon_{it}$, for which the estimated results are shown in Table 15.7.

Table 15.7: Breusch-Pagan LM Test for Random Effects.

Dependent variable: ln(migration)

Variable	*Variance*	*Std. dev.*
x	3.087	1.757
u	1.287	1.134
ε	0.102	0.319
Test: var(u) = 0	(01) = 8990.61	Prob >= 0.00

The Hausman specification test value between the fixed effects least square estimates and the random effects generalised least squares estimates, presented in Table 15.8, strongly rejects the null hypothesis that the difference in coefficients is not systematic, and hence the random effects model is not applicable. Though the results of the Hausman test rule is in favour of fixed effects method, the R^2 value for LSDV is 0.0512 or 5.12 percent is very low (Table 15.6).

Table 15.8: Hausman Specification Test for Fixed Effects and Random Effects Estimations.

Variable	*LSDV* (β_{FE})	*RE (GLS)* (β_{RE})	*Difference* (β_{FE}- β_{RE})	$\sqrt{diag(\Omega_{FE} - \Omega_{RE})}$ *std. error*
lnOGDP	-1.340	-1.602	0.262	0.110
lnDGDP	2.568	2.479	0.089	0.131
lnOUemp	0.258	0.234	0.024	0.002
lnDUemp	-0.181	-0.108	-0.073	0.023
lnOPop	0.0408	2.214	-2.173	0.425
lnDPop	-1.545	-2.080	0.536	0.571
Test: H_o: difference in coefficients not systematic				
β_{FE} consistent under H_0 and H_1		β_{RE} inconsistent under H_1 efficient under H_o		
$\chi^2 = (\beta_{FE} - \beta_{RE})'(V_{FE} - R_{RE})^{-1}(\beta_{FE} - \beta_{RE})$ = 58.54				Prob>χ^2 =0.00

From the empirical analysis, it is evident that the random effects GLS estimates for all independent variables are statistically significant. Also, the random effects method has a better explanatory power (R^2=43.89 percent) than those of the fixed effects techniques. Though pooled or LSDV estimations have relatively higher power than the random effects estimator, they do not take into account the differences between cross-sections or over time periods. The pooled OLS assumes that all the intercept terms for all cross-sections are homogenous, whereas country-wise regression should have different intercept terms for different countries. Therefore, it is reasonable to conclude that the random effects (GLS) estimation of the panel of migration data may be a better estimation strategy as also the random effects model produced the estimates that are in line with the assumptions about how each exogenous variable influence migration.

15.5 Conclusion

International migration in OECD countries is sizable and a host of push and pull factors influence migration. This paper tries to identify the factors associated with migration between 11 select OECD countries over 15 years from 2002 to 2016, a panel data of 1650 observations. The exogenous variables considered are the GDP, unemployment rate, population and distance of both origin and destination countries, which are lagged by one year since the migrants would decide on the choice of leaving their origin country based on prior knowledge of the conditions in the sending and receiving countries. An extended gravity model has been estimated using panel data estimation methods of pooled ordinary least squares, fixed effects within-group, between-group and least squares dummy variable, and random effects generalised least squares estimations. A host of tests, the F-test, chi-square test, Breusch Pagan LM test and Hausman specification teat are applied for model fitness.

In the pooled OLS method, the estimates for distance, origin and destination population sizes, origin and destination unemployment rates and destination gross domestic product are statistically significant, whereas estimate for origin gross domestic product is not significant. In fixed effects within-group estimation method, distance not included, all coefficient estimates are statistically significant. In the fixed effects between-group method, the estimates for distance, origin population size and unemployment rate, destination unemployment rate are statistically significant while the other estimates are not. In the fixed effects LSDV method, all estimates of the regression coefficients are statistically significant, distance being omitted. In the random effects GLS estimation, all coefficients are statistically significant. Based on the tests, the random effects GLS estimation method is identified as a suitable estimation technique for migration in OECD countries.

From the estimated results, this paper has observed that distance between two countries affects migration negatively. The greater the distance, lesser will be the number of people willing to migrate from their home country. The GDP, being a measure of economic growth, is a strong pull factor of migration since people migrate due to the urge of residing in a country with better economic growth and living facilities. The empirical results in this paper show that high GDP in the origin country discourages migration, while high GDP in the destination country has a positive effect on migration. The unemployment rate in the origin country directly influences migration while the same in the destination country is inversely related to the number of out-migrants in the home country. This is because high unemployment rate in any country means that job prospects are less, so the migrants will have the incentive to migrate to countries with higher options of employment. The unemployment rate acts as a push factor of migration. The origin and destination population sizes influence the number of outgoing migrants directly. If the rate of increase in origin population is higher than that of the destination country, the chances of migration are higher.

16

The Impact of Corruption and Governance on Economic Growth: Panel Data Analysis

16.1 Introduction

Corruption is a global phenomenon which is endemic to governments all over the world. The World Bank cites corruption as the single most important obstacle to development. It is a subversive force that can topple the most entrenched regimes and it corrodes currencies, markets and investments. Corruption exists in a wide array of illicit behaviour, such as bribery, extortion, fraud, nepotism, graft, speed money, pilferage, theft, and embezzlement, falsification of records, kickbacks, influence peddling, and campaign contributions. While corruption is commonly attributed to the public sector in India, it also exists in other sectors under the sphere of governance, such as political parties, private business sector and NGOs. Corruption poses a major threat to economic growth through reducing the public and private sector efficiency when it enables people to assume positions of power through patronage rather than ability and merit. Even the scale of corruption in institutions and agencies outside the government and political system are no less. Corruption in private business, autonomous institutions/enterprises, civil society and media are widespread and equally affect a nation's social and economic health. Corruption undermines the rule of law, democratic governance, accountability and sustainable development. Corruption has a negative impact on political and economic institutions that are already fragile and contributes to failures in governance and development. Corruption breaches the contract between citizens and public officials, and this has grave consequences for government functioning. Indeed, corruption is a consequence of a collapse of governance and is also a cause of its continued failure.

There is no uniform definition of corruption, because what is regarded as corruption depends on the existing laws and regulations guiding certain actions. Some countries define corruption in the broadest form while others legislated on the narrow definition of the term corruption. However, it is generally accepted that corruption means the misuse or the abuse of public office for private gain. According to Tanzi (1998), corruption is the intentional noncompliance with arm's length relationship aimed at deriving some advantage from this behaviour for oneself or for related individuals. The Transparency International defines corruption as "the misuse of public power for private benefit". Irrespective of how a nation perceives the definition of corruption in its economy, corruption is a deterrent to economic growth and social development of a nation, hence a stumbling block to its well-being and progress.

The Figure 16.1 and Table 16.1 present the level of corruption around the world in the year 2018 where the Corruption Perception Index (CPI) scale ranges from 0 to 100 according to the Transparency International.

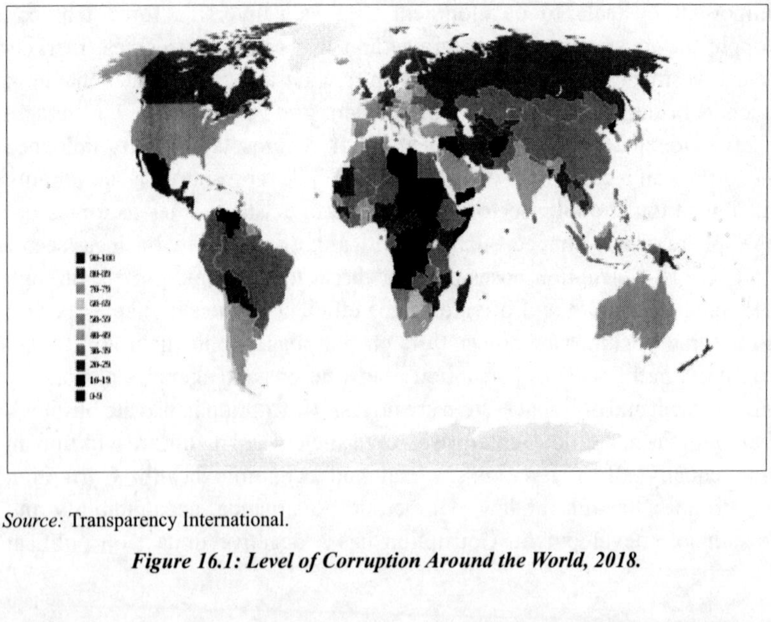

Source: Transparency International.

Figure 16.1: Level of Corruption Around the World, 2018.

According to the Transparency International Denmark is the least corrupted with a CPI score of 88 and Somalia is the most corrupted country with a CPI score of 10 among 180 countries around the world in 2018. The Figure 16.2 presents the rank of India in CPI ranking above 75 in recent years. The Figure 16.3 presents the trend in corruption index scores over the years in India. The level of corruption in India has increased from a low CPI score of around 25 in 1996 to a high score of about 41 in 2011, and thereafter declining in recent years. Still the level of corruption in India is high, and in 2018, India ranks 78 among 180 countries with a score of 41 out of 100 in 2018.

Table 16.1: Least and Most Corrupted Countries in the World, 2018.

Low corruption countries			*High corruption countries*		
Rank	***CPI***	***Country***	***Rank***	***CPI***	***Country***
1	88	Denmark	73	43	South Africa
2	87	New Zealand	78	41	India
3	85	Finland	87	39	China
3	85	Sweden	89	38	Sri Lanka
3	85	Switzerland	105	35	Brazil
3	85	Singapore	117	13	Pakistan
7	82	Norway	138	28	Russia
8	82	Netherlands	176	14	Yeman
9	81	Luxembourg	176	14	North Korea
11	80	Germany	178	13	Syria
22	71	USA	178	13	South Sudan
25	68	Bhutan	180	10	Somalia

Source: Transparency International.

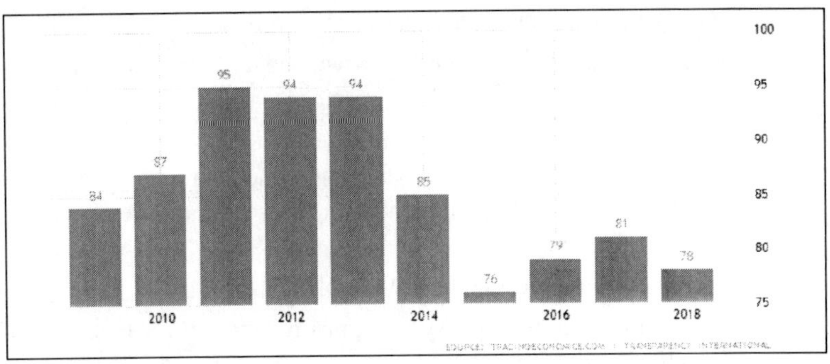

Source: Transparency International.

Figure 16.2: Trend in Corruption Perception Index of India.

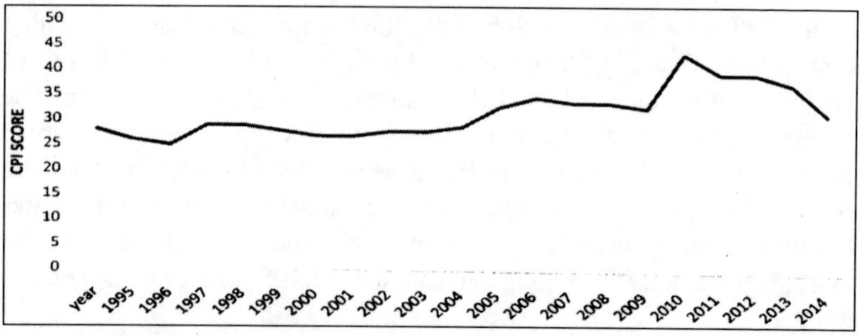

Source: Transparency International.

Figure 16.3: Corruption Perception Index of India (Score)

Frequently, the political and governance systems of a country are cited as the root cause for corruption. Good governance is widely considered to be the solution to most of the problems the country is facing, including corruption. There is no universal acceptance of what constitutes a good governance mechanism, but a sort of agreement does exist on the broad elements of governance as processes and institutions by which authorities are exercised in a country or a region. A good governance covers all aspects of the interface between individuals and business on one hand and government on the other. The Planning Commission of India in its 11th plan says that governance should cover the following distinct dimensions:

- Constitutionally protected right to elect government at various levels in a fair manner, with effective participation by all sections of the population.
- The governments at all levels must be accountable and transparent. Closely related to accountability is the need to eliminate corruption, widely seen as a major deficiency in governance.
- The government must be effective and efficient in delivering social and economic public services, which are its primary responsibilities.
- Local governments (panchayats and municipalities) should be empowered to function efficiently for local economic development and social justice.
- The rule of law must be firmly established.
- The entire administrative system must function in a manner which is to be fair and inclusive.

It is a matter of great concern that the world's largest democracy, India, with a comprehensive constitution and a vibrant civil society has performed so badly on internationally accepted governance indicators. It is also perplexing to see that the largest democracy and third largest economy with rapid economic growth and many-fold increase in budgetary allocations for social sector expenditure, India's ranking in the world in terms Human Development Index (HDI) remains pathetic, ranking lower than even poor and underdeveloped countries. It seems that something must have gone terribly wrong in the democratic governance of the country, for the country has not been able to redistribute fruits of its democracy and rapid economic growth to the majority of its population. Due to corruption and/or otherwise, benefits of growth have remained accumulated in few influential hands. That is why perhaps India has the dubious distinction of having some of the largest numbers of billionaires amidst largest number of the poor in the world. Indeed, an increase in the number of billionaires is indicative of the country's robust macroeconomic performance, but at the same time, a disproportionate decline in poverty is certainly suspicious and is indicative of corruption in governance.

Corruption and governance lie on a continuum but occupy opposite poles, and in fact corruption is the antithesis of good governance. Whereas governance, with its end goal of creating a good government, aims to serve the interest of the largest number of people, corruption, through the use of public office and resources, serves the narrow interest of few families and allies. Good governance with transparency and accountability is fundamental for democracy. Good governance entails an administration that is sensitive and responsive to the needs of the people and is effective in coping with emerging challenges in society by framing and implementing appropriate laws and measures. It includes strict rules for accountability. Good governance largely depends on the extent to which the general citizenry perceives a government to be legitimate i.e. committed to improving the general public welfare, deliver public services, and equitable in its conduct, favouring no special interests or groups. Hence, democratic governance is a necessary requirement to fight corruption.

Generally, some factors which by their very nature (e.g. rigid system, social immobility) cause corruption and some intermediary and accentuating factors (e.g. ignorance, illiteracy, procedural) which provide impetus to corruption. Some of the causative factors of corruption are:

- political factors such as voice and accountability, government effectiveness, political stability, absence of violence.
- institutional factors such as rule of law and regulatory quality.
- social inequalities of patriarchy, caste, language, region and religion.

- centralised democracy, undemocratic dynasty culture, opaque and unaccountable political parties.
- colonial bureaucracy with rigid and discretionary powers, and deeply rooted patronage system.
- ineffective judicial system.

Some of the intermediary/accentuating factors of corruption are:

- outdated rules of governance of police, private sector, religious institutions and NGOs).
- uninformed citizens with widespread illiteracy, unawareness of rights, roles and responsibilities.
- large scale public sector and public procurement policies.:
- lack of self-accountable media and civil society.

Given that there exists a large scale corruption and the level of corruption affects growth and development, and there are evidences that corruption affects economic growth through political institutions and governance, and there are various institutional and regulatory mechanisms to combat corruption, an understanding of the nexus between corruption, political institutions and economic growth in the modern context is warranted. Hence, this paper investigates the effect of corruption and governance on economic growth around the world. Specifically, this paper estimates the effects of voice and accountability, government effectiveness, rule of law, political stability and absence of violence and regulatory quality, and corruption on economic growth. In the empirical analysis, this paper uses a panel data on 110 emerging countries of the world for 15 years from 1999 to 2014). The data are collected from the Political Risk Services (PRS) and the World Bank. The panel fixed effects and random effects models are estimated and the appropriate model is identified by the Hausman test.

16.2 A Brief Review of Recent Literature

Research on the causes and consequences of corruption is not a recent phenomenon; it has a long history in economics dating back to at least with a seminal contribution of the rent seeking literature. This section focuses on the econometric analyses on the consequences of corruption for governance and economic growth.

Akai, Horiuchi and Sakata (2005) estimate the short-run and long-run effects of corruption on economic growth in the US during the period 1991-2000 using a state level cross section data and applying the two stage least square (2SLS) method. Theoretical studies suggest that government failure is a function of corruption, and corruption should have detrimental effect on economic growth in the long-run, and at the same time, corruption may counteract government failure and promote economic growth in the short-run, given exogenously determined suboptimal bureaucratic rules and regulations. The paper measures the rate of economic growth for various time spans, short (1998-2000), middle (1995-2000) and long (1991-2000), and separately estimate the effect of corruption on growth using previously uninvestigated state level cross section data. The 2SLS estimates, with a carefully selected set of instruments, shows that the effect of corruption on economic growth is indeed negative and statistically significant in the middle and long-spans but insignificant in the short-span.

Del Monte and Papagni (2001; 2007) analyse the long-run consequences of bureaucratic corruption by estimating the effect of corruption on productivity of public investment in 20 regions of Italy using a dynamic panel data approach. A model of economic growth with public inputs to private production and private inputs to public goods is formulated in which the bureaucrats buy from the private sector for production of public goods with some degree of discretion. The aim of an illegal agreement between the exchanging parties is to profit from the lack of information and the governments fight corruption through costly public purchases monitoring. The extent of corruption is a decision variable in the maximisation of expected revenue. This model finds support in the panel data analysis of the Italian regions. The effect of corruption on public investment productivity is significant and distinct from a direct negative effective of corruption on the growth rate.

Akinlabi, Hamed and Awoniyi (2011) examine the causality and effect of corruption on foreign direct investment inflow and economic growth in Nigeria. Using the time series data covering 1990 and 2009 and employing the Granger causality test and OLS method, the paper finds there is an inverse relationship between FDI inflow and corruption in Nigeria. A large volume of FDI inflow is associated with a low level of corruption, the exchange rate depreciation and inflation rate are significant determinants of FDI inflow to Nigeria. Also, there is a significant positive relationship between FDI inflow and economic growth in Nigeria.

Adenike (2013) study the impact of corruption on economic growth in Nigeria using annual time series data for the period 1980-2009 applying regression, Granger causality test and impulse response function methods. The empirical results show that in Nigeria corruption per worker exerts a negative influence on output per worker directly and also indirectly on foreign private investment, expenditure on education and capital expenditure per worker. Furthermore, the study reveals that there is a one-sided causality where the direction of influence runs from output per worker to corruption per worker. The study therefore recommends a strategy of actions in various sectors in combating corruption in the Nigerian economy as against a single action, establishment of anti-corruption agency.

Zidi and Dhifallah (2013) study governance and economic growth for a group of 30 developing countries over the period 1998-2011. The paper investigates the impact of the quality of political institutions on economic growth linking between corruption, governance and economic performance using panel data method. The estimated results show that improving the quality of political institutions decreases the level of corruption and boosts sustainable economic growth in developing countries. The paper concludes that the governance increases government accountably to citizens and also strengthens their commitment to policies chosen especially in the fight against corruption.

In India, Dutta, Kar and Roy (2013) study the effect of corruption on the informal sector using a cross section data for 20 Indian states and applying the OLS method. India has a huge informal sector and the extent of corruption in every sector is remarkably high. In fact, stifling bureaucratic interference and corruption at every stage of any activity is one of the main reasons behind high participation in informal and unregulated sectors. Also, for economies characterised by high inequality and poverty, corruption is a useful tool for the government to pacify social unrest, allowing a lower level of governance with substantial corruption in the system. Indeed, the estimated empirical results show that higher corruption increases level of employment in the informal sector. Further result reveals that the higher the level of lagged state domestic product, the positive impact of corruption on the size of the informal sector is nullified.

16.3 Data and Methodology

The main objective of the study is to examine the impact of corruption and governance on economic growth. Towards this end, this paper uses a panel data for 110 emerging countries over 15 years from 1999 to 2014. This paper considers seven variables for empirical estimation viz. growth rate, corruption and governance variables voice and accountability of the citizens, political stability and absence of violence, effectiveness of government, quality of regulations and rule of law. The data on growth rate is obtained from the World Bank World Development Indicators and the data on corruption, political institutions and governance are collected from the Political Risk Services Group database. The panel estimation methods of fixed effects and random effects methods are used in the empirical analysis. Panel data contains the same countries in each cross section repeated over time. Unlike the separate time series and pooled cross section estimations, the panel data controls for the country specific unobservable heterogeneity and time-invariant variables, and the correlation between the omitted variables and the error term.

The Political Risk Services (PRS) or the 'Coplin-O'Leary Country Risk Rating System' is the methodology developed by William Coplin and Michael O'Leary at the Maxwell School of Citizenship and Public Affairs, Syracuse University with the U.S. Department of State, the Central Intelligence Agency, and other government agencies and major multinational corporations. Political Risk Services is the most widely accepted system of completely independent political risk forecasting. For each country, data are collected in a specific format across 17 categories which are then converted into 0-3 scores (low, very high or best, worst). The numerical scores are then converted to create alphabetical ratings and are reported for each country.

Panel Data Method

In the fixed effects model, the individual heterogeneity is assumed to be constant or fixed and uncorrelated with other explanatory variables. These fixed effect variables, which are indicative of the economic behaviour of countries, are used to control each country being different from another. If individual fixed effects are omitted, then the omitted variable bias will cause biased and inconsistent coefficient estimates of the explanatory variables. Therefore, the fixed effects model takes the time-invariant country effects in the constant term of the regression. The panel data model can be specified as:

$$y_{it} = \alpha + \beta x_{it} + \lambda_i + u_{it} \tag{16.1}$$

The fixed effects model is specified as:

$$y_{it} = \alpha_i + \beta x_{it} + u_{it} \tag{16.2}$$

where α_i includes the country specific fixed effects (λ_i).

When the individual country effects are not controlled and are uncorrelated with explanatory variables, then the country effects can be specified as a country specific random element and included as a regressor in the estimating equation. The random effects model can be specified as:

$$y_{it} = \beta x_{it} + \varepsilon_{it} \tag{16.3}$$

where $\varepsilon_{it} = (\lambda_i + u_{it})$, the individual fixed effects is a part of the error term. The random effects panel model is estimated by the generalised least squares method.

As both the fixed effects and random effects models can be estimated on the panel data, the appropriate model for the given data is decided by the Hausman specification test. The Hausman test is based on the fact that the random effects model should be preferred as it takes into account the time effects (between variations) and the random country specific effects whereas in the fixed effects model considers only cross section (within variations) and time effects are assumed to be constant. If the zero-correlation OLS assumption $[Cov(\lambda_i, x_{it}) = 0]$ holds, then the Hausman test is to test the difference in the estimates of fixed effects model versus random effects model for significance. The null hypothesis of Hausman test is constrained by insignificance of fixed effects regression model. The Hausman test is specified as:

$$H = (\hat{\beta}_{RE} - \hat{\beta}_{FE})' \Omega^{-1} (\hat{\beta}_{RE} - \hat{\beta}_{FE}) \sim \chi^2_k \qquad (16.4)$$

where Ω^{-1} is the variance-covariance matrix and the test statistics is distributed as chi square. If chi-square statistic rejects the null hypothesis (random effects regression), the fixed effects model is the choice otherwise random effects occur.

16.4 Empirical Analysis

In the empirical analysis of the effect of corruption and governance on economic growth, the annual growth rate of the country is the dependent variable. The definition of the variables used in the study and their descriptive statistics are presented in Table 16.2. In the 110 emerging economies, the average growth rate is 2.8 percent and the mean corruption score is 0.38. All the governance variable scores are above average, except the effectiveness of government.

Table 16.2: Descriptive Statistics of Variables in the Corruption and Governance Analysis.

Variable	*Description*	*Mean*	*Std. dev.*
GR (annual growth rate)	Growth rate of real GDP of countries (2010 base)	2.780	5.627
CR (level of corruption)	Extent of public power for personal interests and private profit in terms of wealth and gain (0-1 score)	0.386	0.145
VA (voice and accountability)	Ability of a country's citizens to participate and choose the government, based on a number of indicators measuring various aspects of the political process, civil liberties and human rights (0-1 score)	0.595	0.227

PV (political stability and absence of violence)	The likelihood that the government in power will be destabilised or overthrown by unconstitutional means and/or violent or threatened by the public such as terrorism (0-1 score)	0.711	0.114
GE (government effectiveness)	Aspects of quality and availability of public service, the bureaucracy, the competence of civil servants, the independence of the administration of political pressure and the credibility and transparency of the government's reform commitments and policies (0-1 score)	0.473	0.226
RQ (regulatory quality)	Policies and measures of bank supervision and monitoring as well as the perception of the blockage imposed by excessive regulation in areas such as foreign trade and business climate (0-1 score)	0.630	0.202
RL (rule of law)	Indicators that measures the confidence of citizens in accordance with the laws and rules of society (0-1 score)	0.568	0.192
Obs.		1750	

The Table 16.3 presents the fixed effects and random effects panel regression estimates for the impact of corruption and governance on economic growth. In both fixed effects and random effects estimates, the effect of corruption on economic growth is significantly negative, clearly indicating that corruption is harmful to the growth of the economy. An increase in corruption reduces growth rate by 3.5 to 4.15 percent. Political stability and absence of violence has a statistically significant positive effect on growth rate, where the poor governance by the government has a negative effect on economic growth. An increase in political stability and absence of violence would increase growth by 4.5 units. A unit increase in government effectiveness will decrease the growth rate by 4 units. In the random effects model, the effects of the quality of regulation and rule of law are significantly positive. An increase in regulatory quality will increase economic growth rate by 2.15 percent and an increase in rule of law affect the annual growth by 1.75 units.

Table 16.3: Panel Fixed Effects and Random Effects Estimates of Corruption and Governance on Economic Growth.

Dependent variable: Growth rate

Variable	*Fixed effects*	*Random effects*
CR	-3.574** (2.37)	-4.156*** (3.38)
VA	1.718 (0.90)	0.919 (0.56)
PV	4.477** (1.98)	1.725 (1.04)
GE	-4.015* (1.86)	-1.629 (1.63)
RQ	1.817 (1.62)	2.215** (2.35)

RL	-0.680 (0.33)	1.754* (1.67)
Constant	1.097 (0.55)	0.910 (0.40)
σ_u	2.192	1.476
σ_ε	5.391	6.388
ρ	0.141	0.070
F-value/chi²	8.23	30.47
Prob>F/chi²	0.00	0.00

Note: Absolute t-values in parentheses. *** significant at 1 percent level ** significant at 5 percent level * significant at 10 percent level.

The Hausman's specification test result for the appropriateness of the fixed effects and the random effects models is presented Table 16.4. The null hypothesis being the preferred model is random effects vs the alternative hypothesis being the acceptance of fixed effects model. It basically tests whether the unique errors (u_i) are correlated with the regressors, and the null hypothesis is they are not. The Hausman test leads to the conclusion that the random effects model is more suitable for the data as the test result shows p-value as 0.617 which is higher than 0.05.

Table 16.4: Hausman Specification Test.

Variable	*Fixed effects*	*Random effects*	*Difference*	*Std. error*
CR	-3.574	-4.176	0.602	0.839
VA	1.718	0.923	0.791	1.449
PV	4.477	1.801	2.676	1.568
GE	-4.015	-1.557	2.458	1.904
RQ	1.817	2.213	-0.397	0.727
RL	-0.680	1.761	2.440	1.721
Constant	1.097	0.910	0.188	1.672
Hausman test: H_0: difference in coefficients not systematic.				
β_{FE}: consistent under H_0 and H_1				
β_{RE}: efficient under H_0 and inconsistent under H_1				
Test: $H = (\beta_{FE} - \beta_{RE})'(V_{FE} - R_{RE})^{-1}(\beta_{FE} - \beta_{RE}) \sim \chi^2 = 5.35$				
Prob.>chi²= 0.62				

The Breusch Pagan Lagrangian Multiplier test for random effects model is given by: The null hypothesis in the LM test is that variance across entities is zero i.e. no significant difference across units (no panel effect):

H_0: $\sigma_u^2 = 0$ or correlation between ε_{it} and $\varepsilon_{is} = 0$.

H_1: $\sigma_u^2 \neq 0$ or random effects method is applicable.

The LM is distributed as a chi-squared distribution. The estimated Breusch Pagan LM test result presented in Table 16.5 shows LM at 0.0001, meaning there is a significant difference across the countries and thus random effect model is accepted over the fixed effects regression.

Table 16.5: Breusch-Pagan LM Test for Random Effects Estimation.

Dependent variable: Growth rate

Variable	*Variance*	*Std. dev.*
x	36404.1	190.757
u	29.164	5.400
ε	37377.77	193.333
Test: var(u) = 0	χ^2 (01) = 13027.40	Prob > χ^2 = 0.00

16.5 Conclusion

The quality of political institutions is a rule of the game more important in determining the form of economic behaviour of countries. Similarly, corruption has been one of the main institutional failures characterising emerging countries, and there is no doubt that corruption has a detrimental impact on economic performance. The quality of governance, coupled with corruption, is significant in explaining the performance of economies. This paper has focused on empirically analysing the interaction between the quality of political institutions, corruption and economic performance in 110 emerging countries over the period of 15 years from 1999-2014. The data are collected from World Bank and Political Risk Services database. Empirically, this paper followed the fixed effects and random effects panel regression methods of estimation. The estimated results show that corruption impacts economic growth negatively while good governance is associated positively with economic growth. The effect of regulations and rule of law on economic growth is positive while space for voice and accountability and political stability and absence of violence have insignificant effects on growth rate. Therefore, it is clear that corruption is detrimental in countries with low income levels that are less integrated into the global economy and are generally the most populous. The weak and undemocratic political institutions and lack of democracy increases corruption. Thus, these institutional failures that characterise developing countries tend to destabilise their long-term economic growth. Hence, a great deal of democratisation and decentralisation would be better for improving economic growth in the emerging economies.

Appendix 16

Table 16A: List of 110 Emerging Countries in the Study on Corruption, Governance and Economic Growth

Albania	Czech Republic	Latvia	Saudi Arabia
Algeria	Dominican	Liberia	Senegal
Angola	Republic	Libya	Serbia
Argentina	Ecuador	Lithuania	Sierra Leone
Armenia	Egypt	Madagascar	Singapore
Azerbaijan	El Salvador	Malawi	Slovakia
Bahamas	Estonia	Malaysia	Slovenia
Bahrain	Ethiopia	Mali	South Africa
Bangladesh	Gabon	Malta and Gozo	Sri Lanka
Bolivia	Gambia	Myanmar	Sudan
Botswana	Ghana	Mexico	Suriname
Brazil	Guatemala	Moldova	Syria
Brunei	Guinea	Mongolia	Taiwan
Bulgaria	Guinea Bissau	Morocco	Tanzania
Cameroon	Guyana	Mozambique	Thailand
Chile	Haiti	Namibia	Togo
China	Honduras	Nicaragua	Trinidad and Tobago
Colombia	Hong Kong	Niger	Tunisia
Democratic	Hungary	Nigeria	Turkey
Republic Congo	India	Oman	Uganda
(Kinshasha)	Indonesia	Pakistan	Ukraine
Republic of	Iran	Panama	United Arab
Congo	Iraq	Papua New Guinea	Emirates
(Brazzaville)	Israel	Paraguay	Uruguay
Costa Rica	Jamaica	Peru	Venezuela
Cote D' Ivoire	Jordon	Philippines	Vietnam
Croatia	Kazakhstan	Poland	Yemen United
Cuba	Kenya	Romania	Zambia
Cyprus	Kuwait	Russia	Zimbabwe

17

The Effect of Unemployment on Crime: Panel Data Analysis of Vehicle Theft

17.1 Introduction

Persistence of unemployment is one of the major characteristics of India. Despite the efforts of the governments and with many government programmes, the unemployment situation is grim, and in fact, it is increasing, especially the educated unemployment. Unemployment is a situation where in the person willing to work fails to find a job that earns him/her a living. Unemployment has been considered as one of the biggest problems of India. The United Nations Labour Report 2017 reports that "Unemployment in India is projected to increase from 17.7 million in 2016 to 17.8 million in 2017 and 18 million in the year 2018. The reasons for this persistent unemployment scenario are (i) high population (ii) defective education system (iii) excessive burden on agriculture (iv) low productivity in agriculture sector combined with lack of alternative opportunities for agricultural worker (v) unskilled workforce and much more. Though education level in the recent years has improved, skill development is still a crucial issue. India has the largest population of youth in the world, majority without skills and training. Around 65 percent of population of India is under the age of 35, and the impact of unemployment and lack of job opportunities have the worst effect on the youths in India.

It is practically impossible to imagine a better India with such a big number of unemployed youths in the country. A major consequence of this massive unemployment situation is its direct impact on crimes and unlawful activities of youths. The growing crime rate is a result of the deterioration of living standards and lack of gainful employment. Since the very beginning of civilisation, the one thing that disrupts humanity is the growing crime rates. With the magnitude of crime blowing over, lot of effort put into eliminating crime and yet the crime rates have only increased with time. Crime is no longer viewed as only one problem to a given society. Rather it is an integral part of understanding a nation's socio, cultural, political, and economic situation. India is no exception. Crime exists in India in various forms such as murder, extortion, drug trafficking, money laundering, fraud, human trafficking, poaching, prostitution, etc.

People steal and commit various crimes to acquire quick money. The unemployed youth's inability of finding money to fulfill the materialistic desires makes them more prone to committing crimes like burglary and robbery. The emotional structures of the unemployed people crumble down owing to rise of desires and decline of measures to look after the family. Apart from unemployment, a host of factors influence the level of crime in a society. In fact, the Scottish Centre for Crime and Justice Research (SCCJR) found that people do not engage in criminal activities when they are underemployed or completely unemployed. The criminal psychology takes birth in the minds of people who cannot find work without any socially acceptable reasons. There is lesser property crime when people have part-time jobs as they are occupied with work rather than sitting idle.

Increasing crime rates hinder development of the society in many ways. For instance, the increase in crime rate compels the government to devote resources in policing, litigation and prevention, which could have been invested in poverty alleviation, increasing jobs, health, education, productive sectors, etc. Huge sums of money are spent on building prisons, purchasing instruments to combat crime as well as making payment to people involved in crime control and justice system. In this way, increasing criminal activities increase expenses of the government thereby hindering the development of society.

Further, the number of people dying yearly due to criminal activities increases with the increase in crime rate in the country. Crimes lead to the death of people either directly or indirectly. Also, properties are destroyed due to crimes committed. Destruction of properties due to vandalism, juvenile offenses and other violent crimes is one of the serious impacts of crimes in the societies. The commission of crimes in the society also results in an increase in the cost of living in the society. This comes about in several ways such as the cost is taken by the society to prevent crimes, cost incurred to investigate and prosecute criminal as well as the cost incurred by the society in keeping those imprisoned for criminal doings.

The Figure 17.1 presents the share various types of crimes in India classified under the Indian Penal Code (IPC). It consists of violent crimes and property crimes. The crimes in India consists of violent crimes like murder, property crimes like theft, burglary and cheating. The major type of crime in India is property crime, theft accounting for a major share of 17 percent in the overall crime that took place in India in the year 2016, followed by negligent driving (12 percent). Deaths caused by negligence, burglary, cruelty by husband, cheating, kidnapping, assault on women and rioting constitute around 5 to 2 percent each of all crimes committed in India. Among the major property crimes, as shown in Figure 17.2, the motor vehicle theft constitutes 33 percent, followed by 17 percent of burglary thefts. The auto thefts share in the total property crime is high, as it is often reported for insurance reasons, while other property crimes are not always reported (Freeman, 1999). Moreover, the auto theft is largely committed by youths, especially the unemployed youths.

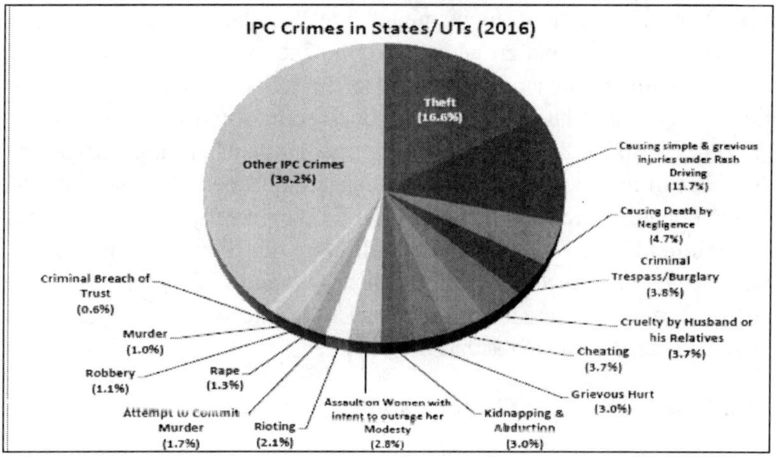

Source: National Crime Records Bureau, 2016.

Figure 17.1: Crime in India, 2016.

India being one of the countries with high crime rates, it is necessary to examine if unemployment fuels the crime rate in the country. Both the variables have been fluctuating over the years and there is no similar trend in crime rates and unemployment rate in India which could lead to the conclusion that there is no systematic relationship between unemployment and crime. However, a closer look is warranted in the light of increasing

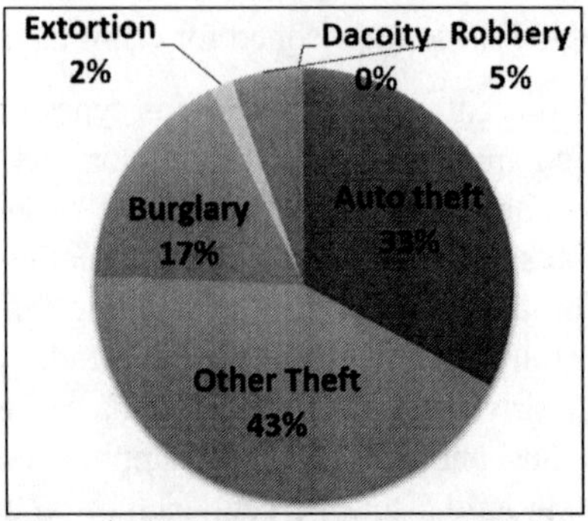

Source – National Crime Records Bureau (NCRB).

Figure 17.2: Major Property Crimes in India, 2016.

crimes in India in recent years. Previous attempts to validate the unemployment - crime hypothesis, though consider various independent variables, largely ignore the rate of change of unemployment which could act as an important variable to study the effect of unemployment over time. This paper attempts to examine the relationship between changes in unemployment rate and crime rate over a panel of four years from 2012 to 2016. Further, this study also analyse the relationship between school enrolment rate and the crime rate. As property crimes constitute a major part of crimes in India, this paper studies property related crimes, particularly the crime of motor vehicle theft. The data are obtained from the National Crime Records Bureau (NCRB), Annual Employment and Unemployment Survey, and U-DISE (Unified District Information System for Education. Empirically, the effects of unemployment rate and school enrolment rate on crime rate are estimated by the panel fixed effects and random effects model and the Hausman test has been applied.

17.2 A Brief Review of Recent Studies

Theoretically, crime is a causation activity. The criminological theories seek to explain the causes of crime in terms of biology and sociology. The biological theories attempt to locate the causes of crime within the individual suggest that there are identifiable differences between offenders and non-offenders. The earlier biological explanations of crime assume that some people are 'born criminals', who are physiologically distinct from non-criminals. However, contemporary approaches to the biology of crime do not seek criminal behaviour in terms of measuring physical features of the body. Rather, they focus on biochemical conditions (poor diet or hormone imbalance), neurophysiological conditions (learning disabilities caused by brain damage), genetic inheritance and/or abnormality, and intelligence. In other words, the criminal is 'other': in some way different or abnormal to non-criminals.

The sociological approaches suggest that crime is shaped by factors external to the individual, such as their experiences within the neighbourhood, the peer group, and the family. Contemporary theories of crime emphasise place and space, such as the defensible space theory, which examines how the design of physical space is related to crime, broken windows theory, which looks the relationship between low level disorder and crime, and routine activities theory, which considers how opportunities to commit crime are shaped by between people's everyday movements through space and time. Economic theories of crime focus on the costs and benefits of committing crime, placing emphasise on the opportunity costs. The main cost of crime is not the money involved but the probability of crime being detected and caught, and the severity of punishment if caught. If the chance of crime being caught is less, the incentive to commit a crime is high.

There have been two major schools of thought on the specific unemployment-crime relationship, one focusing on the 'supply of offenders' and the other emphasises the 'supply of victims'. Sociologists and criminologists focus on the supply of suitable victims. As higher unemployment rate is correlated with a wider decrease in production and consumption, there is less new merchandise in the 'market' to be stolen. Economists on the other hand focus on explaining the economic behaviour of potential offenders and the way they react to changes in economic conditions. In offender is more likely to commit a criminal act during a period of unemployment in order to maintain a certain standard of living.

Since Gary Becker (1968), there have been numerous contributors to the literature on economics of crime. Becker focus on the neoclassical type decision making process of potential criminals use a simple cost-benefit analysis in which criminals make their decisions by considering the benefit of committing a crime and subtracting from that the probability of being caught multiplied by the severity of punishment if caught. Becker argues that potential criminals establish a baseline from their individual risk preferences that helps them decide whether or not they will commit a certain crime. Building on the crime model of Becker (1968), Ehrlich (1996) develops a theory on the 'supply of offenses'. In this 'market model' of crime, the net return per offense equals expected payoff minus direct costs of activity minus opportunity cost of illegitimate activity over illegitimate activity over minus the probability of conviction multiplied by the severity of punishment. That is, net return from crime = nominal financial gain - [direct cost + wage foregone - (probability conviction x punishment)]. Therefore, the net return per offense must exceed some level before the individual commits a crime, depending on each person's risk preference and utility and disutility associated with the illegal activity. The Ehrlich model for the supply of illegitimate activity has been widely used for analysing various crimes over the years.

The Britt's (1994) theory on the relationship between crime and unemployment builds on two opposite premises - motivational perspective and opportunity perspective. The motivational perspective states that as the economic condition deteriorates people are motivated to resort to crime as a source of income. On the other hand, the opportunity perspective sees crime as a supply of potential offenders and suitable victims. During rough economic periods people and places become less suitable victims because they themselves do not have money or excess material goods and personal property is more guarded, and therefore, a negative relationship between economic circumstances and crime should exist. The motivational perspective is the intuitive theory that economists expect to exist in the relationship between unemployment and crime, while Britt's results show that the opportunity perspective has the dominant effect across crimes.

There is an extensive empirical literature on the relationship between unemployment rate and crime rate. Although the approach of this literature is the same, the empirical results on this relationship turn out dissimilar. Melick (2003) attempt to understand which has an overriding effect in the motor vehicle theft and unemployment relationship - motivational perspective or opportunity perspective, in a state level analysis in the US. He uses a cross sectional time series data for twenty years for ten states in the United States. The unemployment rate is used to capture opportunity perspective while change in the unemployment rate captures motivational perspective. The panel fixed effects estimates show that there is significant negative relationship between crime and unemployment due to opportunity effect and positive relationship between crime and change in unemployment rate due to motivational perspective.

Edmark (2005) analyse a panel data of counties over the years 1988-1999 to study the effects of unemployment on property crime rates in Sweden using the fixed-effects method. The results show that unemployment has a positive and significant effect on property crimes. Among the covariates, the coefficients for the clear-up rate, population density and divorce rate are significant for most of the property crimes. Surprisingly, the coefficient for population density is large, a reduction in population density of

1 percent is estimated to lead to an increase in aggregate property crime by almost 1.4 percent.

Raphael and Winter-Ebmer (2001) analyse the unemployment-crime relationship a panel of US states for the period 1971-1997. The OLS regression estimates on seven felony offences show that the effect of unemployment is positive and significant on all types of property crimes. However, the results for violent crime are mixed. The two-stage least squares (2SLS) estimates, that use the state military contracts and a measure of state exposure to oil shocks as instruments for unemployment rates, also show that unemployment exerts a consistent, positive, and highly significant effect on the total property crime rates and the 2SLS estimates exceed the OLS effects.

Lin (2008) focus on the relation between unemployment and crime, applying the instrumental variable technique for the panel data of 49 US states covering the period 1974-2000. The study considers seven crime categories as dependent variables and the total number of prisoners and consumption of ethanol per person among the independent variables, with real exchange rates and oil prices as the instrumental variables. The estimated results show that unemployment has a positive and significant, but relatively small, effect on property crimes.

Goa, Liu and Kouassi (2017) examines the contemporaneous effect of unemployment on crime rates in the US state of Indiana using a panel dataset of 23 sample counties for the years 2006-2013. The panel fixed-effects results show that unemployment has a negative effect on violent crime rate. The paper argues that this is because during unemployment people are less likely to be outside but more like to stay within their properties, and therefore, a higher unemployment rate reduces the number of potential targets of violent crime activities. It is also observed that males and youths of age 14-25 contribute positively to both violent crimes and property crimes, providing evidence in support of the criminal opportunity effect theory.

17.3 Data and Methodology

In an attempt to examine the relationship between unemployment and crime in India, this paper uses a panel data for 28 states in India (except the newly created Telengana) for the time period from 2012 to 2016. The variables considered are motor vehicle theft rate, unemployment rate, school enrolment rate and change in the unemployment rate. The relevant data on motor vehicles theft are obtained from the National Crime Records Bureau (NCRB), on unemployment from the Annual Employment and

Unemployment Surveys, and the enrolment data from the U-DISE (Unified District Information System for Education).

Panel Data Method

In the empirical analysis of the determinants of crime in India, the panel data methodology is followed. Panel data is a longitudinal data that combines cross-section and time-series data containing observations of multiple time periods for the same units. The panel data considers explicitly the individual-specific heterogeneity, more variation, less collinearity and more degrees of freedom, and is best suited than cross-sectional data for studying the dynamics of change. The panel estimation techniques are pooled regression, least squares dummy variable regression, fixed effects and random effects regression methods.

The pooled panel regression model regards each observation as unrelated to the others over panels and time. The pooled regression model is specified as:

$$y_{it} = \alpha + \beta x_{it} + \lambda_i + u_{it} \tag{17.1}$$

where λ_i represents the individual effects. Though the estimates are efficient, the pooled model does not encompass the individual effects as it is assumed to be constant. In the individual effects are correlated with the error term, the pooled regression will produce biased estimates.

The fixed effects model is a useful specification for explaining cross section heterogeneity in panel data. The fixed effects model explores the unemployment-crime relationship assuming that some unobservables within the cross section may impact the outcome and bias the estimates, and hence they have to be controlled. It is also assumed that such time-invariant characteristics are unique to the individual unit and is not correlated with other individual characteristics and the error term. The time-invariant individual effects are added with the constant term and the net effects of other explanatory variables are estimated. The fixed effects regression model is specified as:

$$y_{it} = (\alpha + \lambda_i) + \beta x_{it} + u_{it} \tag{17.2}$$

The fixed effects model can be estimated in three ways: least squares dummy variable (LSDV), within-group and between-group regressions.

In the LSDV estimation, the individual effects are assumed to be fixed over time in each cross-section and hence each cross sectional unit is introduced as dummy variables in the estimating equation. The LSDV regression model can be specified as:

$$y_{it} = \beta x_{it} + D\lambda_i + u_{it} \tag{17.3}$$

where D represents dummy for every unobserved λ_i. However, the LSDV inserts as many dummies as the cross section units and hence so many parameters have to be additionally estimated, enlarging the number of parameter estimates and reducing degrees of freedom regression model, and sometimes leading to dummy variable trap.

Instead of knowing the statistical properties of the unobserved heterogeneity, the individual effects could also be eliminated by simply taking the cross section (within group) average. Thus, the within-group fixed effects regression model can be specified as:

$$(y_{it} - \bar{y}_i) = \beta(x_{it} - \bar{x}_i) + +(u_{it} - \bar{u}_i) \tag{17.4}$$

This time averaging within each cross section eliminates all the time invariant variables thus eliminating the λ_i from the estimating equation. Then, the regression parameters can be simply estimated using the within group averages as:

$$\hat{\beta}_W = \frac{\sum_{i=1}^{n}\sum_{t=1}^{T}(x_{it}-\bar{x}_i)(y_{it}-\bar{y}_i)}{\sum_{i=1}^{n}\sum_{t=1}^{T}(x_{it}-\bar{x}_i)^2} = \frac{w_{xy}}{w_{xx}} \tag{17.5}$$

In the between-group fixed effects method, instead of eliminating the individual effects from the regression, the effects of λ_i are amplified by averaging out all the within-cross section variations, leaving only between-cross section variations. Thus, there will be no estimate for those variables which are constant across cross section units. The between-group fixed effects regression model can be specified as:

$$\bar{y}_i = \beta\bar{x}_i + \bar{u}_i \tag{17.6}$$

This shows the variation of the group means around the overall means and the parameters can be estimated as:

$$\hat{\beta}_B = \frac{\sum_{i=1}^{n}\sum_{t=1}^{T}\bar{x}_i-\bar{x})(\bar{y}_i-\bar{y})}{\sum_{i=1}^{n}\sum_{t=1}^{T}\bar{x}_i-\bar{x})^2} = \frac{B_{xy}}{B_{xx}} \tag{17.7}$$

However, in all the three fixed effects estimations, the assumption is that the error terms are uncorrelated. If the error terms are correlated, then the fixed effects estimation is not suitable as the estimates will be biased and inconsistent.

Unlike the fixed effects models where the individual effects are assumed to be constant and eliminated from estimation by averaging, the random effects regression model assumes that the individual effects λ_i are random and hence have a distribution, and are uncorrelated with the independent variables. An advantage of random effects regression is that the time invariant variables need not be absorbed by the intercept. As λ_i is now random and unobserved, it becomes a part of the error term and hence a distribution function can be specified for the composite error term. The random effects model can be specified as:

$$y_{it} = \alpha + \beta x_{it} + \varepsilon_{it} \tag{17.8}$$

where $\varepsilon_{it} = (\lambda_i + u_{it})$. However, the OLS estimators of the random effects model are inefficient as the condition of serial independence is not met i.e. $Cov(u_{it},u_{is})=\sigma^2 \neq 0$. To avoid inefficiency, the generalised least squares (GLS) method of estimation is to be used.

As the random effects model has the advantage of incorporating the randomness of the individual heterogeneity, the random effects model gives consistent, albeit inefficient, estimates of the parameters. However, if there are omitted variables, the individual specific component λ_i might be correlated with the independent variables in the random effects model, to which the fixed effect model is robust. At the same time, the fixed effects model estimates are consistent, but inefficient, as the λ_i are assumed to be constant and uncorrelated with the error term. Therefore, the choice between fixed effects and random effects panel regression estimation methods is critical. Hausman (1978) has devised a test to choose between the two on the basis that both the random and fixed effects estimators should be approximately the same if the zero-correlation assumption $[Cov(\lambda_i,x_{it})=0]$ holds, but different if the assumption is false. The Hausman test defines the null and alternative hypotheses as:

H_0: The appropriate model is random effects. There is no correlation between the error term and the independent variables in the panel data model i.e. $Cov(\lambda_i,x_{it})=0$.

H_1: The appropriate model is fixed effects. The correlation between the error term and the independent variables in the panel data model is statistically significant i.e. $Cov(\lambda_i,x_{it})\neq 0$.

The Hausman statistic is calculated as:

$$H = (\hat{\beta}_{RE} - \hat{\beta}_{FE})'\,\Omega^{-1}(\hat{\beta}_{RE} - \hat{\beta}_{FE}) \sim \chi^2_k \tag{17.9}$$

Under the null hypothesis, both the estimators are unbiased and consistent. But the random effects estimator is more efficient and so the standard error $(\hat{\beta}_{FE})$>standard error $(\hat{\beta}_{RE})$>. The H statistic is compared with the critical values for the χ^2 distribution for k degrees of freedom. The null hypothesis is rejected if the Hausman statistic is higher than its critical value. And the conclusion is that the fixed effects model is more appropriate.

17.4 Empirical Analysis

The Table 17.1 presents the descriptive statistics of the variables used in the analysis of the relationship between unemployment and crime in India. The dependent variable considered is the motor vehicle theft rate and the independent variables are unemployment rate, school enrolment, and change in the unemployment rate which captures the motivation for theft over time. The Table 17.1 shows that the average motor vehicle theft rate is 39 per 100,000 inhabitants in India. The highest motor vehicle theft rate of 90 has been reported in Mizoram and the least motor vehicle theft rate of 6.4 has been recorded in Tripura in the year 2016. The average unemployment rate has been 4. 65 percent, least in Chhattisgarh with 1.6 percent and high in Goa in 2012. The rate of change in the unemployment rate is substantial, 31 percent over the five years. The mean school enrolment has been 69.17 percent, with the highest of 3.68 crores enrolled in Uttar Pradesh in 2015 and lowest enrolment of 1.05 lakh is in Sikkim in 2016.

Table 17.1: Descriptive Statistics of Variable in the Relationship between Unemployment and Crime Analysis.

Variable	*Description*	*Mean*	*Std. dev.*
Mvt	Number of motor vehicles stolen per 1,00,000 inhabitants	28.96	16.74
Unemp	Labour force without work (percent)	4.65	2.99
Enrl	Number of students enrolled in all types and classes of schools (lakhs)	69.17	79.22
Dunemp	Change in the unemployment rate	31.05	71.31
Obs.		140	

The paper mainly focuses on the relationship between crime rate and unemployment rate from the motivational perspective and opportunity perspective as put forward by Britt (1994). The testing hypothesis is that the effect of unemployment on crime is positive, since unemployed seek some standard of living with quick money acquired by theft as unemployment motivates individuals to commit crime. The panel model is estimated by pooled OLS, LSDV, within group fixed effects, between group fixed effects and random effects regression methods. The estimating panel regression model is specified as:

$$Mvt_{it} + \beta_0 + \beta_1 Unemp_{it} + \beta_2 \ln{(Enrl)_{it}} + v_{it} \tag{17.10}$$

where v_{it} represents u_{it} for OLS, LSDV, within group fixed effects, between group fixed effects models and ε_{it} for random effects model.

The Table 17.2 presents the panel estimates of all specifications. The estimated pooled regression coefficients of unemployment and school enrolment are negative, but statistically insignificant. As the pooled regression is simply an OLS regression, it does not take into account the unobserved heterogeneity. The F-statistic is poor and also insignificant. The R-square value is just 1 percent showing that the pooled OLS regression is not the best way to estimate a panel data.

The LSDV regression captures the unobserved heterogeneity which are unique characteristics of a state by the inclusion of state dummies in the estimation. In the LSDV regression, the effect of unemployment rate on crime rate is positive and highly significant and the impact of school enrolment on crime is negative and significant at 10 percent level. For every percentage point increase in the unemployment rate there will be about 1.63 more stolen vehicles per 100,000 inhabitants, and a percent increase in school enrolment will decrease the motor vehicle theft by 11.17 percent. This result suggests that the motivational perspective outweighs the opportunity perspective for crime in India. Most of the state dummies are negative and significant, compared to the reference state Andhra Pradesh. The F-value is 62.69 and statistically significant showing the fit of the LSDV model.

The within group fixed effects estimates also confirm the LSDV estimates. The unemployment rate and crime are significantly positively related and there is a significant negative relation between school enrolment and crime rate. These two variables explain about 23 percent of within states variations in crime rate in India. The significance of the F-statistic rejects the null hypothesis that the coefficients on the regressors are all jointly zero, suggesting the fit of the specified model.

The between group fixed effects panel regression estimates show an insignificant negative relationship between unemployment and crime and school enrolment and crime. While the within state effects explain the crime rate variations by 22 percent, the between states effect is only 0.5 percent of variations in crime rate in India. Further, the insignificant F-statistic of 0.79 implies that the coefficients of the regressors are all jointly zero, and hence the between group regression model is not appropriate to estimate the relationship between unemployment and crime.

In the random effects panel regression model, in which the randomness of state heterogeneity is accounted for, the effect of unemployment rate on motor vehicle theft is positive and highly significant. A one percent increase in the unemployment rate will increase the motor vehicle rate by almost 1.5 times. The school enrolment coefficient is negative and significant at 10 percent level showing that motor vehicle theft rates will fall by 0.75 percent with one percent increase in school enrolment in India.

The estimated σ_u is 16.34 and σ_ε is 4.49 and, by assertion, the correlation between state heterogeneity (λ_i) and the independent variables (x_{it}) is zero. The rho (ρ) value of 0.93 shows that 92 percent of variations in the crime rate is due to differences across the panels. The significant Wald-chi square value of 27.4 rejects the hypothesis the coefficients in the model are zero, and hence the model is correctly specified.

Table 17.2: Panel Regression Estimates of Crime in India.

Dependent variable: Mvt

Variable	*Pooled regression*	*LSDV*	*Within fixed effects#*	*Between fixed effects*	*Random effects*	*Fixed effects regression@*
Uemp	-0.716 (0.502)	1.63*** (0.28)	1.63*** (0.28)	-1.43 (1.27)	1.43*** (0.27)	1.75*** (0.28)
lnEnrl	-1.61 (0.94)	-11.17* (6.7)	-11.17* (6.7)	-2.08 (2.14)	-0.75* (1.95)	-7.33 (8.3)
Dunemp	-	-	-	-	-	-1.32*** (0.01)
Year2013	-	-	-		-	-1.47 (1.1)
Year2014 -			- -	-	-	-1.05 (1.4)
Year2015	-	-	-	--	-	-1.53 (1.3)
Year2016	-	-	-		-	-2.20* (1.3)
Constant	56.20*** (15.15)	20.76*** (5.66)	-	-	-	-
F-value/Wald chi^2	1.23	16.88	16.88	1.79	27.43	6.77
Prob>F/ chi^2	0.166	0.00	0.000	0.46	0.00	0.000
σ_u	-	-	-	-	16.34	-
σ_ε	-	-	-	-	4.49	-
ρ	-	-	-	-	0.930	
Within R^2	-	-	0.235	0.217	0.224	-
Between R^2	-	-	0.005	0.060	0.011	-
Overall R^2	-	-	0.006	0.023	0.002	-
Adj. R^2/R^2	0.10	0.92	-	-	-	0.31

Note: Standard errors in parentheses. # state dummies included. @ year dummies included. *** significant at 1 percent level ** significant at 5 percent level *** significant at 10 percent level.

The appropriate panel model for the data to be chosen is decided by the Hausman test where the null hypothesis is that the preferred model is random effects and the alternative is the fixed effects. It basically tests whether the unique errors (u_i) are correlated with the regressors, for which the null hypothesis is that they are not. The Table 17.3 shows that the Hausman test rejects the null hypothesis as the chi-square values are significantly high. Therefore, the fixed effects model which produces consistent coefficient estimates is fit for the data.

Table 17.3: Hausman Specification Test for Fixed Effects vs Random Effects.

Variable	$\widehat{\beta}_{FE}$	$\widehat{\beta}_{RE}$	$\widehat{\beta}_{FE} - \widehat{\beta}_{RE}$	$\sqrt{diag(V_{FE} - V_{RE})}$ *std. error*
Unemp	1.63	1.43	0.20	0.60
Enrl	-11.17	-0.75	-10.41	8.01
β_{FE} consistent under H_0 and H_1		β_{RE} inconsistent under H_1 efficient under H_o		
Test: H_o: difference in coefficients not systematic				
χ^2=$(\beta_{FE} - \beta_{RE})'(V_{FE} - R_{RE})^{-1}(\beta_{FE} - \beta_{RE})$= 24.13				Prob>χ^2 =0.00

Since the results from the Hausman test shows that fixed effect model is consistent, the panel model is reestimated by including the time dummies to capture the changes in crime rate over time. The inclusion of year effects in the regression eliminates the influence of factors that cause year-to-year changes in the crime rate. The expanded panel regression model is specified as:

$$Mvt_{it} + \beta_0 + \beta_1 Unemp_{it} + \beta_2 \ln(Enrl)_{it} + \beta_3 Dunemp + \beta_4 2013 + \beta_4 2014 + \beta_5 20015 + \beta_6 2016 + v_{it} \quad (17.11)$$

where year 2012 is the reference category. A new variable, the change in unemployment rate over time (Dunemp) is also included to see how change in unemployment over time affects the crime rate. The estimated results are presented in the last column of Table17. 3. It can be seen that both the positive effect of unemployment and the negative of school education on crime rate increases with the inclusion of the year dummies and changes in unemployment rate. The coefficient of unemployment is statistically significant.

However, the effect of the changes in the unemployment rate on crime rate is negative and statistically significant. As the unemployment rate increases over years, the crime rate decreases by 1.32 times which almost nullifying the positive effect of the unemployment rate. The year dummies are also negative, but statistically insignificant, showing that over the years the effect of unemployment on motor vehicle theft decreases. In the year 2013, the motor vehicle theft rate was 1.47 lesser than that of the previous year. And in 2016, the theft rate is a negative 2.20. The results of this study are in contradiction with the motivation perspective of crime. However, with increasing unemployment, people themselves do not have money and much material goods that make victims less suitable for theft. Moreover, the unemployed people will guard their personal property with more vigil, providing less opportunity for stealing. Thus, the contradicting result is to be seen from the view point of the opportunity perspective of crimes that states that there is a negative relationship between unemployment and crime. As unemployment becomes stationary at a higher level, motor vehicle theft drops considerably. The estimates of this paper show that during periods of stationary unemployment levels the motivational effect dominates while during periods of changing in unemployment rates the opportunity effect dominates.

17.5 Conclusion

In the history, crime often hampers the development of the society. Crime is a harmful act, whether blue collar or white collar crime, the omissions against the public is viewed as criminal activities which the state wishes to prevent with severe punishments of fine, imprisonment, and/or death. Criminal activities may be violent like murder or property crime like theft. Among the many types of property crime, the motor vehicle thefts are among the highest reported crimes. There is common view that most motor vehicle thefts are committed by youngsters, especially the unemployed. In pursuit of living requirements or maintaining some standard of living or quick money, the unemployed engage in thefts. The motor vehicles become easy targets as the vehicle is in open place and can be quickly changed and sold with some criminal nexus. Unlike other property crimes, the risk involved is less as the target is known and open and visible and can be quickly steeled and disposed. The reporting of motor vehicles is high for reasons of insurance claim.

The relationship between unemployment and crime is explained by some theories in terms of the 'supply of offenders' and 'supply of victims'. Economic theories of crime focus on the costs and benefits of crime, the costs being the opportunity cost in terms of the probabilities of crime caught and the quantum of punishment. Sociological theories explain the unemployment-crime relation in terms of motivational perspective and opportunity perspective. The motivational perspective posits that as the economic condition deteriorates the unemployed are motivated to resort to crime as a source of income. The opportunity perspective sees crime as a supply of potential offenders and suitable victims. Thus, there exists a market for crime with potential offenders and victims, the theft offender being mostly the unemployed youth.

In order to examine the effect of unemployment on crime in India, this paper uses the motor vehicle theft as the crime. The period of study is from 2012 to 2016 and the variables in the study include motor vehicle theft rate, unemployment rate, school enrolment and the change in the rate of unemployment rate. The state level data are collected from the NCRB, Employment- Unemployment Survey of India and DISE. The panel data methodologies of pooled regression, LSDV, fixed effects and random effects methods have been used in the empirical analysis of the effect of unemployment on crime. The Hausman test shows that fixed effect model gives consistent estimates. In all panel estimates unemployment rate has a significant positive on motor vehicle theft and school enrolment effect on crime is a significant negative. An increase in unemployment rate increase motor vehicles theft by 1.4 to 1.7 times and an increase in school enrolment decreases the motor vehicle theft by 2 to 11 percent. However, the change in unemployment rate reduces motor vehicle theft almost equally. These opposing effects of unemployment on crime show the dominance of opportunity effect over the motivational effect. This new insight, the fluctuation in unemployment rates, suggests that the focus should be redirected from view of 'supply of offenders' to the 'supply of victims'.

Thus, though higher unemployment causes higher crime rates, some safety nets like unemployment insurance, part-time job, earning while learning, etc. that has been installed to aid people through difficult times, certainly desist unemployed youths from committing unlawful activities. Even with long spells of unemployment, youths should be guarded against the opportunity to commit a criminal act in the long-run.

Appendix 17

Table 17: A Panel LSDV Estimates of Crime in India.

Dependent variable: Mvt

Variable	*Estimate*	*Variable*	*Estimate*
Uemp	1.63*** (0.28)	Maharashtra	18.11*** (4.2)
ln(Enrl)	-11.17* (6.7)	Manipur	-27.19 (25.6)
Arunachal Pradesh	-41.53 (29.0)	Meghalaya	-35.04 (22.8)
Assam	-4.55 (6.2)	Mizoram	1.20 (32.63)
Bihar	-11.87** (6.03)	Nagaland	-55.66** (28.1)
Chhattisgarh	-16.82** (7.75)	Odisha	-14.33*** (5.3)
Goa	-43.45 (34.3)	Punjab	-22.68*** (8.9)
Gujarat	-8.64** (3.4)	Rajasthan	10.14*** (2.9)
Haryana	28.88*** (9.4)	Sikkim	-74.59** (38.2)
Himachal Pradesh	-46.92** (20.2)	Tamil Nadu	-14.05*** (3.1)
Jammu & Kashmir	-43.25*** (15.2)	Tripura	-59.26** (24.7)
Jharkhand	-18.02*** (5.2)	Uttar Pradesh	0.69 (9.9)

Karnataka	-1.85 (3.7)	Uttarakhand	-38.90** (16.0)
Kerala	-42.20*** (9.7)	West Bengal	-8.25** (3.37)
Madhya Pradesh	6.51* (3.5)	Constant	20.76*** (5.66)
F-value	16.88		
Prob>F	0.00		
R^2	0.92		

Note: Standard errors in parentheses. *** significant at 1 percent level** significant at 5 percent level *** significant at 10 percent level.

18

The Determinants of Tax Efforts: Panel Data Analysis of Own Tax Revenue of States

18.1 Introduction

The constitution of India provides independent revenue raising and spending power to both the central and state governments. It also admits the existence of vertical fiscal imbalances in taxing power that exist because of unequal assignment of resources and responsibilities among different tiers of government (Roy and Raychaudhuri, 2007). Federal fiscal transfers are justified to offset the fiscal disadvantages of states that arise from low taxable capacity and low unit cost of providing public services. Federal transfers help states to reduce the vertical and horizontal fiscal imbalances and to achieve equity and efficiency. Even though transfers supplement state revenues to achieve equity and efficiency, they are not substitutes for states own revenues. The federal transfers are shared by the centre with states through many channels: (i) finance commission that distributes the divisible taxes and provides grants-in-aid, (ii) planning commission that makes transfers in the form of state plans, and (iii) various central ministries.

Since expenditure of states exceeds their tax revenue, inter-governmental transfers make an important and significant part of the states' total revenue. The Table 18.1 presents sources of revenue of states in India and the relative share of the various components in total revenue during the period 1991-92 to 2010-11. These components consist of states' own tax revenue, transfers from central government and various ministries, borrowing and other revenue sources. In states, the own tax revenue forms 39.3 percent of their total revenue in 2010-2011. Among the tax revenues of states, a major part, about 85 percent, comes from state sales tax, tax on property and capital transactions and state excise tax. All other taxes such as motor vehicle tax and entertainment tax are minor taxes. Generally, between 1991-92 and 2010-11, the state taxes revenue sources remained more or less at the same level and the central transfers declined from 42 percent of state revenues to 33 percent. As the dependence of states on central transfers has declined, and own tax revenue has not increased over time, the states have resorted to the loans, which have increased from 5 percent to 15 percent during this period.

Table 18.1: Sources of Revenue for States in India (percent).

Source	*1991-92*	*2001-02*	*2010-11*
1. Own tax revenue	33.2	33.7	39.3
Sales tax	19.5	20.0	23.8
State excise tax	5.0	4.5	5.0
Property and capital transaction tax	3.1	3.5	5.2
Vehicle tax	1.7	2.0	2.1
Tax on duties on electricity	1.5	1.3	1.5
Tax on goods and passengers	1.1	1.0	1.0
Tax on profession trades and callings	0.4	0.8	0.3
Agricultural income tax	0.2	0.02	0.0
Entertainment tax	0.3	0.2	0.1
2. Total transfers	41.9	32.6	33.4
Central tax transfers	15.6	14.3	18.7
Grants	14.1	11.7	13.9
Plan grants	11.1	8.0	9.8
Non-plan grants	3.0	3.7	4.2
Central loans	12.1	6.7	0.8
3. Internal loans	4.7	18.3	14.5
Market loans	3.1	5.2	8.9
4. Other sources	41.9	15.4	12.8

Source: Reserve Bank of India: Statistics on State Finances (2012).

In understanding the inter-governmental transfers mechanism and the rules applied in transferring resources from centre to states in India, it is very important to know the criteria used by different finance commissions and the planning commission. So far, 15 Finance Commissions have been in force in India and each commission has followed different criteria while the planning commission of India follows a different mechanism for central transfers to states. The Finance Commissions of India have been using criteria like population, poverty, backwardness, income distance, inverse income, area, infrastructure, fiscal discipline, tax effort and forest cover of states as main criteria for determining the shares of the states in the central tax pool of income tax and excise duty for fiscal capacity equalisation and vertical transfers. In addition to tax devolution to the states, the union government also gives grants-in-aid to states on the basis of the difference between the assessed expenditure and the sum of the projected own revenues and shares in central taxes to fill the revenue gaps of states. The Table 18.2 summarises the transfer criteria of the finance commissions of India in giving grants-in-aid and sharing income tax and excise tax between the centre and states.

Table 18.2: Transfer Criteria of Finance Commissions for Grants to States in India.

Finance commission	***Transfers and criteria***	
First Finance Commission (1952-57)	Grants	For four states - Assam, Bihar, Odisha, West Bengal - to cover their deficits during 1951-56
		For eight states to improve their primary education facilities
	Income tax	55 percent in the proceeds; 80 percent on the basis of the population, 20 percent on the basis of revenue collection of the state
	Excise duty	40 percent of the net proceeds on the basis of population
Second Finance Commission (1957-62)	Grants	Larger grants in aid for meeting development
	Income tax	60 percent in the proceeds; 90 percent on the basis of population, 10 percent on the basis of revenue collection
	Excise duty	25 percent of the net proceeds
Third Finance Commission (1962-66)	Grants	Rs. 550 crores to all states except Maharashtra to cover part of their revenue expenditure
		Rs. 45 crores for all states for improvement of communications
	Income tax	60 percent in the proceeds; 80 percent on the basis of population and 20 percent on the basis of revenue collection of the state
	Excise duty	20 percent of net proceeds
Fourth Finance Commission (1966-69)	Grants	Rs. 610 crores to cover deficits during the period 1966-71
	Income tax	70 percent in the proceeds; 80 percent on the basis of population, 20 percent on the basis of revenue collection of the state income taxes
	Excise duty	20 percent of net proceeds

Fifth Finance Commission (1969-74)	Grants	Rs. 638 crores to cover deficits during the period 1969-74
	Income tax	75 percent in the proceeds; population criterion of devolution of income tax
	Excise duty	No change
Sixth Finance Commission (1974-79)	Grants	Rs. 2510 crores for 14 out of 21 states to cover non-plan revenue deficit
	Income tax	80 percent in the proceeds; population criterion of devolution of income tax
	Excise duty	No change
Seventh Finance Commission (1978-84)	Grants	Rs. 1600 crores to cover deficits of a few poor states during the period 1980-85 and to upgrade the standard of administration
	Income tax	85 percent in the proceeds; population criterion of devolution, of income tax
	Excise duty	40 percent of the net proceeds; 25 percent weight equally for population, increase in per capita income, percentage of poor in each state; a formula for income equalisation between states
Eighth Finance Commission (1984-89)	Grants	Rs. 1556 crores to cover deficits for the period 1985-90; Rs. 915 crores to certain states to upgrade the standard of administration
	Income tax	85 percent of the net proceeds as states share; 10 percent on the basis of income tax collection; Out of remaining 90 percent, 25 percent on the basis of population, 25 percent on the basis of inverse of per capita income of the state multiplied by population, 50 percent on the basis of the distance of per capita income of a state from the highest per capita income state multiplied by the population of the state
	Excise duty	44 percent of the net proceeds; 5 percent to deficit states
Ninth Finance Commission (1989-95)	Grants	Rs. 15017 crores to cover deficits of plan and non-plan revenue account during 1990-95; special annual grant of Rs. 603 crores towards centre's contribution for the calamity relief fund totaling Rs. 3015crores for five years 1990-95; Rs. 122 crores to Madhya Pradesh towards expenditure on rehabilitation and relief of victims of Bhopal gas leak
	Income tax	85 percent in the proceeds; followed the 8th Finance Commission formula; added the backwardness of states on the basis of scheduled caste and scheduled tribe population and the number of agricultural labourers in states as in 1981 census
	Excise duty	45 percent in the proceeds; 25 percent on the basis of 1971 census; 12.5 percent on the basis of index of backwardness; 33.5 percent on the basis of per capita income of the state from highest per capita income state; 12.5 percent on the basis of income adjusted total population; 16.5 percent among states with deficits, after taking into account their shares from all shareable taxes

Tenth Finance Commission (1995-2000)	Grants	Rs. 20300 crores; Rs. 7583 crores to such states for meeting special requirement; Rs. 5380 crores to local bodies like municipalities and panchayats; Rs. 6304 crores to Calamity Relief Fund
	Income tax	77.5 percent of the net proceeds as states share; 20 percent on the basis of population of 1971; 60 percent on the basis of distance of per capita income of a state from that of the state having highest per capita income; 5 percent on the basis of area adjusted; 5 percent on the basis of an index of infrastructure; 10 percent on the basis of tax effort
	Excise duty	47.5 percent of net proceeds to be shared among states on the basis of the same formula used in sharing income tax; 40 percent distributed among major states; 7.5 percent distributed among deficit states
	Additional excise duty	50 percent on the basis of population; 40 percent on the basis of state domestic product; 10 percent on the basis of state sales tax collection
Eleventh Finance Commission (2000-2005)	Grants	Rs. 35359 crores for states facing revenue deficit after devolution of grants; Rs. 4793 crores for certain states for up gradation of administration and special problems; Rs. 8000 crores to panchayats and Rs. 2000 crores to municipalities for five years 2000-2005
	Share of union tax revenues	29.5 percent share to states in the net proceeds of union taxes and duties
	Income tax	20 percent on the basis of population; 62.5 percent on the basis of distance of per capita income of a state from that of the state having highest per capita income; 7.5 percent on the basis of (i) 7.5 percent weight to index of infrastructure, and (ii) 7.5 percent weight to fiscal discipline
	Excise duty	47.5 percent of net proceeds to be shared among states on the basis of the same formula used in sharing income tax; 40 percent distributed among major states; 7.5 percent distributed among deficit states
Twelfth Finance Commission (2005-10)	Grants	Rs. 142639 crores from non-plan revenue account; Rs. 56856 crores non-plan revenue deficit grant to 15 states; Rs. 10172 crores for education sector to eight states; Rs. 5887 crores for health sector for seven states; Rs. 15000 crores for roads and bridges; Rs. 20000 crores for the panchayati raj institutions; Rs. 4000 crores for urban local bodies; Rs. 21333 crores Calamity Relief Fund
	Share of union tax revenues	30.5 percent share to states in the net proceeds of union taxes and duties; Rs. 755751 crores share of central taxes and grants-in-aid
Thirteenth Finance Commission (2010-15)	Share of union tax revenues	32 percent share to states in the net proceeds of union taxes and duties; criteria: 47.5 percent income distance; 25 percent 1971 population; 15 percent fiscal discipline 10 percent area

Fourteenth Finance Commission (2015-20)	Grants	Rs. 38.48 lakh crores; grants to local bodies - 90 percent weight of 2011 population; 10 percent weight of area; 90:10 ratio of basic to performance grant for panchayats; 80:20 ratio for municipalities
	Share of union tax revenues	42 percent share to states in the net proceeds of union taxes and duties; criteria: 50 percent income distance; 17.5 percent 1971 population; 15 percent area; 10 percent 2011 demographic change; 7.5 percent forest cover
Fifteenth Finance Commission (2020-25)	Yet to recommend	

On the other hand, the Planning Commission of India transfers resources on the basis of population, per capita income, tax effort, fiscal management, literacy, land reform, etc. The transfer of the planning commission is based on a formula where 30 percent of the transfers are in the form of grants and 70 percent as loans. The grants and loans are tied together; states have to accept loans with grants. The criteria used by the planning commission in transferring resources to the states are: 60 percent on the basis of population of the state; 15 percent on the basis: (i) 7.5 percent on the basis of tax effort, fiscal management (include the speed of utilization of committed foreign aid and state's performance of revenue collection) and progress in respect of national objectives, and (ii) 7.5 percent to meet special problems of the states such as population control, literacy and land reform; 25 percent on the basis of per capita state domestic product (SDP) based on a formula: (i) 20 percent to only states with less than average per capita SDP on the basis of the inverse formula, and (ii) 5 percent according to the distance formula. The inverse formula is specified as:

$$Inverse\ formula: \frac{\frac{P_i}{Y_i}}{\Sigma\left(\frac{P_i}{Y_i}\right)} \quad (18.1)$$

which is inversely related to the per capita income of the state. The distance formula is specified as:

$$Distance\ formula: \frac{(Y_h - Y_i)P_i}{\Sigma[(Y_h - Y_i)P_i]} \quad (18.2)$$

where Y_i and Y_h denote the per capita SDP of the ith and the richest state in India respectively, P_i denotes the population of the state. The indicator increases as the distance of income of the state from the richest state increases.

The Tables 18.3 and 18.3b present the share on individual states in the union transfers. The share of the general category states has been as high as 97 percent, declined later to 86 percent and then risen again above 90 percent in recent Finance Commission awards. The share of special category states has also changed accordingly from a high of 13 percent to a range of 7-8 percent. Within the general category states, the share of middle income states has been falling and the share of low income states has been rising largely at the cost of the high income states.

Table 18.3a: Share in Central Taxes and Duties to States Recommended by Finance Commissions of India - General Category States.

State	*1st FC*	*2nd FC*	*3rd FC*	*4th FC*	*5th FC*	*6th FC*
Andhra Pradesh	4.8	8.22	7.8	7.56	7.55	8.03
Bihar	11.75	8.71	9.34	9.11	11.05	10.40
Chhattisgarh	-	-	-	-	-	-
Goa	-	-	-	-	-	-
Gujarat	-	4.20	6.02	5.58	5.01	5.19
Haryana	-	-	-	1.57	1.64	1.70
Jharkhand	-	-	-	-	-	-
Karnataka	1.04	5.11	5.08	5.15	4.98	5.40
Kerala	0.39	3.43	4.08	3.87	3.98	3.82
Madhya Pradesh	6.29	6.63	7.01	6.78	7.45	7.66
Maharashtra	18.75	12.90	11.20	11.88	10.57	10.02
Odisha	4.23	3.53	4.52	3.98	3.97	3.84
Punjab	4.05	4.78	5.53	2.93	2.46	2.38
Rajasthan	3.79	4.17	4.61	4.44	4.64	4.70
Tamil Nadu	11.39	8.56	7.48	7.90	7.56	7.59
Uttar Pradesh	18.81	16.63	13.87	14.86	16.77	16.20
West Bengal	11.99	9.33	8.78	8.94	8.17	8.28
Total	**97.29**	**96.19**	**95.40**	**94.54**	**95.79**	**95.21**
	7th FC	*8th FC*	*9th FC*	*10th FC*	*11th FC*	*12th FC*
Andhra Pradesh	7.81	7.72	7.48	7.91	7.70	7.36
Bihar	11.18	11.23	11.00	11.29	14.60	11.03
Chhattisgarh	-	-	-	-	-	2.65
Goa	-	-	0.39	0.25	0.21	0.26
Gujarat	5.01	3.97	3.86	3.88	2.82	3.57
Haryana	1.60	1.20	1.29	1.24	0.94	1.08
Jharkhand	-	-	-	-	-	3.36
Karnataka	5.23	4.80	4.51	4.86	4.93	4.46
Kerala	3.98	3.53	3.32	3.50	3.06	2.67
Madhya Pradesh	7.98	7,81	7.44	7.40	8.84	6.71

Maharashtra	8.91	7.33	6.87	6.23	4.63	5.00
Odisha	4.24	4.38	5.25	4.97	5.47	5.61
Punjab	2.18	1.71	1.72	1.53	1.15	1.30
Rajasthan	4.91	4.31	5.25	4.97	5.47	5.61
Tamil Nadu	7.68	6.85	6.84	6.12	5.39	5.31
Uttar Pradesh	16.65	16.58	15.79	16.25	19.80	19.26
West Bengal	8.18	7.90	7.12	6.84	8.12	7.06
Total	**95.22**	**89.32**	**87.73**	**86.54**	**92.70**	**91.83**

Source: Reports of Finance Commissions, Government of India.

Table 18.3b: Share in Central Taxes and Duties to States Recommended by Finance Commissions of India – Special Category States

State	*1st FC*	*2nd FC*	*3rd FC*	*4th FC*	*5th FC*	*6th FC*
Arunachal Pradesh	-	-	-	-	-	-
Assam	2.71	2.69	3.24	2.89	2.39	2.61
Himachal Pradesh	-	-	-	-	0.49	0.61
Jammu & Kashmir	-	1.13	1.29	1.51	0.91	0.83
Manipur	-	-	-	-	0.07	0.19
Meghalaya	-	-	-	-	0.17	0.18
Mizoram	-	-	-	-	-	-
Nagaland	-	-	0.07	1.05	0.08	0.10
Sikkim	-	-	-	-	-	-
Tripura	-	-	-	-	0.11	0.28
Uttaranchal	-	-	-	-	-	-
Total	**2.71**	**3.81**	**4.60**	**5.46**	**4.21**	**4.79**
	7th FC	*8th FC*	*9th FC*	*10th FC*	*11th FC*	*12th FC*
Arunachal Pradesh	-	-	0.60	0.66	0.24	0.29
Assam	2.58	3.51	3.38	3.42	3.28	3.24
Himachal Pradesh	0.57	1.49	1.44	1.81	0.68	0.52
Jammu & Kashmir	0.83	2.07	2.52	2.86	1.29	1.30
Manipur	0.20	0.84	0.81	0.82	0.37	0.36
Meghalaya	0.19	0.68	0.64	0.74	0.34	0.37
Mizoram	-	-	0.73	0.68	0.20	0.24
Nagaland	0.09	0.91	0.89	1.06	0.22	0.26
Sikkim	-	0.18	0.18	0.27	0.18	0.23
Tripura	0.31	1.00	1.09	1.13	0.49	0.43
Uttaranchal	-	-	-	-	-	0.94
Total	**4.78**	**10.68**	**12.27**	**13.46**	**7.30**	**8.17**

Source: Reports of Finance Commissions, Government of India.

As the Table 18.4 shows there have been large variations in transfers received by individual states. Among the non-special category states, Bihar and Orissa received the largest proportion of transfers in 2010-11. Bihar shows an increasing dependence on central transfers whereas a declining trend is observed in the case of Orissa, Uttar Pradesh, Rajasthan and West Bengal. States least dependent on central transfers are the high income states, mainly Punjab, Haryana and Gujarat. The intergovernmental transfers are a major source of revenue for all the special category states. Nagaland received the highest funds in 2010-11 followed by Manipur while Himachal Pradesh and Uttaranchal have received lowest funds.

Table 18.4: Central Fiscal Transfers as Proportion of States Aggregate Revenue.

State	*1991*	*2001*	*2010*	*State*	*1991*	*2001*	*2010*
General category states				Goa	0.43	0.12	0.16
Bihar	0.61	0.57	0.68	Punjab	0.31	0.13	0.16
Odisha	0.55	0.45	0.48	Gujarat	0.21	0.20	0.15
Jharkhand	-	0.45	0.46	Special category states			
Uttar Pradesh	0.55	0.43	0.42	Nagaland	0.87	0.82	0.83
Madhya Pradesh	0.44	0.36	0.41	Manipur	0.85	0.80	0.81
Chhattisgarh	-	0.35	0.41	Arunachal Pradesh	0.92	0.79	0.80
Rajasthan	0.40	0.31	0.34	Meghalaya	0.78	0.73	0.76
West Bengal	0.47	0.33	0.33	Tripura	0.87	0.74	0.75
Andhra Pradesh	0.40	0.32	0.27	Jammu & Kashmir	0.80	0.77	0.69
Karnataka	0.28	0.30	0.26	Mizoram	0.96	0.70	0.66
Tamil Nadu	0.30	0.21	0.22	Assam	0.69	0.59	0.59
Kerala	0.39	0.25	0.19	Sikkim	0.75	0.33	0.52
Maharashtra	0.27	0.12	0.18	Himachal Pradesh	0.37	0.55	0.45
Haryana	0.24	0.12	0.16	Uttaranchal	-	0.42	0.42

The financial transfers from the union government to states have been designed to fill the fiscal gap in the state budgets. The relationship between union transfers and state's own tax revenue is interlinked in the sense that the transfer policies may encourage or discourage the tax effort of the states. When the size such central transfers is more than the required financial assistance by the states, such states are discouraged in their own revenue efforts and vice versa. Thus, the central financial transfers create revenue substitution effect in the state's budget. Hence, this paper aims to analyse the effects of central transfers on state's own revenue income or own tax revenue. This paper uses a state-wise panel for 15 major states of India for 30 years from 1980-81 to 2009-10 consisting of 444 observations.

The variables considered are own tax revenue, total revenue, grants from the centre, share in central taxes and revenue expenditure, NSDP and NSDP per capita. In the empirical analysis, the panel data methodology of fixed effects and random effects regression models are used along with the Hausman specification test.

18.2 A Brief Review of Recent Studies

Vasishtha and Rajaraman (2000) investigate the impact of state grants on the tax effort of rural local governments (panchayats) in Kerala using data for 1993-94. They regress own tax revenue separately on total grants and untied grants, after controlling for the population as a tax capacity proxy, for each district. They also regress own tax per capita on untied grants per capita in a separate specification and find a significant negative impact of total grants and untied grants on the own tax revenue of panchayats in many districts of the state. Though this study is exclusively related to state-local transfers, it provides vital inferences on the impact of transfers on tax efforts of the recipient government.

Panda (2009) examines the incentive effects of federal transfers on states' own-revenue using the fixed and random effects panel regression models in India. The estimated results show that per capita resource transfers from the centre are significantly and negatively associated with states' own revenue, own tax revenue and own non-tax revenue in per capita terms, irrespective of linear and log specifications. This result indicates that central transfers have a dampening effect on states' revenue efforts. Further, the results show that the incentive criteria for tax effort as used in the Finance Commission devolutions and in the Gadgil formula used by the Planning Commission are not reflected in the system and it has failed to induce the desired positive revenue pattern in states. The paper suggests assigning a higher weight to tax effort in the devolution formula and for more effective coordination among different channels in designing criteria and incentives.

Sharma (2011) examines the concept of Vertical Fiscal Imbalance (VFI). The paper derives the estimates of VFl by comparing the revenues and expenditures of two levels of government, much like accounting or deficit measurements. The paper aims to clarify the multiple usages of the symbolically loaded terms VFI and VFG (vertical fiscal gap) by critically engaging the fundamental assumptions and premises underlying these similar notions. The paper proposes an alternative conceptual framework and introduces the concepts of Vertical Fiscal Asymmetry (VFA) and Vertical Fiscal Difference (VFD) that have the potential to better structure public debate on issues of vertical fiscal relations and stimulate a sensible appreciation of the problem and possible remedies.

Bhatt and Scaramozzino (2015) analyse the relationship between transfers, state domestic product, and fiscal deficit in India for a panel of states for the period 1990-2010. Generally, the system of federal transfers has been criticised on the grounds that it distorts the incentives for states to promote fiscal discipline. The paper finds a positive long-run relationship and bidirectional causality between primary/gross fiscal deficits and non-plan transfers. Further, a negative long-run relationship and one-way causality between state domestic product and transfers are observed, with causality going from state domestic product to transfers. These results are also confirmed by the multivariate cointegration analysis, which finds a long-run relationship between fiscal transfers, state product per capita and the primary deficit of the states. The evidence in the paper is consistent with the system of fiscal transfers being gap filling.

18.3 Data and Methodology

The data used in this study is state-wise panel data for 30 years from 1980-81 to 2009-10, having 444 observations, collected from various government databases. The 15 states considered are Andhra Pradesh, Bihar, Goa, Gujarat Haryana, Karnataka, Kerala, Madhya Pradesh, Maharashtra, Odisha, Punjab, Rajasthan, Tamil Nadu, Uttar Pradesh and West Bengal. The data for the variables own tax revenue, total revenue, grants from the centre, share in central taxes and revenue expenditure are obtained from the Reserve Bank of India Handbook of Statistics on State Finances, and the data on variables NSDP and NSDP per capita are collected from Finance Ministry's Economic Surveys.

Panel Data Method

Panel data consists of repeated data on the same observations over a time i.e. repeated cross sectional time series. The major advantage of panel data over a cross section is that it allows great flexibility in modeling differences in behaviour across individuals as it controls for both the time invariant observed and unobserved individual heterogeneity. The basic framework is a regression model of the form:

$$y_{it} = \alpha z_i + \beta x_{it} + u_{it} \qquad i = 1, \dots, n \quad t = 1, \dots, T_i \tag{18.1}$$

The observed heterogeneity or individual effect is z which contains a constant term and a set of individual or group specific variables which are observed such as race, sex, location, etc. and unobserved such as family specific characteristics, individual heterogeneity in skill preferences, etc. If all the observed and unobserved individual or group specific heterogeneity are taken to be constant over time, the model is a classical regression model, then the entire model can be estimated by the ordinary least squares method. The complications arise when the unobserved heterogeneity is correlated with the error term, then OLS estimation will produce biased (inconsistent and inefficient) estimates. Generally, a panel data is estimated by pooled data, least squares dummy variables, fixed effects and random effects regression models.

Pooled Regression: If z contains only a constant term, then OLS estimation provides consistent and efficient estimates of the common α and the slope vector β. The assumptions of the pooled model are:

$$y_{it} = \alpha + \beta x_{it} + u_{it} \tag{18.2}$$

$$E(u_{it}|x_{it}) = 0E(u_{it}^2) = \sigma_u^2 Cov(u_{it}, x_{it}) = 0 \tag{18.3}$$

The pooled regression is also called as population averaged model as the presence of any latent heterogeneity is averaged out. To the pooled data, the least squares regression is applied under the assumptions of zero conditional mean of the error, homoscedasticity, independence across observations and strict homogeneity of x.

Fixed Effects Regression: If z is unobserved, but correlated with x, then the least squares estimator of β is biased and inconsistent as a consequence of an omitted variable bias. In this instance, the observable individual effects are assumed to be fixed or remain constant over time and such a fixed effects model is specified as:

$$y_{it} = \alpha_i + \beta x_{it} + u_{it} \tag{18.4}$$

where $\alpha_i = \alpha z_i$ is a group specific constant term. However, the omitted unobservable individual effects, λ_i, may be correlated with the x variables. That is:

$$E(\lambda_i|x_{it}) = c(x_i) \Rightarrow E(u_{it}|x_{it}) \neq 0 \tag{18.5}$$

Because the conditional mean is the same in every period, the model is written as:

$$y_{it} = \beta x_{it} + c(x_i) + [\lambda_i - c(x_i)] + u_{it} \tag{18.6}$$

$$y_{it} = \alpha_i + \beta x_{it} + [\lambda_i - c(x_i)] + u_{it} \tag{18.7}$$

By construction the bracketed term is uncorrelated with x and is absorbed in the disturbance term. Hence, the fixed effects panel regression model is specified as in equation (18.4). The fixed effects regression model captures the differences in the constant term α_i and each α_i is treated as an anonymous parameter to be estimated. The fixed effects regression models the differences between cross sectional units strictly as parametric shifts of the regression function. However, estimating so many constant terms as there are cross sectional observations is costly in terms of degrees of freedom lost.

Random Effects Regression: If the unobserved individual heterogeneity, however formulated, is assumed to be uncorrelated with x, then the individual specific constant terms may be assumed as randomly distributed across cross sectional units. This is tantamount to assuming that sampled cross sectional units are drawn from a large population. As there is no need to estimate each of the α_i separately, the number of parameters to be estimated is reduced drastically. Thus, a linear regression model can be estimated with a compound disturbance that may be consistent, although inefficiently, by least squares. This random effects regression approach specifies that λ_i is a group specific random element similar to u_{it} but there is a single draw that enters the regression identically in each period. A reformulation of the regression model can be specified as:

$$y_{it} = \beta x_{it} + E(\alpha z_i) + [\alpha z_i - E(\alpha z_i)] + u_{it} \quad (18.8)$$

$$y_{it} = \beta x_{it} + \alpha + \lambda_i + u_{it} \quad (18.9)$$

where the single constant term is the mean of the unobserved heterogeneity $[\alpha]E(z_i)$. The component λ_i is the random heterogeneity specific to the ith observation and is constant through time. The assumptions of the random effects regression model are:

$$\begin{aligned} &E(u_{it}|x_{it}) = E(\lambda_i|x_{it}) = 0 \\ &E(u_{it}^2) = \sigma_u^2 E(\lambda_i^2) = \sigma_\lambda^2 \\ &E(u_{it}\lambda_j|x_{it}) = 0 \quad for\ all\ i,t,j \\ &E(u_{it}u_{js}|x_{it}) = 0 \quad if\ t \neq s\ and\ i \neq j \\ &E(u_i u_j|x_{it}) = 0 \quad if\ i \neq j \end{aligned} \quad (18.10)$$

In terms of group specific observations, $\mathbf{y}_i$, $\mathbf{x}_i$, $\lambda_i\mathbf{i}$ and $\mathbf{u}_i$ for T observations, the composite error term is specified as:

$$\varepsilon_{it} = (u_{it} + \lambda_i) \text{ and } \varepsilon_i = [\varepsilon_{i1}, \varepsilon_{i2}, \ldots, \varepsilon_{iT}]' \quad (18.11)$$

The assumptions for this formulation are:

$$\begin{aligned} &E(\varepsilon_{it}|\boldsymbol{x}) = \sigma_u^2 + \sigma_\lambda^2 \\ &E(\varepsilon_{it}\varepsilon_{is}|\boldsymbol{x}) = \sigma_\lambda^2 \quad if\ t \neq s \\ &E(\varepsilon_{it}\varepsilon_{is}|\boldsymbol{x}) = \sigma_\lambda^2 \quad for\ all\ t\ and\ s\ if\ i \neq j \end{aligned} \quad (18.12)$$

For the T observations of cross sectional unit i:

$$E(\varepsilon_i\varepsilon_i'|\boldsymbol{x}) = \Sigma = \begin{bmatrix} \sigma_u^2 + \sigma_\lambda^2 & \sigma_\lambda^2 & \ldots\sigma_\lambda^2 \\ \sigma_\lambda^2 & \sigma_u^2 + \sigma_\lambda^2 & \ldots\sigma_\lambda^2 \\ \ldots & \ldots & \ldots\ldots \\ \sigma_\lambda^2 & \sigma_\lambda^2\ldots & \sigma_u^2 + \sigma_\lambda^2 \end{bmatrix} \quad (18.13)$$

$$\Sigma = \sigma_u^2 \boldsymbol{I}_T + \sigma_\lambda^2 \boldsymbol{i}_T \boldsymbol{i}_T' \qquad (18.14)$$

where $\mathbf{i}_T$ is a Tx1 column vector of 1s. As cross section units i and j are independent, the covariance matrix of the disturbance term for the full nT observations is:

$$\boldsymbol{\Omega} = \begin{bmatrix} \Sigma & \mathbf{0} & \ldots \mathbf{0} \\ \mathbf{0} & \Sigma & \ldots \mathbf{0} \\ \ldots & \ldots & \ldots\ldots \\ \mathbf{0} & \mathbf{0}\ldots & \Sigma \end{bmatrix} = \mathrm{I}_n \otimes \Sigma \qquad (18.15)$$

Then, the estimates of slope parameters $\hat{\boldsymbol{\beta}}$ are obtained from the generalised least squares (GLS) estimation as:

$$\hat{\boldsymbol{\beta}} = (\boldsymbol{x}'\boldsymbol{\Omega}^{-1}\boldsymbol{x})'\boldsymbol{x}'\boldsymbol{\Omega}^{-1}\boldsymbol{y} = \left[\sum_{i=1}^{n} \boldsymbol{x}_i'\boldsymbol{\Omega}^{-1}\boldsymbol{x}_i\right]^{-1} \sum_{i=1}^{n} \boldsymbol{x}_i'\boldsymbol{\Omega}^{-1}\boldsymbol{y}_i \qquad (18.16)$$

Thus, the GLS estimator, like the OLS estimator, is a matrix weighted average of the within and between cross sectional units estimators.

Hausman Specification Test: The crucial distinction between fixed and random effects is whether the unobserved individual effect embodies elements that are correlated with the regressors in the model, not whether these effects are stochastic or not. There is little justification for treating the individual effects as uncorrelated with the other regressors, and hence the random effects model suffers from the inconsistency due to possible correlation between the included variables and the random effect. On the other hand, the fixed effects estimation shifts only the intercepts leaving the slope coefficients unchanged, thus there is no difference between the two different estimation methodologies. Moreover, too many parameters need to be estimated as there are cross sectional units. A pertinent question is which one is appropriate in the empirical estimation. Hausman (1978) argues that under the hypothesis of no correlation, the OLS, fixed effects and random effects estimators are consistent, but OLS is inefficient, whereas under the alternative, fixed effect is consistent, but the random effect is not. Therefore, under the null hypothesis, the two estimates should not differ systematically and hence a test is proposed on the difference.

The Hausman specification test tests the covariance matrix of the difference vector $[\hat{\beta}_{FE} - \hat{\beta}_{RE}]$ for orthogonality of the common effects and the regressors:

$$Var[\hat{\beta}_{FE} - \hat{\beta}_{RE}] = var(\hat{\beta}_{FE}) + var(\hat{\beta}_{RE}) - cov(\hat{\beta}_{FE}, \hat{\beta}_{RE}) - cov(\hat{\beta}_{RE}, \hat{\beta}_{FE}) \qquad (18.17)$$

If there is no difference between the two estimators, as Hausman shows, then the covariance of an efficient estimator with its difference from an inefficient estimator is zero:

$$Cov[(\hat{\beta}_{FE} - \hat{\beta}_{RE}), \hat{\beta}_{RE}] = cov(\hat{\beta}_{FE} - \hat{\beta}_{RE}) - var(\hat{\beta}_{RE}) = 0 \qquad (18.18)$$

$$Cov(\hat{\beta}_{FE} - \hat{\beta}_{RE}) = var(\hat{\beta}_{RE}) \qquad (18.19)$$

$$Var[\hat{\beta}_{FE} - \hat{\beta}_{RE}] = var(\hat{\beta}_{FE}) - var(\hat{\beta}_{RE}) = \Psi \quad (18.20)$$

where Ψ is the covariance matrix for the test. Under the null hypothesis, the chi-square test is based on the Wald criterion:

$$W = \chi^2 = [\hat{\beta}_{FE} - \hat{\beta}_{RE}]' \hat{\Psi}^{-1} [\hat{\beta}_{FE} - \hat{\beta}_{RE}] \quad (18.21)$$

The estimated covariance matrices of the slope estimator in the fixed effects model and the estimated covariance matrix in the random effects model, exclusive of the constant term are used in $\hat{\Psi}$. Though the Hausman test is a useful device for determining the preferred specification of the common effects model, it does not guarantee that the difference of the two covariance matrices will be positive definite in a finite sample i.e. nothing is there to prevent the statistic Ψ from being negative. Hence, the random effects model is not rejected, since the likeness of the covariance matrices is what is causing the problem, and under the alternative (fixed effects) hypothesis, they may be significantly dissimilar. Therefore, it is useful, using the results of the fixed and random effect models, to recover the coefficient vector and estimated the asymptotic covariance matrix, $\hat{\beta}_{FE}$ and V_{FE} from the fixed effects results and the $\hat{\beta}_{RE}$ and V_{RE} (excluding the constant term). The test statistic is:

$$H = [\hat{\beta}_{FE} - \hat{\beta}_{RE}]' [V_{FE} - V_{RE}]^{-1} [\hat{\beta}_{FE} - \hat{\beta}_{RE}] \quad (18.22)$$

If the computed value of the testing statistic is greater than the critical value, the null hypothesis of random effects model is rejected and the fixed effects model is the preferred specification for data.

18.4 Empirical Analysis

In the empirical analysis, own tax revenue of states as a ratio of NSDP is specified as a function of grants from the centre as a ratio of the total revenue, share in central taxes as a ratio of revenue, revenue expenditure as a ratio of NSDP and per capita NSDP. As the observations for a state may not be independent, panel data regression techniques are used to control for the individual differences. The Table 18.5 presents the definition and the descriptive statistics of the variables used in the empirical analysis.

Table 18.5: Descriptive Statistics of Variables in the Tax Efforts of States Analysi.

Variable	*Definition*	*Mean*	*Std. dev.*
STR/NSDP	Own tax revenue of state as a ratio of NSDP	0.084	0.031
GRANTS/NSDP	Grants from the centre as a ratio of the state total revenue	0.243	0.191
SCT/REV	Share in central taxes as a ratio of state revenue	0.414	0.409

REVEXP/NSDP	Revenue expenditure of state as a ratio of NSDP	0.192	0.083
NSDPpc	Per capita net state domestic product (Rs. at current prices)	1.538	1.855
Obs.		444	

The estimating empirical specification is:

$$STR/NSDP_{it} = \beta_0 + \beta_1 NSDP_{it} + \beta_2 GRANTS/REV_{it} + \beta_3 SCT/REV_{it} + \beta_4 REVEXP/NSDP_{it} + +u_{it} \quad (18.23)$$

The Table 18.6 presents the estimates of pooled OLS, fixed effects and random effects panel regression models. The pooled OLS regression estimates show that a unit increase in grants from the centre will lead to a significant reduction of 4.8 percent in the tax effort of the states. Similarly, an increase in the share in central taxes will lead to a significant reduction in the tax effort of states by 1.9 percent. The revenue expenditure as a ratio of NSDP is also highly significant and the coefficient indicates a positive impact on tax efforts of states. However, the coefficient of per capita NSDP has insignificant on states tax efforts.

Table 18.6: Panel Regression Estimates of Tax Efforts of States in India.

Dependent variable: STR/NSDP

Variable	*Pooled regression*	*Fixed effects*	*Random effects*
NSDPpc	0.00013 (0.31)	0.0092*** (3.04)	0.00093*** (2.96)
GRANTS/NSDP	-0.048*** (7.53)	-0.0057*** (3.06)	-0.0098*** (2.78)
SCT/REV	-0.193*** (6.53)	-0.0077*** (2.67)	-0.011*** (3.61)
REVEXP/NSDP	0.308*** (3.37)	0.324*** (5.18)	0.322*** (4.80)
Constant	0.044*** (9.87)	0.025*** (7.52)	0.027*** (9.04)
Within R-square	-	0.856	0.855
Between R-square	-	0.063	0.145
R-square	0.75	0.61	0.645
ρ-value $[\sigma_u^2/(\sigma_u^2 - \sigma_\varepsilon^2)]$	-	0.745	0.410
Hausman test	-	67.32	
Pro>Chi^2 (p-value)	-	0.00	

Note: Absolute t-values in parentheses. *** significant at 1 percent.

The fixed effects regression that controls the state-wise heterogeneity of differences in economic, social and demographic factors, estimates show that NSDP per capita and revenue expenditure as a ratio of NSDP are statistically significant and positively influences the tax efforts of states. The coefficient of per capita NSDP, showing the tax capacity of sub-national units and the ability of states to raise tax revenue, implies that a unit increase in per capita NSDP leads to an increase of 1 percent increase in tax revenues of the states. Similarly, one unit increase in revenue expenditure as a ratio of NSDP leads to 32 percent increase in tax effort of the states. This implies that an increase in current expenditure of states will pressure the government to increase its effort to collect more taxes as they have to find a way to finance the additional expenditure. The estimated coefficient of grants as a ratio of revenue is significantly and negatively associated with tax effort of states. A one unit increase in grants, given the total revenue of the state, will reduce the tax effort of the state by half a percent. This clearly states that grants from central government have an adverse effect on revenue mobilisation of states. The significant negative coefficient of the share in central taxes as a ratio of the total revenue of states shows that an increase in it will dampen the tax collection efforts of states.

The rho value for the fixed effects model shows that the group errors are correlated with regressors. The rho is the inter-class correlation which indicates the percentage of variance due to difference across panels. The rho value of 0.745 shows that 75 percent of the variance in revenue generation of states is due to differences across panels implying that there exists a wide inequality across the states of India in their tax efforts. There is a situation of the states being polar opposites; on one hand, there are states which exhibit a very promising situation of revenue generation and, on the other hand, there are states with an alarmingly low tax efforts with a dire need of policy level overhaul to address revenue gaps. The within R-square value shows that nearly 85.61 percent variance in revenue collection is mainly explained by transfers and revenue expenditure.

In the random effects regression, the NSDP per capita and revenue expenditure as a ratio of NSDP have statistically significant positive effect on the tax efforts of states. However, an increase in per capita NSDP has only a marginal impact on the tax efforts of states. A one unit increase in revenue expenditure as a ratio of NSDP leads to 32 percent increase in tax effort of the states. An increase both in union grants and share in central taxes decreases the tax efforts of states showing the dampening effect on the tax collection efforts of states. The rho value of the random effects model shows that about 41 percent of the variance in revenue generation of states is due to differences across panels and the between R-square value shows that nearly 14 percent variance in own tax revenue of states is due to differences across panels.

As both the fixed effects and random effects models produced estimates that are very close, the appropriateness of the models for data are checked with the Hausman specification test. The mill hypothesis for the Hausman test is that there is random effect or differences between the models are not systematic whereas alternative hypothesis states that there is no differences and presence of fixed effect. The calculated chi-square value for the Hausman test is highly significant and hence the null hypothesis of random effect is rejected and the alternative hypothesis of fixed effects model as appropriate for data is accepted.

18.5 Conclusion

Bridging the development gap between the economically and socially divergent regions and allocating resources, especially the tax revenues in a federal economy like India, is a challenging task. A common way of dealing with this task is to provide additional financial support to the poorer states from the central revenue collections in order to help them develop and compete with their richer counterparts. Therefore, in a federal setup, the concepts of vertical and horizontal equity and efficiency are important considerations for such transfers. As the sub-national governments also have their own sources of revenue, there could be a temptation to seek less revenue mobilisation by the states, thus lacking efficiency, and the centre may direct transfers to those states with the largest fiscal imbalances or less revenue. This would undermine the credibility of the central government when it tries to enforce a binding budget constraint on the state governments and it could lead to a reduced effort by states to adhere to fiscal policy norms. The states with higher tax potential may tend to rely more on the central transfers and might not efficiently use their tax potential to generate more revenue.

This paper analyses the effect of federal transfers on own tax revenue of states using a panel data set of transfers and taxes for 15 states of India for 30 years from 1980-81 to 2009-10. The estimated negative relationship between transfers, grant from the centre and share in central transfers, and revenue mobilisation of states indicates revenue substitution by states; more central government assistance means less dependence on own tax revenue. Indian states increasingly depend on central grants, rather than improving efforts to increase their own revenues even when they have high tax potential or even when they are in dire need of financial assistance. Thus, the central transfers adversely affect the incentives of states to mobilise their own resources indicating that central transfers have a dampening effect on states revenue efforts.

The panel analysis of this paper also shows a strong positive relationship between NSDP per capita and tax revenue showing high tax potential of the states. However, the NSDP per capita alone cannot be taken as a measure of tax capacity or the revenue base. This is because not all services are under the purview of state taxes and also agricultural income is included in NSDP but does not fetch any income tax for states. Further, the incentive criterion for tax effort as used both in the Finance Commissions devolutions and in the Gadgil formula used by the Planning Commission is not reflected in the federal system of India, and it has failed to induce a desired positive revenue generation in states.

Higher union transfers are justified to low state income states where the tax collection is low, may be due to a low tax base or capacity factors, in order to reduce the vertical and horizontal fiscal imbalances. A higher transfer is a way to enable a state to provide a level of services at par with other states. However, the dependence of richer states also on the union financial transfers is to be discouraged. In the long-run, the effects of central transfers must be either neutral or should encourage own revenue efforts of states in India.

19

The Causal Effect of Labour Market Reforms on Unemployment and Wages: Panel TSLS Estimation

19.1 Introduction

The labour market operates with the supply and demand for labour wherein the supply of labour is provided by employees/individuals and demand by employers/entrepreneurs. In a liberal economy, the governments regulate the functioning of the labour markets with employment protection legislation, tax wedge, unionisation, unemployment benefits, etc. such labour market regulations that enhance and secure working environment are generally referred as labour market institutions. The labour market regulations that started in the second half of 19th century with strong industrialisation growth in Western Europe and North America, expanded to comprehensive labour codes, rules for trade unions and collective bargaining, unemployment insurance, active labour market programmes and employment legislations in developed countries, subsequently expanded to developing countries also with liberalisation, privatisation and globalisation in the 20th century.

The high job creation and low unemployment in the United States relative to Europe raised questions whether Europe's more stringent labour regulations, more powerful unions, more extensive collective bargaining and more generous unemployment insurance regimes contribute to the employment performance in developed countries. However, empirical studies on the impact of labour market regulations on employment and wages are rather scanty. Studies by European Commission and Organisation of Economic Cooperation and Development (OECD) countries blame labour market regulations for increasing unemployment. They point out that more rigid labour market institutions negatively impact job creation and increases unemployment. Moreover, the slowing economic growth in the world leading economies such as United States, European Union and OECD countries has made it worse for other economies around the world.

The Figure 19.1 presents the evolution of labour market regulations in the OECD countries between 2000 and 2012. The average union density, average tax wedge, and average employment protection in OECD countries have declined over time, reflecting the well-known mitigation of labour market regulations. The sharp decline in the union density during the thirteen years indicates the de-unionisation in OECD countries.

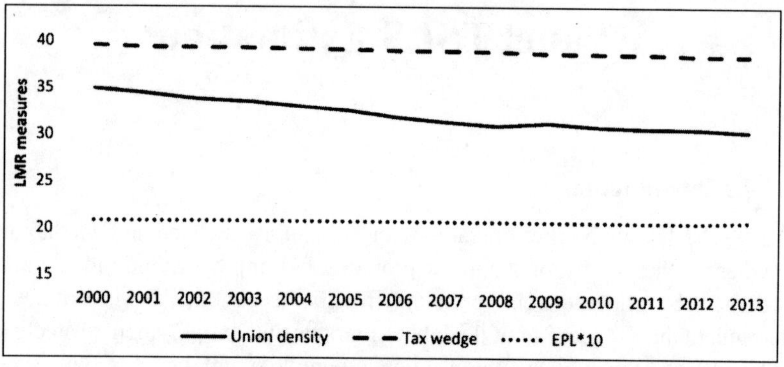

Figure 19.1: Labour Market Regulations in OECD Countries, 2000-2012.

With changing production technologies and methods of production, continuous labour reforms are taking place throughout the world. The western industrialised OECD economies are in the forefront of legislating labour market reforms. The labour market regulations are aimed at protecting labour interests especially wages hiring and firing conditions and most importantly to tackle the unemployment situation in the wake of globalisation and automation of the production processes. In some economies the labour market legislations are rigid while in some economies they are flexible. A more flexible labour market reduces the labour market regulations will eventually worsen the working environment of the labourers. This reduces the labourers' willingness to work and therefore increases unemployment. That is, the supply of labour in the market reduces. On the other hand, the demand for labour by firms increases due to relaxation of labour market regulations. As a result, there is a supply-demand gap in the labour market and hence the increasing in unemployment in OECD countries in recent years. How far these labour market regulations impact the wage rates and unemployment is a question for empirical investigation.

The objective of this paper is to examine the impact of labour market reforms on the unemployment and on wage payments in OECD countries. In the empirical analysis, this paper uses data for 17 OECD countries over a period of 13 years (2000 to 2012) obtained from the OECD and World Bank sources. The variables considered are labour market regulation indicators like union density, tax wedge and employment protection, unemployment rate, hourly pay for work, and macroeconomic variables total factor productivity, annual GDP growth rate, research and development expenditure and fertility rate. In the empirical analysis, the two-stage-least-squares (2SLS) method is used for the estimation of simultaneous system of labour demand and labour supply. The simultaneous equation model facilitates the estimation of the effect of labour market reforms on the wage (hourly pay for work) and the unemployment rate. The labour demand function used is the unemployment function which has independent variables labour market regulations measured union density, employment protection legislation and tax wedge, and demand shocks measured by GDP growth, total factor productivity growth, research and development expenditure and labour productivity growth. The labour supply function is the wage function represented by total hourly pay for time work which has independent variables labour market regulations measured by union density, employment protection legislation and tax wedge, and supply shocks measured by the fertility rate.

19.2 A Brief Review of Recent Studies

Di Tella and MacCulloch (2002) attempt to explain the effect of labour market flexibility and labour force participation on the performance of the labour market. The panel data used on hiring and firing restrictions is a survey data of business people in 21 OECD countries covering the period 1984-1990. The Lazear's parsimonious reduced form model is used in the estimation, controlling country and time fixed effects, and in the dynamic panel data estimation, GLS and GMM techniques are employed. The estimated results show that increasing labour market flexibility increases both the employment rate and the rate of participation in the labour force. In the short run, the estimated effects are larger in the female labour market relative to labour market for males, although both groups have similar long-run coefficients. The results are viewed as more labour market flexibility leads to lower unemployment rates and lower rates of long-term unemployment.

Huang et al. (2013) focus on the unemployment driven by labour market reforms in Europe in 15 European countries over the period 1985 to 2009. The paper analyses the impact of labour market regulations on wage payments and unemployment rate using the 2SLS method. It is hypothesised that labour supply is discouraged by decreases in union density, replacement rate, and tax wedge while de-unionisation and tax system reforms enhance labour demand. The estimated results show that replacement rate is the only measure of labour market regulation that affects labour supply, but not the demand side. Further, the effect of labour market institutions on the behaviour of labour demand outweighs the effect on labour suppliers, which pushes up the wage rate and mitigates the unemployment problem. Thus, when adopting labour market reforms particular attention need to be paid to the adjustment of the replacement rate in order to avoid overly depressing labour supply to lowering the unemployment rate without hurting wage payments or discouraging labour supply.

Zribi, Temmi and Zrelli (2014) examine the impact of policies aimed at increasing labour market flexibility on unemployment, especially youth unemployment after the Great Recession. It is observed that the youth unemployment rates in most countries are at least twice as high as the total unemployment rate. The unbalanced panel dataset of 92 countries over the period 2000 to 2010, taken from International Labour Organisation, World Development Indicators and Fraser Institute Economic Freedom of the World databases, has been divided as two subgroups of 32 developed and 60 developing countries. The static and dynamic models are estimated using the Feasible Generalised Least Squares (FGLS) and GMM methods. The estimated results show that most of the macroeconomic and demographic variables and labour market flexibility indicators reduce general and youth unemployment rates. The effect of labour market regulations in developed countries is significantly higher than in the developing countries. The collective bargaining, mandated cost of worker dismissal and conscription does not seem to play an important role on youth unemployment.

Turrini, Koltay, Pierlni, Goifard and Kiss (2014) analyse the determinants and impact of labour market reforms in the European Union with reference to the 2008 crisis. They note that European Union countries with similar institutional settings tend to follow analogous reform patterns. In these countries' reforms are more frequent when the environment is characterised by unsatisfactory labour market outcomes, notably high and growing unemployment, and a high initial level of regulations or fiscal burden on labour. The LABREF database on EU over the period 2000-2011 that contains a large set of information on reform characteristics has been used. In the empirical estimation, pooled regression analysis with Impulse Response Function (IRF) and Least Squares Dummy Variables (LSDV) methods have been applied. The effect of selected reforms on aggregate labour market outcomes has been found supportive of common priors: tax and benefit reforms tend to be followed, after a time lag, by improved activity rates and lower unemployment. Further, it is observed that the overall reforms activism has increased during the crises period.

Gur (2015) studies factors that affect unemployment in the BRIC (Brazil, Russia, India and China) countries, the recent attention-grabbing emerging markets of the world. The panel fixed effects regression has been applied for estimation of the BRIC country data collected from the World Bank, OECD and Bloomberg database, for the period 2001-2012. The estimated results show that the most important cause of increasing unemployment in the BRIC countries is inflation followed by population growth. Further, growths in gross domestic product, trade volume, total investment and industrial product are the main economic factors that lead to a reduction of unemployment in BRIC economies.

19.3 Data and Methodology

In this paper, a panel data of 17 OECD countries spanning over 13 years from 2000 to 2012 collected from the OECD database and WB indicators is used in the empirical analysis applying the 2SLS method. The 17 OECD counties considered are Austria, Belgium, Canada, Denmark, Finland, France, Germany, Ireland, Italy, Japan, Netherlands, New Zealand, Portugal, Spain, Sweden, Switzerland, United Kingdom and United States. The dependent variables are unemployment rate and total hourly pay for time worked. The independent variables are labour market regulation variables, demand shock variables, and supply shock variables.

The 2SLS method consists of a set of structural equations and an estimating reduced form equation. The structural disturbance terms u should satisfy the usual stochastic assumptions such as zero mean, constant variance and zero covariance. The reduced form disturbance terms v should also satisfy the same since v's are linear combination of u's. In the structural equations, the variables in the model are of two kinds: exogenous variables and endogenous variables. The exogenous variables are variables that are determined outside the system and the endogenous variables are variables are determined within the system of equations. The endogeneity problem arises in a multiple regression model when the explanatory variables are correlated with the error term, for several reasons including omitted variable bias, measurement error and simultaneity/reverse causation (x causes y, y causes x). With endogeneity, the OLS estimation, which assumes independence of explanatory variables from the error term, will produce inconsistent estimates. Simultaneous causality bias can be eliminated with instrumental regression. When there are two or more instruments for an endogenous variable, the two stage least squares estimation method is applied. The 2SLS method is a reduced form equation expressing endogenous variables in terms of instrumental variables or exogenous variables that remove the simultaneous equation bias can give consistent estimates. The instruments, say z, must satisfy two conditions: (i) instrument relevance: $cov(x,z) \neq 0$, and (ii) instrument exogeneity $cov(x,u) = 0$, where z is the instrument and x is the endogenous variable and u is the error term. That is, the instrumented variable z must be correlated with explanatory variable x and at the same time must not be correlated with error term u. This implies that z affects y, the independent variable, only through x. The identification and selection of appropriate instruments is challenging task.

Panel Two Stage Least Squares Method

The structural equation is specified as:

$$y = \beta_0 + \beta_1 x_1 + \beta_2 x_2 + u \tag{19.1}$$

where y is the dependent variable, x_1 is endogenous variables, x_2 is exogenous variables, β's are parameters to be estimated and u is the error term. By instrumenting the endogenous variables x_1 with m instrumental variables, along with all exogenous variables, the reduced form estimating equation can be written as:

$$y_1 = \beta_2 x_2 + \delta_1 z_1 + \cdots + \delta_m z_m + v \tag{19.2}$$

Substituting value of x_1 from reduced form estimation in the structural equation:

$$y = \beta_1(\hat{x}_1 + v) + \beta_2 x_2 + u \tag{19.3}$$

$$y = \delta z + (u + v\beta_1) \tag{19.4}$$

where $z = [x_x, x_2]$ and $\delta = \begin{bmatrix}\beta_1\\ \beta_2\end{bmatrix}$.

$$\text{Let } \alpha = \begin{bmatrix}\alpha_1\\ \alpha_2\end{bmatrix} = (z'z)^{-1}z'(\delta z + u + v\beta_1) \tag{19.5}$$

$$\alpha = \delta + (z'z)^{-1}z^{'}(\delta z + u + v\beta_1) = \delta + (z'z)^{-1}z'u \tag{19.6}$$

$$Plim\ \alpha = \delta + Plim\left(\frac{1}{n}(z'z)^{-1}\right) Plim\left(\frac{1}{n}z'u\right) \tag{19.7}$$

$$\text{As } Plim\left(\frac{1}{n}z'u\right) = 0,\ Plim\ \alpha = \delta \tag{19.8}$$

This is the two stage least squares (2SLS) estimation procedure which is consistent and α is the consistent estimator of δ.

In simultaneous equations methods, identification of structural equations and endogeneity and exogeneity of variables are tested with specification tests. The Durbin and Wu-Hausman tests of endogeneity are performed to determine whether the regressors in the model are exogenous or not. The difference between the Durbin and Wu-Hausman tests is that the former uses estimates of the variance of the error term assuming the variables being tested are exogenous, while the later uses estimates of the error variance assuming the variables being tested are endogenous. The idea of Wu-Hausman test for endogeneity is to see whether the estimates of OLS and IV methods are different (Hausman, 1978). The test is to estimate an auxiliary regression in the first stage:

$$x_1 = \delta_1 z_1 + \delta_2 z_2 + v \tag{19.9}$$

The residuals $\hat{v}$ of equation (19.9) are then included as an additional explanatory variable in equation (19.1):

$$y = \beta_0 + \beta_1 x_1 + \beta_2 x_2 + \gamma_1 \hat{v} + \varepsilon \tag{19.10}$$

Then test the hypothesis whether γ_1 equals zero or not. This implies that x_1 could be correlated with u through v. The null hypothesis is that the residual $\hat{v}_i$ is zero and therefore x_1 is exogenous. Therefore, if $\gamma_1=0$, then x_1 is an exogenous variable and when $\gamma_1 \neq 0$, then x_1 is endogenous variable.

The identification test of simultaneous equations method uses the order condition. In order for identification of a given model, the order condition states that $K\text{-}k \geq m\text{-}1$, where M is the number of endogenous variables in the model, m is the number of endogenous variables in a given equation, K is the number of exogenous variables in the model, and k is the number of exogenous variables in a given equation. The equations may be under-identified, exactly-identified or over-identified. The 2SLS is usually used for estimating over-identified equations.

Exogeneity cannot be tested as it involves a correlation between the instrumental variable and an unobserved error. If there is more than one instrument, then whether some of them are uncorrelated with the structural error can be tested. The Sargan test is used to test for the over-identifying restrictions. The test hypothesis is that whether all the instruments (z's) are uncorrelated with u against the alternative at least one z is correlated with u. The logic underlying the test is that the residuals should be independent of the instruments as required by the estimation procedure. The Sargan test procedure consists of: (i) estimate the structural equation by 2SLS and obtain the residuals $\hat{u}$, (ii) regress $\hat{u}$ on all exogenous variables and obtain the R-square (R^2), and (iii) calculate $nR^2 \sim \chi^2$ (chi-square) distribution with number of over-identifying parameters equal to the number of instruments less the number of endogenous variables in the equation. If the test statistic exceeds the critical value, the null hypothesis is rejected and at least some of the IVs are not exogenous. A high R^2 in step 2 would indicate that the residuals are not independent of the instruments leading to a rejection of the model specification or instruments.

19.4 Empirical Analysis

The empirical models of structural and reduced form equations for labour supply and labour demand functions are estimated using the 2SLS method. The labour supply (L_s) and labour demand (L_d) are expressed as functions of wage, labour market regulations (LMR) consisting of three measures - union density, employment protection and tax wedge - with supply shocks (fertility) and demand shocks - GDP growth rate, technological shocks (R&D expenditure), total factor productivity and labour productivity respectively.

$$Labour\ supply: \frac{L_s}{L} = f_s(Wage, LMR, S) \qquad (19.11)$$

$$Labour\ demand: \frac{L_d}{L} = f_d(Wage, LMR, D) \qquad (19.12)$$

where is L equilibrium employment rare and L is total labour force. By definition, unemployment rate is the percentage of total labour force that is unemployed but actively seeking employment and willing to work. Hence,

$$Unemployment\ rate = \left(1 - \frac{L}{L}\right) \qquad (19.13)$$

At equilibrium, there exists labour supply function and labour demand functions from which an expression for wage rate is derived, which may then be considered as the transformed labour supply function. Similarly, an expression for unemployment rate is derived and considered as the transformed labour demand function.

$$Labour\ supply\ function: Wage = \phi_s(Unemployment, LMR, S) \qquad (19.14)$$

$$Labour\ demand\ function: Unemployment = \phi_d(Wage, LMR, D) \qquad (19.15)$$

The equations (19.14) and (19.15) are empirically specified as:

$$Wage = \beta_0 + \beta_1 Unemp + \beta_2 Union + \beta_3 EPL + \beta_4 Tax + \beta_5 Fertility + u_1 \qquad (19.16)$$

$$Unemployment = \alpha_0 + \alpha_1 Wage + \alpha_2 Union + \alpha_3 EPL + \alpha_4 Tax + \alpha_5 R\&D + \alpha_6 GR + \alpha_7 TFP + \alpha_7 LP + u_2 \qquad (19.17)$$

The equations (19.17) and (19.18) are simultaneous equations and are to be estimated by the 2SLS method. Wage rate and unemployment rate are the two endogenous variables in the model.

Empirically, in the first stage estimation the reduced form equations of labour supply (wage) and labour demand (unemployment rate) are derived. Then the endogenous variables on all exogenous variables present in the model are regressed obtaining the predicted values for wage rate and unemployment rate:

$$Wage = \delta_0 + \delta_1 Union + \delta_2 EPL + \delta_3 Tax + \delta_4 Fertility + \delta_5 R\&D + \delta_6 GR + \delta_7 TFP + \delta_7 LP + \varepsilon_1 \quad (19.18)$$

$$Unemployment = \delta_0 + \delta_1 Union + \delta_2 EPL + \delta_3 Tax + \delta_4 Fertility + \delta_5 R\&D + \delta_6 GR + \delta_7 TFP + \delta_7 LP + \varepsilon_2 \quad (19.19)$$

In the second stage estimation, the structural form equations are estimated regressing the original model by replacing two the endogenous variables, wage rate and unemployment rate by their predicted values. The empirical estimation obtained thus in this stage are the 2SLS estimates:

$$Wage = \beta_0 + \beta_1 \widehat{Unemp} + \beta_2 Union + \beta_3 EPL + \beta_4 Tax + \beta_5 Fertility + u_1 \quad (19.20)$$

$$Unemployment = \alpha_0 + \alpha_1 \widehat{Wage} + \alpha_2 Union + \alpha_3 EPL + \alpha_4 Tax + \alpha_5 R\&D + \alpha_6 GR + \alpha_7 TFP + \alpha_7 LP + u_2 \quad (19.21)$$

The Table 19.1 presents the descriptive statistics of the variables used in the empirical analysis of the effect of labour market regulations on wages and unemployment.

Table 19.1: Descriptive Statistics of Variables in the Labour Market Regulations Analysis.

Variable	*Description*	*Mean*	*Std. dev.*
Wage rate	Total hourly pay for time worked (US$)	14.401	6.58
Unemployment rate	Share of labour force that is without work but seeking employment (percent)	7.202	3.09
Union density	Ratio of wage and salary earners that are trade union members to the total number of wage and salary earners (percent)	32.103	20.56
Employment protection legislation	The procedures and costs involved in dismissing or hiring workers (score 1-6 with 6 being the most protected level)	2.094	0.91
Tax wedge	Difference between what employees takes home in earnings and what it costs to employ them – measure of the extent to which tax on labour income discourages employment (percent of labour cost)	39.110	10.04
GDP growth rate	Growth rate of annual GDP (percent)	1.631	2.49
R&D expenditure	Gross domestic expenditure on research and development (percent of GDP)	2.093	0.81
Total factor productivity	The residual of GDP growth that cannot be explained by growth in labour and capital inputs (percent)	0.528	1.53
Labour productivity	Real GDP produced by an hour of labour work (percent)	1.296	1.66
Fertility rate	Number of births per woman	2.007	0.88
N	No. of observations	221	

The estimated results of the panel fixed effects and random effects reduced form regression models are presented in Table 19.2. Among the measures of labour market regulations, the union density and tax wedge are the most important factors in determining wage payment and the unemployment rate. In the fixed effects estimates, the tax wedge has a significant positive impact on wage. A 10 percent increase in tax wedge would increase wages by about 2 percent, thus decreasing labour supply. The union density has negative impact on unemployment, a percent increase in union membership decreases unemployment around 1 percent. The employment protection legislations have contradictory effects on wages and unemployment and in fixed and random effects models, but insignificant in both estimations. It seems more rigid labour market regulations with improved working conditions may provide more effects to the legislative measures.

Table 19.2: Panel Regression Estimates of Reduced Form Wage Rate and Unemployment Rate Equations.

Variable	*Fixed effects*		*Random effects*	
	Wage rate	*Unemployment rate*	*Wage rate*	*Unemployment rate*
Union density	-0.119 (0.07)	-1.442*** (0.14)	-0.175 (0.06)	-0.044* (0.02)
Tax wedge	0.215** (0.10)	-0.268 (0.19)	-0.289** (0.13)	0.106** (0.65)
EPL	-1.093 (1.28)	1.692 (2,42)	0.283 (1.56)	-0.834 (0.64)
TFP	1.137*** (0.21)	1.023*** (0.38)	0.710 (0.50)	1.271*** (0.22)
LP	-0.073 (0.14)	-0.378 (0.27)	-0.836*** (0.35)	-0.087 (0.16)
R&D expenditure	0.631 (0.695)	3.164*** (1.31)	6.704*** (1.22)	-0.308 (0.52)
GDP growth rate	-0.806*** (0.08)	-0.694*** (0.16)	-0.476*** (0.19)	0.918*** (0.08)
Fertility rate	-5.441*** (0.96)	5.920*** (1.78)	-0.756*** (1.38)	0.309 (0.57)

Note: Standard errors in parentheses. *** significant at 1 percent level ** significant at 5 percent level * significant at 10 percent level.

The macroeconomic shocks variables like total factor productivity and R&D expenditure have positive effects on both wages and unemployment, whereas the effects of GDP growth rate, labour productivity on wages and unemployment are negative. An increase in fertility rate decreases the wage rate, while increasing the unemployment rate. The technological shocks push up the wage rate, but also increase the unemployment problem. Specifically, a percent enhancement in TFP tends to increase wage payments and unemployment rate equally by about 1 percent. A one percent enhancement in R&D increases unemployment by 3 percent, implying rapid improvement in technologies such as automation observed in many OECD countries in the 21st century have increased the wage payments along with high unemployment rates. The growth in GDP in OECD has negative impact on wage payments and has reduced unemployment problem in OECD countries. The supply shock represented by fertility rate increases labour supply which in effect reduces wage payments and increases unemployment problem in the OECD countries.

In the random effects on reduced-form estimates union density and tax wedge have a negative effect on the wage rate, while union has a negative impact on unemployment rate and tax wedge shows has a positive effect on unemployment rate. This shows that more labour market flexibility will boost wage rate and undermines the unemployment rate. However, the labour market regulations have differential impact on the market players. Hence, reforming labour markets with legislations need an understanding of how reforms alter both labour demand and labour supply decisions. Further, technological shock (TFP and R&D) push up the wage rate as well as the unemployment problem. A one percent increase in R&D tends to increase wages by 6.7 percent and TFP increases unemployment by 1.27 percent. The growth in GDP in OECD has negative impact on both wage payments and unemployment rate. An increase in supply shock variable fertility rate increases the labour supply which in effect reduces wage payments and increases unemployment problem in OECD countries.

The estimates of two stage least squares (2SLS) method are presented in Table 19.3. The empirical random effects estimation of labour supply function and demand function are mostly insignificant. However, the estimation of random effects is necessary to choose between fixed and random effects estimations. For this the Hausman specification test is used where the null hypothesis is that the preferred model is random effects model and the alternative hypothesis is fixed effects as the appropriate model. If the chi-square value is significant (Prob.>chi2 smaller than .05), the null hypothesis of random effects model is rejected and fixed effects model is accepted. The Hausman test for wage rate and unemployment rate equations reports chi-square values of 397.06 and 8.71 with respective Prob>chi2 as 0.0000 and 0.46. As both Prob>chi2 for wage and unemployment specifications are less than 0.5, the fixed effects model is used for discussion.

Table 19.3: 2SLS Panel Regression Estimates of Wage Rate and Unemployment Rate Equations.

Variable	*2SLS fixed effects*		*2SLS random effects*	
	Wage rate	*Unemployment rate*	*Wage rate*	*Unemployment rate*
Wage rate	-	-0.909*** (0.33)	-	2.825 (2.56)
Unemployment rate	0.949*** (0.17)	-	0.606*** (0.22)	-
Union density	-1.495*** (0.13)	-1.444*** (0.48)	-0.048 (0.06)	-0.685 (3.08)
Tax wedge	-0.442** (0.20)	-0.031 (0.22)	-0.189 (0.13)	1.137 (4.19)
EPL	1.828 (2.58)	1.462 (2,85)	-1.257 (1.58)	-2.218 (6.53)
TFP	-	2.077*** (0.53)	-	-0.716 (8.22)
LP	-	-0.42 (0.33)	-	2.11 (9.05)
R&D expenditure	-	3.539* (1.95)	-	-2.05 (4.20)
GDP growth rate	-	-1.44*** (0.27)	-	0.385 (5.28)
Fertility rate	6.265*** (2.13)	-	-1.671 (1.42)	-
Test statistics	Wage equation		Unemployment equation	
Hausman test	397.06		8.71	
Chi-square value	[0.00]		[0.46]	
Endogeneity test	9.90 [0.001]		32.28 [0.00]	
Sargan statistic	8.43 [0.03]		0.00	

Note: Standard errors in parentheses. p-values in square brackets. *** significant at 1 percent level ** significant at 5 percent level * significant at 10 percent level.

In the 2SLS coefficient estimates of wage equation, the unemployment rate is significant at 1 percent level and is positively related to wage payments. A 1 percent increase in unemployment rate increases wage by the same proportion. The labour market regulation variables union density and tax wedge are statistically significant at 1 percent and 5 percent levels respectively. The union density is negatively related to wage rate, specifically a 1 percent increase in union membership decreases wage rate by 1.5 percent. The tax wedge of labour market regulation is also negatively related with wage rate. A 10 percent increase in tax wedge would decrease wage payments by 4.4 percent, implying an employee can have more take-home earnings. However, the employment protection variable is not significant implying changes in employment protection legislations may not have any significant impact on wage. On the whole, the labour market regulations in OECD have discouraged workers from joining labour market due to decline in the work environment.

The supply shock variable fertility rate is statistically significant and positively related to wage rate. An increasing fertility rate shifts the labour supply outward and increases wage payments. Specifically, a 1 percent increase in fertility rate increases wage by 6.26 percent. The Sargan statistic reports p-value of 0.03. The null hypothesis of Sargan statistics test for overidentification i.e. all instruments (z's) are uncorrelated with u is rejected, implying there are at least one z correlated with u in the labour supply equation. Thus, the wage equation is over-identified. The endogeneity test reports p-value 0.001, rejecting the null hypothesis that variables are exogenous, thus unemployment rate is an endogenous variable in wage equation.

In the fixed effects estimates of unemployment equation in Table 19.3, the wage rate is significant at 1 percent level and is negatively related to the unemployment rate. A 1 percent increase in wage rate would decrease unemployment rate by almost equally. Among the labour market regulation variables, only union density is statistically significant. An increase in trade union membership has a negative impact on unemployment rate. Specifically, a 1 percent increase in union density would decreases unemployment rate by 1.4 percent. The other two measures of labour market regulation, tax wedge and employment protection, are insignificant. The effect of demand shocks is mixed. The GDP growth rate has a statistically significant negative effect on unemployment rate. A 1 percent increase in GDP growth would decrease unemployment by 1.4 percent. The total factor productivity (TFP) and expenditure on research and development are positively related to unemployment rate. A 1 percent increase in total factor productivity leads to a 2 percent increase in the unemployment rate. The labour productivity is negatively related to unemployment rate and is statistically insignificant. This shows that the decreasing demand for unskilled labours outweighs the increasing demand for skilled labours. The Sargan test statistic is 0.00 for the labour demand function, showing that the unemployment equation is exactly identified, and hence the validity of instruments cannot be tested. The endogeneity test reports p-value of 0.00, rejecting the null hypothesis that variables are exogenous. Thus, wage rate is an endogenous variable in the unemployment equation.

19.5 Conclusion

With changing production technologies and methods of production, continuous labour reforms are taking place throughout the world. The western industrialised OECD economies are in the forefront of legislating labour market reforms. The labour market regulations are aimed at protecting labour interests especially wages hiring and firing conditions and most importantly to tackle the unemployment situation in the wake of globalisation and automation of the production processes. In some economies the labour market legislations are rigid while in some economies they are flexible. A more flexible labour market reduces the labour market regulations will eventually worsen the working environment of the labourers. This reduces the labourers' willingness to work and therefore increases unemployment. That is, the supply of labour in the market reduces. On the other hand, the demand for labour by firms increases due to relaxation of labour market regulations. As a result, there is a supply-demand gap in the labour market and hence the increasing in unemployment in OECD countries in recent years. How far these labour market regulations impact the wage rates and unemployment is a question for empirical investigation. This paper examines the effects of labour market reforms on unemployment and wage payments in 17 OECD countries using a panel data for the period 2000 to 2012. The labour market regulations are measured by the union density, tax wedge, and an index of employment protection laws. Treating wage rates and unemployment rates as endogenous variable, this paper applied the two stage least squares fixed effects regression method in the empirical analysis.

The main results of this paper can be summarised as follows. The de-unionisation in OECD countries has discouraged labour supply and increased unemployment problem. In the OECD countries, the workers bargaining powers in defending their rights have weakened and the reduction in tax wedge has raised wage payments as well as the disposable income of the workers. The labour market regulations have discouraged workers from joining the labour force since regulations make the working conditions tough. Though the flexibility of the labour market has increased the labour demand in the OECD countries, it has also aggravated the unemployment problem among workers. The empirical estimates show that the employment protection laws have no significant impact on wages and employment in the workers in OECD countries. The total factor productivity and research and development expenditure have a positive impact on unemployment rates in the OECD countries. The technological changes that results from an increase in TFP and R&D lead to an increased demand for skilled labour, which leaves the unskilled labour unemployed implying that the aggregate unemployment level increases. One way to address the supply-demand gap in the labour market arising due to labour market regulations in OECD countries is to provide incentives like pensions, bonuses, paid leaves, insurance, etc. for the labourers so that they will be encouraged to join the labour market.

20

The Determinants of Child Mortality: Panel Instrumental Variable Estimation with Endogeneity of Child Mortality and Fertility

20.1 Introduction

Child mortality rates such as infant mortality rates and neonatal mortality rates are generally accepted as measures of health of population as well as quality of health care. Though mortality rates refer to the risk of infant deaths, it is widely used as a crude indicator of the general population health, socio-economic status of the community and the level of penetration of quality health care services. The child mortality rates are related to other factors that are likely to impact the population health in general, such the level of economic development, standards of living, social welfare, morbidity rates and the environment. The child mortality rates, along with fertility rates, is one of the immediate determinants of population growth of a country. The relationship between mortality and fertility rates controls the population growth in a dynamic equilibrium and directs the demographic structure of population as well as the demographic transition.

There are several evidences to show that there has been a rapid reduction in child mortality rates over the course of modernisation characterised by decline in poverty and improvements in health. The trend in child mortality across continents, presented in Figure 20.1, shows a continuous is fall in child mortality throughout the world. The global child mortality fell from 18.2 percent in 1960 to 4.3 percent in 2015. The child mortality in rich countries is less than 1 percent of the total rates of mortality. Major reductions in the child mortality rates can be observed in developing countries like Brazil and China by over 10 fold over the last 4 decades. Even in sub-Saharan Africa child mortality has been continuously falling for the last 50 years from an alarming rate of one in every four to one in every ten child deaths to birth. From Figure 20.1 it can also be observed that the mortality rates prevalent in the sub-Saharan African countries were higher than the global average in the 1950s and is still remaining higher than the global average, even though it has seen a significant fall in child mortality rates over the years. Similarly, Asian country child mortality rates were higher than the global average in the initial years, however, Asian countries has seen a rapid decline and has managed to remain below the global average in recent years. Further, the European and American countries remain very low in child mortality rates compared to the global average (Roser, 2018).

The Figure 20.2 and Table 20.1 show the trends in decline in child mortality rates by income level. It can be observed that the rate of decline in child mortality rates has been very minimal at low levels of child mortality; this is primarily because of inherent convexity in the relationship between income and mortality rates. At low levels of child mortality rates, additional increase in income will tend to have a minimal impact on decline in child

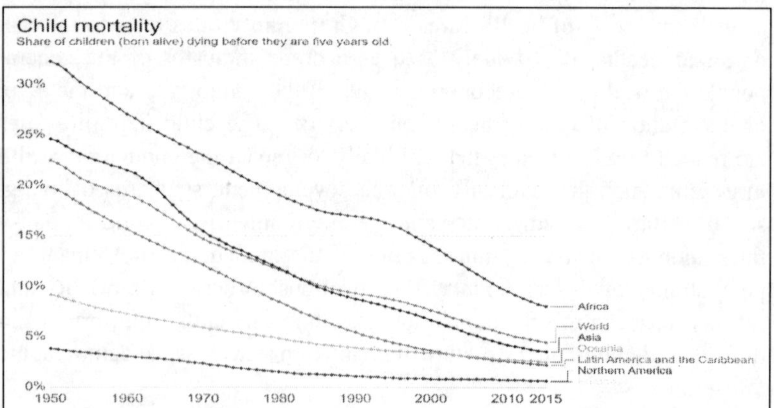

Source: UN Population Division (2017).

Figure 20.1: Child Mortality Rates by Continent.
(Share of children (born alive) dying before five years old)

mortality rates. And at high rates of child mortality additional increase in income would rapidly decrease the mortality rates and the effects tend to subside with additional increase in income. The Figure 20.2 shows the high income country child mortality rates which little lesser than 5 percent in the 1960s has remained a little above 1 percent in 2012, indicating a slow decline. However, the decline in child mortality rates of low income and lower middle income countries has been rapid compared to the decline in the world child mortality rates. The mortality rates of these countries which were above 25 percent in the 1960s fell to below 10 percent in 2012.

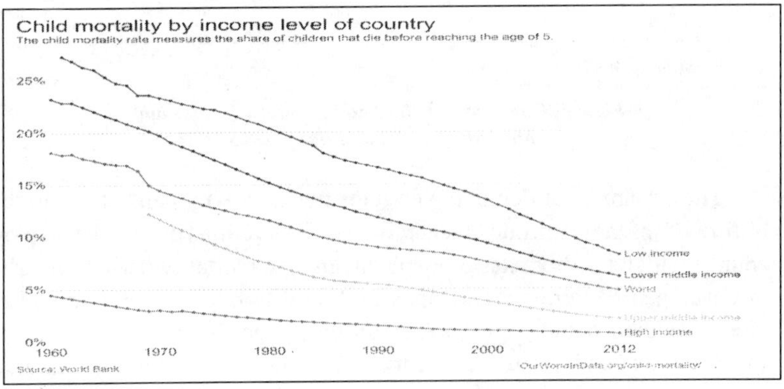

Source: World Bank (2012).

Figure 20.2: Child Mortality Rates by Income.

(Share of children dying before reaching the age of 5)

Table 20.1: Child Mortality Rates by Income for 217 Countries, 1960-2012.

Countries	***1960***	***1970***	***1980***	***1990***	***2000***	***2012***
High income	4.46	2.99	2.09	1.45	0.97	0.62
Low income	27.32	23.28	20.41	16.56	13.42	8.54
Lower middle income	23.27	19.76	15.16	11.18	9.3	6.12
Upper middle income	13.5	11.69	7.44	5.43	3.79	2.02
World	18.1	14.16	11.57	8.98	7.54	4.78

Source: World Bank (2012).

The convexity in the relation between levels of economic development as measured by the per capita income and general health levels as measured by child mortality rates is shown in Figure 20.3. This is linearised by considering the logs of both variables. The convex relation between income and child mortality rate is primarily because, at very low levels of income there persists very high levels of child mortality rates, however with small increase in income the mortality rates fall at very rapid levels and later with additional increase in income the marginal effects tends to fade away.

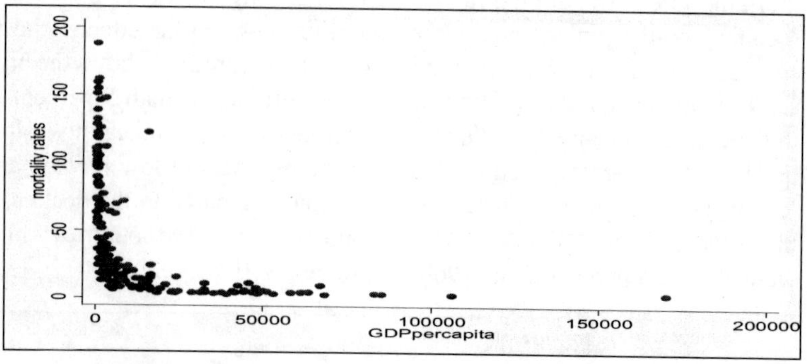

Source: World Bank (2015).

Figure 20.3: Convex Relationship between Income and Mortality for 85 Countries in 2015.

The dynamics of demographic transition primarily depends upon the birth rates and the death rates. Generally, it is observed that in most developing countries high fertility rates is coupled with high mortality rates. Similarly, in developed countries there exists low fertility rates and low mortality rates. Standard demographic transition theory posits that mortality rates for infants and children drive fertility rates, intermediated through cultural, social and psychological processes. Those social processes have the effect of keeping population size stable. Under conditions of high mortality, high fertility rates are required to keep population from shrinking. When there is a transition from high to low mortality rates, fertility rates decrease. May studies also suggest that the relationship between fertility and mortality is bi-directional. One side of the argument is that as the number of children per woman increases the time and resources that is shared between the children gets reduced and this could increase the probability of child dying at an early age. The other side of the argument is that as the mortality risks are high, given the parental expectation of the ideal number of births, higher would be the fertility rates to cope up with the expected levels births.

Therefore, when the mortality risks are high the fertility rates also tend to be higher. First, parental expectations of child loss might be expressed in terms of insurance or hoarding behaviour causing fertility to be higher than if survival were assured. In terms of the life cycle theory, the parents face a trade-off between the number of children and the quality of care given to each child. Rise in the child birth reduces available time and energy to invest in each individual child, increasing their likelihood of dying. At the same time, with post-natal investment in offspring, the death of an existing offspring releases time and energy for the mother to invest in additional child, a placement offspring. Initially, fertility and child mortality around the world were so high that on average every woman lost 1 of her children before they could celebrate their 5th birthday. With the decline of child mortality and fertility this became very rare; in 2015 Swedish women lost on average 0.006 children before they were 5 years old. It is known that one in every two children dies and if the expected level of children that they wish to have is three, then their total number of births would naturally be six.

Similarly, strong relationship exists between overall economic development and the levels of death rates. Economic development generally depicted by the gross domestic income per capita is also the best single indicator of the standard of living, As GDP per capita is weighted by the population, economic development influences mortality rates. Also, studies have observed that the relationship between income per head and levels of mortality is convex, that is a small gain in income per head in low income countries tend to produce a decline in the mortality rates and the effect tends to flatten out as the income per head increases. It is also observed that only in situations where a country shares their health technology to control death rates, that mortality has become significantly disassociated from economic levels. For example, in Ceylon, Mauritius and British Guiana, low cost public health services provided during the post war era has resulted in significant decrease in the death rates despite any significant increase in the levels of living.

Among all the factors associated with child mortality, the female literacy has been the single most important factor in reducing child mortality. There is an inverse relationship between the levels of female literacy and infant mortality rates. Shetty and Shetty (2017) argue that female literacy is an empowerment as well as an emancipator; literate females enjoy greater autonomy and are more involved in decision making. Literate women are able to adopt a healthier life style and this has a great positive impact on mother's as well as child's health, thereby reducing child mortality rates as well as maternal mortality rates. The benefits of education of women are many and varied; one prime benefit is healthier children which again reduces the risk of child death. Education among females improves the nutrition intake and personal hygiene, which has a significant impact on their own health as well as the health of their off-springs. Short birth intervals and unintended pregnancies pose serious risk to the mother and her infants by causing high risk of pregnancy related complications and self-induced abortions. Therefore, education among females improves awareness to such problems and the knowledge of immunisation, mitigating child mortality risks. Countries which have progressed more on the female literacy front reduce infant mortality at a faster. States and countries which have a higher percentage of literate women perform better on developmental and social indices, Women's education is also often cited as one of the most valuable tools to reduce poverty.

The Figure 20.4 shows the various causal links that exists between a woman's education, child mortality and economic development (Browne and Barrett, 1991). The links shown are primarily health related know-how.

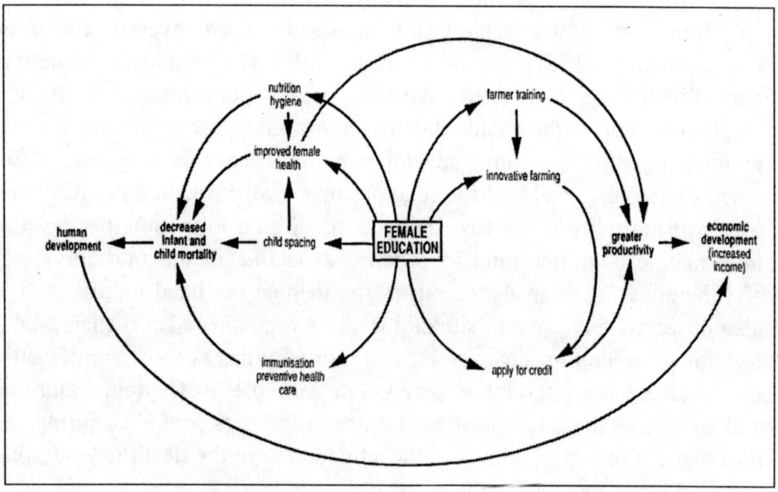

Source: Browne and Barrett (1991).

Figure 20.4: Causation Structure of Female Education on Child Mortality.

The objective of this paper is to analyse the impact of the major factors that influence the child mortality rates. Specifically, this paper estimates the effects of economic development, inequality, fertility, female literacy and female labour force participation on child mortality rates across countries and over time. The panel data used in this paper for 85 countries is derived from various sources including the World Development Reports and population databases. Empirically, a fixed effects instrumental variable method is used.

20.2. A Brief Review of Recent Studies

As early as 1970s, Preston (1975) estimates the relative contribution of economic factors to increases in life expectancy, the opposite of mortality, exploring the cross-sectional relationships between national life expectancies and income per capita during three different decades of 20th century - 1900s, 1930s and 1960s. The study plots logistic curves that specify the relation between life expectancy at birth and national income per heads. The curves thus estimated produced an upward sloping concave curves, shifting upward for each cross section that was estimated. Also, the simple correlation between life expectancy and the logarithm of income per head is 0.885 in the 1930s and 0.880 in the 1960s. At higher income levels the shift is unmistakable; it amounts to some 10-12 years of life expectancy at incomes between $100 and $500 and progressively less thereafter due to the concavity in their relationship. A comparison of the curves horizontally and vertically suggested that, in order to attain a particular value of life expectancy between 40 and 60, a range that includes a large majority of the current world population, a nation required an income level approximately 2-6 times higher in the 1930s than in the 1960s.

Hobcraft, Mcdonald and Rutstein (1984) analyse five socio-economic correlates of infant and child mortality using the World Fertility Survey for 28 developing countries. The study considers variations in mortality for the first five years of children for each of the following variables: mother's education, mother's work status, husband's occupation, husband's education and place of residence. A multivariate approach to assess the relative importance of each of the five variables reveals that the mortality differences are most strongly associated with mother's education and occupation and the differences increase with age through the first five years of life of the child. The mother's education is strongly associated with mortality during the first five years of life particularly in Asian countries. Child mortality for few African countries is relatively strongly associated with husband's occupation and education. The mortality differences between the first and fourth birthday of children are often appallingly large by socioeconomic differences.

Torre and Myrskyla (2014) consider age specific mortality rates and life expectancy as response variables, for the age groups of 1-14, 15-49, 50-64 and 65 89, to estimate the effects GDP per capita and income inequality using a panel data for the period 1975-2006. The study observes that the GDP per head and unobserved period and country factors, income inequality, measured by the Gini index, are strongly and positively associated with male and female mortality upto age 15. For women the association vanishes at older ages, but for men persists upto age 50. These findings suggest that policies decreasing income inequality may improve the health of children and young-to middle-aged men.

Gerdtham, U.-G. and M. Johannesson (2004) examine whether mortality is related to individual income, mean community income and inequality in community income, controlling for initial health status and personal characteristics. The regression analysis is based on data of over 40000 individuals who were followed up for 1-17 years. The dependent variable in the regression analysis is the survival time in years and the survival status at the end of the follow up period. To estimate the effect of income and other covariates on mortality risk, a Cox proportional hazard model is estimated. The estimates of the Cox model show that the individual income is highly significant with a negative sign, implying that the mortality risk decreases with higher income. Further, the study suggests that the relationship is highly nonlinear with a decreasing effect of income at higher income levels. The other relationships are not statistically significant.

Miller and Paxson (2006) explore the relationship between relative income and mortality in the US using a semi-aggregated data on mortality rates of people categorised by age, race, gender and place of residence for 1980 and 1990. The study develops an empirical model in which the individual health is a function of own income and the incomes of those who live in the same geographical area. The study observes no significant relation of mortality with having relatively wealthy neighbours, holding own income fixed. However, for working-aged black males having relatively wealthy neighbours is associated with lower mortality. For example, among younger (aged 25–64) black men, an increase in income of others is estimated to have a beneficial effect on mortality that is 40 percent as large as an equivalent increase in own income.

Haines (1998) uses an instrumental variable technique to analyse the bi-directional relationship between child mortality and fertility rates. The instrument, the proportion of death, is regressed on fertility rates to obtain the fitted values, which is then regressed with the original first stage regression equation. The estimated coefficient is a good predictor of the replacement or the hoarding effect.

Saurabh, Sarkar and Pandey (2013) investigate the relationship of male and female literacy rates with crude birth rates and infant mortality rates in the states and union territories of India. The estimated regression coefficients show that CBR is significantly inversely related with female literacy rate, while the male literacy rate is not significantly related to CBR. The IMR of the states are also inversely related to their female literacy rate, whereas male literacy rate is not significant. As the educated women are known to take informed reproductive and healthcare decisions, female literacy is highly important for both population stabilisation and better infant health care which is reflected in lower birth rates and infant mortality rates respectively.

Westoff and Bankole (2001) argue that as one of the major proximate determinants of fertility, contraceptive prevelence is expected to be stringly negatively associated with fertility. To analyse the differences in the relationship between contraceptive usage and fertility rates in sub-Saharan Afica and other regions, they consider three measures of fertility: births in last 12 months, proportion currently pregnant and total fertility rate. The study finds the correlation of -0.368 between total fertility rate and contraceptive usage for sub-Saharan Africa, however for other regions it is -0.807. They advance various hypotheses to account for this anomaly: African women use more traditional methods with higher failure rates; contraception is used more for spacing than for limiting births implying more discontinuation; total fertility rate may be insensitive to more recent rapid increases in contraceptive prevalence. The study concludes that the populations in sub-Saharan Africa is clearly at the beginning of their fertility transition and can be compared with Asian and Latin American populations at much more advanced stages of the transition. By comparing the correlation for the same regions that are surveyed more than once, the study discerns a clear trend in sub-Saharan Africa toward a higher correlation over time.

The World Health Organisation (2015) reports that around 25-40 percent of maternal deaths could be eliminated if unplanned pregnancies are prevented. When the use of contraceptives is low in a country, the total fertility rate – average number of children per woman during her life time – is often high. The Contraceptive Prevalence Rates (CPR) in countries with a high MMR and a low proportion of skilled care at birth are usually low. The Total Fertility Rate (TFR) in countries with a low CPR is usually high. Most of the countries with a high total fertility rate often have limited choice of contraceptive methods.

20.3. Data and Methodology

This paper uses a cross-country panel data for 85 countries for two years 2000 and 2015 from the World Bank database to analyse the determinants of the mortality rates under the age of five. The child mortality rate is expressed as a function of fertility rate, per capita income, income inequality and female literacy and labour force participation rates. However, as there is a bi-directional causality between fertility rates and child mortality rates, contraceptive prevalence rate enters as an instrumental variable is the method of estimation. The dependent variable, under five mortality rate is the number of children that died before reaching the age of five per 1000 children. The fertility rate is the number of children that would be born to a woman if she were to live to the end of her childbearing years and bear children in accordance with age specific fertility rates of specified years. The female literacy rate is the percentage of females aged 15 and above who can both read and write. The GDP per capita is the per person value of the goods and services produced within a country during a given year (weighted by the population of the country at constant 2010 USD).The Gini index measures the area between the Lorenz curve and the line of absolute equality, expressed as a percentage of the maximum area under the line. The female labour force participation shows the extent to which women are active in the labour force. The contraceptive prevalence rate, included as instrumental variable, is the percentage of women aged 15-49 years who are married or in union and who are practicing or whose sexual partners are practicing any form of contraception.

Panel Instrumental Variable Method

The major advantage of a panel data set over a cross-section is that it allows greater flexibility in modeling differences in behaviour across individuals. The heterogeneity or individual effects λ_i may be observed or unobserved. The empirical analysis begins with the pooled OLS method:

$$y_{it} = \alpha + \beta x_{it} + \lambda_i + u_{it} \tag{20.1}$$

In the panel data context, the pooled regression model is the population averaged model as, under the classical model assumptions, any latent heterogeneity is averaged out.

If λ_i are taken to be constant over time, then first differencing is just one of the many ways to eliminate the individual effect λ_i. An alternative method is the fixed effects or within transformation. For each *i*, averaging equation (20.1) over time yields:

$$\bar{y}_i = \beta \bar{x}_i + \bar{u}_i \tag{20.2}$$

where $\bar{y} = T^{-1} \sum_{t=1}^{T} y_{it}$. Subtracting equation (20.2) from equation (20.1) eliminates the unobserved individual heterogeneity λ_i which is fixed over time. The resulting time-demeaned transformed equation is:

$$(y_{it} - \bar{y}_i) = \beta(x_{it} - \bar{x}_i) + (u_{it} - \bar{u}_i) \tag{20.3}$$

As the unobserved individual effect λ_i has disappeared, equation (20.3) can be estimated by the pooled OLS on the time-demeaned variable as fixed effects estimator or the within estimator. However, when λ_i is correlated with x_i, the least squares estimator of β is biased and inconsistent as a consequence of an omitted variable. If there exist some observable fixed effects, $\alpha_i = z_i\alpha$, the fixed effects model approach takes α_i to be a group-specific constant term in the regression model. Then, the model:

$$y_{it} = \alpha_i + \beta x_{it} + u_{it} \tag{20.4}$$

specifies an estimable conditional mean.

If the unobserved individual heterogeneity λ_i, however formulated, is uncorrelated with x_i, then the model can be formulated as a linear regression model with a compound disturbance term:

$$y_{it} = \beta x_{it} + E[z_i\alpha - E(z_i\alpha)] + \varepsilon_{it} \tag{20.5}$$

$$y_{it} = \beta x_{it} + \alpha + u_i + \varepsilon_{it} \tag{20.6}$$

This random effects approach specifies that u_i is a group-specific random element. The crucial distinction between fixed and random effects is whether the unobserved individual effect embodies elements that are correlated with the regressors in the model, not whether these effects are stochastic or not. The random effects model, as a linear regression model with a compound disturbance, may be consistently, although inefficiently, estimated by least squares.

However, when there is endogenous regressor in the model, the covariance between the endogenous variable and error term is not zero, hence the OLS type estimates tend to over-estimate the parameters and therefore the estimates biased and inconsistent. The problem of endogeneity arises when there is bi-directional causality between the dependent and the independent variable as the error u is directly affecting the regressors x and therefore indirectly affecting the dependent variable y. The structural equations of the model can be specified as:

$$x_{it} = \beta_0 + \beta_1 y_{it} + \beta_2 z_{ti} + u_{it} \tag{20.7}$$

$$y_{it} = \alpha_0 + \alpha_1 x_{it} + e_{it} \tag{20.8}$$

Inserting equation (20.8) in equation (20.7) implies that x_{it} is a function of e_{it} and hence $cov\ (x_{it}|e_{it}) \neq 0$. Similarly, plugging equation (20.7) in equation (20.8) shows that y_{it} is a function of u_{it}, and hence $cov\ (y_{it}|u_{it}) \neq 0$.

Therefore, the correlation between the endogenous variable x and error term u to be removed using an instrumental variable (IV) estimation method. The IV is a variable z that has the property that changes in z are associated with changes in x but do not lead to change in y and not correlated with u, thus introducing only exogenous variation in x. The IV estimation considers the covariance between the instrument z and the dependent variable y:

$$cov(z_i, y_i) = cov[z_i, (\beta_0 + X'\hat{\beta} + u_i)] = cov(z_i, \beta_0) + \hat{\beta}cov(z_i, x_i) + cov(z_i, u_i) \tag{20.9}$$

By the assumption of instrumental variable method, the IV is uncorrelated with the error term:

$$cov(z_i, u_i) = 0 \Rightarrow cov(z_i, y_i) \Rightarrow \hat{\beta} cov(z_i, x_i) \Rightarrow \hat{\beta} = \frac{cov(z_i, y_i)}{cov(z_i, x_i)} \quad (20.10)$$

The IV estimation is also a two stage least squares estimation. Specifying the model as structural equations:

$$y = \beta_1 x_1 + \beta_2 x_2 + u \quad (20.11)$$

where y is the vector of the dependent variable, x_1 is the matrix endogenous variable and x_2 is a matrix of exogenous variable. The structural equations model involves a combined set of $x = [x_1, x_2]$ of both endogenous and the exogenous independent variables. The set of instruments are specified for only exogenous variables as $z = [z_1, x_2]$ where z_1 is an instrument for x_1 and x_2 is an instrument for itself. The 2SLS method replaces the endogenous variable with the predicted values of this endogenous variable when regressed on the instrument chosen. First, the first stage equation with only exogenous regressors is estimated:

$$x_1 = \gamma_1 z + \gamma_2 x_2 + \varepsilon \quad (20.12)$$

Then, the fitted values of are substituted in the structural equation:

$$y = \hat{\beta}_1 \hat{x}_1 + \hat{\beta}_2 x_2 + u \quad (20.13)$$

The fixed effects model allows the unobserved individual effects to be correlated with the included variables and the differences between units are parametric shifts of the regression function. In the random effects model the individual specific constant terms are randomly distributed across cross-sectional units, thereby greatly reducing the number of parameters to be estimated. An inevitable question is which should be used? From a purely practical standpoint, the dummy variable approach is costly in terms of degrees of freedom lost. On the other hand, the fixed effects approach is superior as there is little justification for treating the individual effects as uncorrelated with the other regressors, as is assumed in the random effects model. The random effects treatment, therefore, may suffer from the inconsistency due to this correlation between the included variables and the random effect.

The specification test devised by Hausman (1978) is used to test for orthogonality of the common effects and the regressors. The test is based on the idea that under the hypothesis of no correlation, OLS, fixed effects and random effects estimators are consistent, but OLS is inefficient, whereas under the alternative, fixed effect is consistent, but the random effect is not. Therefore, under the null hypothesis, the two estimates should not differ systematically, and a test can be based on the difference. The other essential ingredient for the test is the covariance matrix of the difference vector $[\hat{\beta}_{FE} - \hat{\beta}_{RE}]$:

$$var[\hat{\beta}_{FE} - \hat{\beta}_{RE}] = var[\hat{\beta}_{FE}] + var[\hat{\beta}_{RE}] - cov[\hat{\beta}_{FE}, \hat{\beta}_{RE}] - cov[\hat{\beta}_{RE}, \hat{\beta}_{FE}] \quad (20.14)$$

Hausman's essential result is that the covariance of an efficient estimator with its difference from an inefficient estimator is zero, which implies that:

$$cov[(\hat{\beta}_{FE} - \hat{\beta}_{RE}), \hat{\beta}_{RE}] = cov[\hat{\beta}_{FE}, \hat{\beta}_{RE}] - var[\hat{\beta}_{RE}] = 0 \\ \Rightarrow Cov[\hat{\beta}_{FE}, \hat{\beta}_{RE}] = var[\hat{\beta}_{RE}] \quad (20.15)$$

Inserting equation (20.15) in equation (20.14) produces the covariance matrix for the Hausman test:

$$var[\hat{\beta}_{FE} - \hat{\beta}_{RE}] = var[\hat{\beta}_{FE}] - var[\hat{\beta}_{RE}] = \psi \quad (20.16)$$

The test statistic is thus:

$$H = (b_{FE} - \hat{\beta}_{RE})' (\psi_{FE} - \psi_{RE})^{-1} (b_{FE} - \hat{\beta}_{RE}) \quad (20.17)$$

The chi-squared test is based on the Wald criterion:

$$W = \chi^2(k-1) = [b - \hat{\beta}]\psi^{-1}[b - \hat{\beta}] \quad (20.18)$$

For the fixed effects model, the estimated covariance matrix ψ is the slope estimator and for the random effects model, estimated covariance matrix ψ excludes the constant term. The null hypothesis and alternative hypothesis for Hausman test is specified as $H_0: b = \hat{\beta}$ and $H_1: b \neq \hat{\beta}$. When computed value of the testing statistic is greater than the critical value, the null hypothesis of the random effects model is rejected and the preferred specification for the data is the fixed effects model.

20.4. Empirical Analysis

The estimating empirical panel model specifies an endogenous relationship between child mortality rate and fertility rate, along with other covariates like per capita income, Gini index, female literacy rate and female labour force participation rate. The theoretical argument for endogeneity of the variables is that higher the fertility rates, the parents will have less time and resources to devote to the new born child hence causing to the death of that child at an early age. In the other direction, higher the mortality rates the parents would give birth to more children to meet their required number of births. When there is bidirectional causality between two variables, then the error terms will be correlated with the current endogenous variable, the fertility rate. Therefore, the instrumental variable method is used when there is bidirectional causality between the two variables. The structural equations are given as:

$$lnCMR_{it} = \beta_0 + \beta_1 lnGDPPC_{it} + \beta_2 lnGI_{it} + \beta_3 LR_{it} + \beta_4 FR_{it} + \beta_5 FLPR_{it} + \lambda_i + u_{it} \quad (20.19)$$

$$FR_{it} = \alpha_0 + \alpha_1 lnMR_{it} + \delta_i + \varepsilon_{it} \quad (20.20)$$

where λ_i represents the individual heterogeneity. Plugging equation (20.20) into equation (20.19) implies that the mortality rates is a function of ε_{it}. Hence, the $\text{cov}\,(lnMR_{it} \mid \varepsilon_{it}) \neq 0$. Similarly, plugging in equation (20.19) into equation (20.20) implies that the fertility rate is a function of u_{it}. Hence, the $\text{cov}(FR_{it} \mid u_{it}) \neq 0$. Therefore, an instrumental variable which is uncorrelated with the error term u_{it} and associated with the endogenous covariate is introduced.

The instrument that is used for the fertility rate which is the endogenous variable is the contraceptive prevalence rate (CPR). There are several studies that show a strong negative relationship between the contraceptive prevalence rate and the fertility rate. The condition that is to be satisfied by CPR as the instrumental variable are:

$E(CPR_{it}, u_{it}) = 0$, the CPR is uncorrelated with the error term.

$E(CPR_{it}, FR_{it}) \neq 0$, the CPR is correlated with the endogenous variable, the fertility rate.

As the CPR is not a direct cause of child mortality rate, the $\text{Cov}(MR_{it} \mid FR_{it}) = 0$.

In other words, the CPR is not included in the structural equation.

Comparing the estimated effects with and without instruments, the degree of upward and downward biases due to the non-zero covariance that exists between the time invariant unobserved heterogeneity and the covariates can be ascertained.

The Table 20.2 presents the descriptive statistics of the variables used in the IV analysis of the determinants of child mortality for panel data of 85 countries for 2000 and 2015. The mean of child mortality rate is 68.1 with a standard deviation of 49.61. The high standard deviation signifies the significance of the time variant and invariant as well as observed and unobserved heterogeneity within and between the countries. For example, the differences in the national income between countries can explain the high standard deviation in the child mortality rates. The high variation in the national income is explained by the standard deviations in the GDP per capita, which is US$ 7880.46, with a mean of US$ 3137.42. Similarly, the female literacy also has high standard deviation of 27.14 with a mean of 66.26. The mean of Gini index that measures income inequality is 38 with a standard deviation of 9.24. The labour force participation rate has a mean of 40.65 and a standard deviation of 9.051.

Table 20.2: Descriptive Statistics of Variables in the Child Mortality Analysis.

Variable	*Mean*	*Std. dev.*
Child mortality rate (CMR)	68.61	49.61
Fertility rate (FR)	3.88	1.63
GDP per capita (GDPPC)	3137.42	7880.46
Gini index (GI)	38	9.24
Female literacy rate (FLPR)	66.26	27.14
Female labour participation rate (FLR)	40.65	9.051
N	170	

The null hypothesis of Hausman's test is that there is random effect or differences between the models are not systematic whereas the alternative hypothesis states that there is no differences and presence of fixed effects. The chi-square value for the Hausman's test is highly significant confirming that the difference in the coefficients of the fixed and random effects model are significant, which suggests that there exists a strong relation between time invariant unobserved individual heterogeneity and the covariates in the model. Hence, the null hypothesis that there is random effect is rejected and hence the fixed effects model is the appropriate model. Thus, the fixed effects model is considered to be an appropriate model to obtain unbiased and consistent estimates. The fixed effect model control the country-wise heterogeneity due to differences in economic, social and demographic factors across regions. The country-wise time invariant unobserved heterogeneity can be the life styles that a particular country may follow, levels of immunity to diseases, gender bias, general hygiene, knowledge of implementing health related techniques into child rearing etc.

In the fixed effects model, the within R-square value for the model is 0.78 showing about 78 percent variation in child mortality rates in each of the countries is mainly explained by their per capita income, fertility rates and female literacy rates through time. Similarly, the between group R-square shows states that 83 percent of the variation in child mortality rates between countries are explained by the covariates that enter into the model. The rho value of 0.94 shows that about 94 percent of the variance in child mortality is due to differences across panels. This statistic indicates that there exists a wide inequality across the countries around the world showing polar opposites; on one hand, there are countries which exhibit a very promising situation of child mortality, and on the other hand, there are nations with alarming situation with regard to child mortality.

The panel estimates presented in Table 20.3 show that log of GDP per capita and female literacy rate are significantly negatively related to the log of mortality rate of the countries around the world. This is in line with the findings of Torre and Myrskyla (2014). Per capita income shows the general economic development in the countries which could significantly reduce the levels of child mortality rates. A one unit increase in per capita GDP leads to a decrease of 0.29 units of log of child mortality rate. An increase in per capita GDP induces the ability of countries to obtain higher standards of living thus contributing to declining child mortality. Also, a one unit increase in female literacy rate leads to 0.008 unit decrease in child mortality rates of the countries. Literate mothers are able to incorporate healthy life styles and hence female literacy has a significant impact on the child health. This finding is in line with the findings of Saurabh, Sarkar and Pandey (2013).

Table 20.3: Panel IV Estimates of Child Mortality Rate for 85 Countries.

Variable	*Pooled OLS*	*Fixed effects*		*Random effects*
		Not instrumented	*Instrumented*	
Fertility rate	0.224* (0.04)	0.097** (0.05)	0.318* (0.09)	0.273* (0.06)
Ln(GDP per capita)	-0.354* (0.03)	-0.353* (0.29)	-0.297* (0.04)	-0.308* (0.03)
Ln(Gini index)	0.717* (0.15)	0.102 (0.17)	0.141 (0.19)	0.360* (0.14)
Female literacy rate	-0.006* (0.002)	-0.008** (0.003)	-0.007* (0.003)	-0.005*** (0.002)
Female labour force participation rate	-0.002 (0.003)	0.0005 (0.12)	0.009 (0.14)	0.003 (0.004)
Constant	5.120* (0.50)	6.32* (1.06)	4.37* (1.41)	3.90* (0.77)
R-square (within)	-	0.82	0.78	0.79
R- square (between)	-	0.83	0.83	0.85
R-square	0.86	0.84	0.83	0.85
Rho-value	-	0.94	0.93	0.91
No. of obs.	170			
No. of countries	85			

Note: Standard errors in parentheses. * significant at 1 percent level ** significant at 5 percent level *** significant at 10 percent level.

The estimated effect of fertility rate is highly significant in all specifications and is positively associated with child mortality rates. A unit increase in total fertility rate induces an increase of 0.318 units in child mortality rates. The fertility rate is instrumented with the contraceptive prevalence rate to obtain the unbiased estimate of the impact of fertility rate on child mortality rate. In order asses the strength of the instrumental variable and the identification of the structural equation, three tests are considered: Anderson-Canon Lagrange Multiplier, Wald F and Sargan-Hansen tests for identification. The test results presented in Table 20.4 confirms that the equation is not under identified, since the computed Wald F-statistic is greater than the critical value. Therefore, the instrument contraceptive prevalence rate is a strong instrument for the endogenous regressor fertility rate.

Table 20.4: Identification Test Statistics.

Identification test	*Test statistic*	*Test statistic value*
Under identification	A-C LM statistic	19.918 (0.00)
Weak identification	Wald F statistic	24.629
Overidentification	Sargan-Hansen statistic	21.236 (0.00)

Note: p-values in parentheses.

Even though in the fixed effects model the Gini coefficient is not significant enough to explain the variation in child mortality, the estimated coefficient shows a positive relation between the two, similar to Torre and Myrskyla (2014) which is statistically significant in their study. This means that as income inequality rises child mortality rate also increases. However, the literature is not able to identify the exact dynamics through which inequality affects the child death rates. Similarly, female labour force participation rate has no statistically significant impact on child mortality rates.

20.5. Conclusion

This paper investigates the effects of per capita income, income inequality, female literacy rate, fertility rates and female labour force participation rate on child mortality rate in a panel of 85 countries between 2000 and 2015. The study uses fixed effects instrumental variable method of estimation the fertility rate is an endogenous variable in the model. The empirical estimates show significant negative effect of per capita income and female literacy rate and a strong positive impact of fertility rate on child mortality in the pane countries. However, the analysis also finds no significant role for income inequality and female labour force participation in controlling child mortality. Thus, in countries where there is persistent child mortality, the policies should focus on bringing down the fertility rates through education especially female literacy and more so on the usage of contraceptive usage. The strong positive relationship between overall economic development and the levels of death rates strengthen the argument the economic development is the best contraceptive. Increasing income per capita also encompasses other components of living standards, such as health and life style changes. Undoubtedly, controlling child mortality rates is an advantage to the population with considerably less pressure on the resource use and even greater advantage to the growth of an economy.

21

The Causality Among Foreign Direct Investment, Energy Consumption, Carbon Emissions and Economic Growth: Panel Quantile Regression Estimation

21.1. Introduction

The growing climate change and global warming have emerged as one of the most serious problems facing the international community (Wang et al. 2014). The accumulation of greenhouse gas (GHG) emissions, most notably the carbon dioxide (CO2) emissions from industries, is the most significant cause for global warming (Zhang et al. 2014). Since the industrial revolution, the levels of CO_2 emissions from human activities have been continuously increasing and the burning of fossil fuels and deforestation have been identified as the primary cause of increased CO_2 concentrations in the atmosphere. In the wake of rapid industrialisation in the post-war era and the rush for economic growth, high demand for energy consumption and the consequent CO_2 emissions in a large number of developed and developing countries pose serious problems for development agenda in the post-globalisation strategies. Specifically, carbon emission is the main cause of environmental degradation, a consequence of economic growth.

Though energy consumption caused by economic growth is the decisive factor in environmental pollution, energy consumption and economic growth alone may not explain the whole CO_2 emissions. Other factors such as foreign direct investment, a necessary input for economic growth, are also associated with carbon emissions. Invariably, most developing countries vie for attracting FDI as a source of industrialisation and economic growth. Developed countries also encourage shifting of their industries to other countries as a way to reduce energy consumption thereby reducing pollution and developing green environment in their countries. Therefore, the FDI channel is also encouraged in both developed and developing countries.

Research on the analysis of the relationship between economic growth and energy consumption as well as CO_2 emissions and environmental degradation try to establish the causality and estimate the causal effects. Empirical studies use both time series and panel data and apply cointegration techniques including unit root, cointegration, and causality tests. This paper aims to analyse the causal relationship between economic growth, FDI, energy consumption, and CO_2 emissions in five ASEAN (Association of Southeast Asian Nations) countries (ASEAN-5) - Indonesia, Malaysia, Philippines, Singapore, and Thailand - the original founding members of ASEAN in 1967 and remain the most influential members of ASEAN in the 21st century. The main objective of this paper is to estimate the impact of FDI, economic growth and energy consumption on carbon emissions in ASEAN-5 economies. Further, this paper examines whether the effects are the same at all levels or vary across the emission distribution i.e. differential effects with the most and least emissions.

In terms of per capita income in 2011, Singapore (US$ 34,758) ranked the highest, followed by Malaysia (US$ 6318), Thailand (US$ 3163), Indonesia (US$ 1570) and Philippines (US$ 1403). The average annual economic growth rate in ASEAN economies has been above 5 percent between 2000 to 2013, far exceeding the OECD average growth (1.6 percent) and comparable to the growth experienced by India (7.2 percent) and Africa (4.8 percent). The Figure 21.1 presents the time series of GDP per capita

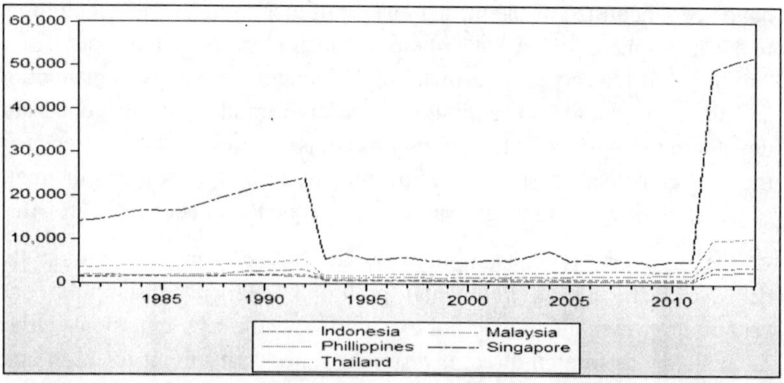

Figure 21.1: GDP per capita in ASEAN-5 Countries (in constant 2010 US$).

for the ASEAN-5 countries. Overall, a persistent growth of GDP per capita level is observed in all ASEAN-5 countries, though Singapore stands atop.

The Figure 21.2 depicts the time series of FDI for the ASEAN-5countries. The FDI inflow in Singapore is not only higher but also has been increasing faster than that in the other four countries ASEAN economies where there has been only a slight increase in the FDI inflows over the years.

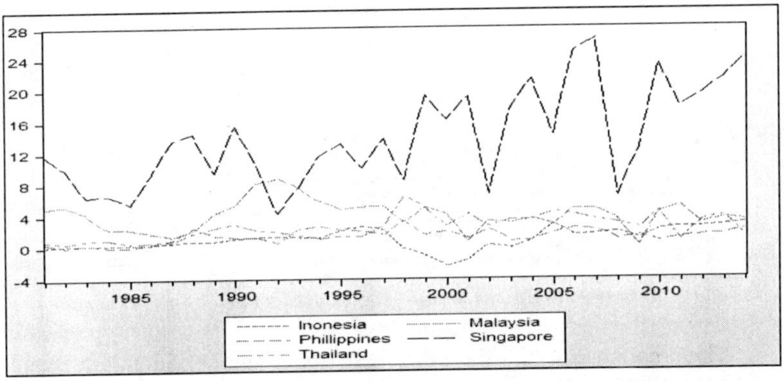

Figure 21.2: FDI Inflow in ASEAN-5 Countries (share of net FDI inflow in GDP).

The Figure 21.3 presents the time series of energy consumption of the ASEAN-5 countries. All the five countries show increasing trend of energy consumption over the years. However, since 1994, Singapore shows a unique feature with regard to energy consumption. Since 1994, the level of energy consumption in Singapore has been declining in the face of continuous increase in economic growth. Further, the energy consumption in Malaysia and Thailand are steadily growing, the same in Indonesia and Philippines do not show any increasing trend.

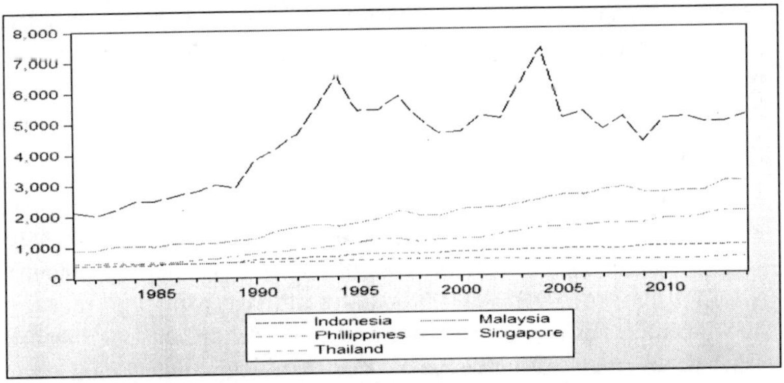

Figure 21.3: Energy Consumption in ASEAN-5 Countries (kg of oil equivalents).

The Figure 21.4 depicts the trend in carbon emissions in the ASEAN-5 countries. The carbon emissions closely follow the trends in energy consumption in these economies. In Singapore there has been a persistent decrease since 1997 in carbon emissions. A persistent increase in the emissions level can be observed in the other four countries.

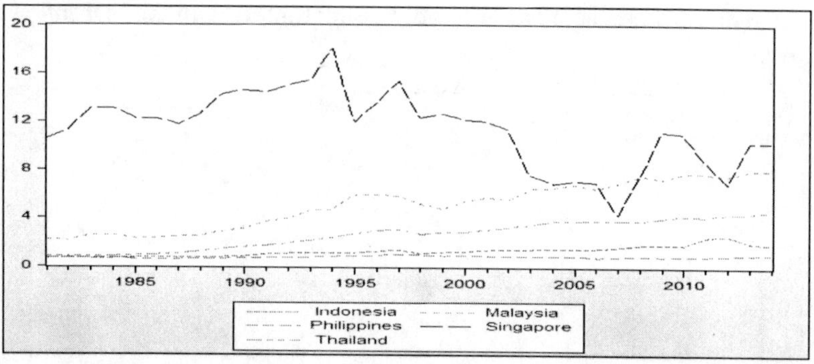

Fig 21.4: Carbon Emissions in ASEAN-5 Countries (metric tons per capita).

Thus, compared with the other ASEAN countries, Singapore stands atop with high GDP per capita, FDI inflow and energy consumption, but declining trends in carbon emissions and energy consumption. Singapore is a developed country and follow improved energy usage efficiency. Thus, Singapore shows the Environmental Kuznets Curve hypothesis i.e. an inverted U-shaped relationship between environmental pollution and income. As the other four ASEAN-5 countries are developing countries, there is increasing trends in economic growth, energy consumption and carbon emissions.

21.2. A Brief Review of Recent Studies

Perman and Stern (2003) examine the U-shaped relation between various indicators of environmental degradation such as sulfur emissions and income per capita for 74 countries over a span of 31 years. The cointegration test indicates no cointegration relationship between environmental degradation and income.

Hassain (2011) examines the dynamic causal relationships between carbon dioxide emissions, energy consumption, economic growth, trade openness and urbanisation for a panel of Newly Industrialised Countries (NIC) for the period 1971-2007. The four different panel unit root tests show that all panel variables are integrated of order one and the Johansen Fisher panel cointegration test show that there is a cointegration vector among the variables. The Granger causality test shows no evidence of long-run causal relationship, but there is unidirectional short-run causal relationship from economic growth and trade openness to carbon dioxide emissions, from economic growth to energy consumption, from trade openness to economic growth, from urbanisation to economic growth and from trade openness to urbanisation. The results show that the long-run elasticity of carbon dioxide emissions with respect to energy consumption (1.22) is higher than the short-run elasticity of (0.60). This indicates that over time high energy consumption in the newly industrialised countries gives rise to more carbon dioxide emissions and the environment gets polluted more.

Arouri et al. (2012) investigate the relationship between carbon dioxide (CO_2) emissions, energy consumption and real GDP for 12 middle-east and African (MANA) countries for the period 1981-2005. The panel unit roots test show that the MENA countries are cross sectionally correlated and the cointegration results shows a long-term relationship between CO_2 emissions and potential determinants. The error correction model (ECM) results also show evidence of positive causality from energy consumption to CO_2 emissions. Further, the causality from GDP to CO_2 emissions depends on the level of economic growth and the real GDP exhibits a quadratic relationship with CO_2 emissions satisfying the Environment Kuznets Curve (EKC) hypothesis in majority of the MANA countries.

Zhang and Lin (2012) investigate the impact of economic indicators on pollution (CO_2 emissions) in China during the period 1995-2010 using panel fixed effects model. They use demographic intensity, urbanisation, GDP, industrial production, production of services and energy consumption as economic indicators. The results show that demographic intensity, GDP, industrial production, and energy consumption have an impact on CO_2 emissions.

Omri (2013) study the impact of economic activity on environmental degradation in the middle-east and African (MANA) countries for the period 1990-2011. He utilises CO_2 emissions as an indicator of pollution and labour, capital, population, financial development, and GDP as indicators of economic activities. The regression results lend support for the presence of a positive and significant impact of the GDP and negative impact of financial development and capital on CO_2 emissions.

Rafindadi et al. (2014) study the causal relationship between pollution and economic activity in Asia-Pacific countries for the period 1975-2012. employing panel fixed effects estimation method. In this study, pollution is measured by CO_2 emissions and economic indicators are the GDP, water, added value of natural resources and energy consumption. The estimated results show the existence of a positive and significant relationship between CO_2 emissions and GDP. And energy consumption affects pollution positively.

21.3. Data and Methodology

In order to examine the determinants of carbon emissions in the ASEAN-5 countries - Indonesia, Malaysia, Philippines, Singapore and Thailand - this paper uses a panel of annual data for 34 years for these five ASEAN economies on FDI, economic growth, energy consumption and carbon emissions in these economies for the period 1981 to 2014. The data are collected from the 2015 World Development Indicators of the World Bank. All the variables used are transformed into natural logarithms to reduce to effect of heteroscedasticity. The Table 21.1 presents the description and measurement of the variables used in the empirical analysis.

Table 21.1: Description of the Variables used in the Carbon Emissions Analysis.

Variable	*Description and measurement*
CO2	Carbon dioxide emissions (metric tons per capita)
ENC	Energy consumption (kg of oil equivalent per capita)
GDPpc	Economic growth - GDP per capita US$ at 2010 constant prices)
POP	Population of the country
TROPEN	Trade openness (percent of GDP)
FDI	Foreign direct investment - net inflows (percent of GDP)
FINDEV	Financial development - domestic credit to the private sector(percent of GDP)

Source: World Bank (2015): World Bank Indicators, 2015.

Empirically, as the data are time series, a prerequisite is to test for stationarity to determine if the data series are stationary or not. The panel cointegration is to examine the long-run and short-run relationship between the variables. The dynamic relationship among the variables are analysed by panel quantile regression method to understand the differential effects at different quantiles of the carbon emissions distribution. The panel-based unit root tests for the stationarity of the series are those of Quah (1994), Breitung (2000), Breitung and Mayer (1994), Levin, Lin and Chu (2002), Im, Pesaran and Shin (2003), Fisher-type tests using ADF and PP tests (Phillips and Perron, 1988; Maddala and Wu, 1999; Hadri, 2000; Choi, 2001).

Panel Data Method

A panel unit root test is based on the following univariate regression:

$$\Delta y_{it} = \rho_i y_{it-1} + \delta x_{it} + u_{it} \quad i = 1, \ldots, N \quad t = 1, \ldots, T \tag{21.1}$$

where x_{it} are the exogenous variables in the model including any fixed effects or individual trends, ρ_i are the autoregressive coefficients and the errors u_{it} are assumed to be mutually independent idiosyncratic disturbance. If $|\rho_i|<1$, y_i is said to be weakly (trend) stationary. On the other hand, if $|\rho_i|=1$, then y_i contains a unit root.

Augmented Dickey-Fuller Unit Root Test: The ADF test is based on the following univariate regression:

$$\Delta y_{it} = \rho_i y_{it-1} + \sum_{k=1}^{p_i} \gamma_{ik} \Delta y_{it-k} + \delta_i x_{it} + u_{it} \tag{22.2}$$

Assuming a common $\alpha=\rho-1$ and allowing the lag order p_i for the difference terms to vary across cross sections, the null and alternative hypotheses for the test unit root test are specified as:

Null hypothesis: H_0: $\alpha = 0$ (presence of unit root)

Alternative hypothesis: H_1: $\alpha < 0$ (no unit root)

However, the individual unit root tests have limited power as there may be too many unit roots in a panel data.

Levin-Lin-Chu Test: The Levin-Lin-Chu Test (LLC) suggests the following hypotheses:

Null hypothesis: H_0: each time series contains a unit root

Alternative hypothesis: H_1: each time series is stationary

where the lag order p is permitted to vary across individuals. The procedure is to first run the Augmented Dickey-Fuller (ADF) unit root test for each cross-section on the equation (21.2)

Then, run two auxiliary regressions:

$$\Delta y_{it} \text{ on } \Delta y_{it-k} \text{ and } x_{it} \text{ to obtain the residuals } \hat{e}_{it} \tag{21.3}$$

$$y_{i,t-1} \text{ on } \Delta y_{it-k} \text{ and } x_{it} \text{ to obtain the residuals } \hat{v}_{it-1} \tag{21.4}$$

The next step is to standardise the as:

$$\tilde{e}_{it} = \hat{e}_{it} / \hat{\sigma}_{ui} \tag{21.5}$$

$$\tilde{v}_{it-1} = \hat{v}_{it} / \hat{\sigma}_{ui} \tag{21.6}$$

where σ_{ui} denotes the standard error from each ADF. The final step is to run the pooled OLS regression:

$$\tilde{e}_{it} = \rho\tilde{v}_{it-1} + \hat{u}_{it} \quad (21.7)$$

The Levin-Lin-Chu null hypothesis for panel unit root test is: H_0: ρ=0.

Breitung test: In the Breitung panel unit root test, only the autoregressive portion, not the deterministic terms, are included in the Levin-Lin-Chu test procedure. Applying forward orthogonalisation transformation i.e. subtracting the mean of the future observations from each of the first T-1 observations ($\tilde{y}$), to the residuals $\hat{e}_{it}$, the transformed residuals are obtained as:

$$e^*_{it} = \rho v^*_{it-1} + u^*_{it} \quad (21.8)$$

Then, the pooled regression is estimated as:

$$\Delta y^*_{it} = \sqrt{\frac{T-t}{T-t+1}}\left(\Delta\tilde{y}_{it} - \frac{\Delta\tilde{y}_{it-1}+\cdots+\Delta\tilde{y}_{iT}}{T-t}\right) = \alpha y^*_{it-1} + \varepsilon_{it} \quad (21.9)$$

Then test for the significance of α.

Im-Pesaran-Shin (IPS) test: The Im, Pesaran and Shin panel unit root test specifies a separate ADF regression for each cross section and the hypotheses are specified as:

Null hypothesis: H_0: α=0, for all i

Alternative hypothesis: $H_1: \begin{cases} \alpha_i = 0 & for\ i = 1, \ldots, N_1 \\ \alpha_i < 0 & for\ i = N_1 + 1, \ldots, N \end{cases}$ (21.10)

Fisher-ADF and Fisher-Phillips-Perron tests: The Fisher-type test uses p-values from unit root tests for each cross-section i. The Fisher is as follows:

$$P = -2\sum_{i=1}^{N} lnp_i \quad (21.11)$$

The next step is to test for the existence of a long-run cointegration among CO_2 and other variables using panel cointegration tests. The panel cointegration tests are based on the following panel regression model:

$$y_{it} = \alpha_i + \delta_i t + \beta_{mi} x_{mit} + e_{it} i = 1, \ldots, N;\ t = 1, \ldots, T;\ m = 1, \ldots, M \quad (21.12)$$

where i represents the cross section units, t the time and m the number of regressors. In this setup, α is the individual specific intercept or fixed effects parameter which varies across individual cross-sectional units and δ_i is individual specific time effects. The residual based panel cointegration test of Pedroni (1999; 2004) uses the first difference of the panel regression:

$$\Delta y_{it} = \beta_{mi}\Delta x_{mit} + \eta_{it} \quad (21.13)$$

The long-run variance of the estimated residuals from the first differenced panel regression is computed as:

$$\hat{\psi}_{it}^2 = \frac{1}{T}\sum_{t=1}^{T}\hat{\eta}_{it}^2 + \frac{2}{T}\sum_{k=1}^{p_i}\left(1 - \frac{k}{p_i+1}\right)\sum_{t=k+1}^{T}\hat{\eta}_{it}\hat{\eta}_{it-k} \tag{21.14}$$

The panel-ρ and group-ρ statistics are obtained from the panel regression residuals from equation (21.12):

$$\hat{e}_{it} = \hat{\rho}_i\hat{e}_{it-1} + \hat{\mu}_{it} \tag{21.15}$$

The long-run variance ($\hat{\sigma}_i^2$) and the contemporaneous variance ($\hat{s}_i^2$) of $\hat{\mu}_{it}$ are then computed as:

$$\hat{\sigma}_i^2 = \frac{1}{T}\sum_{t=1}^{T}\hat{\mu}_{it} \tag{21.16}$$

$$\hat{s}_i^2 = \frac{1}{T}\sum_{t=1}^{T}\hat{\mu}_{it} + \frac{2}{T}\sum_{k=1}^{p_i}\left(1 - \frac{k}{p_i+1}\right)\sum_{t=k+1}^{T}\hat{\mu}_{it}\hat{\mu}_{it-k} \tag{21.17}$$

Then, compute λi as:

$$\lambda_i = \frac{1}{2}(\hat{\sigma}_i^2 - \hat{s}_i^2) \tag{21.18}$$

The panel-t and group-t statistics are again computed from the panel regression residuals from equation (21.12):

$$\hat{e}_{it} = \hat{\rho}_i\hat{e}_{it-1} + \sum_{k=1}^{p_i}\hat{\rho}_{ik}\Delta\hat{e}_{it-k} + \hat{\mu}_{it}^* \tag{21.19}$$

The variance of ($\hat{\mu}_{it}^*$) is computed as:

$$\hat{s}_i^{*2} = \frac{1}{T}\sum_{t=1}^{T}\hat{\mu}_{it}^{*2} \text{ and } \tilde{s}_{NT}^{*2} \equiv \frac{1}{N}\sum_{i=1}^{N}\hat{s}_i^{*2} \tag{21.20}$$

Pedroni (1999; 2004) computes the panel cointegration statistics from panel-ρ, panel-t, group-ρ and group-t statistics and show that the test statistics are standard normally distributed. Then, the null hypothesis of no cointegration for the panel cointegration test is the same for each statistic:

Null hypothesis: H_0: $\rho_i = 1\ \forall i$

However, there is a difference in the alternative hypothesis for the between-dimension-based and within-dimension based panel cointegration tests. The between-dimension based statistics does not require common value of ρ:

Alternative hypothesis: H_1: $\rho_i < 1\ \forall i$

The within-dimension-based statistics requires a common value for $\rho_i = \rho$:

Alternative hypothesis: H_1: $\rho_i = \rho < 1\ \forall i$

Under the alternative hypothesis, all the panel cointegration test statistics diverge to negative infinity. Thus, the left tail of the standard normal distribution is used to reject the null hypothesis.

Panel Quantile Regression Method

To estimate the differential effects at different points of the distribution function, the quantile regression method, proposed by Koenker and Bassett (1978), is used. The quantile regression is a generalisation of median regression analysis to other quantiles of the distribution function and is robust to outliers and heavy distributions. The conditional quantile of y_i given x_i is as follows:

$$Q_{yi}(\tau|x_i) = \beta_\tau x_i^T \tag{21.21}$$

The unobserved heterogeneity is controlled by the fixed effects panel quantile regression, which estimates the conditional heterogeneous covariance effects of carbon emissions drivers. The fixed effects panel quantile regression is specified as:

$$Q_{yit}(\tau_k|\alpha_i, x_{it}) = \alpha_i + \beta_{\tau_k} x_i^T \tag{21.22}$$

where k indicates the quantiles. However, the fixed effects panel quantile regression has a drawback of the incidental parameters problem with the inclusion of a considerable amount of fixed effects (α_i) and the estimates are inconsistent with large cross sections and less time period (Lancaster, 2000). Moreover, the fixed effects panel quantile regression method to eliminate the observed fixed effects relying on the basis of linear operators is unfeasible in the conditional quantile regression method (Canay, 2011). To overcome these problems, Koenker (2004) proposes joint estimation of the unobservable fixed effect as parameters along with the covariate effects for different quantiles. This method imposes a penalty on the minimisation to address the computational problem of estimating a mass of parameters specifically. The parameter estimate is calculated as follows:

$$\underset{\alpha,\beta}{Min} \sum_{i=1}^{N} \sum_{t=1}^{T} \sum_{k=1}^{K} \omega_k \rho_{\tau_k} \left[y_{it} - \alpha_i - \beta_{\tau_k} x_i^T\right] + \lambda \sum_{i=1}^{N} |\alpha_i| \tag{21.23}$$

where ρ_{τ_k} is the quantile loss function, ω_k is the relative weight given to the k-th quantile that controls for the contribution of the k-th quantile on the estimation of the fixed effects, λ is the tuning parameter that reduces the individual effects to zero to improve the performance of the estimate of β. If λ term goes to zero, then the penalty term disappears, and the usual fixed effects estimator is the result. However, if the λ term goes to infinity, then the model is estimated without individual effects. Alexander et al. (2011) and Lamarche (2010; 2011) propose equally weighted quantiles $\omega_k = 1/K$. The estimating empirical panel conditional quantile function for τ^{th} quantile is specified as:

$$Q_{CO_{2_{it}}}(\tau_k|\alpha_i, \gamma_t, x_{it}) = \alpha_i + \gamma_t + \beta_{1\tau} FDI_{it} + \beta_{2\tau} GDPpc_{it} + \beta_{3\tau} ENC_{it} + \beta_{4\tau} TROPEN_{it} + \beta_{5\tau} FINDEV + \beta_{6\tau} POP_{it_{it}} + \varepsilon_{it} \tag{21.23}$$

where the carbon dioxide emissions indicator is estimated as a function of energy consumption, foreign direct investment and economic growth along with other control variables.

21.4. Empirical Analysis

The Table 21.2 presents the descriptive statistics of the variables used to estimate the effects of FDI, economic growth and energy consumption on carbon emissions in the ASEAN-5 economies. The distributions of all of the variables are skewed, and the kurtosis values show that the seven series distributions are more concentrated with longer tails. The Jarque-Bera tests strongly reject the null hypothesis of normality, indicating the non-normality of the unconditional distribution of all the variables.

Table 21.2: Descriptive Statistics of Variables in the Carbon Emissions Analysis.

Variable	*Description*	*Mean*@	*Median*#	*Jarque-Bera*
CO_2	Carbon dioxide (CO_2) emissions from consumption of oil, gas and coal based on standard global average conversion factors (metric tons per capita)	4.250 (4.261)	2.461 [1.257] (3.503)	46.578***
GDPpc	Gross domestic product real per capita (constant 2010 US$)	4338.417 (7738.343)	1719.264 [4.266] (23.901)	3610.083***
FDI	Foreign direct investment of cross-border investment made by a resident in one economy (net inflows) (% of GDP US$)	4.488 (5.692)	2.403 [1.999] (6.538)	201.958***
ENC	Energy consumption of commercially traded fuels including modern renewable used to generate electricity (kg of oil equivalent per capita)	1711.155 (387.097)	1003.582 [1.454] (4.121)	68.771***
FINDEV	Financial development measured by domestic credit to the private sector (% of GDP US$)	72.306 (40.290)	77.802 [0.219] (1.931)	9.448***
TROPEN	Trade openness of removal or reduction of tariff obstacles such as duties and surcharges, and nontariff obstacles such as licensing rules, quotas and other requirements (% of GDP US$)	175.623 (439.987)	92.247 [10.083] (116.005)	9333.501***
POP	Total population of the country within the scope of census	29117845 (55266094)	1126233 [2.331] (7.951)	327.651
Obs.	170			

Note: @standard deviations in parentheses. # skewness in brackets and kurtosis in parentheses. *** significant at 1 percent level.

The Table 21.3 presents the results of the panel unit root tests. The panel unit root test results indicate that the null hypothesis of the existence of a unit root could not be rejected for all variables at the levels, except the FDI. However, the unit root null hypothesis for all variables at the first difference could be completely rejected at 1 percent level of significance. Therefore, an empirical analysis that uses the first difference sequence is necessary. As the results of the panel unit root tests indicate that the variables contain a panel unit root, the Johansen Fisher panel co integration test is used to examine whether there is long-run relationship among the variables. The Johansen panel cointegration test results presented in Table 21.4 indicate the existence of cointegrating vectors using one lag length.

Table 21.3: Panel Unit Root Tests.

Variable	*Levin-Lin-Chu*	*Breitung*	*Im- Pesaran-Shin*	*Fisher-Augmented Dicky-Fuller*	*Fisher- Phillips-Perron*
At level					
CO_2	0.020	-1.844	-1.317	15.738	11.450
GDPpc	5.779	3.636	4.543	0.206	0.292
FDI	-0.898***	-3.257	-2.626	25.260	37.140***
ENC	0.234	-1.089	-0.259	11.468	13.121
FINDEV	-0.084	-1.404	0.312	6.654	4.058
TROPEN	-6.945	-7.580	-4.572	37.750	81.197
POP	4.967	2.948	4.288	0.246	0.337
At first difference					
CO_2	-5.182***	-4.212***	-6.255***	54.195***	84.350***
GDPpc	-7.181***	-2.496***	-5.105***	42.287***	84.864***
FDI	-3.685***	-6.181***	-8.418***	75.121***	61.104***
ENC	-5.103***	-4.833***	-5.994***	51.110***	12..701***
FINDEV	-1.467***	-5.454***	-3.410***	28.868***	48.424***
TROPEN	-11.860***	-14.320***	-11.002***	98.714***	13.170***
POP	-7.242***	-3.020***	-5.184***	42.985***	84.306***

Note: *** significant at 1 percent level.

Table 21.4: Johansen Panel Cointegration Test.

Hypothesised no. of CEs	*Trace value*	*Prob.*	*Max-eigen value*	*Prob.*
None	97.05***	0.0000	52.86***	0.0000
At most 1	49.78***	0.0000	42.58***	0.0000
At most 2	19.27***	0.0370	14.09	0.1691
At most 3	10.02	0.4390	5.880	0.8252
At most 4	7.452	0.6822	8.278	0.6017
At most 5	4.693	0.9107	5.061	0.8870
At most 6	6.442	0.7769	6.442	0.7769

Note: significant at 1 percent level.

To facilitate comparisons, the carbon emission model is first estimated by the OLS pooled regression and fixed effects regression methods and the estimated results are presented in Table 21.5. The fixed effects model controls for the time specific and spatially invariant variables, whose omission could bias the estimates in the typical time series OLS estimation. The fixed effects estimates show that GDP has a positive and significant effect on carbon emissions. Similarly, energy consumption is positively related with carbon emissions. These two results together imply that economic growth necessitates environmental degradation. The effects of FDI and domestic investments on carbon emissions are insignificantly negative. The estimated relationship between FDI and pollution support the effect hypothesis and provide no evidence for the FDI's deteriorating impact on environmental. However, these estimated average effects do not provide a more complete picture of the influence at different points of the distribution of carbon emissions. Therefore, panel quantile regression is to be estimated to understand the heterogeneous effects across the different percentiles in the conditional distribution of carbon emissions.

Table 21.5: Pooled Regression and Panel Fixed Effects Estimates of Carbon Emissions.
Dependent variable: Carbon emissions

Variable	*OLS pooled regression*	*OLS fixed effects*
lnGDPpc	0.456***(6.22)	0.524*** (6.66)
lnFDI	-0.020 (0.88)	-0.011(0.51)
lnENC	0.526*** (6.35)	0.414*** (4.83)
lnTROPN	0.045 (1.23)	0.052 (1.36)
lnFINDEV	0.217*** (5.39)	0.090 (1.33)
lnPOP	-0.034*** (5.07)	-0.043*** (6.15)
Constant	-7.066*** (31.59)	-6.253*** (13.08)

Note: Absolute t-values in parentheses. *** significant at 1 percent level
** significant at 5 percent level.

The Table 21.6 presents the estimated results of the panel quantile regression. The estimated quantile coefficients of lnGDPpc are highly significant and have a positive sign at all quantiles. The effect of economic growth increases on carbon emission increases with every quantile from 2 percent at 10th quantile to 7 percent at the 95th quantile. Similarly, the coefficients of lnENC are also highly significant at all quantiles and the effect on carbon emissions is consistently positive, but slightly decreases over the quantiles from 5 percent at the 10th quantile to 4 percent at the 95th quantile. Both these results together imply that as economy grows energy consumption increases which causes more carbon emissions. At the higher levels of energy consumption, a tilt towards renewable sources of energy and better technology use for emission control are adopted and hence less carbon emissions. A higher economic growth level can mitigate the increase in carbon emissions in high-emissions countries. Thus, the quantile regression results of the relationship between economic growth and environment observed in the ASEAN-5 economies does not lend support for the U-shaped Environmental Kuznets Curve (EKC) hypothesis.

Table 21.6: Panel Quantile Regression Estimates of Carbon Emissions.

Dependent variable: Carbon emissions

Variable	*10th*	*30th*	*40th*	*50th*	*70th*	*90th*	*95th*
lnGDPpc	0.19* (1.80)	0.51*** (3.27)	0.59*** (5.38)	0.61*** (6.50)	0.65 (0.08)	0.71*** (11.11)	0.71*** (11.65)
lnFDI	0.009 (0.32)	-0.003 (0.15)	-0.007 (0.49)	-0.006 (0.44)	-0.009 (0.66)	-0.007 (0.45)	0.01 (1.13)
lnENC	0.56*** (3.96)	0.55*** (3.49)	0.52*** (4.88)	0.51*** (5.70)	0.47 (0.08)	0.45*** (5.24)	0.48*** (5.37)
lnTROPN	0.02 (0.61)	0.02 (0.67)	-0.002 (0.08)	0.006 (0.20)	0.01 (0.02)	0.03 (0.89)	0.002 (0.14)
lnFINDEV	0.39*** (6.74)	0.22*** (6.89)	0.19*** (7.55)	0.16*** (7.10)	0.13 (0.02)	0.07* (1.96)	0.02 (0.38)
lnPOP	-0.02** (2.05)	-0.04*** (3.28)	-0.04*** (5.25)	-0.04 (0.007)	-0.05 (0.005)	-0.05*** (11.11)	-0.06*** (11.37)
Constant	-6.37*** (19.51)	-7.51*** (53.25)	-7.64*** (56.97)	-7.56*** (54.44)	-7.50*** (50.97)	-7.44*** (35.08)	-7.30*** (33.35)

Note: Absolute t-values in parentheses. *** significant at 1 percent level ** significant at 5 percent level.

The impact of FDI on carbon emissions is statistically insignificant at all the quantiles. Probably at the lower quantiles, FDI is insufficient to support the pollution haven hypothesis in the low-emissions countries and at the higher quantiles, the influence of FDI on carbon emissions is negated by the global standards. These results support the halo-effect hypothesis in high-emission countries. Also, the insignificant impact of FDI at lower quantiles mean that most FDI likely investments in non-polluting sectors of low-emissions countries. In high-emissions environments, the FDI inflow may develop technology and innovations in production methods mostly by multinational companies. These more advanced technologies tend to disseminate cleaner technology that will be less harmful to the environment and such technologies may also be indirectly passed on to domestic firms via backward or forward linkages. Therefore, in high-emissions countries, an increase in FDI improves the regions environmental quality. The results show that effect hypothesis is valid in high-emissions ASEAN-5countries.

The other results are also informative. The impact of the population size on carbon emissions is significantly negative both at lower quantiles and at higher quantiles; at the median quantile, population becomes insignificant. These results imply that a larger population size leads to higher carbon emissions in low-emissions countries whereas the opposite holds true in high-emissions countries. The effect of financial development, similar to economic growth, is positive at all quantiles. The coefficients of private sector investments are significant at lower quantiles, but become insignificant at higher quantiles. Moreover, the effects of financial investments on carbon emissions decreases from 4 percent at the lower quantile to almost zero percent at the 95th quantile, again confirming the concern for environmental quality at higher development levels. Trade openness has no significant effect on carbon emissions in the ASEAN-5 economies.

In order to examine the significance of the heterogeneity of the parameters across quantiles of the panel quantile regression model, the inter-quantile tests are performed. The Wald tests are used to check for slope equality across quantiles. The variance-covariance matrix of the corresponding coefficients is obtained from the bootstrap procedure. The Table 21.7 and Figure 21.5 present the results of the test of equality of the coefficients between the lower quantiles and the upper quantiles. The test is whether the slope coefficient at the 10th quantile is the same as that in the middle quantile (50th quantile) and in the higher quantiles (95th quantile). The tests reject the hypothesis of parameter homogeneity except in the cases of energy consumption. Thus, there is a differential effect of FDI, economic growth, financial development and population on the distribution of carbon emissions in ASEAN-5 countries.

Table 21.7: Wald Test for Equality of Slope Parameters at Quantiles.

Variable	*10th quantile vs 50th quantile*		*10th quantile vs 95th quantile*	
	Test statistic	*p-value*	*Test statistic*	*p-value*
lnGDPpc	0.053	0.166	8.707***	0.051
lnFDI	1.009**	0.026	3.018*	0.016
lnENC	6.644	0.182	0.482	0.090
lnTROPN	8.046**	0.034	0.003***	0.020
lnFINDEV	3.429**	0.056	1.0154**	0.041
lnPOP	5.007	0.012	8.057**	0.004

Note: ** significant at 5 percent levels.

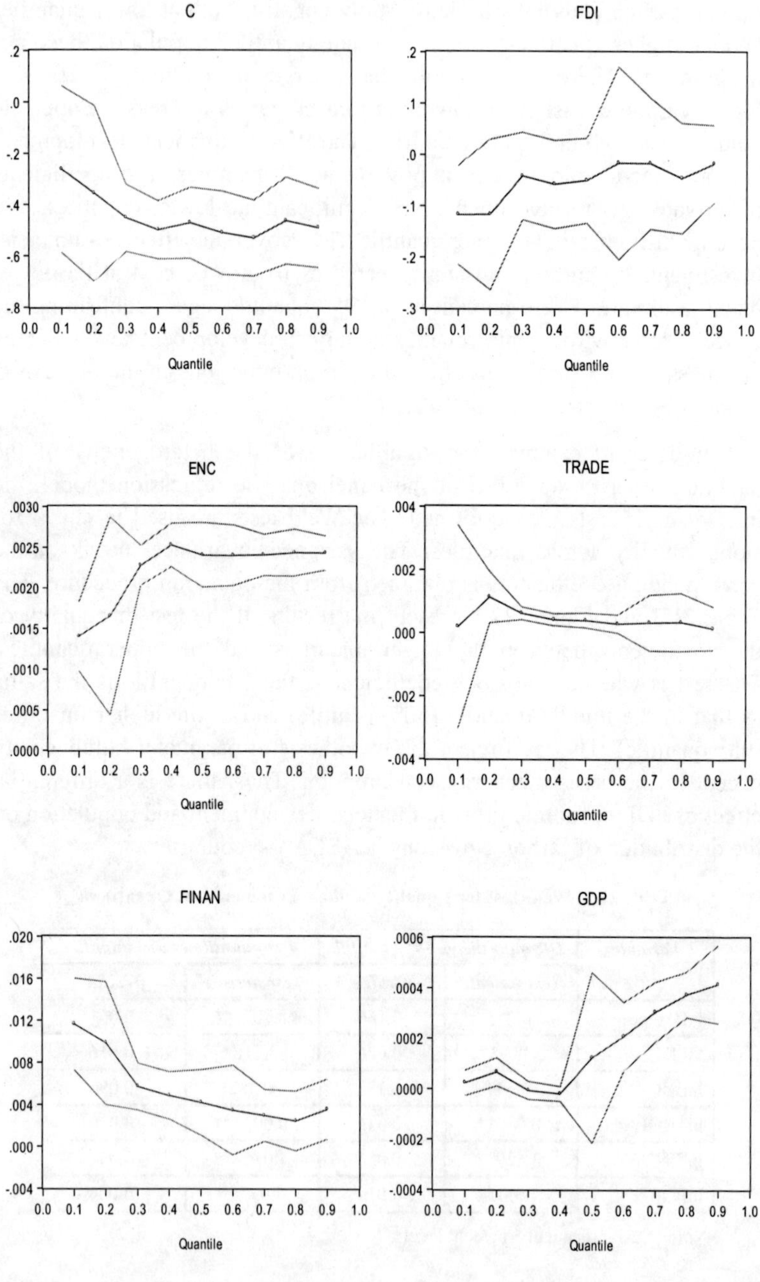
C
.2
.0
-.2
-.4
-.6
-.8
0.0 0.1 0.2 0.3 0.4 0.5 0.6 0.7 0.8 0.9 1.0
Quantile
FDI
.2
.1
.0
-.1
-.2
-.3
0.0 0.1 0.2 0.3 0.4 0.5 0.6 0.7 0.8 0.9 1.0
Quantile
ENC
.0030
.0025
.0020
.0015
.0010
.0005
.0000
0.0 0.1 0.2 0.3 0.4 0.5 0.6 0.7 0.8 0.9 1.0
Quantile
TRADE
.004
.002
.000
-.002
-.004
0.0 0.1 0.2 0.3 0.4 0.5 0.6 0.7 0.8 0.9 1.0
Quantile
FINAN
.020
.016
.012
.008
.004
.000
-.004
0.0 0.1 0.2 0.3 0.4 0.5 0.6 0.7 0.8 0.9 1.0
Quantile
GDP
.0006
.0004
.0002
.0000
-.0002
-.0004
0.0 0.1 0.2 0.3 0.4 0.5 0.6 0.7 0.8 0.9 1.0
Quantile

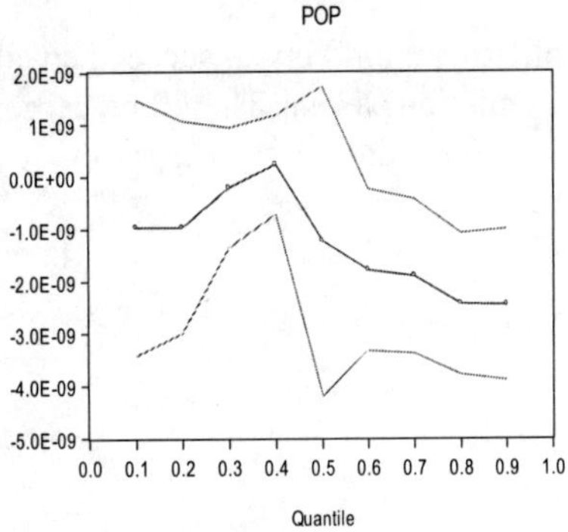

Figure 21.5: Heterogeneity in Panel Quantile Regression Estimates.

21.5. Conclusion

The main aim of this paper is to estimate the effect of FDI, economic growth and energy consumption on carbon emissions in five ASEAN (Association of Southeast Asian Nations - Indonesia, Malaysia, Philippines, Singapore, and Thailand) countries. The paper used a panel data from the five ASEAN-5 counties for the period 1981 to 2014 and applied the panel quantile regression method to understand the differential effects of the factors on carbon emissions at different quantiles of the distribution. The estimated empirical results show that the impacts of various factors on carbon emission in ASEAN-5 economies are evidently heterogeneous. The quantile results are further confirmed by the Wald test that supports the observed differences along the estimated coefficients are significant across quantiles. Economic growth and energy consumption increase carbon emissions significantly in high-emission ASEAN countries. However, at higher levels of energy consumption, adoption of green renewable energy and emission control technology mitigate the increase in carbon emissions. The quantile estimates of this paper do not lend support to the U-shaped Environmental Kuznets Curve (EKC) hypothesis.

At the same time, the insignificant effect of FDI on carbon emissions also does not lend sufficient support to the pollution haven hypothesis in lower-emission ASEAN countries. However, the negative influence of FDI on carbon emissions at the middle quantiles supports the halo effect hypothesis. An increase in FDI may improve the regions environmental quality. In addition, high financial development which indicates private investments increases carbon emissions trade openness has no influence on carbon emissions in ASEAN-5 economies. Therefore, uniform carbon emissions control policies are unlikely to succeed equally across countries with different carbon emissions levels. Therefore, carbon emissions control measures should be tailored differently across low-emissions and high-emissions economies.

22

The Effect of Bilateral Investment Treaty on Foreign Direct Investment: Dynamic Panel GMM-IV Estimation

22.1. Introduction

Foreign direct investment (FDI) is recognised as the most powerful engine of the recent trends in economic growth. The FDI inflows enable capital-poor countries to bridge the gap of domestic savings and investment and build up physical capital in third world countries. The FDI also create employment opportunities, develop productive capacity, enhance skills of local labour through transfer of technology and managerial know-how, and integrate the domestic economy with the global economy. The FDI is an integral part in the introduction and familiarisation of modern technology and management skills from developed countries. Thus, it is in the interest of every nation to boost their FDI inflows. For effective and substantial FDI inflows, sustained economic growth of either the source nation or the host nation is vital. Further, the macroeconomic environment has an impact on the FDI inflows. The variables like GDP, growth rate, inflation, political stability, international trade and technology transfer agreements, exchange rate, skilled labour are the most important factors that influence the flows of FDI to an economy. There also may be some factors that are difficult to be controlled by the governments in determining the FDI inflows.

Generally, the investors seek to ensure if the investment if profitable; an investor might consider inflation rate as a crucial determinant for FDI since it can reduce the value of investments over time. This makes investment costly and unstable. There also can be political constraints restricting the flows of FDI. The political environment is particularly relevant to determine the financial openness of the FDI receiving economies and they might influence the minds of investors. The political constraints affect the decision making of an investor as it may make their investment unproductive and uncertain. Less political discretion is supposed to render credible commitments to (foreign) investors more likely. It creates reciprocation in the direction of investment and trade by setting up foreseen barriers which changes the challenges and opportunities for investors.

In order to protect the interests of the foreign investors, the governments generally direct their policies towards some control measures that determine the FDIs. One among the few control variables is Bilateral Investment Treaty (BIT). The BIT is to protect the interests of foreign investors against the threat of appropriation by the government of the host country, empowering individual private parties to take international arbitral proceedings against host nations under their terms. In this respect, India has one of the largest BIT networks with other counties around the world. As shown in Figure 22.1, a good number of India's BITs were signed with many counties in the 1990s and the early 2000s. The signing of BITS is to show that India is competitive and appropriately reform-minded and to signal that the environment is investment friendly so as to deserve a good destination for FDI, as well as much in tune with a trend that was being followed by many countries all over the world.

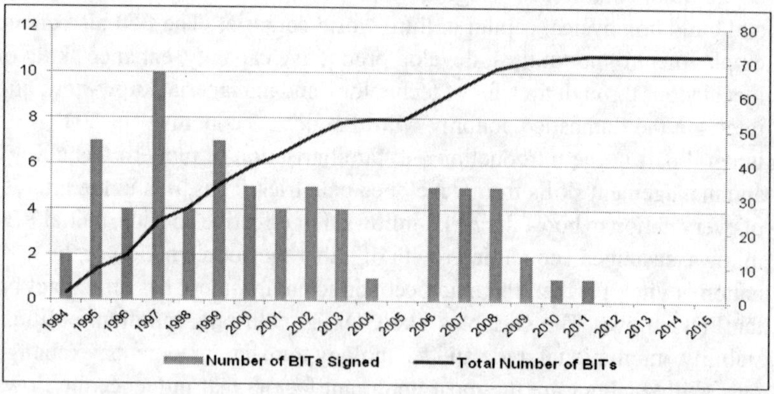

Source: UNCTAD.

Figure 22.1: Trend in Bilateral Investment Treaties of India, 1994-2015.

The BITs promote investment by increasing investor confidence on account of the protections enabled by the international agreements.

The BITs substitute weaker domestic rights in developing nations. In order to enforce such agreements, the international tribunals may charge heavy fines which not only creates a financial pressure but also a regulatory pressure on the host economy. Therefore, from this view, the FDI inflows from investors will be greater when a BIT exists than when it does not. As the BITs are heterogeneous, a BIT with a nation is subject to several clauses which may vary for each nation. As the clauses increase, the possibility for an investor to claim a BIT may also increase, in other words, it is difficult to regulate a policy with greater constraints rising due to an international agreement. However, there is also a negative and a more discouraging side of BITs. The efficiency of a BIT in order to facilitate an international investor requires not only protection but a scope of growth and long-term sustainability of the business. Also, in case of a failure by the government, once a nation loses in the international tribunal such as International Centre of Settlement of Investment Disputes (ICSID), it might lead to a negative impact for an investor in line of their operations with the same nation. It is observed that that once the claim of an investor gets registered with the in the international tribunal for arbitration, the FDI flows with the country declines, showing the rising uncertainty and distrust of an investor. The costs and benefits of a ratified BIT is shown in Table 22.1.

Table 22.1: Costs and Benefits of BITs for the Host Country.

Costs of BIT	*Benefits of BIT*
Loss of sovereignty: loss of regulatory policy autonomy to serve domestic purpose	Attracting FDI
	Signaling liberalisation policy orientation to some domestic audiences without intention of ratification
Potential costs of being sued including financial costs of litigations, loss of future FDI due to ICSID litigations	Strengthening intergovernmental political ties
	Behaving in a way that is consistent with the accepted norm of treating foreign investors

The Figure 22.2 shows the variation in the FDI inflows after the lodgement of first claim against a BIT. Before the lodgement of a claim, the difference between protected and non-protected investor is seen to be constant where a BIT protected investor has higher flows of FDI. After the lodgement of a claim against a host nation, the difference between the protected and non-protected investor increases. However, as can be noted from Figure 20.2, by asking for a claim, the magnitude of flows of the protected investors does not go below the protected investors which make BITs influencing the FDI inflows positively. Both the protected and non-protected BIT investors continue to invest at a similar magnitude. Thus, it can be seen that in the global context the relation between BIT and FDI is positive even after claims by an investor.

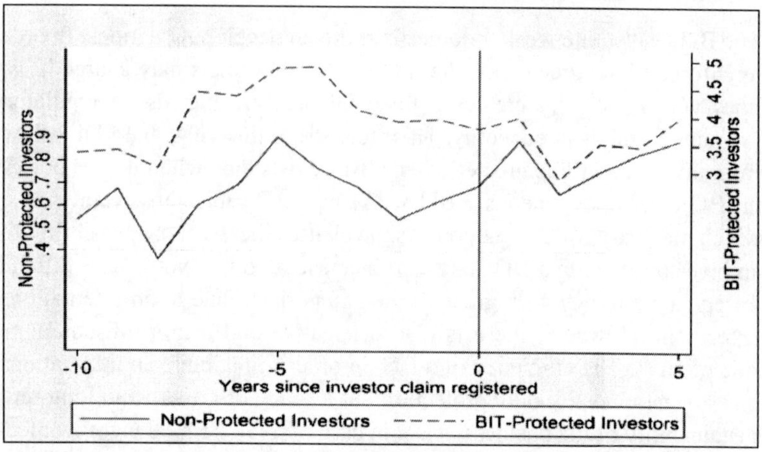

Figure 22.2: FDI Trend Around Lodgement of First Claim Against Host Economy.

Thus, though the BITs constrain host nations for international arbitration, the continued FDI inflows even after lodging of claims by investors in international tribunals, the nature of the relationship between BITs and FDI inflows needs examination, especially in the context of developmental aims such as technology transfer and human resource development with FDI. Therefore, it is relevant to examine the behaviour and determinants of FDI inflows when the BITs are taking place. It is useful for the governments to understand whether this tool which they perceive as a working instrument to encourage FDI is true in its actual form. Hence, the main objectives of this paper are to identify the determinants of FDI inflows in India and to analyse the impact of BITs on FDI inflows in India. The paper uses panel data for 76 countries for the time period 2000-2016. The data for the empirical analysis have been extracted from various databases like UNCTAD, World Bank, POLCON index and Chinn-Ito datasets. The empirical analysis uses a dynamic panel data methodology and the estimation method followed is the Generalised Method of Moments (GMM).

22.2. A Brief Review of Recent Studies

It seems the positive impact of BITs on FDI inflows strongly depends on a supportive political-economic environment. Tobin and Rose-Ackerman (2011) studying the possible consequences of BITs, focus on political and economic factors as complements to BITs in 176 countries for the time period of 1984-2000 applying the OLS method. They observe that that the BITs have a positive impact on FDI inflows only in countries with a stable business environment and BITs do not seem to encourage FDI except at low levels of political risk.

In contrast, Neumayer and Spess (2005), analysing the issue of BITs affecting the FDI in 119 countries for the time period 1970-2001 applying the panel fixed effects model, observe that developing host countries that have agreed to a larger number of BITs have attracted higher FDI inflows. In particular, countries with a weaker domestic institutional quality stand out most to gain from BITs. While Tobin and Rose-Ackerman reject the view that BITs are a substitute for a favourable local business environment, whereas Neumayer and Spess report some evidence to this effect.

Ranjan (2010) describes the bilateral investment treaty programmes of India in the light of global experience. The paper argues that the effects of BITs on investment flows may vary from country to country and may also be different for different periods of time and thus there cannot be a general proposition that signing BITs invariably result in more investment inflows. The study observes that that foreign investment is more related to macroeconomic factors such as overall economic stability, location advantage, level of infrastructure and other related factors. According to the paper, there can also be negative results of entering into BIT as the treaties may unduly constrain regulatory discretion.

Busse, Koniger and Nunnenkamp (2010) investigate the role of BIT in promoting FDI in a gravity type model using a panel data from World Bank and UNCTAD database for the time period 1978-2004 and applying estimating techniques such pooled OLS, Poisson Pseudo Maximum Likelihood (PPML) and Generalised Method of Moments (GMM). The dependent variable is the ratio of FDI flows to a particular country to the FDI flows to all the countries, and the independent variables include real GDP growth, inflation, trade openness, GDP per capita, Free Trade Agreement (FTA), Double Taxation Treaty (DTT), common currency and BIT. The empirical results show that there is a positive impact of BIT for the foreign investors as they shift their preferences for investing to a country which has signed a BIT.

Buthe and Milner (2008) examine the political factors that affect the FDI flows focusing on the relationship between trade and investment for a panel of 122 developing countries for the time period 1970-2000 using a gravity type model. Using an index variable POLCON as a measure of political violence and instability and instrumental variables estimation method, the paper suggests that the political factors, which should increase the predictability of politics by reducing the risk of policy change, boost inward FDI significantly. Similarly, the BITs, GATT and PTAs have shown positive impact for boosting the foreign investors to invest in the host nation.

Mina (2015) examines the role of political risk guarantees, which bilateral investment treaties serve, in debt accumulation in 68 low and middle income countries for the time period 1984-2011 using OLS and GMM estimation methodologies. The paper empirically finds that signed bilateral investment treaties with OECD countries have a positive influence on total and guaranteed debt accumulation. The results suggest that the role of bilateral investment treaties extends beyond attracting FDI to international lending.

Aisbett, Busee and Nunnenkamp (2018) analyse the impact on FDI of claims by investors against hosts for alleged violation of BIT obligations using a gravity model for data covering the time period 1980-2010 and applying two way fixed effects estimation method. The paper finds that FDI flows to developing host countries decline when they are taken before the International Centre of Settlement of Investment Disputes (ICSID), in particular when they lose a dispute in arbitration. The paper finds that when a host faces a claim, FDI from sources with a BIT in place falls significantly more than that from unprotected sources.

The Table 22.2 summaries the findings of the literature on the relationship between BITs and FDI. The empirical studies show that the bilateral investment treaties do impact FDI inflows. However, the significance of the BITs affecting FDI is limited to stable business and political environment. It can also be inferred that the BIT can be expected to be a tool for the government of the host nation to work in order to generate FDI.

Table 22.2: Summary of Empirical Findings on the Relationship between BITs and FDI.

Study	*Data*	*Model*	*Findings*
Hallward-Driemeier (2003)	FDI flows from 20 OECD countries into 31 developing countries, 1980-2000	OLS	BITs do not attract additional FDI
Grosse and Trevino (2005)	FDI inflows in Central and Eastern European region, 1990-1999	OLS	BITs along with institutional improvements provide an assurance of equal treatment to both domestic as well as foreign investor
Neumayer and Spess (2005)	119 developing countries, 1970-2001	Fixed and random effects	Larger the number of BITs negotiated better the flow of FDI

(Contd...)

Buthe and Milner (2008)	BITs to which developing countries are party, 1970-2000	Fixed effects	Greater the number of BITs more the FDI received
Guerin (2011)	FDI outflows in European Union, 1992-2007	OLS and fixed effects	BITs encourage EU FDI outflows up to 35 percent with a partner economy
Mina (2015)	FDI in Gulf Cooperation Countries (GCC) which negotiate BITs, 1984-2002	GMM	Negative impact of BITs on FDI, domestic property rights protection institutions matter more

22.3. Data and Methodology

This paper uses a panel data for 76 countries for the time period 2000-2016 extracted from the World Bank, UNCTAD, Chinn-ito.com, and DIPP. The variables considered are foreign direct investment (FDI), bilateral investment treaties (BIT), Chinn-Ito (KAOPEN) index, POLCON index, inflation ate and gross domestic product. The dependent variable is FDI inflows, the amount of foreign investment made to host country by the source country. The annual inward FDI flows, is the sum of the year's new direct investment in a host country by capital owners that are foreign to that country (net of direct investments withdrawn by foreign capital owners), calculated as a percentage of GDP. The FDI as a percentage of GDP has been taken in order to eliminate the need to deflate the dependent variable and to make it comparable across countries and across time.

As this paper uses BITs signed by India with other countries as an important determinant of FDI inflows to India, the Table 22.3 shows the frequency of the countries signing BIT with India in the time period 2000-2016. It can be seen that a large number of BITs have been signed before the year 2000. A total number of 51 BITs have been recorded in the data out of 81 BITs which have been signed by India with other countries.

Table 22.3: Distribution of Countries Signed BIT with India, 2000-2016.

Year	*BIT signed*	*BIT not signed*	*Year*	*BIT signed*	*BIT not signed*
2000	30	46	2009	48	28
2001	33	43	2010	49	27
2002	38	38	2011	50	26
2003	39	37	2012	50	26
2004	40	36	2013	51	25
2005	40	36	2014	51	25
2006	43	33	2015	51	25
2007	46	30	2016	51	25
2008	47	29			

The independent variables considered are as follows. BIT (bilateral investment treaty) - a treaty between two nations to mutually protect the investors from both countries in order to facilitate their investments in the host country. The BIT in this model has been taken as a dummy variable. If the BIT is assigned on a given year, it is 1, otherwise 0.GDP growth rate - the annual percentage growth rate of GDP at market prices on constant local currency. GDP is the sum of gross value added by the residents in the economy plus any product taxes and minus the any subsidies not included in the values of the products. It is calculated without making deductions for depreciation of fabricated assets or for depletion and degradation of natural resources. Inflation rate is the annualised percentage change in the general price index over time. Inflation rate is the percentage increase in the price of goods and services which is taken annually. The Chinn-Ito Index (KAOPEN) is an index measuring a country's degree of capital account openness (Chinn and Ito, 2006; 2008). KAOPEN is based on the binary dummy variables that codify the tabulation of restrictions on cross-border financial transactions reported in the IMF's annual report on exchange arrangements and exchange restrictions (IMF-AREAER). This index takes on higher values the more open the country is to cross-border capital transactions. By construction, the series has a mean of zero. It ranges from -2 to 3 with higher digit showing openness of capital.

Political Constraint Index (POLCON) is a direct measure of the feasibility of a change in policy given the structure of a nation's political institutions (the number of veto points) and the preferences of the actors that inhabit them (the partisan alignment of various veto points and the heterogeneity or homogeneity of the preferences within each branch). The institutional development of host countries can be verified by political constraints on the executive branch. The POLCON focuses on the political discretion of the executive branch. Chinn-Ito index for financial openness of nation can also be considered as a determinant of FDI. The index is based on several dummy variables, including the presence of multiple exchange rates, capital account transactions and requirements to surrender export proceeds. This index is calculated so that higher index values indicate greater openness to cross-border capital transactions (with a mean of zero). Thus, POLCON is included as poor institutions may discourage FDI by giving rise to uncertainty. The indicator ranges from zero (total political discretion) to one (no political discretion). The Table 22.4 presents the mean values of the variables by country classification.

Table 22.4: Descriptive Statistics of the Variables by Classification of Countries.

Variable	*Developed OECD members*	*Developed non-OECD members*	*Developing OECD countries*	*Developing non-OECD countries*
FDI	260.72 (458.44)	755.04 (1338.77)	4.97 (5.48)	175.92 (998.54)
GDP growth rate	1.98 (1.22)	3.94 (1.48)	3.11 (1.33)	3.84 (3.20)
Inflation rate	1.91 (1.01)	2.22 (1.82)	4.71 (0.22)	7.50 (6.47)
Chinn-Ito index	1.79 (0.95)	0.51 (0.70)	1.79 (0.40)	0.01 (0.32)
POLCON	0.48 (0.08)	0.23 (0.20)	0.31 (0.14)	0.14 (0.20)
BIT signed countries	20	1	1	29
BIT not signed countries	8	4	1	12

Note: Standard deviations in parentheses.
Country classifications: Developed OECD economies: Australia, Austria, Belgium, Canada, Czech Republic, France, Germany, Greece, Iceland, Ireland, Israel, Italy, Japan, Liechtenstein, Luxemburg, Netherlands, New Zealand, Norway, Poland, Portugal, South Korea, Spain, Sweden, Switzerland, USA, UK; Developed non-OECD economies - Cyprus, Hong Kong, Isle of Man, Malta, Denmark, Finland, Singapore; Developing OECD economies - Chile, Hungary. Developing non-OECD economies: Bahamas, Bahrain, Belarus, Brazil, Bulgaria, Cayman Islands, Channel Islands, China, Columbia, Egypt, Indonesia, Jordan, Kazakhstan, Kenya, Kuwait, Lebanon, Malaysia, Maldives, Mauritius, Mexico, Morocco, Nepal, Nigeria, Oman, Panama, Philippines, Qatar, Russia, Saudi Arabia, Seychelles, South Africa, Sri Lanka, Thailand, The Bermudas, Turkey, UAE, Ukraine, Uruguay, Vietnam, Virgin Islands, Yemen.

Dynamic Panel GMM Model

This paper uses a dynamic panel data model in the empirical analysis as it allows for more flexibility, imposes less restrictions and permits modeling individual differences across cross-section units. Also, the issues of serial correlation of error terms and endogeneity due to individual specific fixed effects in the model are taken care by the panel estimation. The FDI inflow from country i in year t is to be determined in part by the FDI inflows from country i in year t-1, hence, it is a dynamic panel dataset. Since this study is observing FDI inflows into India from its partner countries over time, it is likely that the model will have country specific fixed effects, leading to the problem of unobserved heterogeneity. Since this is a dynamic model, it is likely that the error terms will not be white noise, and will be serially correlated. To correct for serial correlation and country specific fixed effects, Generalised Methods of Moments (GMM) estimation is used to estimate the endogenous dynamic panel data model. With GMM estimation, suitable instruments can easily be found which can then be tested for exogeneity with respect to the error term which includes any individual specific effects. An instrumental variable is a proxy variable that removes the correlation between regressor and error term which permits consistent estimation of the coefficients. A valid instrument therefore has to satisfy both instrument relevance (variation in the instrument is related to the variation in the explanatory variable) and instrument exogeneity (part of the variation in the explanatory variable is captured by the exogenous instrumental variable). In the dynamic panel data model, the lagged values of the dependent variable themselves serves as valid instruments for the lagged variable.

A general panel data model is specified as:

$$y_{it} = \beta x_{it} + u_{it} i = 1, \ldots, N; \;\; t = 1, \ldots, T \tag{22.1}$$

The error term u_{it} is assumed to follow a one-way error component model:

$$u_{it} = \alpha_i + \varepsilon_{it} \tag{22.2}$$

where α_i is the (unobserved) individual effects, x_{it} is a vector of K_1 explanatory variables, z_i is a vector of K_2 time-invariant explanatory variables. The terms $\alpha_i \sim IID(0, \sigma_\alpha^2)$ and $\varepsilon_{it} \sim IID(0, \sigma_\varepsilon^2)$ are independent of each other and among themselves.A dynamic panel data model is characterised by the presence of a lagged dependent variable among the regressors:

$$y_{it} = \delta y_{it-1} + \beta x_{it} + \gamma z_i + \alpha_i + \varepsilon_{it} i = 1, \ldots, N; \;\; t = 1, \ldots, T \tag{22.3}$$

with $E(\varepsilon_{it}) = 0$, $E(\varepsilon_{it}\varepsilon_{is}) = \sigma_\varepsilon^2$ if j = i and t = s, $E(\varepsilon_{it}\varepsilon_{is}) = 0$ otherwise, $E(\alpha_i) = 0$, $E(\alpha_i x_{it}) = 0$. It is also to be noted that $y_{it-2}(\text{or} y_{it-2} y_{it-3})$ is not the only instrument for $(y_{it-1} y_{it-2})$. In fact, Arellano and Bond (1991) note that all y_{it-2-j} satisfy the conditions $E[y_{it-2-j}(y_{it-1} - y_{it-2}] \neq 0$ and $E[y_{it-2-j}(\varepsilon y_{it} - \varepsilon_{it-1}] = 0$. Therefore, they all are legitimate instruments for $(y_{it-1} y_{it-2})$.

In the GMM estimation, the moment conditions are created by taking the orthogonal deviations. These equations contain parameters to be estimated. For the purpose of estimation, the following assumptions for GMM are specified: Convergence of empirical moment – the data generating process is assumed to meet the law of large numbers. The empirical moments converge in probability to its population counterpart:

$$\overline{m}_n(\theta_0) = 1/n \textstyle\sum_{i=1}^{n} m_i(\theta_0) \rightarrow 0 \tag{22.4}$$

Asymptotic distribution of empirical moments - empirical moments obey central limit theorem, and finite asymptotic covariance matrix converges to normal distribution:

$$\sqrt{n} m_i(\theta_0) \rightarrow N[0, \phi] \tag{22.5}$$

Identification - considering n as the number of equations and k as the number of parameters, for any $n \geq k$, if $\boldsymbol{\theta}_1$ and θ_2 are different parameter vectors, then:

$$\bar{m}_n(\theta_1) \neq \bar{m}_n(\theta_2) \tag{22.6}$$

Hence, all $\boldsymbol{\theta}_i$ are unique. Probability limit of GMM is uniquely minimised at true parameters, $\boldsymbol{\theta}_0$.

To eliminate the unobservable country specific (individual) effects, the GMM estimator takes the first difference:

$$\Delta y_{it} = \delta \Delta y_{it-1} + \beta \Delta x_{it} + \Delta \varepsilon_{it} \tag{22.7}$$

Even when the unobservable country effects is eliminated with differencing, there can still be an endogeneity bias arising from the correlation between the lagged difference of the dependent variable and the error term. In this case instrumental variables are used. The differenced GMM estimator uses the lagged levels of the explanatory variables as instruments on the conditions that the error term of the differenced equation is not serially correlated and that the lagged levels of the explanatory variables are weakly exogenous. The moment conditions therefore are written as:

$$E[W(\varepsilon_{it}\varepsilon_{it-1})] = 0 \qquad s \geq 2;\; t = 3, \dots, T \tag{22.8}$$

$$E[V(\varepsilon_{it}\varepsilon_{it-1})] = 0 \qquad s \geq 2;\; t = 3, \dots, T \tag{22.9}$$

where W is written as:

$$\begin{bmatrix} [y_{i1}] & \cdots & & 0 \\ \vdots & [y_{i1} \quad y_{i2}] & & \vdots \\ \vdots & \vdots & & \vdots \\ 0 & \cdots & [y_{i1} & \cdots \quad y_{iT-2}] \end{bmatrix} \tag{22.10}$$

and V is written as:

$$V = \begin{bmatrix} [x_{i1}] & \cdots & & 0 \\ \vdots & [x_{i1} \quad x_{i2}] & & \vdots \\ \vdots & \vdots & & \vdots \\ 0 & \cdots & [x_{i1} & \cdots \quad x_{iT-2}] \end{bmatrix} \tag{22.11}$$

When the dependent variable is highly persistent over time, the differenced GMM suffer from weak instrument problem and its asymptotic properties may be affected. Blundell and Bond (2000) propose a system GMM estimator using the lagged differences of explanatory variables as instruments, instead of lagged differences of the dependent variable, assuming the absence of serial correlation in the error term, and between these instruments and the error term. Then, the moment conditions are written as:

$$E[\Delta y_{it-s}(u_{it})] = 0 \qquad s \geq 2; \; t = 3, \dots, T \tag{20.12}$$

$$E[\Delta x_{it-s}(u_{it})] = 0 \qquad s \geq 2; \; t = 3, \dots, T \tag{20.13}$$

which can be represented in a general for as:

$$E[m_l(y_{it}, x_{it}, \theta)] = E[m_{il}(\theta)] = 0 \tag{20.14}$$

where θ represents the β_i parameters to be estimated. This creates a set of M moment equations with K parameters. In the present paper case, we need to estimate β_2, β_3, β_4 and β_5. Therefore, in order to have a unique solution for the given parameters the criterion of weighted sum of squares can be used:

$$q = \overline{m}(\theta)' W_n \overline{m}(\theta) \tag{20.15}$$

where $$\overline{m}(\theta) = 1/n \textstyle\sum_{i=1}^{n} m_l(y_i, x_{i,} \theta) \tag{20.16}$$

and W_n is a positive definite matrix proportional to the asymptotic covariance matrix of the moment condition $m_l(\theta)$.

GMM can be extended to any number of moment conditions. For the purpose of estimation, this study chooses both the difference GMM and the system GMM estimators which use first differences and the orthogonal condition.

With the application of GMM, a test of over identification of the model is applied in this paper. This test is taken as the number of variables in the model is increasing with each model it may create a situation that there might not be a parameter value β such that the moment condition $E[m_l(y_i, x_i, \beta)]=0$ holds. Thus, the over identifying restrictions are testable. For example, taking the linear model $y=\beta_1 x_1 + \beta_2 x_2 + u$ with $E(x_1 u)=0$ with and $E(x_2 u)=0$. It is possible that $\beta_2 = 0$, so that the linear equation may be written as $y = \beta_1 c_1 + u$. However, it is possible that $\beta_2 \neq 0$ and in this case it would be impossible to find a value of β_1 so that both $E[x_1 (y-\beta_1 x_1)] = 0$ and $E[x_2 (y - \beta_2 x_2)] = 0$ hold simultaneously. In this sense, an exclusion restriction can be seen as an over identifying restriction.

With IV estimation, the Sargan test is a test of the validity of the instruments. It is a test of over identifying restrictions. The hypothesis being tested by Sargan test is that the IVs are uncorrelated with some set of residuals and therefore they are acceptable instruments and the excluded instruments are correctly excluded from the estimating equation.

The criterion function at the parameter estimates is:

$$J_n = J_n(\beta) \rightarrow \chi_l^2 \tag{22.17}$$

The degrees of freedom of the asymptotic distribution are the number of over identifying restrictions. Under the null hypothesis that the over-identifying restrictions are valid, the Sargan statistic is distributed as a χ^2 (p-k), where k is the number of estimated coefficients and p is the instrument rank. The hypothesis being tested is, given z are the IVs:

H_0: $(z,u) = 0 \rightarrow J = 0$, the over-identification restrictions are valid.

H_1:$(z,u) \neq 0 \rightarrow J \neq 0$, the over-identification restrictions are not valid.

If the statistic J exceeds the chi-square critical value, the model is rejected. Thus, in case of alternative hypothesis, the restrictions applied by the estimation are bearable and the fit of the model can be considered good. The GMM over identification test is a very useful by-product of the GMM methodology and thus the J statistic is taken in GMM estimation. However, based on this information alone, it is unclear the problem with in the model that is estimated as the reason for over identification of the restrictions is not known, and therefore it is typically a cause for concern. In the empirical analysis, the Sargan – Hansen J Test has been used in order to verify the over identification of the restrictions imposed over the instruments.

22.4 Empirical Analysis

The dependent variable used in this paper is the FDI inflow and the independent variables used are GDP growth rate, inflation rate, Chinn-Ito index, political constraints index and the bilateral investment treaty. The dependent variable FDI is measured on a ratio scale as FDI inflow to India for a country i as a ratio to the country's GDP. The independent variable GDP growth rate and inflation rate are measured on the interval scale where the interval values are from -100 percent to 100 percent. The CHIN-ITO index taking the value ranging from – 2 to +3 and the POLCON (0, 1) index are also measured on interval scale. The dummy variables BIT, OECD are measured on a nominal scale. The descriptive statistics of the variables used in the empirical estimation are presented in Table 22.5.

Table 22.5: Descriptive Statistics of Variables in the Determination of FDI.

Variable	*Description*	*Mean*	*Std. dev.*
FDI	FDI flow of country to India as a share of its GDP	0.0094	0.02626
GDPGR	GDP growth rate of a country	3.146	6.222
INF	Inflation rate of a country	5.03	9.795
CHINN-ITO	Financial openness index of a country	0.748	1.142
POLCON	Political constraints index of a country	0.316	0.217
BIT	If bilateral investment treaty signed=1, 0 otherwise	0.585	0.492
OECD	If a member of OECD=1, 0 otherwise	0.379	0.485
DEV	If a developed country=1, 0 otherwise	0.462	0.498

From the Table 22.5, the following statements can be inferred. India receives around 1 percent of FDI inflow as percentage share from a country's GDP with a standard deviation of 2 percent. The average GDP growth rate and inflation rate of the nations in the data are 3.14 percent and 5 percent respectively. The value of Chin-Ito (KAOPEN) index is 0.75 which falls in the middle of a range of [-2, 3] showing neutral openness of nations but with a greater degree of deviation (1.14). The POLCON index is deviating from 0.1 to 0.5 with an average of 0.3, showing lesser political discretion in the countries. The dummy variable BIT shows in about 58.5 percent of 76 countries from where FDI flows, India has signed BITs. Further, India receives FDI from 38 percent of the countries are OECD and from 46 percent of the developed countries as a whole.

The empirical specification of the estimating equation is,

$$FDI_{it} = \alpha + \beta_1 FDI_{it-1} + \beta_2 GDP_{it} + \beta_3 INF_{it} + \beta_4 BIT_{it} + \beta_5 CHIN - ITO_{it} + \beta_6 POLCON_{it} + \beta_7 OECD_{it} + \beta_8 DEV_{it} + u_{it} \tag{22.18}$$

The pooled regression estimates are presented Table 22.6. The effect of BIT on FDI inflows is positive and statistically significant. Every BIT signed by India increases FDI by about 1.4 percent. While the GDP growth rate and Chinn-Ito index of openness effects positive FDI, inflation and political discretion dampens FDI inflows. However, none of these variables are statistically significant. Also, the very low R-square value shows that the OLS estimates are poor and shows a low goodness of fit of the model. The OLS results are biased as it cannot control the serial correlation and country specific fixed effects. Therefore, GMM is used as an estimation technique which solves these problems and also accommodates a dynamic model.

Table 22.6: OLS Estimates for FDI Inflows in India, 2000-2016.

Variable	*Spec.1*	*Spec.2*	*Spec.3*	*Spec.4*
Inflation	-0.0001 (0.582)	-0.0003 (1.220)	-0.0001 (0.610)	-0.0003 (1.137)
GDP growth rate	0.0002 (0.549)	0.00003 (0.086)	0.0002 (0.557)	0.00007 (0.190)
BIT	0.014*** (2.808)	0.015*** (3.021)	0.014*** (2.791)	0.014*** (2.770)
Chinn-Ito	-	-0.0062*** (2.722)	-	-0.0074*** (2.937)
POLCON	-	-	-0.0023 (0.194)	0.0152 (1.118)
Constant	0.0007 (0.155)	0.006 (1.29)	0.001 (0.244)	0.002 (0.483)
R squared (within)	0.006	0.01	0.006	0.01
F-value	2.83***	3.99***	2.13	3.44***
No. of obs.	1095	1241	1241	1241

Note: Absolute t-values in parentheses. *** significant at 1 percent level.

The Table 22.7 presents the GMM estimates of the determinants of FDI inflows in India during 2000-2016. The models have been estimated by differenced GMM and by system GMM. It is observed by Mina (2013) and Busse, Koniger and Nunnenkamp (2010) that system GMM performs better than differenced GMM since the latter suffers from poor finite sample properties. Also, in the present analysis, the differenced GMM may not be suitable as the variable BIT changes its values only in the periods of signing of the BIT. While in the differenced GMM, the sign of intercept coefficients is positive whereas in system GMM it is negative. The differenced GMM estimates show that, when the explanatory variables are zero, the FDI inflow in India from each investor nation at any time period is 0.9 percent of their share of GDP. In the system GMM estimation, it is however seen that FDI is negative, showing FDI outflows from India.

Table 22.7: GMM Estimates for FDI Inflows in India, 2000 2016

Variable	*Differenced*	*System 1*	*System 2*	*System 3*
FDI (-1)	0.68*** (3.97)	0.68*** (7.70)	0.72*** (6.57)	0.66*** (7.03)
Inflation	0.0004*** (7.97)	0.0004*** (3.33)	0.0003*** (3.37)	0.001*** (7.32)
GDP growth rate	0.006*** (5.42)	0.006*** (3.80)	0.003*** (8.47)	0.006*** (5.25)

(Contd...)

BIT	-0.06*** (6.24)	-0.06*** (6.65)	-0.03*** (3.25)	-0.16*** (5.19)
OECD	-	-	-	-2.82 (1.73)
DEV	-	-	-	-0.21*** (49.86)
Chinn-Ito	-0.07*** (6.59)	-0.07*** (7.72)	-	-0.07*** (4.15)
POLCON	0.26*** (8.48)	0.26*** (12.73)	0.18*** (17.97)	0.28*** (15.23)
Constant	0.009*** (3.76)	-0.02*** (8.10)	-0.004*** (8605)	-0.08*** (6.50)
J statistic (p-values)	51.53 (0.33)	57.65 (0.21)	62.43*** (0.05)	61.01*** (0.05)
No. of obs.	1095	1095	1095	1095

Note: Absolute t-values in parentheses. *** significant at 1 percent level.

The main variable, the dummy variable BIT shows a statistically significant negative impact on FDI inflows to India. The signing of a BIT by India with the source country reduces in the FDI inflow to India by intercept by 0.06 percent. In the case of India, the negative effect of BIT may be because of the inefficiencies of the BIT signed or due to the apprehension of insecurity of the investors even after the signing of BITs with the source country. Studies like Busse et al. (2010) and Buthe and Milner (2008) find that BIT has been positively associated with the FDI inflows. Tobin and Rose-Ackerman (2011) find this relationship to be week. Further, Mina (2015) and (Aisbett et al. 2018) find a negative relationship between BIT and FDI. Most of these studies use cross-country analysis with BIT and FDI flows. However, the present paper considers the analysis of the interaction of a single country (India) with its experiences with BIT. During the period 2000-2016, it could be seen that a countless number of arbitration cases emerged with India such as the Dabhol power case (2001), White Industries case (2002), Sistema JFSC (2012) and others. It can be noted that due to these cases emerging there was raising insecurity for foreign investors. According to Aisbett et al. (2018), when a host nation (like Indian case) faces a claim, FDI from source countries with a BIT in place falls significantly more than that from unprotected sources. As observed from Figure 22.2, it could be seen that the distrust of investors increases with arbitration proceedings on the BIT resulting in lesser difference between protected and non-protected investors of BIT. Thus, it could be seen that there is a drastic increase in the distrust of foreign investors due to arbitration proceedings with BITs.

In the GMM estimates, the coefficients of the lagged FDI are positive and statistically significant in all specifications. An increase in previous year FDI increases the current year FDI by 6.8 to 7.2 percent. Similarly, an increase in the GDP growth rate pushes India's FDI inflows positively. A unit increase in the percentage of GDP growth rate of a country significantly increases the percentage ratio of FDI inflows to India by 0.6 percent. Further, inflation has also significant positive effect by enhancing FDI inflows in India. As a unit increase in the percentage of inflation rate of a country increases the percentage ratio of FDI to GDP by 0.04 percent. In India's case, a country's inflation pushes investors to consider investing in India, except, perhaps inflation carries to a very miser magnitude of change in FDI.

The financial openness variable (Chinn-Ito index) explains the financial borders of a country. In case of India, as a foreign country is more financially open it may choose not invest in India. A unit increase in the Chinn-Ito index of a country decreases the percentage ratio of FDI to GDP by 7 percent. Thus, the decision of a nation not to invest in India because of financial openness of that economy is also an important determinant of FDI inflows to India. The political constraints (POLCON) index is one of the variables which have a significant positive impact. This also has the highest impact in the decision making of an investor. A unit increase in the political stability or less political discretion of a country decreases the percentage ratio of FDI to GDP by 26 percent. Thus, countries with less political discretion in their investment outflows have higher tendency to invest in India. In the case of an OECD member country, the effect on FDI inflows to India is statistically insignificant negative. The coefficient of the dummy variable DEV shows that a developed nation may not be interested in investing in India as much as a developing nation.

The J statistic shows that the specifications have p-values significant at 1 percent for over identification of restrictions. Thus, the test for over-identification of GMM instruments suggests that instruments are uncorrelated with the error term and they are exogenous in the system.

22.5. Conclusion

The objective of this paper is to identify the determinants of FDI and their effect on FDI inflows to India, with specific focus on the effect of bilateral investment treaty (BIT). The paper has used a dynamic panel data GMM-IV analysis on 76 counties for the time period 2000-2016. To analyse the impact of the determining variables on FDI, pooled OLS, differenced GMM and system GMM estimation methods have been employed. As the

OLS estimation suffers from serial correlation and endogeneity bias, the estimates of differenced GMM and system GMM have been compared and interpreted.

The empirical estimates of bilateral investment treaties show a significant negative effect on the FDI inflows in India. The sample period is also the time period when India's first arbitration cases emerged that includes the Dabhol power case. These arbitration cases under BIT have led to an impact for the foreign investors not to invest in India. Thus, it is to be seen that the BITs have been inefficient and they are not able to establish a strong foundation for creating confidence and risk-free environment for international investors. The empirical results further show while the lagged FDI has significant positive effect on FDI inflows to India, the factors like GDP growth, inflation rate contribute very low to India's FDI inflows. The financial openness of the source nations has been reducing FDI inflows to India. However, as shown by the POLCON index, the countries with lesser political constraints have positive FDI outflow towards India. Also, as opposed to domestic variables, the Chinn-Ito index and POLCON index have greater share of change in FDI inflows to India.

References

Abdullah, H., M. Azam and S.K. Zakariya (2016) "The Impact of Environmental Quality on Public Health Expenditure in Malaysia", *Asia Pacific Journal of Advanced Business and Social Studies*, 2, 2, 365-379.

Abuya, B.A., E.O. Onsomu, J.K. Kimani and D. Moore (2011) "Influence of Maternal Education on Child Immunization and Stunting in Kenya", *Maternal and Child Health Journal*, 15, 8, 1389-1399.

Adams, R. and J. Page (2005) "Do International Migration and Remittances Reduce Poverty in Developing Countries?", *World Development*, 33, 10, 1645-1669.

Addison, E.K.Y (2004) "The Macroeconomic Impact of Remittances", Paper presented at the Conference on Migration and Development in Ghana, September 14-16, 2004, Ghana.

Adenike, E.T. (2013) "An Econometric Analysis of the Impact of Corruption on Economic Growth in Nigeria", *Journal of Business Management and Economics*, 4, 3, 54-65.

Adetunji, M.O. and M.O. Rauf (2012) "Analysis of Household Demand for Meat in Southwest, Nigeria", *Global Journal of Science Frontier Research Agriculture & Biology*, 12, 1, 1-9.

Adjasi, C.K.D. and N.B. Biekpe (2005) "Stock Market Returns and Exchange Rate Dynamics in Selected African Countries: A Bivariate Analysis", *African Finance Journal*, 2, 6, 17-28.

Adjasi, C.K.D. and C.A. Yartey (2007) "Stock Market Development in Sub-Saharan Africa: Critical Issues and Challenges", IMF Working Paper No. 07/209, International Monetary Fund.

Aepli, M. and R. Finger (2013) "Determinants of Sheep and Goat Meat Consumption in Switzerland", *Agricultural and Food Economics*, 1, 1, Article 11.

Aggarwal, R. (1981) "Exchange Rates and Stock Prices: A Study of U. S. Capital Market under Floating Exchange Rates", *Akron Business and Economic Review*, 12, 1, 7-12.

Agrawal, G., A.K. Srivastav and A. Srivastav (2010) "A Study of Exchange Rates Movement and Stock Market Volatility", *International Journal of Business and Management*, 5, 12, 62-73.

Aguilera, M.B. (2003) "The Impact of the Worker: How Social Capital Influence the Job Tenure of formerly Undocumented Mexican Immigrants", *Sociological Inquiry*, 73, 1, 52-83.

Aguilera, M.B. (2008) "Personal Networks and the Incomes of Men and Women in the United States: Do Personal Networks Provide Higher Returns for Men or Women?", *Research in Social Stratification and Mobility*, 26, 3, 221-233.

Ahmed, A.E.M. and S.Z. Suliman (2011) "The Long-Run Relationship between Money Supply, Real GDP, and Price Level: Empirical Evidence from Sudan", *Journal of Business Studies Quarterly*, 2, 2, 68-79.

Aisbett, E., M. Busse and P. Nunnenkamp (2018) "Bilateral Investment Treaties as Deterrents of Host-country Discretion: The Impact of Investor-State Disputes on Foreign Direct Investment in Developing Countries, *Review of World Economics*, 154, 1, 119-155.

Ajayi, R.A. and M. Mougoue (1996) "On the Dynamic Relation between Stock Prices and Exchange Rates", *Journal of Financial Research*, 19, 2, 193-207.

Ajayi, R.A., J. Friedman and S.M. Mehdian (1998) "On the Relationship between Stock Returns and Exchange Rates: Tests of Granger Causality", *Global Finance Journal*, 9, 2, 241-251.

Akai, N., Y. Horiuchi and M. Sakata (2005) "Short-run and Long-run Effects of Corruption on Economic Growth: Evidence from State-Level Cross-Section Data for the United State", Osaka, Japan: Osaka International University Press.

Akgiray, V. (1989) "Conditional Heteroskedasticity in Time Series of Stock Returns: Evidence and Forecasts", *Journal of Business*, 62, 1, 55-80.

Akinlabi, A.O., B. Hamed and M.A. Awoniyi (2011) "Corruption, Foreign Direct Investment and Economic Growth in Nigeria: An Empirical Investigation", *Journal of Research in International Business Management*, 1, 9, 278-292.

Akkihal, R. H. Smith and R. Adkins (1997) "The Economics of Corruption in Developing countries", *Coastal Business Journal*, 1, 1, 39-44.

Alexander, M., M. Harding and C. Lamarche (2011) "Quantile Regression for Time-Series-Cross Section Data", *International Journal of Statistics and Management Systems*, 6, 1, 47-72.

Aliyu, S.U.R. and A.O. Elijah (2011) "How Corruption Affects Economic Growth in Nigeria", *Journal of Global Business Management*, 4, 2, 143-154.

Andrienko, Y. and S. Guriev (2004) "Determinants of Interregional Mobility in Russia: *Economics of Transition*, 12, 1, 1-27.

Ang, J.B. and W.J. McKibbin (2007) "Financial liberalization, Financial sector Development and Growth: Evidence from Malaysia", *Journal of Development Economics*, 84, 1, 215-233.

Angrist, J.D. and J. Pischke (2008) *Mostly Harmless Econometrics: An Empiricist's Companion*, Princeton: Princeton University Press.

Anjomani, A. (2002) "Regional Growth and Interstate Migration", *Socio-Economic Planning Sciences*, 36, 4, 239-265.

Ansari, M.S. (2012) "Indian Capital Market Review: Issues, Dimensions and Performance Analysis", *Journal of Economics*, 3, 2, 181-191.

Apte, P. (1998) "Currency Exposure and Stock Prices", *Journal of Foreign Exchange and International Finance*, 12, 2, 135-143.

Apte, P. (2002) "The Inter-relationship between Stock Markets and the Foreign Exchange Market", *Prajnan*, 30, 1, 17-29.

Arouri, Md.El-.H., A.B. Youssef and C. Rault (2012) "Energy Consumption, Economic Growth and CO_2 Emissions in Middle East and North African Countries", *Energy Policy*, 45, 342-349.

Asare, E., G. Nakakeeto and S. Eduardo (2018) "Determinants of the Choice of a Savings Option: The Case of African Households", Paper presented at the Southern Agricultural Economics Association (SAEA) Annual Meeting, Jacksonville FL, Texas, February 2-6, 2018.

Ashenfelter, O., C. Harmon and H. Oosterbeek (1999) "A Review of Estimates of the Schooling/Earnings Relationship, with Tests for Publication Bias", *Labour Economics*, 6, 4, 453-470.

Babalola, S. (2008) "Determinants of the Uptake of the Full Dose of Diphtheria-Pertussis-Tetanus (DPT3) Vaccines in Northern nigeria: A Multilevel Analysis", *Matern and Child Health Journal*, 13, 4, 550-558.

Bagdigen, M. and H. Cetintas (2004) "Causality between Public Expenditure and Economic Growth: The Turkish Case", *Journal of Economic and Social Research*, 6, 1, 53-72.

Bahmani-Oskooee, M. and A. Sohrabian (1992) "Stock Prices and the Effective Exchange Rate of the Dollar", *Applied Economics*, 24, 4, 459-464.

Balogun, S.A., H.A. Yusuff, K.Q. Yusuf, A.M. Al-Shenqiti, M.T. Balogun and P. Tettey (2017) "Maternal Education and Child Immunization: The Mediating Roles of Maternal Literacy and Socioeconomic Status", *Pan African Medical Journal*, 24, 26, 217.

Banerjee, A., S. Mullainathan and R. Hanna (2012) "Corruption", NBER Working Paper No. 17968.

Barbieri, L. (2008) "Panel Cointegration Tests: A Survey", *Review of International Social Science*, 116, 1, 3-36.

Barbieri, L. (2009) "Panel Unit Root Tests under Cross-Sectional Dependence: An Overview", *Journal of Statistics: Advances in Theory and Applications*, 1, 2, 117-158.

Bardhan, P. (1997) "Corruption and Development: A Review of Issues", *Journal of Economic Literature*, 35, 3, 1320-1346.

Bardhan, P. and D. Mookherjee (2006) "Corruption and Decentralization of Infrastructure Delivery in Developing Countries", *Economic Journal*, 116, 1,107-133.

Bargain, O., S.K. Bhaumik, M. Chakrabarthy and Z. Zhao (2009) "Earnings Differences between Chinese and Indian Wage Earners, 1987-2004", *Review of Income and Wealth*, 55, s1, 562-587.

Barma, S.C and C.K. Mukhopadhyay (2009) "Money and Price Relationship in the Economy of Bangladesh (A Time Series Analysis with Vector Autoregressive Model)", *Osmania Journal of International Business Studies*, 4, 2, 64-83.

Barro, R. J. (1990) "Government Spending in a Simple Model of Endogenous Growth", *Journal of Political Economy*, 98, 5, S103-S125.

Barro, R.J. and X. Sala-i-Martin (1992) "Public Finance in Models of Economic Growth", *Review of Economic Studies*, 59, 4, 645-661.

Bartlett, R.L. and C. Callahan (1984) "Wage Determination and Marital Status: Another Look", *Industrial Relations*, 23, 1, 90-96.

Bartov, E. and G.M. Bodnar (1994) "Firm Valuation, Earnings Expectations and the Exchange-Rate Exposure Effect", *Journal of Finance*, 49, 5, 1755-1785.

Basaleem, H.O, K.A. Al-Sakkaf and K. Shumsuddin (2010) "Immunization Coverage and Its Determinants among Children", *Saudi Medical Journal*, 31, 11, 1221-1226.

Bayar, A.A. and B.Y. Ilhan (2016) Determinants of Household Education Expenditures: Do Poor Spend Less on Education?", *Topics in Middle Eastern and African Economies18.*

Beck, T., A. Demigric-Kunt and R. Levine (2007) "Finance Inequality and Poor", *Journal of Economic Growth*, 12, 1, 27-49.

Becker, G.S. (1964) *Human Capital: A Theoretical and Empirical Analysis, with Special Reference to Education*, Chicago: University of Chicago Press.

Becker, G.S. (1968) "Crime and Punishment: An Economic Approach", *Journal of Political Economy*, 76, 2, 169-217.

Becker, G.S. (1973) "A Theory of Marriage: Part I", *Journal of Political Economy*, 81, 4, 813-846.

Becker, G.S. (1974) "A Theory of Marriage: Part II", *Journal of Political Economy*, 82, 2, S11-S26.

Bell, C. and P.L. Rousseau (2001) "Post-Independence in India: A Case of Finance Led Industrialization?", *Journal of Development Economics*, 65, 1, 153-175.

Bemel-Verdugo, L.E., D. Furceri and D. Guillaume (2012) "Labor Market Flexibility and Unemployment: New Empirical Evidence of Static and Dynamic Effects", *Comparative Economic Studies*, 54, 251-273.

Benham, L. (1974) "Benefits of Women's Education Within Marriage", *Journal of Political Economy*, 82, 2, Part II, S57-S71.

Betcherman, G. (2013) "Labor Market Institutions: A Review of the Literature", Background Paper for the World Development Report 2013.

Bhalotra, S. and B. Zamora (2010) "Social Divisions in Education in India", in A. Sharif and R. Basant (eds.): *Handbook of Muslims in India: Empirical and Policy Perspectives*, Delhi: Oxford University Press, 165-198.

Bhatt, A. and P. Scaramozzino (2015) "Fiscal Transfers and Fiscal Discipline in India: An Empirical Investigation", *Public Finance Review*, 43, 1, 53-81.

Bhaumik, S.K. and M. Chakrabarty (2008) "Does Move to Market Have an Impact on Earnings Gap Across Gender? Some Evidence from India", *Applied Economics Letters*, 15, 8, 601-605.

Bhaumik, S.K. and M. Chakrabarty (2009) "Is Education the Panacea for Economic Deprivation of Muslims? Evidence from Wage Earners in India, 1987-2004", *Journal of Asian Economics*, 20, 2, 137-149.

Bhaumik, S.K. and M. Chakrabarty (2010) "Mother or Motherland: Can a Government Have an Impact on Educational Attainment of the Population? Preliminary Evidence from India", William Davidson Institute Working Paper Number 987.

Bhaumik, S.K. and M. Chakrabarty (2012) "Whither Human Capital? The Woeful Tale of Transition to Tertiary Education in India", *Applied Economic Letters*, 19, 9, 835-838.

Bhaumik, S.K. and M. Chakrabarty (2013) "Educational Attainment in India: What Drives Transition?", *ICRA's Bulletin - Money and Finance*, February, 95-112.

Biswas, A.K. (2005) "Corruption: A Good Challenge to the Governance in India", *International Journal of Innovative Research and Development*, 1, 5. 1-15.

Blazquez-Fernandez, D. Cantarero-Prieto and M. Pascual-Saez (2019) "On the Nexus of Air Pollution and Health Expenditures: New Empirical Evidence", *Gaceta Sanitaria*, 33, 4, 389-394.

Blundell, R. and S. Bond (2000) "GMM Estimation with Persistent Panel Data: An Application to Production Functions", *Econometric Reviews*, 19, 3, 321-340.

Boachie, M.K., I.O. Mensah, P. Sobiesuo, M. Immurana, A.-A. Iddrisu and I. Kyei-Brobbey (2014) "Determinants of Public Health Expenditure in Ghana: A Cointegration Analysis", *Journal of Behavioural Finance Entrepreneurship Account Transport*, 2, 2, 35-40.

Bodnar, G.M. and S.M. Bartram (2007) "The Exchange Rate Exposure Puzzle", *Managerial Finance*, 33, 9, 642-666.

Bongaarts, J. (2017) "The Effect of Contraception on Fertility: Is Sub-Saharan Africa Different?", *Demographic Research*, 37, 6, 129-146.

Borooah, V.K. (2006) "What makes People Happy? Some Evidence from Ireland", *Journal of Happiness Studies*, 7, 4, 427-465.

Bose, N., M.H. Emranul and D. Osborn (2007) "Public Expenditure and Economic Growth: Disaggregated Analysis for Developing Countries", Manchester School, 75, 5, 533-556.

Branson, W.H. (1983) "Macroeconomic Determinants of Real Exchange Rate Risk", in R.J. Herring (ed.): *Managing Foreign Exchange Risk*, Cambridge: Cambridge University Press.

Branson, W.H. and D.W. Henderson (1985) "The Specification and Influence of Assets", in R.W. Jones and P.B. Kenen (eds.): *Handbook of International Economics, Volume 2*, Amsterdam: Elsevier, 749-805.

Breitung, J. (2000) "The Local Power of Some Unit Root Tests for Panel Data", B.H. Baltagi, T.B. Fombay and R. Carter (eds.): *Nonstationary Panels, Panel Cointegration, and Dynamic Panels, Advances in Econometrics, Volume 15*, London: Emerald Publishing, 161-178.

Breitung, J. and W. Meyer (1994) "Testing for Unit Roots in Panel Data: Are Wages on Different Bargaining Levels Cointegrated?", *Applied Economics*, 26, 4, 353-361.

Breitung J. and M.H. Pesaran (2008) "Unit Roots and Cointegration in Panels", in L. Matyas and P. Sevestre (eds.): *The Econometrics of Panel Data, Advanced Studies in Theoretical and Applied Econometrics, Volume 46*, Berlin, Heidelberg: Springer-Verlag, 279-322.

Breusch, T.S. (1978) "Testing for autocorrelation in Dynamic Linear Models", *Australian Economic Papers*, 17, 31, 334-355.

Breusch, T.S. and A.R. Pagan (1979) "A Simple Test for Heteroskedasticity and Random Coefficient Variation, *Econometrica*, 47, 5, 1287-1294.

Britt, C.L. (1997) "Reconsidering the Unemployment and Crime Relationship: Variation by Age Group and Historical Period', *Journal of Quantitative Criminology*, 13, 4, 405-428.

Browne, A.W. and H.R. Barrett (1991) "Female Education in Sub-Saharan Africa: The Key to Development?", *Comparative Education*, 27, 3, 275-285.

Bunea, D. (2012) "Modern Gravity Models of Internal Migration: The Case of Romania", *Theoretical and Applied Economics*, 18, 4, 127-144.

Busse, M., J. Koniger and P. Nunnenkamp (2010) "FDI Promotion Through Bilateral Investment Treaties: More Than A Bit?", *Review of World Economics*, 146, 1, 147-177.

Buthe, T. (2010) "Politics and Institutions in the Regulation of Global Capital: A Review Article", *Review of International Organizations*, 3, 2, 207-220.

Buthe, T. and H.V. Milner (2008) "The Politics of Foreign Direct Investment into Developing Countries: Increasing FDI Through International Trade Agreements", *American Journal of Political Science*, 52, 4, 741-762.

Caldwell, J.C. (1979) "Education as a Factor in Mortality Decline: An Examination of Nigerian Data", *Population Studies*, 33, 3395- 413.

Canay, I. (2011) "A Simple Approach to Quantile Regression for Panel Data", *Econometrics Journal*, 14, 3, 368-386.

Card, D. (1999) "The Causal Effect of Education on Earnings", in O. Ashen felter and D. Card (eds.): *Handbook of Labor Economics, Volume 3A*, Amsterdam: Elsevier, 1801-1863.

Card, D. (2001) "Estimating the Return to Schooling: Progress on Some Persistent Econometric Problems", *Econometrica*, 69, 5, 1127-1160.

Carling, J. (2008) "The Determinants of Migrant Remittances", *Oxford Review of Economic Policy*, 24, 3, 581-598.

Chakraborty, I. (2010) "Financial Development and Economic Growth in India", *South Asia Economic Journal*, 11, 2, 287-308.

Chandrasekhar, S., P. Geetha Rani and S. Sahoo (2016) "Household Expenditure on Higher Education in India: What Do We Know and What Do Recent Data have to Say?", WP 2016-030, IGIDR, Mumbai.

Chaudhri, D.P. and R. Jha (2011) "Child Poverty, Demographic Transition and Gender Bias in Education in India, Household Data Analysis (1993-94 and 2004-05)", *Indian Economic Journal*, 59, 2, 1-28.

Chaudhri, D.P. and R. Jha (2012) "Child Poverty and Compulsory Elementary Education in India: Policy Insights from Household Data Analysis", *Indian Journal of Human Development*, 6, 1, 5-30.

Chen, G. and S. Hamori (2009) "Economic Returns to Schooling in Urban China: OLS and the Instrumental Variables Approach", *China Economic Review*, 20, 2, 143-152.

Chen, Y. and S. Feng (2011) "Parental Education and Wages: Evidence from China", *Frontiers of Economics in China*, 6, 4, 568-591.

Chen, Z. and M. Jin (2017) "Financial Inclusion in China: Use of Credit", *Journal of Family and Economic Issues*, 38, 4, 528-540.

Chiricos, T.G. (1987) "Rates of Crime and Unemployment: An Analysis of Aggregate Research Evidence", *Social Problems*, 34, 2, 187-212.

Choi, I. (2001) "Unit Root Tests for Panel Data", *Journal of International Money and Finance*, 20, 2, 249-272.

Choi, J.J. and M. Rajan (1997) "A Joint Test of Market Segmentation and Exchange Risk Factor in International Capital Markets", *Journal of International Business Studies*, 28, 1, 29-49.

Chude, N.P. and D.I. Chude (2013) "Impact of Government Expenditure on Economic Growth in Nigeria", *International Journal of Business and Management Review*, 1, 4, 64-71.

Cihak, M., A. Demirguc-Kunt, E. Feyen and R. Levine (2012) "Benchmarking Financial Systems Around the World", Working Paper Series No. 6175, World Bank.

Clark, A.E. and C. Senik (2011) "Will GDP Growth Increase Happiness in Developing Countries?", in R. Peccoud (ed.): *Measure For Measure: How Well Do We Measure Development?*, Paris: STIN, 99-176.

Clark, A.E., P. Frijters and M.A. Shields (2008) "Relative Income, Happiness and Utility: An Explanation of Easterlin Paradox and Other Puzzles", *Journal of Economic Literature*, 46, 1, 95-144.

Como, M. (2011) "Do Happier People Make More Money? An Empirical Study of the Effect of a Person's Happiness on Their Income", *The Park Place Economist*, 19, 1, Article 8.

Consultative Group to Assist the Poor (CGAP) (2017) *The Consultative Group to Assist the Poorest: A Microfinance Program*, Washington, D.C.: World Bank.

Cox, D. (1987) "Motives for Private Income Transfers", *Journal of Political Economy*, 95, 3, 508-546.

Cox, D. and E. Jimenez (1990) "Achieving Social Objectives Through Private Transfers: A Review", *World Bank Research Observer*, 5, 2, 205-218.

Cox, D., B. Hansen and E. Jimenez (2004), "How Responsive Are Private Transfers to Income? Evidence from a Laissez-Faire Economy", *Journal of Public Economics*, 88, 9-10, 2193-2219.

Das, S. (2003) "Modeling Money, Price and Output in India: A Vector Auto Regressive and Moving Average (VARMA) Approach", *Applied Economics*, 35, 10, 1219-1225.

Deaton, A. (2008) "Income, Health and Well-being around the World: Evidence from the Gallup World Poll", *Journal of Economic Perspective*, 22, 2, 53-72.

Del Monte, A. and E. Papagni (2007) "The Determinants of Corruption in Italy: Regional Panel Data Analysis", *European Journal of Political Economy*, 23, 2, 379-396.

Del Monte, A. and E. Papagni (2001) "Public Expenditure, Corruption, and Economic Growth: The Case of Italy", *European Journal of Political Economy*, 17, 1, 1-16.

Demetriades, P. and K. Hussein (1996) "Does Financial Development Cause Economic Growth? Time Series Evidence from 16 Countries", *Journal of Development Economics*, 51, 2, 387-411.

Demigric-Kunt, A., L. Klapper, D. Singer and P. Van Oudheusden (2015) "The Global Findex Database: Measuring Financial Inclusion Around the World", World Bank Policy Reaserch Working Paper No.7255, World Bank.

Desai, S. and S. Alva (1998) "Maternal Education and Child Health: Is There a Strong Casual Relationship?", *Demography*, 35, 1, 71-81.

Di Tella, R. and R. MacCulloch (2002) "The Consequence of Labor Market Flexibility: Panel Evidence Based on Survey Data", *European Economic Review*, 49, 1225-1259.

Dickey, D. and W.A. Fuller (1979) "Distribution of the Estimators for Autoregressive Time Series with a Unit Root", *Journal of the American Statistical Association*, 74, 366, 427-431.

Dickey, D.A and W.A. Fuller (1981) "Likelihood Ratio Statistics for Autoregressive Time Series", *Econometrica*, 49, 4, 1057-1072.

Diks, C. and V. Panchenko (2006) "A New Statistic and Practical Guidelines for Nonparametric Granger Causality Testing", *Journal of Economic Dynamics and Control*, 30, 9-10, 1647-1669.

Diog, A. and S. McIvor (1999) "Corruption and Its Control in the Development Context: An Analysis and Selective Review of Literature", *Third World Quarterly*, 20, 3, 357-376.

Donnelly, R. and E. Sheehy (1996) "The Share Price Reaction of U.K. Exporters to Exchange Rate Movements", *Journal of International Business Studies*, 27, 1, 157-165.

Dornbusch, R. and S. Fischer (1980) "Exchange Rates and the Current Account", *American Economic Review*, 70, 5, 960-971.

Dutta, N., S. Kar and S. Roy (2013) "Informal Sector and Corruption: An Empirical Investigation for India", *International Review of Economics and Finance*, 27, 357-373.

Dutta, P. (2017) "Measuring Financial Inclusion in West Bengal: Policy Framework for Inclusive Growth", *Great Lakes Herald*, 11, 1, 39-59.

Easterlin, R.A. (1974) "Does Economic Growth Improve the Human Lot? Some Empirical Evidence", in P.A. David and M.W. Reder (eds.): *Nations and Households in Economic Growth*, New York: Academic Press, 89-125.

Edgerton, J.D., L.W. Roberts and S. von Below (2012) "Education and Quality of Life", in K.C. Land, A.C. Michalos and M.J. Sirgy (eds.): *Handbook of Social Indicators and Quality of Life Research*, Dordrecht: Springer, 265-296.

Edmark, K. (2005) "Unemployment and Crime: Is There a Connection", *Scandinavian Journal of Economics*, 107, 2, 353-373.

Ehrlich, I. (1996) "Crime, Punishment, and Market for Offences", *Journal of Economic Perspectives*, 10, 1, 43-67.

Elliott, C. and D. Ellingworth (1996) "The Relationship between Unemployment and Crime: A Cross Sectional Analysis Employing the British Crime Survey 1992", *International Journal of Management*, 17, 6/7, 81-88.

Emokaro, C.O. and O. Dibiah (2014) "Demand Analysis for Chicken Meat, Beef and Fish Among Urban Households in Edo and Delta States, Nigeria", *Journal of Applied and Natural Science*, 6, 1, 239-245.

Engel, R.F. and C.W.J. Granger (1987) "Co-Integration and Error Correction: Representation, Estimation, and Testing", *Econometrica*, 55, 2, 251-276.

Enofe, A.O., A. Oriaifoh, I. Akolo and C.L. Oriaifoh (2016) "Corruption and Nigeria Economic Growth", *International journal of Advanced Academic Research,* 2, 4, 26-35.

Eozenou, P. (2008) "The Determinants of Private Transfers in Rural Vietnam", mimeo, IFPRI and European University Institute.

Etzo, I. (2011) "The Determinants of the Recent Interregional Migration Flows in Italy: A Panel Data Analysis", *Journal of Regional Science*, 51, 5, 948-966.

Ewah, S.O.E, A.E. Esang and J.U. Bassey (2009) "Appraisal of Capital Market Efficiency on Economic Growth in Nigeria", *International Journal of Business and Management*, 4, 12, 219-228.

Fanta, A. and K. Mutsonziwa (2016) "Gender and Financial Inclusion: Analysis of Financial Inclusion of Women in the SADC Region", Johannesburg, South Africa: Finmark Trust for CGAP.

Fattahi, M. (2015) "The Role of Urbanization Rate in the Relationship between Air Pollution and Health Expenditures: A Dynamic Panel Data Approach", *International Letter of Society Humanist Science*, 53, 68-72.

Fattahi, M., A. Assari, H. Sadeghi and H. Agharpour (2013) "Air Pollution and Public Health Expenditure: Compare Developed and Developing Countries", *Journal of Economic Development Research*, 11, 3, 111-132.

Fernandez, R. (2003) "Sorting, Education and Inequality", in M. Dewatripont, L.P. Hansen and S.J. Turnovsky (eds.): Advances in Economics and Econometrics: Theory and Applications, Cambridge: Cambridge University Press, 1-40.

Fialova, K. (2011) "Labor Market Institutions and Their Effect on Labor Market Performance in OECD and European Countries", World Bank Working Paper No. 103794.

Fischer, S. (1993) "The Role of Macroeconomic Factors in Growth", *Journal of Monetary Economics*, 32, 3, 485-512.

Forshaw, J., S.M. Gerver, M. Gill, E. Cooper, L. Manikam and H. Ward (2017) "The Global Effect of Maternal Education on Complete Childhood Vaccination: A Systematic Review and Meta-analysis", *BioMed Central: Infectious Diseases*, 17, Article 801, 1-16.

Frankel J.A. (1983) "Monetary and Portfolio Balance Models of Exchange Rate Determination", in J.S. Bhandari and B.H. Putnam (eds.): *Economic Interdependence and Flexible Exchange Rates*, Cambridge: MIT Press, 84-114.

Frederiksen, H. (1966) "Determinants and Consequences of Mortality and Fertility Trends", *Public Health Report*, 81, 8, 715-727.

Freeman, R. (1999) "The Economics of Crime", in O. Ashen felter and D. Card (eds.): *Handbook of Labor Economics, Volume 3, Part C*, Amsterdam: Elsevier, 3529-3571.

Frey, B.S. and A. Stutzer (2005) "Happiness Research: State and Prospects", *Review of Social Economy*, 63, 2, 207-228.

Gandhi, V.P. and Y.Z. Zhang (2010) "Rising Demand for Livestock Products in India: Nature, Patterns and Implications", *Australasian Agribusiness Review*, 18, 1, 1-32.

Gangal, V.L.N. and H. Gupta (2013) "Public Expenditure and Economic Growth A Case Study of India", *Global Journal of Management and Business Studies*, 3, 2, 191-196.

Gerdtham, U.-G. and M. Johannesson (2004) "Absolute Income, Relative Income, Income Inequality and Mortality", *Journal of Human Resources*, 39, 1, 228-247.

Gertler, P. and P. Glewwe (1989) *The Willingness to Pay for Education in Developing Countries: Evidence from Rural Peru*, Living Standards Measurement Study WP54, World Bank, Washington, D.C.

Ghatak, S., A. Mulhern and J. Watson (2008) "Inter-Regional Migration in Transition Economies: The Case of Poland", *Review of Development Economics*, 12, 1, 209-222.

Ghosh, S. (2010) "Examining Carbon Emission Economic Growth Nexus for India: A Multivariate Cointegration Approach", *Energy Policy*, 38, 6, 3008- 3014.

Gitaharie, B., L. Soelistianingsih and T. Djutaharta (2014) "Financial Inclusion: Household Access to Credit in Indonesia", Working Paper No. 201401, Faculty of Economics and business, University of Indonesia.

Glewee, P.W. (1991) *The Economics of School Quality Investments in Developing Countries: An Empirical Study of Ghana*, London: MacMillan Press.

Glewwe, P.W. (2002) "Schools and Skills in Developing Countries: Education Policies and Socioeconomic Outcomes", *Journal of Economic Literature*, 40, 2, 436-482.

Goa, G., B. Liu and I. Kouassi (2017) "The Contemporaneous Effect of Unemployment on Crime Rates: The Case of Indiana", *Southwestern Economic Review*, 44, 99-108.

Godfrey, L.G. (1978) "Testing Against General Autoregressive and Moving Average Error Models When the Regressors Include Lagged Dependent Variables", *Econometrica*, 45, 6, 1293-1301.

Goldberg, J. and J. Smith (2008) "The Effects of Education on Labour Market Outcomes", in E. Fiske and H. Ladd (eds.): *Handbook of Education Finance and Policy*, London: Routledge, 730-742.

Goldsmith, R.W. (1969) *Financial Structure and Development*, New Haven: Yale University Press.

Gould, B.W. (2002) "Household Composition and Food Expenditure in China", *Agribusiness*, 18, 3, 387-402.

Government of India (2012) "Household Consumer Expenditure Survey, NSSO 68th Round", Ministry of Statistics and Programme Implementation, GOI.

Government of India (2014) *National Health Mission*, Ministry of Health and Family Welfare, Government of India.

Granger, C.W.J. (1969) "Investigating Causal Relations by Econometric Models and Cross-Spectral Methods", *Econometrica*, 37, 3, 424-438.

Granger, C.W.J., B.-N. Huang and Ch-W. Yang (2000) "A Bivariate Causality between Stock Prices and Exchange Rates: Evidence from Recent Asianflu", *Quarterly Review of Economics and Finance*, 40, 3, 337-354.

Greenwood, J. and B.D. Smith (1997) "Financial Markets in Development and the Development of Financial Markets", *Journal of Economic Dynamics and Control*, 21, 1, 145-181.

Greenwood, J., N. Guner, G. Kocharkov and C. Santos (2014) "Marry Your Like: Assortative Mating and Income Inequality", *American Economic Review*, 104, 5, 348-353.

Greenwood, M.J. (1985) "Human Migration: Theory, Models, and Empirical Studies", *Journal of Regional Science*, 25, 4, 521-544.

Griliches, Z. (1977a) "Estimating the Returns to Schooling: Some Econometric Problems", *Econometrica*, 45, 1, 1-22.

Griliches, Z. (1977b) "Education, Income, and Ability: Rejoinder", *Journal of Political Economy*, 85, 1, 215.

Griliches, Z. and W.M. Mason (1972) "Education, Income, and Ability", *Journal of Political Economy*, 80, 3, S74-S103.

Gur, B. (2015) "An Analysis of Unemployment Determinants in BRIC Countries", *International Journal of Business and Social Science*, 6, 1, 192-198.

Hadri, K. (2000) "Testing for Unit Roots in Heterogeneous Panel Data", *Econometrics Journal*, 3, 2, 148-161.

Haines, M.R. (1998) *From Death to Birth, Mortality Decline and Reproductive Change,* Washington D.C.: National Academy Press.

Hajdu, T. and G. Hajdu (2014) "Income and Subjective Well Being: How Important is the Methodology", *Hungarian Statistical Review, Special Number 18*, 110-127.

Halkos, G.E. and M.K. Trigoni (2010) "Financial Development and Economic Growth: Evidence from the European Union", *Managerial Finance*, 36, 11, 949-957.

Hanushek, E.A. and L. Wobmann (2010) "Education and Economic Growth", in P. Peterson, E. Baker and B. McGraw (eds.): *International Encyclopaedia of Education, Volume 2*, Oxford: Elsevier, 245-252.

Hau, H. and H. Rey (2006) "Exchange Rates, Equity Prices, and Capital Flows", *Review of Financial Studies*, 19, 1, 273-317.

Hauser, R.M., J.R. Warren, M.-H. Huang and W.Y. Carter (2000) "Occupational Status, Education, and Social Mobility in the Meritocracy", in K. Arrow, S. Bowles and S. Durlauf (eds.): *Meritocracy and Economic Inequality*, Princeton: Princeton University Press, 179-229.

Hausman, J. (1978) "Specification Tests in Econometrics", *Econometrica*, 6, 46, 1251-1271.

Hobcraft, J.N., J.W. Mcdonald and S.O. Rutstein (1984) "Socio-Economic Factors in Infant and Child Mortality: A Cross-National Comparison", *Population Studies*, 38, 2, 193-223.

Hossain, Md.S. (2011) "Panel Estimation for CO_2 Emissions, Energy Consumption, Economic Growth, Trade Openness and Urbanization of Newly Industrialized Countries", *Energy Policy*, 39, 11, 6991-6999.

Huang, E.L-H. and J.H.-Y.Huang (2013) "Labor Market Reforms on the Unemployment Rate and Wage Payments in Europe", *Empirical Economic Letters*, 12, 1365-1374.

Hupkova, D. and P. Bielik (2009) "Estimating Demand Elasticities of Meat Demand in Slovakia", *Acta Agriculturae Scandinavica, Section C- Economy*, 7.

Hussain, M.N. (2014) "Empirical Econometric Analysis of Relationship between Fiscal-Monetary Policies and Output on SAARC Countries", *Journal of Developing Areas*, 48, 4, 209-224.

Im, K.S., M.H. Pesaran and Y. Shin (2003) "Testing for Unit Roots in Heterogeneous Panels", *Journal of Econometrics*, 115, 1, 53-74.

Inglehart, R., R. Foa, C. Peterson and C. Welzel (2008) "Development, Freedom and Rising Happiness: A Global Perspective", *Perspectives on Psychological Science*, 3, 264-285.

Jagadeesh Babu, A., A. Rupa Sundari, G. Triveni and J. Indumathi (2010) "Study on Meat Consumption Patterns in Rural Households of Chittor District of A.P", *Tamilnadu Journal of Veterinary & Animal Sciences*, 6, 4,183-187.

Jarque, C.M. and A.K. Bera (1980) "Efficient Tests for Normality, Homoskedasticity and Serial Independence of Regression Residuals", *Economic Letters*, 6, 3, 255-259.

Jarque, C.M. and A.K. Bera (1987) "A Test for Normality of Observations and Regression Residuals", *International Statistical Review*, 55, 2, 163-172.

Jegajeevan, S. (2012) "Return Volatility and Asymmetric News Effect in Sri Lankan Stock Market", *Staff Studies, Central Bank of Sri Lanka*, 40, 1, 37-57.

Jency, S. (2017) "Trends of Capital Market in India", *International Journal of Economics and Management Studies*, 4, 3, 15-19.

Jerrett, M., J. Eyles, C. Dufournaud and S. Birch (2003) "Environmental Influences on Healthcare Expenditures: An Exploratory Analysis from Ontario, Canada", *Journal of Epidemiology and Community Health*",57, 5, 334-338.

Jie, H. (2008) "Industrialization, Environment and Health: The Impacts of Industrial SO_2 Emission on Public Health in China", *Chinese Journal of Population Resources and Environment*, 6, 1, 14-24.

Jirata, M.T., J.C. Chelule and R.O. Odhiambo (2014) "Deriving Some Estimators of Panel Data Regression Models with Individual Effects", *International Journal of Science and Research*, 3, 5, 53-59.

Johansen, S. (1988) "Statistical Analysis of Cointegrating Vectors", *Journal of Economic Dynamics and Control*, 12, 2-3, 231-254.

Johansen, S. and K. Juselius (1990) "Maximum Likelihood Estimation and Inference on Cointegration - With Applications to the Demand for Money", *Oxford Bulletin of Economics and Statistics*, 52, 2, 169-210.

Jorion, P. (1990) "*The Exchange Rate Exposure of US Multinationals", Journal of Business*, 63, 3, 331-345.

Jorion, P. (1991) "*The Pricing of Exchange Rate Risk in the Stock Market", Journal of Financial and Quantitative Analysis*, 26, 3, 363-376.

Joseph, N. (2002) "Modelling the Impacts of Interest Rate and Exchange Rate Changes on UK Stock Returns", *Derivatives Use, Trading and Regulation*, 7, 4, 306-323.

Jung, J. and W.W. Koo (2000) "AN Econometric Analysis of Demand for Meat and Fish Products in Korea", Agricultural Economics Report No. 439.

Kar, S. and K. Mandal (2014) "Re-examining the Finance-Growth Relationship for a Developing Economy: A Time Series Analysis of Post-Reform India", *Journal of Developing Areas*, 48, 1, 83-105.

Karli, B. and A. Bilgic (2007) "Factor Affecting Meat and Meat Products Consumption Quantities in Sanliurfa Province, Turkey", *Akdeniz Universitesi Ziraat Fakultesi Dergisi*, 20, 1, 127-136.

Karoui, A. (2006) "The Correlation between FX Rate Volatility and Stock Exchange Returns Volatility: An Emerging Markets Overview", Paper presented at 13th Global finance Conference, Ottawa, Canada.

Karunanayake, I., A. Valadkhani and M. O'Brien (2010) "Financial Crises and International Stock Volatility Transmission", *Australian Economic Papers*, 49, 3, 209-221.

Kaufmann, D. (1997) "Corruption: Some Myths and Facts", *Foreign Policy*, 114-131.

Kavithaa, N.V., N. Vimal Rajkumar and C.M. Sree Lakshmi (2014) "A Study on the Season-wise Variation Consumption Behaviour of Meat in Erode District of Tamil Nadu", *International Journal of Science, Environment and Technology*, 3, 4, 1412-1414.

Kehinde, A.O., I.S. Ademola, I.K. Kayode, A.O. Felix and O.O. Musibau (2013) "Capital Market and Economic Growth in Nigeria - An Empirical Analysis", *Journal of Humanities and Social Science*, 6, 6, 60-68.

Keynes, J.M. (1936) *The General Theory of Employment, Interest and Money*, London: Palgrave Macmillan.

Khan, H.R. (2011) "Financial Inclusion and Financial Stability: Are They Two Sides of the Same Coin?", Address at BANCON (Indian Bankers Association and Indian Overseas Bank Conference), Chennai, November 4, 2011.

Khan, M.S. and A.S. Senhadji (2003) "Financial Development and Economic Growth: An Overview", *Journal of African Economics*, 12, *Supplement 2*, ii89-ii110.

Khan, M.T., S. Zaheer and K. Shafique (2017) "Maternal Education, Empoerment, Economic Status and Child Polio Vaccination Uptake in Pakistan", *British Medical Journal Open*, 7, e013853, 1-7.

Khan, R.E.A. and R. Ali (2015) "Causality Analysis of Volatility in Exchange Rate and Stock Market Prices: A Case Study of Pakistan", *Asian Economic and financial Review*, 5, 5, 805-815.

Khemani, S. (2007) "Does Delegation of Fiscal Policy to an Independent Agency Make a Difference? Evidence from Intergovernmental Transfers in India", *Journal of Development Economics*, 82, 2, 464-484.

Kim, K. (2003) "Dollar Exchange Rate and Stock Price: Evidence from Multivariate Cointegration and Error Correction Model", *Review of Financial Economics*, 12, 3, 301-313.

Kim., S.S., J.A. Frimpong, P.A. Rivers and J.J. Kronenfeld (2007) "Effects of Maternal and Provider Characteristics on Up-to-Date Immunization Status of Children Aged 19 to 35 Months", *American Jornal of Public Health*, 97, 2, 259-266.

King, R.G. and R. Levine (1993) "Finance, Entrepreneurship, and Growth: Theory and Evidence", *Journal of Monetary Economics*, 32, 3, 513-542.

Klein, R. and F. Vella (2010) "Estimating a Class of Triangular Simultaneous Equations Models Without Exclusion Restrictions", *Journal of Econometrics*, 154, 2, 154-164.

Koenker, R. (2005) *Quantile Regression*, Cambridge: Cambridge University Press.

Koenker, R. (2004) "Quantile Regression for Longitudinal Data", *Journal of Multivariate Analysis*, 91, 1, 74-89.

Koenker, R. (2017) "Quantile Regression: 40 Years On", *Annual Review of Economics*, 9, 155-176.

Koenker, R. and G. Bassett (1978) "Regression Quantiles", *Econometrica*, 46, 1, 33-50.

Koenker, R. and K.F. Hallock (2001) "Quantile Regression" *Journal of Economic Perspectives*, 15, 4, 143-156.

Krueger, A.B. and M. Lindahl (2001) "Education for Growth: Why and For Whom?", *Journal of Economic Literature*, 39, 4, 1101-1136.

Kumar, P. and S.C. Aggarwal (2003) "An Econometric Analysis of Causes of Migration in Assam", *Demography India*, 32, 1, 107-122.

Lakshmanasamy, T. (1988a) *Economics of Farm Families: An Econometric Analysis of the Demand for Children*, Ph.D. Thesis, Department of Econometrics, University of Madras, Chennai.

Lakshmanasamy, T. (1988b) "Economic Utility and the Demand for Children: A Theoretical and Empirical Analysis", *Artha Vijnana*, 30, 4, 421-453.

Lakshmanasamy, T. (1989a) "Economic Contribution of Rural Children and the Family Fertility Behaviour: A Rationale for High Fertility in India", *Asian Economic Review*, 31, 1, 51-78.

Lakshmanasamy, T. (1989b) "Old Age, Risk, Security and Children: An Empirical Evidence from Rural India", *Indian Journal of Economics*, 70, 276, 51-68.

Lakshmanasamy, T. (1990) "Family Survival Strategy and Migration: An Analysis of Returns to Migration", *Indian Journal of Social Work*, 51, 3, 473-485.

Lakshmanasamy, T. (1991a) "Income Smoothing, Risk and the Family: Household Relationships as Risk Diversification Strategy", *Journal of Social and Economic Studies*, 63-79.

Lakshmanasamy, T. (1991b) "Hours of Work of Rural Children: Its Determinants and Effect on Fertility", *Indian Journal of Labour Economics*, 34, 1, 54-59.

Lakshmanasamy, T. (1991c) "Demand for Children in Rural Families: Children as Consumption Utility", *Journal of Family Welfare*, 37, 4, 3-12.

Lakshmanasamy, T. (1991d) "Intergenerational Transfers and Wealth Accumulation: Motivations for Savings and the Effects of Annuities", *Indian Journal of Economics*, 71, 283, 465-487.

Lakshmanasamy, T. (1991e) "Risk, Consumption Smoothing and the Family: Portfolio Management of Children and Assets in Rural Families", *Artha Vijnana*, 33, 4, 24-40.

Lakshmanasamy, T. (1991f) "The Demand for Children: A Survey", *Asian Economic Review*, 33, 1, 49-102.

Lakshmanasamy, T. (1991g) "The Family, Risk and Self-Insurance: An Application of Portfolio Selection Model", *Indian Journal of Social Science*, 4, 4, 567-589.

Lakshmanasamy, T. (1991h) "Agricultural Modernisation, Risk, and Migration: Family Strategy for Innovation", in J. Mahender Reddy and S. Kisan Rao (eds.): *Agricultural Development and Rural-Urban Disparities*, New Delhi: Sterling Publishers, 153-165.

Lakshmanasamy, T. (1992) "Income Smoothing, Risk and the Family: Inter-and Intra-Family Relationships as Risk Diversification Strategy", *Indian Economic Journal*, 39, 4, 30-43.

Lakshmanasamy, T. (1993a) "Intrafamily Relations, Migration and Remittances", *Artha Vijnana*, 35, 1, 86-94.

Lakshmanasamy, T. (1993b) "Hours of work of Rural Children: Its Determinants and Effects on Fertility", in B.P.Singh and S.Mahanty (eds.): *Children at Work: Problems and Policy Issues*, New Delhi: B.R. Publishing House, 153-163.

Lakshmanasamy, T. (1993c) "Economic Valuation of Pristine Quality: Some Issues", in Anil Agarwal (ed.): *The Challenge of the Balance: Environmental Economics in India*, New Delhi: Centre for Science and Environment, 42-45.

Lakshmanasamy, T. (1997a) "Educational Infrastructure and Economic Benefits in Tamil Nadu", *IEA 1st Amrit Jubilee (80th) Conference Volume*, 803-810.

Lakshmanasamy, T. (1997b) *Economics of Human Behaviour: Essays in Honour of A.M. Nalla Gounden*, New Delhi: Allied Publishers.

Lakshmanasamy, T. (2000a) "The Household Costs and Willingness to Pay for Higher Education", *Journal of Educational Planning and Administration*, 14, 2, 187-196.

Lakshmanasamy, T. (2000b) "The Economics of Corruption and Development", *IEA Conference (83rd) Volume of the Millennium*, 2000, 681-688.

Lakshmanasamy, T. (2000c) "Education and Economic Growth in a Knowledge Based Economy", in K.B.Powar (ed.): *Higher Education for Human Development*, New Delhi: Association of Indian Universities, 166-181.

Lakshmanasamy, T. (2001a) "Education, Search, Matching and Age at Marriage of Females", *Asian-African Journal of Economics and Econometrics*, 1, 1, 63-77.

Lakshmanasamy, T. (2001b) "Microeconometrics of Selective Samples and Discrete Choice: Contributions of Heckman and McFadden for the Analysis of Microdata", in Department of Economics, Annamalai University (ed.): *Papers on James J.Heckman and Daniel L.McFadden: Nobel Laureates in Economics - 2000*, Annamalai University, 1-25.

Lakshmanasamy, T. (2001c) "The Economics of Corruption and Development", in D.Narasimha Reddy (ed.): *Crime, Corruption and Development*, New Delhi: Deep & Deep Publishers, 24-34.

Lakshmanasamy, T. (2002a) "Nash Bargained Household Decisions: Testing the Economic Models of Family in India", *Indian Economic Journal*, 50, 3-4, 99-115.

Lakshmanasamy, T. (2002b) "Imperfect Information, Knowledge and Development", *IEA 85th Conference Volume*, 135-147.

Lakshmanasamy, T. (2002c) "A Test for the Economic Empowerment of Women", in A.Ranga Reddy (ed.): *Empowerment of Women and Ecological Development*, New Delhi: Serials Publications, 353-373.

Lakshmanasamy, T. (2002d) "Human Capital: An Infrastructure for Economic Growth", in S.Murty (ed.): *Infrastructure and Social Sector Development for Economic Growth*, Jaipur: RBSA Publishers, 91-109.

Lakshmanasamy, T. (2003a) "New Information, New Institutions and Economic Development", *Asian Economic Review*, 45, 3, 425-439.

Lakshmanasamy, T. (2003b) "Testing the Unitary and Nash Bargaining Household Models in India", *Indian Journal of Social and Economic Development*, 5, 2, 197-217.

Lakshmanasamy, T. (2003c) "The Microeconometrics of Selective Samples and Discrete Choice", *India Development Review*, 1, 1, 47-63.

Lakshmanasamy, T. (2003d) "Nash Bargained Household Decisions: Testing the Economic Models of Family in India", *Indian Economic Journal*, 50, 3&4, 99-115.

Lakshmanasamy, T. (2003e) "Household Costs and Willingness to Pay for Higher Education", in J.B.G.Tilak (ed.): *Financing Education in India*, Delhi: Ravi Books, 255-266.

Lakshmanasamy, T. (2003f) "Economic Empowerment of Women: Implications for Household Decision Making Process", in G.Vidya Rani, H.Grija Rani and V.Bhagyalaxmi (eds.): *Status of Women: Post Independence Era*, Warangal: A.S.M. College of Women, 133-148.

Lakshmanasamy, T. (2004a) "Some Critical Issues in Financing of Higher Education", *Perspectives in Education*, 29, 1, 5-22.

Lakshmanasamy, T. (2004b) "Willingness to Pay for Higher Education: An Econometric Analysis using Contingent Valuation Method", *Indian Educational Review*, 40, 2, 3-23.

Lakshmanasamy, T. (2004c) "New Institutions and Economic Development: The Significance of Governance and Social Capital for Economic Growth", *Indian Journal of Economics*, 75, 336, 65-94.

Lakshmanasamy, T. (2004d) "Intergenerational Mobility of Income and Education in India", *Quantonomics*, 1, 1, 9-19.

Lakshmanasamy, T. (2004e) "Social Capital, Institutions and Development", in G.Gopal Reddy and T.L.N.Swamy (eds.): *Institutional Policy Options for Sustainable Agricultural Development*, Hyderabad: Department of Economics, Osmania University, 88-99.

Lakshmanasamy, T. (2005a) "The Economic Theory of Bribery and Corruption", in A. Ranga Reddy (ed.): *Dimensions of Crime and Corruption in India*, New Delhi: Serials Publications, 128-144.

Lakshmanasamy, T. (2005b) "Modernisation and Development: Institutional Reforms under Globalisation", in S. Narsimhan and D.Y. Kim (eds.): *Korea and India: A Forging Relationship*, New Delhi: Manak Publications, 2005, 45-77.

Lakshmanasamy, T. (2006a) "Women's Education, Dowry, Bargaining and Gains to Marriage", *Journal of Educational Planning and Administration*, 20, 1, 27-51.

Lakshmanasamy, T. (2006b) "Demand for Higher Education and Willingness to Pay: An Econometric Analysis using Contingent Valuation Method", *Manpower Journal*, 41, 1, 97-120.

Lakshmanasamy, T. (2006c) "Imperfect Information, Institutions and Development", in D.M. Nachane and B. Chatterjee (eds.): *Economics of Asymmetric Information*, New Delhi: Deep & Deep Publishers, 46-63.

Lakshmanasamy, T. (2007a) "Social Capital, Economic Reforms and Economic Development", in A. Banerjee and R. Arunachalam (eds.): *Indian Economic Reforms and Response of States*, New Delhi: Kanishka Publishers, 260-280.

Lakshmanasamy, T. (2007b) "Women's Education, Dowry, Bargaining and Gains to Marriage", in J.B.G.Tilak (ed.): *Women's Education and Development*, Delhi: Gyan Publishers, 249-281.

Lakshmanasamy, T. (2008a) "Agglomeration Economies, New Economic Geography and Industry Clusters", *Indian Geographical Journal*, 83, 2, 105-120.

Lakshmanasamy, T. (2008b) "Social Exclusion and Inclusion: Meaning, Identification and Strategy", *Journal of Development and Social Change*, 5, 1-2, 193-212.

Lakshmanasamy, T. (2008c) "Understanding Social Exclusion and Empowering for Inclusion", in R.G. Dange (ed.): *Social Exclusion and Inclusive Policies in South Asia*, Kolhapur: Shivaji University, 1-9.

Lakshmanasamy, T. (2009a) "Unequal Chances: The Intergenerational Transmission of Economic Advantage under Marital Sorting" in B. Dutta,T. Ray and E. Somanathan (eds.): *New and Enduring Themes in Development Economics*, New York: World Scientific Publishing, 41-56.

Lakshmanasamy, T. (2009b) "Equality among the Unequal: Choice vs Luck under Individual Heterogeneity and Non-Subordination in Economic Distribution", *International Research Journal of Social Sciences*, 2, 2, 253-271.

Lakshmanasamy, T. (2009c) "Women in Business: Human Capital versus Family Background", *Annamalai Economic Papers*, 20-29.

Lakshmanasamy, T. (2009d) "Financing the Poor and Marginalised: Financial Institutions vs Microfinance", *Journal of Development and Social Change*, 6, 3&4, 59-69.

Lakshmanasamy, T. (2009e) "Social Justice and Welfare State: Including the Excluded", in G. Bhadru Naik and V. Rajasekhar (eds.): *Reservations in the Era of Globalization and Privatization – Emerging Trends and Issues*, Hyderabad: Sree Bhagavan Publications, 2009, 31-47.

Lakshmanasamy, T. (2009f) "Equality and Social Justice: Opportunity vs Choice under Disadvantage", in G. Bhadru Naik and V. Rajasekhar (eds.): *Dr. B.R. Ambedkar's Philosophy of Social Justice and Its Relevance*, Hyderabad: Sree Bhagavan Publications, 76-91.

Lakshmanasamy, T. (2009g) "Innovations, Patents, Spillovers and Development: A Panel Data Analysis of R&D Expenditure and Economic Growth in India", *Indian Geographical Journal*, 84, 1, 29-48.

Lakshmanasamy, T. (2010a) "Are You Satisfied with Your Income? The Economics of Happiness in India", *Journal of Quantitative Economics*, 8, 2, 115-141.

Lakshmanasamy, T. (2010b) "Global ICT Revolution and the Indian Service Sector Growth", *Journal of Development and Social Change*, 7, 1&2, 14-33.

Lakshmanasamy, T. (2010c) "Corruption, Inequality and Poverty: Cracking the Guardian Knot through a Smart Card", in S. Sarkar (ed.): *Tackling Poverty Challenges: Key Approaches and Policy Implications*, Germany: Lambert Academic Publishing.

Lakshmanasamy, T. (2010d) "Positional Aspirations, Relative Income and Happiness: Money and Well-Being under Status Comparison" in G.B. Naik and V. Rajasekhar (eds.): *Buddhism: World Harmony and Peace*, Hyderabad: Sree Bhagavan Publications, 262-284.

Lakshmanasamy, T. (2010e) "Agglomeration Economies and Industry Clusters", in E.M. Thomas and C.J. Unny (eds.): *Industrial Growth Through Clusters*, Department of Economics, Christ College, Irinjalakuda, Thrissur, Kerala, .7-25.

Lakshmanasamy, T. (2010f) "Expanding Opportunity, Widening Inequality and Worsening Income Distribution under Economic (Market) Globalization", in A.K. Thakur and P. Singh (eds.): *Globalisation – Inclusive Growth and Indian Economy: Issues and Policies*, New Delhi: Regal Publications, 1-29.

Lakshmanasamy, T. (2010g) *Population Dynamics and Human Development: Opportunities and Challenges*, Delhi: Bookwell Publishers.

Lakshmanasamy, T. (2010h) "The Poor and Financial Inclusion: A Panel Quantile Regression Analysis of Banking Services in Indian States", *Indian Geographical Journal,* 85, 2, 115-130.

Lakshmanasamy, T. (2011a) "Expanding Opportunity, Widening Inequality and Worsening Income Distribution under Economic (Market) Globalisation", in P. Arunachalam (ed.) *Mahatma Gandhi National Rural Employment Guarantee Programme and Poverty in India*, New Delhi: Serials Publications, 214-242.

Lakshmanasamy, T. (2011b) "Innovations, Patents, Spillovers and Development: A Panel Data Analysis of R&D Expenditure and Economic Growth in India", *Indian Geographical Journal*, 86, 1, June 2011.

Lakshmanasamy, T. (2011c) "The Poor and Financial Inclusion: A Panel Quantile Regression Analysis of Banking Services in Indian States", *Indian Geographical Journal*, 86, 2, December 2011.

Lakshmanasamy, T. (2012a) "Ageing and Security: Savings and Transfers Behaviour of Indian Households", *Indian Journal of Gerontology*, 26, 4, 484-501.

Lakshmanasamy, T. (2012b) "Are Indian Households Impurely Altruistic? Testing for Bequest Motives and Intergenerational Transfers in India", *Indian Economic Journal*, 60, 1, 39-66.

Lakshmanasamy, T. (2012c) "Neuroeconomics: The Science of the Art of Decision Making", *Asian Economic Review*, 54, 1, 49-98.

Lakshmanasamy, T. (2012d) "Economic Development and Transition of Youths: Differential Perceptions of Changing Lifestyles and Behaviour of Youths in India", *Indian Journal of Youth Affairs*, 16, 2, 114-129.

Lakshmanasamy, T. (2012e) "Connecting the Poor to Economic Prosperity", in N. Mani (eds.): *Paradox of Poverty and Economic Prosperity*, New Delhi: Serials Publications, 16-35.

Lakshmanasamy, T. (2012f) "Digital Governance: Potential Uses of NPR and UID as Smart Card for Economic Efficiency", *International Journal of Management Research and Technology*, 6, 1, 101-113.

Lakshmanasamy, T. (2012g) "Savings and Wealth Transfers to Children: An Econometric Analysis of Intergenerational Transfers in India", *Indian Geographical Journal*, 87, 2, 108-137.

Lakshmanasamy, T. (2012h) "Savings and Wealth Transfers to Children: An Econometric Analysis of Intergenerational Transfers in India", *Indian Geographical Journal,* 87, 2, 108-137.

Lakshmanasamy, T. (2013a) "Team Capital and Productivity: A Panel Analysis of the Effect of Unit Specific Nursing Care on Patient Outcome", *Artha Vijnana*, 55, 3, 252-271.

Lakshmanasamy, T. (2013b) "How Deep Are Caste Discrimination and Social Exclusion? Methodologies for Measuring Economic Deprivation of Dalits", *Indian Journal of Dalit and Tribal Studies and Action*, 1, 1, 18-34.

Lakshmanasamy, T. (2013c) "So Near Yet So Far! The Elusive Quest for the Engines of Economic Growth", *Shanlax International Journal of Economics*, 1, 2, 82-90.

Lakshmanasamy, T. (2013d) "Health Capital and the Rights to Health Care", *Shanlax International Journal of Economics, Special Issue on Health Economics*, 98-109.

Lakshmanasamy, T. (2014a) *Economics of Household Non-Market Behaviour: Analysis of Household Relations and Decisions*, Delhi: Bookwell Publishers.

Lakshmanasamy, T. (2014b) "From Wealth of Nations to Wealth of Relations: The Power of Social Networks and the Small World of Economics", *Indian Journal of Economics*. 95, 376, 93-177.

Lakshmanasamy, T. (2014c) "Is Economics in Genes? The Genoeconomics of Economic Behaviour and Economic Development", *Indian Economic Journal*, 61, 4, 593-625.

Lakshmanasamy, T. (2015a) *Economics of Growth, Inequality, Institutions and Development: Reforms, Social Capital, Inclusion and Distribution*, Delhi: Bookwell Publishers.

Lakshmanasamy, T. (2015b) *Applied Microeconometrics of Human Decisions*, Delhi: Bookwell Publishers.

Lakshmanasamy, T. (2015c) "Economic Challenges of Greying Population: Problem or Predicament?", *Ageing and Society: The Indian Journal of Gerontology*, 25, 1-2, 1-26.

Lakshmanasamy, T. (2015d) "Economics of Business Networks: Theory and Empirics of the Structure and Properties of the Network among Trading Firms", *Artha Vijnana*, 57, 1, 49-79.

Lakshmanasamy, T. (2015e) "The Effect of Monsoon Rainfall Shortage on Farmer Suicides in India: A Panel Data Econometric Analysis", *Indian Geographical Journal*, 94, 1, 14-25.

Lakshmanasamy, T. (2015f) "Why the Apple Doesn't Fall for the Poor? The Elusive Invisible Veil between the Poor and the Economic Prosperity", mimeo, Department of Econometrics, University of Madras.

Lakshmanasamy, T. (2016) "Does Conditional Aid Promote Performance? A Regression Discontinuity Analysis of the Impact of GAVI Alliance on Immunisation in Developing Countries", *ArthaVijnana*, 58, 1, 19-55.

Lakshmanasamy, T. (2017a) "Demand for Private Tuition: A Quantile Regression Analysis of Household Expenditure on Private Coaching in India", *Journal of Educational Planning and Administration*, 31, 2, 115-139.

Lakshmanasamy, T. (2017b) "Empirics of Dynamic Network in Actor-Oriented Model: Panel Estimation of the Parameters of Co-evolution of Network and Behavior Effects in Business Relations", *South Asian Journal of Management*, 24, 2, 136-168.

Lakshmanasamy, T. (2018a) "Sex Discrimination in India: A Two Step Estimation and Decomposition of Gender Wage Gap in the Labour Market", *Labour and Development*, 25, 1, 35-58.

Lakshmanasamy, T. (2018b) "Are Commercial Banks in India Technically Efficient? A Multiple Output - Multiple Input Technology Panel Stochastic Ray Frontier Function Estimation", *WEALTH - International Journal of Money, Banking and Finance*, 7, 3, 4-16.

Lakshmanasamy, T. (2018c) "Women's Education, Dowry, Bargaining and Gains to Marriage", in R.M. Sudarshan and J.B.G. Tilak (eds.): *Gender in Contemporary Education Research*, New Delhi: Gyan Publishing House, 225-250.

Lakshmanasamy, T. (2018d) *New and Evolving Economics: Biological and Behavioural Perspectives on Economic Behaviour*, Delhi: Trinity Press.

Lakshmanasamy, T. (2019a) "Is There Educational Mobility in India? A 2SLS-IV Estimation of Intergenerational Effects of Parental Education on Child Education" *Journal of Indian Education*, 44, 4, 161-178.

Lakshmanasamy, T. (2019b) "Does Fiscal Management Induce Prudent Government Expenditure in India? An Econometric Analysis of Causality", *WEALTH - International Journal of Money, Banking and Finance*, 8, 2.

Lakshmanasamy, T. (2019c) "Is There Quantity Rationing for Credit in India? Panel Conditional Fixed Effects Logistic Regression Estimation of Sources of Credit", *Journal of Governance and Public Policy*, 9, 1.

Lakshmanasamy, T. (2019d) "The Effect of Volatility Clustering on Future Volatility: Forecasting Stock Prices and Volatility by GARCH and EGARCH Methods", *WEALTH - International Journal of Money, Banking and Finance*, 9, 1.

Lakshmanasamy, T. (2019e) *Econometrics of Networks and Efficiency: Social Network Analysis of Business Relations and Economic Performance*, Delhi: Bookwell Publishers.

Lakshmanasamy, T. (2020) *Econometric Applications: Empirics of Simultaneous Equations, Time Series, Qualitative Response and Panel Data Models*, Delhi: Kalpaz Publications.

Lakshmanasamy, T. (2020a) "Happiness in India: Distribution of Life Satisfaction by Socioeconomic Status and Demographic Characteristics", *Journal of Economic and Social Development*, 16, 1.

Lakshmanasamy, T. (2020b) "The Relationship between Life Satisfaction and Happiness with Income Within and Across States in India", *Indian Geographical Journal*, 95, 1.

Lakshmanasamy, T. and C. Anil (2012) "Link Loyalty in Social Networks: An Econometric Analysis of Marketing Channel Networks in India", *International Journal of Economics and Business Research*, 4, 5, 501-513.

Lakshmanasamy, T. and C. Anil (2015a) "Product Seasonality and Benefits of Linking with Marketing Networks: A Discriminant Analysis of Dealer Relations in Business", *Journal of Marketing Vistas*, 5, 2, 49-58.

Lakshmanasamy, T. and C. Anil (2015b) "The Effect of Attributes of Distribution Channel Member on Supply Chain Management: An Empirical Analysis of Social Networks in Business", *International Journal of Logistics Systems and Management*, 21, 2, 160-180.

Lakshmanasamy, T. and C. Anil (2015c) "Social Network Analysis of Marketing Intermediaries – An Empirical Analysis", *International Journal of Management and Network Economics*, 3, 3, 181-198.

Lakshmanasamy, T. and C. Anil (2015d) "Relative Rankings and Risks in Marketing Management: An Empirical Analysis of Dealer Perceptions and Trade Factors in Dealer Networks", *Journal of Management Research*, 15, 4, 197-210.

Lakshmanasamy, T. and C. Anil (2016) "Economic Utility on Social Networks: Utility of Linking and Delinking in Dealership Networks", *Journal of Economic Policy and Research*, 11, 1, 70-83.

Lakshmanasamy, T. and R. Arunachalam (2005) "Economic Reforms and Development: Reflections on Economic Paradigms and Public-Private Partnership", in P. Jegadish Gandhi and M.J. Joseph (eds.): *Public-Private Partnership in Nation Building*, New Delhi: Deep and Deep Publications, 22-61.

Lakshmanasamy, T. and R. Arunachalam (2006) "Public-Private Partnership in Development: Some Theoretical and Empirical Reflections", in S.N. Misra and B.K. Sahu (eds.): *Globalisation, Economic Growth and Human Development*, New Delhi: Anmol Publications, 60-80.

Lakshmanasamy, T. and R. Arunachalam (2008) "Vulnerability of Landholdings to Income Shocks", in A. Vinayak Reddy and M. Yadagira Charyulu (eds.): *Indian Agriculture: Challenges of Globalisation*, New Delhi: New Century Publications, 303-322.

Lakshmanasamy, T. and S. Madheswaran (1993) "Determinants of Earnings in Scientific Labour Market", *Journal of Educational Planning and Administration*, 7, 2, 181-196.

Lakshmanasamy, T. and S. Madheswaran (1994) "Education and Earnings among Science Graduates" in West Bengal", *Indian Journal of Regional Science*, 26, 2, 63-75.

Lakshmanasamy, T. and S. Madheswaran (1995a) "Discrimination by Community: Evidence from Indian Scientific and Technical Labour Market", *Indian Journal of Social Science*, 8, 1, 59-77.

Lakshmanasamy, T. and S. Madheswaran (1995b) "Dual Selection Criteria for Simultaneous Decisions: Migration and Sector Choice of Scientific and Technical Females in India', *Indian Journal of Applied Economics*, 4, 3, 89-104.

Lakshmanasamy, T. and S. Madheswaran (1996a) "Occupational Segregation and Earnings Discrimination by Sex: Evidence from India", *Artha Vijnana*, 38, 4, 372-386.

Lakshmanasamy, T. and S. Madheswaran (1996b) "Employment Decision and Earnings: Issues of Self-Selection and Selectivity Bias", *Indian Economic Journal*, 43, 4, 56-72.

Lakshmanasamy, T. and S. Madheswaran (1996c) "Occupational Segregation and Earnings Discrimination by Sex: Evidence from India", *Artha Vijnana*, 38, 4, 372-386.

Lakshmanasamy, T. and S. Madheswaran (2001a) "Household Characteristics, Financial Aid and Financing Higher Education", *Perspectives in Education, Special Issue*, 17, 65-76.

Lakshmanasamy, T. and S. Madheswaran (2001b) "Stochastic Frontier Function and the Measurement of Sex Discrimination", in S. Elumalai (ed.): *Optimization Techniques in Industrial Mathematics*, Chennai: Ramanujan Institute for Advanced Study in Mathematics, University of Madras, 124-135.

Lakshmanasamy, T. and S. Madheswaran (2002) "Asymmetric Information or Ignorance in the Labour Market: A Two-Tiered Earnings Frontier Estimation", *Indian Social Science Review*, 4, 2, 223-237.

Lakshmanasamy, T. and S. Madheswaran (2004) "Determinants of Earnings in Scientific Labour Market", in D. Thakur and D.N.Thakur (eds.): *Vocational and Technical Education*, New Delhi: Deep and Deep Publishers, 565-586.

Lakshmanasamy, T. and K.S. Mandal (1989) "Rural Poverty during 1970s and 1980s", *Yojana*, 33, 23, 8-10.

Lakshmanasamy, T. and K. Maya (2017) "Money and Happiness in India: Are the Poor Unhappy and Rich Happy?", *Indian Economic Journal, Special Issue*, 64, 571-588.

Lakshmanasamy, T. and K. Maya (2020) "Rank Status and Happiness in India: A Panel Ordered Probit Estimation of the Effect of Ordinal Relative Comparison on Well-being", Indian Journal of Health and Well-being, 11, 1.

Lakshmanasamy, T. and A.M. Nalla Gounden (1992) "The Sources of Academic Achievement and School Effectiveness", *New Frontiers in Education*, 22, 1, 89-103.

Lakshmanasamy, T. and C. Ramanurthy (2005) "Corruption in Development Perspectives", in A. Ranga Reddy (ed.): *Dimensions of Crime and Corruption in India*, New Delhi: Serials Publications, 509-533.

Lakshmanasamy, T. and S. Ramasamy (1999) "An Econometric Analysis of the Worker Choice between Public and Private Sector", *Indian Journal of Labour Economics*, 42, 1, 71-83.

Lakshmanasamy, T. and K.C. Roy (2007) "Does Human Capital and Dowry Raise Women's Bargaining in Household Decisions?" in K.C. Roy and C.B. Prasad (eds.): *Governance and Development in Developing Countries*, New York, USA: Nova Science, 141-159.

Lakshmanasamy, T. and K.C. Roy (2012) "Institutional Reforms and Governance Restructuring for Distribution of Gains under Globalisation", in J.A. Mancini (ed.): *Globalisation: Partnerships, Modernisation and Future Perspectives*, New York, USA: Nova Science Publishers, 207-220.

Lakshmanasamy, T. and U. Sankar (1993) *Methodology of Applied Economic Research*, New Delhi: Sterling Publishers.

Lakshmanasamy, T. and K.R. Shanmugam (2000) "Labour Use Efficiency of Banking Sector in India", *Indian Journal of Labour Economics*, 43, 4, 989-999.

Lakshmanasamy, T. and K.R. Shanmugam (2001) "Production Frontiers and Efficiency Measures: An Analysis of the Banking Sector in India", *Asian and African Journal of Economics and Econometrics*, 1, 2, 211-228.

Lakshmanasamy, T. and K.R. Shanmugam (2003) "Technical Efficiency Measures for Single and Multiple Output Technologies", in P. Thangavel (ed.): *Algorithms and Artificial Systems*, Chennai: Allied Publishers, 277-295.

Lakshmanasamy, T. and K. Shanthi (1999) "Family Background, Choice and Participation of Women in Higher Education in Tamil Nadu", in Association of Indian Universities (ed.): *Women Participation in Higher Education*, New Delhi: Association of Indian Universities, 15-26.

Lakshmanasamy, T. and K. Shanthi (2010) "Will the Emerging Asian Giants China and India Overshadow Japan?" in G. Balachandirane (ed.): *Japan in a Resurgent Asia*, New Delhi: Manak Publications Pvt. Ltd, 94-108.

Lakshmanasamy, T. and T.M. Srinivasan (1997) (eds.) *Economics of Human Behaviour: Essays in Honour of A.M. Nalla Gounden*, New Delhi: Allied Publishers.

Lamarche, C. (2010) "Robust Penalized Quantile Regression Estimation for Panel Data", *Journal of Econometrics*, 157, 396-408.

Lamarche, C. (2011) "Measuring the Incentives to Learn in Colombia Using New Quantile Regression Approaches", *Journal of Development Economics*, 96, 2, 278-288.

Lancaster, T. (2000) "The Incidental Parameter Problem since 1948", *Journal of Econometrics*, 95, 2, 391-413.

Lane, J.I., L.A. Salmon and R. Spletzer (2012) *Establishment Wage Differentials*, Washington, D.C.: US Bureau of Labor Statistics.

Lee, E.S. (1966) "A Theory of Migration", *Demography*, 3, 1, 47-57.

Lenka, S.K. (2015) "Measuring Financial Development in India: A PCA Approach", *Theoretical and Applied Economics*, 22, 1, 187-198.

Lenka, S.K. and R. Sharma (2017) "Does Financial Inclusion Spur Economic Growth in India?", *Journal of Developing Areas*, 51, 3, 215-228.

Levi, M. (1994) "Exchange Rates and the Valuation of firms", in Y. Amihud and R.M. Levich (eds.): *Exchange Rates and Corporate Performance*, New York: Irwin.

Levin, A., Ch-F. Lin and Ch-S.J. Chu (2002) "Unit root Tests in Panel Data: Asymptotic and Finite Sample Properties", *Journal of Econometrics*, 108, 1, 1-24.

Levine, R., N. Loayza and T. Beck (2000) "Financial Intermediation and Growth: Causality and Causes", *Journal of Monetary Economics*, 46, 1, 31-77.

Lhoungu, I., B. Mishra and P.S. Suresh (2016) "Public Expenditure and Economic Growth in Nagaland: A Time Series Analysis", *International Journal of Research in Social Sciences*, 6, 10, 839-888.

Lin, M.-L. (2008) "does Unemployment Increase Crime? Evidence from US Sate Data 1974-2000", *Journal of Human Resources*, 43, 2, 413-436.

Litchfield, J., B. Reilly and M. Veneziani (2012) "Analysis of Life Satisfaction in Albania: A Heteroscedastic Ordered Probit Model Approach", *Journal of Economic Behavior and Organization*, 81, 3, 731-741.

Long, J.S. and J. Freese (2001) "Regression Models for Categorical Dependent Variables Using STATA", Stata Press Publication, STATA Corporation.

Lowry, I.S. (1966) *Migration and Metropolitan Growth: Two Analytical Models*, San Francisco: Chandler Publishing Company.

MacKinnon, J.G., A.A. Haug and L. Michelis (1999) "Numerical Distribution Functions of Likelihood Ratio Tests for Cointegration", *Journal of Applied Econometrics*, 14, 5, 563-577.

Maddala, G.S. and S. Wu (1999) "A Comparative Study of Unit root Tests with Panel Data and a New Simple Test", *Oxford Bulletin of Economics and Statistics*, 61, S1, 631-652.

Maina, Y.B. and B.A. Baba (2012) "Determinants of Ruminant Meat Demand in Maiduguri, Borno State, Nigeria", *Greener Journal of Agricultural Sciences*, 2, 8, 381-385.

Majumdar, C. and G. Gupta (2015) "Don't Worry, Be Happy: A Survey of the Economics of Happiness", *Economic and Political Weekly*, 50, 40, 50-62.

Makwana, A.C. (2012) "Foreign Institutional Investment in India", *Quest International Multidisciplinary Research Journal*, 1, 2, 197-201.

Malik, W.S. and M.I. Khawaja (2006) "Money, Output, and Inflation: Evidence from Pakistan", *Pakistan Development Review*, 45, 4, 1277-1286.

Marston, R.C. (2001) "The Effects of Industrial Structure on Economic Exposure", *Journal of International Money and Finance*, 20, 2, 149-164.

Mauro, P. (1995) "Corruption and Growth", *Quarterly Journal of Economics*, 110, 3, 681-712.

Mayasami, R. K. and T.S. Koh (2000) "A Vector Error Correction Model of the Singapore Stock Market", *International Review of Economics and Finance*, 9, 1, 79-96.

Maysami, R.C., L.C. Howe and M.A. Rahmat (2004) "Relationship between Macroeconomic Variables and Stock Market Indices: Cointegration Evidence from Stock Exchange of Singapore's All-S Sector Indices", *Jurnal Pengurusan*, 24, 47-77.

McCandless, G.T. and W.E. Weber (1995) "Some Monetary Facts", *Federal Reserve Bank of Minneapolis Quarterly Review*, 19, 3, 2-11.

McCullagh, P. (1980) "Regression Models for Ordinal Data", *Journal of the Royal Statistical Society, Series B (Methodological)*, 42, 2, 109-142.

McKelvey, D. and W. Zavoina (1975) "A Statistical Model for the Analysis of Ordinal Level Dependent Variables", *Journal of Mathematical Sociology*, 4, 1, 103-120.

Melick, M.D. (2003) "The Relationship between Crime and Unemployment", *The Park Place Economist*, 11, 1, 30-36.

Miller, D.L. and C. Paxson (2006) "Relative Income, Race, and Mortality", *Journal of Health Economics*, 25, 5, 979-1003.

Mina, W. (2015) "Political Risk Guarantees and Capital Flows: The Role of Bilateral Investment Treaties", *Economics: The Open-Access, Open-Assessment E-Journal*, 9, 1-38.

Mincer, J. (1974) *Schooling Experience and Earnings*, New York: Columbia University Press.

Mishra, A., N. Swain and D.K. Malhotra (2007) "Volatility Spillover between Stock and Foreign Exchange Markets: Indian Evidence", *International Journal of Business*, 12, 3, 343-359.

Mishra, A.K. (2004) "Stock Market and Foreign Exchange Market in India: Are They Related?", *South Asia Economic Journal*, 5, 2, 209-232.

Mishra, P.K., M. Malla, S. Mishra, B.B. Pradhan and S.K. Mishra (2010) "Performance of Indian Capital Market - An Empirical Analysis", *European Journal of Economics, Finance and Administrative Sciences*, 23, 1, 49-57.

Mohammadzadeh, Y., H. Ghahramani and E. Nazariyan (2015) "Environmental, Health and Health Care Costs", *Health Information Management Journal*, 12, 4, 495-505.

Mohanamani, P. and T. Sivagnanasithi (2014) "Indian Stock Market and Aggregate Macroeconomic Variables: Time Series Analysis", *Journal of Economics and Finance*, 3, 6, 68-74.

Motiram, S. and L. Osberg (2012) "Demand or Supply for Schooling in Rural India?", *Electronic International Journal of Time Use Research*, 9, 1, 1-27.

Muhammed Juman, B.K. and M.K. Irshad (2015) "An Overview of India Capital Markets", *Bonfring International Journal of Industrial Engineering and Management Science*, 5, 2, 17-23.

Mukhopadhyay, S. (1980) "Birthplace Migration in India: 1961, 1971", *Indian Economic Review*, 15, 3, 185-200.

Muktadir-al-Mukit, D. (2012) "Effects of Interest Rate and Exchange Rate on Volatility of Market Index at Dhaka Stock Exchange", *Journal of Business and Technology*, 7, 2, 1-18.

Musgrave, R.A. (1961) "Approaches to a Fiscal Theory of Political Federalism", in Universities-National Bureau Committee for Economic Research (ed.): *Public Finances: Needs, Sources, and Utilization*, Princeton: Princeton University Press, 97-134.

Musgrave, R.A. (1969) *Fiscal Systems*, New Haven and London: Yale University Press.

Musgrave, R.A. and P.B. Musgrave (1973) *Public Finance in Theory and Practice*, New York: McGraw Hill.

Mwabu, G. and T.P. Schultz (1996) "Education Returns Across Quantiles of the Wage Function: Alternative Explanations for Returns to Education by Race in South Africa", *American Economic Review*, 86, 2, 335-339.

Nachane, D. M. and R.M. Nadkarni (1985) "Empirical Tests of Certain Monetarist Propositions via Causality Theory", *Indian Economic Journal*, 33, 1, 13-41.

Nain, M.Z. and B. Kamaiah (2014) "Financial Development and Economic Growth in India: Some Evidence from Non-Linear Causality Analysis", *Economic Change and Restructuring*, 47, 4, 299-319.

Najang, P. and B. Seifert (1992) "Volatility of Exchange Rates, Interest Rates, and Stock Returns", *Journal of Multinational Financial Management*, 2, 1, 1-19.

Narayan, K.P. (2004) "Reformulating Critical Values for the Bounds F-statistics Approach to Cointegration", Discussion Paper No. 02/04, Department of Economics, Monash University.

Nelson, D.B. (1991) "Conditional Heteroskedasticity in Asset Returns: A New Approach", *Econometrica*, 59, 2, 347-370.

Neumayer, and L. Spess (2005) "Do Bilateral Iinvestment Treaties Increase Foreign direct Investment to Developing Countries", *World Development*, Vol. 33, 10, 1567-1585.

Nock, S.L. (1998a) *Marriage in Men's Lives*, New York: Oxford University Press.

Nock, S.L. (1998b) "The Consequences of Premarital Fatherhood", *American Sociological Review*, 63, 2, 250-263.

NSSO (2011-12) "Household Consumption of Goods and Services in India", NSS 68th Round, Ministry of Statistics and Program Implementation, Government of India.

Odo, S.I., I.C. Ogonna, U.C. Chinyere and C.B. Chibuzor (2016) "Public Expenditure and Economic Growth in South Africa: Long Run and Causality Approach", *Asian Journal of Economics, Business and Accounting*, 1, 2, 1-17.

Omri, A. (2013) "CO_2 Emissions, Energy Consumption and Economic Growth Nexus in MENA Countries: Evidence from Simultaneous Equations Models", *Energy Economics,* 40, 657-664.

Onsomu, E.O., B.A. Abuya, I.N. Okech, D. Moore and J. Collins-McNeil (2015) "Maternal Education and Immunization Status among Children of Kenya", *Maternal and Child Health Journal*, 19, 8, 1724-1733.

Osamwonyi, I.O. and E.I. Evbayiro-Osagie (2012) "The Relationship between Macroeconomic Variables and Stock Market Index in Nigeria", *Journal of Economics*, 3, 1, 55-63.

Oster, S. and J. Agell (2007) "Crime and Unemployment in Turbulent Times", *Journal of European Economic Association*, 5, 4, 752-775.

Ota, M. and P.G. Moffatt (2007) "The Within-Household Schooling Decision: A Study of Children in Rural Andhra Pradesh", *Journal of Population Economics*, 20, 1, 223-239.

Ozurumba, B.A. and E.E. Chigbu (2013) "An Econometric Analysis of Capital Market Performance and Economic Growth in Nigeria", *Interdisciplinary Journal of Contemporary Research in Business*, 4, 10, 165-176.

Pal, K. and R. Mittal (2011) "Impact of Macroeconomic Indicators on Indian Capital Markets", *Journal of Risk Finance*, 12, 2, 84-97.

Pan, M-A., R.C-W. Fox and Y.A. Liu (2007) "Dynamic Linkages between Exchange Rates and Stock Prices: Evidence from East Asian Markets", *International Review of Economics and Business*, 16, 4, 503-520.

Panda, P.K. (2009) "Central Fiscal Transfers and States' Own Revenue Efforts in India: Panel Data Models", *Margin: The Journal of Applied Economic Research*, 3, 3, 223-224.

Panda, P.K. (2016) "Economic and Political Determinants of Central fiscal Transfers in India: A Dynamic Panel Data Analysis of State Level Data", *Journal of Developing Areas*, 50, 2, 329-347.

Paternoster, R. and S.D. Bushway (2001) "Theoretical and Empirical Work on the Relationship between Unemployment and Crime', *Journal of Quantitative Criminology*, 17, 4, 391-407.

Patra, N (2012) "An Analysis of Socioeconomic and Demographic Determinants of Childhood Immunisation in India", in M. Pal *et al.* (eds.): *Gender Issues and Empowerment of Women*, New York: Nova Science Publishers, 205-226.

Patrick, H.T. (1966) "Financial Development and Economic Growth in Underdeveloped Countries", *Economic Development and Cultural Change*, 14, 2, 174-189.

Peacock, A.T. and J. Wiseman (1961) *The Growth of Public Expenditure in the United Kingdom*, Princeton: Princeton University Press.

Pedroni, P. (1999) "Critical Values for Cointegration Tests in Heterogeneous Panels with Multiple Regressors", *Oxford Bulletin of Economics and Statistics*, 61, S1, 653-670.

Pedroni, P. (2001) "Fully-Modified OLS for Heterogeneous Cointegrated Panels", in B.H. Baltagi, T.B. Fombay and R. Carter (eds.): *Nonstationary Panels, Panel Cointegration, and Dynamic Panels, Advances in Econometrics, Volume 15*, London: Emerald Publishing, 93-130.

Pedroni, P. (2004) "Panel Cointegration: Asymptotic and Finite Sample Properties of Pooled Time Series Tests with an Application to the PPP Hypothesis", *Econometric Theory*, 20, 3, 597-625.

Peiris, T.U.I. and T.S.G. Peiris (2011) "Measuring Stock Market Volatility in an Emerging Economy", in *Proceedings of the International Conference on Business and Information*, Sri Lanka: University of Kelaniya.

Perman, R. And D.I. Stern (2003) "Evidence from Panel Unit Root and Cointegration Tests that the Environmental Kuznets Curve Does Not Exist", *Australian Journal of Agricultural and Resource Economics*, 47, 3, 325-347.

Pesaran, M.H., Y. Shin and R.J. Smith (2001) "Bounds Testing Approaches to the Analysis of Level Relationships", *Journal of Applied Econometrics*, 16, 3, 289-326.

Phillips, P. and P. Perron (1988) "Testing for a Unit Root in Time Series Regressions", *Biometrika*, 75, 2, 335-346.

Phukan, R.K., M.P. Barman and J. Mahanta (2008) "Factors Associated with Immunization coverage of Children in Assam, India: Over the Fifty Year of Life", *Journal of Tropical Pediatrics*, 55, 4, 249-252.

Pierce, D.A. (1977) "Relationships - and the Lack Thereof - Between Economic Time Series, with Special Reference to Money and Interest Rates", *Journal of the American Statistical Association*, 72, 357, 11-26.

Poot, J., O. Alimi, M. Cameron and D.C. Mare (2016) "The Gravity Model of Migration: The Successful Comeback of an Ageing Superstar in Regional Science", IZA Discussion Paper No. 10329, Bonn.

Preston, S.H. (1975) "The Changing Relation between Mortality and Level of Economic Development", *Population Studies*, 29, 2, 231-248.

Psacharopoulos, G. (1972) "Rates of Return to Investment in Education Around the World", *Comparative Education Review*, 16, 1, 281-302.

Psacharopoulos, G. (1985) "Returns to Education: A Further International Update and Implications", *Journal of Human Resources*, 20, 4, 583-604.

Psacharupoulos, G. (1986) "Welfare Effects of Government Interventions in Education", *Contemporary Economic Policy*, 4, 3, 51-62.

Psacharupoulos, G. (1994) "Returns to Investment in Education: A Global Update", *World Development*, 22, 9, 1325-1343.

Psacharopoulos, G. and H.A. Patrinos (2018) "Returns to Investment in Education: A Decennial Review of the Global Literature", *Education Economics*, 26, 5, 445-458.

Quah, D. (1994) "Exploiting Cross-Section Variation for Unit Root Inference in Dynamic Data", *Economics Letters*, 44, 1, 9-19.

Racine, J. and Q. Li (2004) "Nonparametric Estimation of Regression Functions with both Categorical and Continuous Data", *Journal of Econometrics*, 119, 1, 99-130.

Raeissi, P., T. Harati-Khalilabad, A. Rezapour, S.Y. Hashemi, A. Mousavi and S. Khodabakhshzadeh (2018) "Effects of Air Pollution on Public and Private Health Expenditure in Iran: A Time Series Study (1972-2014)", *Journal of Preventive Medicine and Public Health*, 51, 3, 140-147.

Rafindadi, A.A., Z. Yusof, K. Zaman, P. Kyophilavong and G. Akhmat (2014) "The Relationship between Air Pollution, Fossil Fuel Energy Consumption, and Water Resources in the Panel of Selected Asia-Pacific Countries", *Environmental Science and Pollution Research*, 21, 19, 11395-11400.

Raghavendra, H.N., S. B. Mahaja bashetti, N. N. Karnool, V. S. Kulkarni and H. Basavaraj (2009) "Meat Consumption Pattern and Its Preference in Dharwad District: A Socio-economic Analysis", *Krishi Kosh: Karnataka Journal of Agricultural Sciences*, 22, 2, 353-358.

Rai, M. (2014) *Corruption and Governance in India - Current Status and Way Forward*, New Delhi: Voluntary Action Network in India.

Rajput, B. (2017) "Financial Institution and Its Determinants: An Empirical Study on the Interstate Variations in India", *International Journal on Arts, Management and Humanaties*, 6, 1, 8-18.

Ramasamy, B. and M.C.H. Yeung (2002) "The Relationship between Exchange Rates and Stock Prices: Implications on Capital Controls", *Asia Pacific Journal of Economics and Business*, 6, 2, 46-60.

Rami, G. (2010) "Causality between Money, Prices and Output in India (1951-2005): A Granger Causality Approach", *Journal of Quantitative Economics*, 8, 2, 20-41.

Rangarajan, C. and R.R. Arif (1990) "Money, Output and Prices - A Macroeconomic Model", *Economic and Political Weekly*, 25, 16, 837-852.

Rangarajan, C. and D.K. Srivastava (2011) *Federalism and Fiscal Transfers in India*, New Delhi: Oxford University Press.

Ranjan, P. (2010) "Indian Investment Treaty Programme in the Light of Global Experiences", *Economic and Political Weekly*, 45, 7, February 13, 68-72.

Rao, M.G. (2002) "State Finances in India: Issues and Challenges", *Economic and Political Weekly*, 37, 31, 3261-3271.

Raphael, S. and R. Winter-Ebmer (2001) "Identifying the Effects of Unemployment on Crime", *Journal of Law and Economics*, 44, 1, 259-283.

Rati Ram (1986) "Government Size and Economic Growth: A New Framework and Some Evidence from Cross-Section and Time-Series Data", *American Economic Review*, 76, 1, 191-203.

Ravenstein, E.G. (1885) "The Laws of Migration", *Journal of the Statistical Society of London*, 48, 2, 167-235.

Rioja, F. and N. Valev (2004) "Does One Size Fit All? A Reexamination of the Finance and Growth Relationship", *Journal of Development Economics*, 74, 2, 429-447.

Robinson, J. (1952) *The Generalization of the General Theory, the Rate of Interest and Other Essays*, London: Macmillan.

Rock, M.T. and H. Bonnet (2004) "The Comparative Politics of Corruption: Accounting for the Asian Paradox in Empirical Studies of Corruption, Growth and Investment", *World Development*, 32, 6, 999-1017.

Rose-Ackerman, S. (1975) "The Economics of Corruption", *Journal of Public Economics*, 4, 2, 187-203.

Rose-Ackerman, S. (1997) "Corruption and Development", in B. Pleskovic and J.E. Stiglitz (eds.): *Annual World Bank Conference on Development Economics*, 35-57.

Rose-Ackerman, S. (1999) *Corruption and Government*, Cambridge, UK: Cambridge University Press.

Roser, M. (2018) "Child Mortality", Published online at OurWorldInData.org at https://ourworldindata.org/child-mortality.

Roy, P. and A. Raychaudhuri (2009) "Intergovernmental Transfer Rules, State Fiscal Policy and Performance in India", in B. Dutta, T. Ray and E. Somanathan (eds.): *New Enduring Themes in Development Economics*, New York: World Scientific Publishing, 369-400.

Rudra, S. (2017) "Immunisation Coverage: India Far Away from Meeting Targets", Observer Research Foundation Expert Speak Article.

Sackey, H.A. (2008) "Private Returns to Education in Ghana: Implications for Investments in Schooling and Migration", AERC Research Paper 174, African Economic Research Consortium, Nairobi, Kenya.

Sahoo, M.K. and M. Gomkale (2015) "Financial Inclusion in India: An Empirical Study of Unorganized Sector in Gujarat", *Inormation Management and Business Review*, 7, 5, 6-17.

Salawu, M.B., A.G Ibrahim, L.O. Lamidi and A.E. Sadeeq (2014) "Consumption and Consumer Preference for Poultry Meat Types in Ibadan Metropolis", *Journal of Economics and Sustainable Development*, 5, 28, 20-25.

Sander, W. (1992) "The Effects of Ethnicity and Religion on Educational Attainment", *Economics of Education Review*, 11, 2, 119-135.

Sandewall, O., D. Cesarini and M. Johannesson (2014) "The Co-Twin Methodology and Returns to Schooling - Testing a Critical Assumption", *Labour Economics*, 26, C, 1-10.

Sargan, J. (1958) "The Estimation of Economic Relationships using Instrumental Variables", *Econometrica*, 26, 3, 393-415.

Sarma, M. and J. Pais (2011) "Financial Inclusion and Development", *Journal of International development*, 23, 5, 613-628.

Saurabh, S., S. Sarkar and D. Pandey (2013) "Female Literacy Rate is a Better Predictor of Birth Rate and Infant Mortality Rate in India", *Jounal of Family Medicine and Primary Care*, 2, 4, 349-353.

Scarpetta, S. (1998) "Labor Market Reforms and Unemployment: Lessons from the Experience of the OECD Countries", ADB Working Paper No. 6444.

Schneider, E., P. Chen and J. Frohn (2008) "A Long-Run Structural Macro-Econometric Model for Germany", *Economics E-Journal*, 2, 16, 1-12.

Schoeni, R.F. (1995) "Marital Status and Earnings in Developed Countries", *Journal of Population Economics*, 8, 4, 351-359.

Schultz, T. W. (1961) "Investment in Human Capital", *American Economic Review*, 51, 1, 1-17.

Schultz, T. W. (1962) *Investment in Human Beings*, Chicago: University of Chicago Press.

Schultz, T.P. (1988) "Education Investments and Returns", in H. Chenery and T.N. Srinivasan (eds.): *Handbook of Development Economics, Volume 1*, Amsterdam: North-Holland Publishing, 543-630.

Schultz, T.P. (1999) "Health and Schooling Investment in Africa" *Journal of Economic Perspectives*, 13, 3, 67-88.

Schultz, T.P. (2003) "Wage Rentals for Reproducible Human Capital: Evidence from Two West African Countries", *Economics and Human Biology*, 1, 3, 331-366.

Schumpeter, J.A. (1911) *The Theory of Economic Development: An Inquiry into Profits, Capital, Credit, Interest, and the Business Cycle*, Cambridge: Harvard University Press.

Sefa Dei, G.J. (2004) *Schooling and Education in Africa: The Case of Ghana*, Trenton: Africa World Press.

Sekmen, F. (2011) "Exchange Rate Volatility and Stock Returns for the U.S.", *African Journal of Business Management*, 2, 22, 9659-9664.

Sham Bhat, K. (1993) "Determinants of Grants in Indian States", *Indian Journal of Economics*, 74, 293, 161-173.

Sham Bhat, K. and V. Nirmala (1993) "Political Economy of Tax Revenue Determination in Indian States", *Indian Journal of Economics*, 73, 290, 383-396.

Shapiro, A.C. (1975) "Exchange Rate Changes, Inflation, and the Value of the Multinational Corporation", *Journal of Finance*, 30, 2, 485-502.

Sharma, B., H. Mahajan and G.D. Velhal (2013) "Immunization Coverage: Role of Sociodemographic Variables", *Advances in Preventive Medicine*, 2013:607935.

Sharma, C. (2011) "Beyond Gaps and Imbalances: Re-structuring the Debate on Intergovernmental Fiscal Relations", *Public Administration*, 90, 1, 99-128.

Shaw, E.S. (1973) *Financial Deepening in Economic Development*, New York: Oxford University Press.

Shera, A., B. Dosti, P. Grabov (2014) "Corruption impact on Economic Growth: An Empirical Analysis", *Journal of Economic Development, Management, IT, Finance and Marketing*, 1,1, 57-77.

Shetty, A. and S. Shetty (2017) "Impact of Female Literacy on Infant Mortality Rate in India", *Current Pediatric Research*, 1, 18, 49-56.

Shleifer, A. and R. Vishny (1993) "Corruption", *Quarterly Journal of Economics*, 108, 3, 599-617.

Sichilima, T., L. Mapemba and G. Tembo (2015) "What Determines Expenditure Allocationto Beef among Lusaka Residents in Zambia? Evidence from Household Survey", *Modern Economy*, 6, 411-422.

Sims, C.A. (1972) "Money, Income, and Causality", *American Economic Review*, 62, 4, 540-552.

Singh B.P. and A.K. Mishra (2015) "Researching the Relationship between Financial and Real Sector in India", *Indian Journal of Economics and Development, 11,* 4,861-868.

Singh, B.P. and A.K. Mishra (2014) "Nexus of Financial Development and Economic Growth in India: Revisiting Schumpeter", *Indian Journal of Economics and Development, 10,* 3, 246-255.

Singh, N. and G. Vasishtha (2004) "Some Patterns in Center-State Fiscal Transfers in India: An Illustrative Analysis", *Economic and Political Weekly*, 39, 45, 4897-4903.

Singh, P. and R.J. Yadav(2000) "Immunization Status of Children in India", *Indian Pediatrics*, 37, 11, 1194-1199.

Singh, P.B. (2013) "Trends in Child Immunization across Geographical Regions in India: Focus on Urban-Rural and Gender differentials", *PLOS One*, 8, 9, e73102, 1-11.

Sinha, D. and Macri, J. (2001) "Financial Development and Economic Growth: The Case of Eight Asian Countries", *International Economics*, 54, 2, 219-234.

Sinha, P. and A.K. Giri (1989) "Consumption of Livestock Products - Analysis and Comparison of Data of NSS 32nd and NSS 38th Round", in Indian Society of Agricultural Economics (ed.): *Livestock Economy of India*, New Delhi: Oxford and IBH Publishing Co.

Solnik, B. (1987) "Using Financial Prices to Test Exchange Rate Models: A Note", *Journal of Finance*, 42, 1, 141-149.

Spence, M. (1973) "Job Market Signaling", *Quarterly Journal of Economics*, 87, 3, 355-374.

Steinberg, M.B.M. (2015) "On the Demand for Education in India", Doctoral Thesis, Department of Economics, Harvard University.

Stevenson, B. and J. Wolfers (2008) "Economic Growth and Happiness: Reassessing the Easterlin Paradox", *Brookings Papers on Economic Activity*, 1, 1-84.

Stouffer, S.A. (1940) "Intervening Opportunities: A Theory Relating Mobility and Distance", *American Sociological Review*, 5, 6, 845-867.

Streatfield, K., M. Singarimbun and I. Diamond (1990) "Maternal Education and Child Immunization", *Demography*, 27, 3, 447-455.

Subhani, S., R. Yaseen, M.A. Khan, G. Jeelani and R. Fatima (2015) "Impact of Mother's Education on Child Immunization: A Comparative Study of India and Pakistan", *Journal of Finance and Economics*, 3, 3, 51-54.

Taiwo, M. and T. Abayomi (2011) "Government expenditure and economic development: Empirical evidence from Nigeria", *European Journal of Business and Management*, 3, 9, 18-28.

Tansel, A. (1997) "Schooling Attainment, Parental Education, and Gender in Cote d'Ivoire and Ghana", *Economic Development and Cultural Change*, 45, 4, 825-856.

Tansel, A. (2002) "Determinants of School Attainment of Boys and Girls in Turkey: Individual, Household and Community Factors", *Economics of Education Review*, 21, 5, 455-470.

Tanzi, V. (1998) "Corruption around the World: Causes, Consequences, Scope and Cures", *IMF Staff Papers*, 45, 4, 559-594.

Tiefenthaler, J. (1997) "The Productivity Gains of Marriage: Effects of Spousal Education on Own Productivity across market Sectors in Brazil", *Economic Development and Cultural Change*, 45, 3, 633-650.

Tilak, J.B.G. (2002) "Determinants of Household Expenditure on Education in Rural India", NCAER Working Paper Series No. 88.

Tobin, J. and S. Rose-Ackerman (2011) "When BITs Have Some Bite: The Political-Economic Environment for Bilateral Investment Treaties, *Review of International Organizations*, 6, 1, 1-32.

Torre, R. and M. Myrskyla (2014) "Income Inequality and Population Health: A Panel Data Analysis on 21 Developed Countries", *Population Studies*, 68, 1, 1-13.

Trivedi, P. and Panda, D. (2014) "Macroeconomic Determinants of Private Transfers to India", *Journal of Quantitative Economics*, 12, 1, 51-76.

Trostel, P. (2002) "Estimates of the Return to Schooling in 28 Countries", *Labour Economics*, 9, 1, 1-16.

Tudorel, A., S. Stancu, M. Nedelcu and A. Matei (2009) "Econometric Models Used for the Corruption Analysis", Munich Personal RePEc Paper 19623.

Turrini, A., G. Koltay, F. Pierini, C. Gotfard and A. Kiss (2014) "A Decade of Labour Market Reforms in the EU: Insights from the LABREF Database", European Economy Economic Papers 522.

Twumasi Baffour, P. (2013) "Determinants of Urban Worker Earnings in Ghana and Tanzania: The Role of Education", CREDIT Research Paper No.13/01, University of Nottingham.

Twumasi Baffour, P. (2015) "Determinants of Urban worker Earnings in Ghana: The Role of Education", *Modern Economy*, 6, 1240-1252.

Ulwodi, D.W. and P.W. Muriu (2017) "Barries of Financial Inclusion in Sub-Saharan Africa", *Journal of Economics and Sustainable Development,* 8, 14, 66-81.

UNICEF (2007) "Achieving Universal Primary Education in Ghana by 2015: A Reality or a Dream?", Division of Policy and Planning, New York: United Nations Children's Fund.

United Nations (2006) *Building Inclusive Financial Sectors for Development*, New York: United Nations.

van Leuvensteijn, M. and A. Parikh (2002) "how Different Are the Determinants of Population versus Labour Migration in Germany", *Applied Economics Letters*, 9, 11, 699-703.

van Wissen, L., L. van der Gaag, P. Rees and J. Stillwell (2008) "In Search of a Modelling Strategy for Projecting Internal Migration in European Countries: Demographic versus Explanatory Approaches", in: J. Poot, B. Waldorf and L. Wissen (eds.):*Migration and Human Capital: Regional and Global Perspectives*, Cheltenham: Edward Elgar, 49-74.

Vandenberg, P.(2010) "Impact of Labor Market Institutions on Unemployment: Results from a Global Panel", ADB Economic Working Paper Series No. 219.

Vasishtha, G. and I. Rajaraman (2000) "Impact of Grants on Tax Effort of Local Government", *Economic and Political Weekly*, 35, 33, 2943-2948.

Veenhoven, R. (since 1984) *World Database of Happiness: Happiness in Nations*, https://worlddatabaseofhappiness.eur.nl.

Vehovar, U. and M. Jager (2003) "Corruption, Quality of Governance and Economic growth: The Slovenian Dilemma between Phoenix and Potemkin", Paper presented at the Conference on Institutions in Transition, Kranjska, Slovenia, June 19-21, 2003.

Wade, R. (1982) "The System of Administrative and Political Corruption: Canal Irrigation in South India", *Journal of Development Studies*, 18, 3, 287-327.

Wagner, A. (1958) [1883] "Three Extracts on Public Finance", in R.A. Musgrave and A.T. Peacock (eds.): *Classics in the Theory of Public Finance*, London: Macmillan, 1-15.

Wang, S., C. Fang, X. Guan, B. Pang and H. Ma (2014) "Urbanization, Energy Consumption, and Carbon dioxide Emissions in China: A Panel Data Analysis of China's Province", *Applied Energy*, 136, 738-749.

Weinstein, J.A. and V.K. Pillai (2001) *Demography: The Science of Population*, Boston, USA: Allyn and Bacon.

Westoff, C.F. and A. Bankole (2001) "The Contraception - Fertility Link in Sub-Saharan Africa and in Other Developing Countries", *DHS Analytical Studies No.4*, 1-21.

Wild, J. and H. Lebdaoui (2014) "Stock Market Performance and Economic Growth in Morocco", *Global Advanced Research Journal of Management and Business Studies*, 3, 5, 207-216.

World Bank (1989) "Basis Education for Self-Employment and Rural Development", Western Africa Region, Washington, D.C.: World Bank.

World Bank (2004) *Millennium Development Goals*, Washington, D.C.: World Bank.

World Bank (2017) *Global Financial Development Database*, Washington, D.C.: World Bank.

World Bank (2017) *The Global Findex Database*, Washington, D.C.: World Bank.

World Health Organisation (2015) *Regional Framework for Reproductive Health in the Western Pacific*, Manila: WHO Regional Office for the Western Pacific Region.

World Health Organisation (2016) *India: WHO and UNICEF Estimates of Immunization Coverage,* Geneva: World Health Organization.

Yadav, R.J. and P. Singh (2004) "Immunization Status of Children and Mothers in the State of Madhya Pradesh", *Indian Journal of Community Medicine*, 29, 3, 147-148.

Yahaya, A., N.M. Nor, M.S. Habibullah, J.A. Ghani and Z.M. Noor (2016) "How Relevant Is Environmental Quality to Per Capita Health Expenditures? Empirical Evidence from Panel of Developing Countries", *Springer Plus*, 5, 925, 1-15.

Yau, H-Y. and C-C. Nieh (2009) "Testing for Cointegration with Threshold Effect between Stock Prices and Exchange Rates in Japan and Taiwan", *Japan and the World Economy*, 21, 3, 292-300.

Yazdi, S.K. and B. Khanalizadeh (2017) "Air Pollution, Economic Growth and Health Care Expenditure", *Economic Research*, 30. 1, 1181-1190.

Yushkina, Y. (2010) "The Determinants of Happiness and Its Changes: An Empirical Analysis Based on Panel Data from Russia, Master's Thesis, Amherst College.

Zhang, C., and Y. Lin (2012) "Panel Estimation for Urbanization, Energy Consumption and CO_2 Emissions: A Regional Analysis in China", *Energy Policy*, 49, C, 488-498.

Zhang, J., C.M. Wang, L. Liu, H. Guo, G.D. Liu, Y.W. Li and S.H. Deng (2014) "Investigation of Carbon dioxide Emission in China by Primary Component Analysis", *Science of the Total Environment*, 472, 239-247.

Zhao, H. (2010) "Dynamic Relationship between Exchange Rate and Stock Price: Evidence from China", *Research in International Business and Finance*, 24, 2, 103-112.

Zhou, Z.Y., Y.R. Wu and W. M. Tian (2005) "Rural Foodgrain Consumption", in Z.Y. Zhou and W.M. Tian (eds.): *Grains in China: Foodgrain, Feedgrain and World Trade*, Aldershot: Ashgate, 42-64.

Zidi, A. and S.M. Dhifallah (2013) "Corruption, Governance and Economic Growth in Developing Countries: Analysis by Panel Data", *International Journal of Management and Business Studies*, 3, 2, 25-30.

Zribi, T.El-G., H. Temmi and N. Zrelli (2014) "Can Labor Market Flexibility Affect Unemployment? A Panel Data Analysis", *Journal of Human Resource Management and Labor Studies*, 2, 1, 17-40.

Zubair, A. (2013) "Causal Relationship between Stock Market Index and Exchange Rate: Evidence from Nigeria", *Journal of Applied Statistics*, 4, 2, 87-110.